CW01081857

French Film History,
1895–1946

WISCONSIN FILM STUDIES

Patrick McGilligan, *series editor*

French Film History,
1895–1946

Richard Neupert

THE UNIVERSITY OF WISCONSIN PRESS

The University of Wisconsin Press
728 State Street, Suite 443
Madison, Wisconsin 53706
uwpress.wisc.edu

Gray's Inn House, 127 Clerkenwell Road
London ECIR 5DB, United Kingdom
eurospanbookstore.com

Printed in the United States of America
This book may be available in a digital edition.

Library of Congress Cataloging-in-Publication Data

Names: Neupert, Richard John, author.
Title: French film history, 1895–1946 / Richard Neupert.
Other titles: Wisconsin film studies.
Description: Madison, Wisconsin : The University of Wisconsin Press, [2022] |
Series: Wisconsin film studies | Includes bibliographical references and index.
Identifiers: LCCN 2021041542 | ISBN 9780299337704 (hardcover)
Subjects: LCSH: Motion pictures—France—History.
Classification: LCC PN1993.5.F7 N478 2022 | DDC 791.450944—dc23/eng/20211027
LC record available at https://lccn.loc.gov/2021041542

For Cathy and Sophie, *toujours*

Contents

Illustrations

Acknowledgments

I grew up in Monona, Wisconsin, far from France, but just across the lake from Madison and the University of Wisconsin (UW). I began attending UW campus 16mm film society screenings in high school, where I discovered foreign films. In college at UW, I took French classes due to my new interest in Jean Renoir, Jean Gabin, Agnès Varda, and the New Wave, thanks in part to Rose Avila's engaging French courses. But it was in graduate school at UW–Madison that everything fell into place. My amazing classes with David Bordwell, Vance Kepley Jr., J. J. Murphy, Tino Balio, and Kristin Thompson were rounded out by Peter Schofer's French film class. They all still help and counsel me to this day. Fellow grad students Matthew Bernstein, Jim Peterson, Kevin Hagopian, and Leslie Midkiff-Debauche shaped my critical and historical approaches. Peter Schofer also found funding for my year of PhD classes in Paris. There, Rick Altman, Jacques Aumont, Michel Marie, Christian Metz, and Marc Vernet guided and inspired me, while Eric Smoodin, Emily Calmer, and B. Z. Petroff ran with me to screenings in far-flung cinemas, at the two cinematheques, and at Paris III, Censier. Research trips to Paris, Lyon, and Brussels have continued to reveal new titles and paths of inquiry ever since.

As always, I am thankful for a wide range of support from friends, colleagues, and institutions for this project. At the University of Georgia, generous travel and research funding from the Charles H. Wheatley professorship, the University of Georgia Foundation, and the Franklin College of Arts and Sciences proved crucial. My department head, David Saltz, is always supportive, and Steven Carroll and Clay Chastain helped with all sorts of practical issues, including budgets and illustrations. Mike Hussey, Jonathan Krell, Nate Kohn, Christopher Sieving, Jed Rasula, and Martin Kagel have proven themselves to be creative and encouraging colleagues. Reference librarian Kristin Nielsen and the library staff, especially the interlibrary loan office, have all been essential to this study. Moreover, back in Madison, everyone at the University of Wisconsin Press has been a pleasure to work with, including Dennis Lloyd, Jacqulyn Teoh, Holly McArthur, Terry Emmrich, Jennifer Conn, Sheila McMahon, and Adam Mehring.

I want to acknowledge that it has proven difficult to find space to highlight adequately every scholar working on a given film or topic. Notes were eliminated to streamline the text, and I encourage readers to follow up points of interest by consulting the in-text citations and the valuable array of sources in the bibliography. Unless otherwise cited, translations from French are mine. French film scholarship is a particularly lively and rewarding area of study, and I appreciate all the critics, theorists, and historians contributing to our field and discipline. Kelley Conway, Eric Smoodin, Marc Vernet, Ginette Vincendeau, and Martin O'Shaugnessy have been especially invaluable. My very good friends Jim Peterson, Sue Collins, and Matthew and Natalie Bernstein continually offer much-needed and appreciated advice and encouragement.

Finally, this project would not have been possible without the brilliant contributions and suggestions from my wife, Catherine Jones, who is always ready to proof passages, translate tricky expressions, and watch yet another French movie that proves the obsessive allure of lasting love.

French Film History,
1895–1946

CHAPTER I

Science and Visual Culture in Nineteenth-Century France

F rench cinema has been vibrant and influential throughout its long, rich history, from the 1890s right up to today. Its powerful cultural significance has also been firmly established in film criticism and theory. More than just a string of well-known movies, recognizable stars, or talented auteurs, French cinema is a resilient, dynamic cluster of systems involving a wide range of pertinent institutions, aesthetic options, companies, and modes of production. It is precisely this active mix of mechanisms and the resulting array of stories and styles that lie at the heart of this study. French cinema did not fall from the skies or sprout up naturally from the ground. It has been carefully constructed and continues to shift, grow, and transform with every new writer, director, producer, actor, and movie and with each new spectator and critic. This book addresses the creative and often unexpected trajectory of French cinema, which continues to be one of the most provocative and engaging cinemas in the world.

French Film History, 1895–1946 concentrates on films produced within the geographic territory of France, but as we shall see, right from the beginning, French cinema depended on talent, influences, resources, and financing from outside its borders. Thomas Elsaesser reminds us that a national cinema functions as a brand, encouraging cultural loyalty as well as institutional and government support. But a "national" cinema is also an economic venture in a global industrial setting with a mobile workforce (36). French films and filmmakers have always benefited from international cooperation at every level. For instance, the canonical French Surrealist film *An Andalusian Dog* (*Un chien andalou*, 1929) was made by two immigrants, Luis Buñuel and Salvador Dalí, and was bankrolled by Buñuel's mother in Spain. Furthermore,

French talent often traveled in search of new opportunities and spread "French" traits around the world. Already in the 1910s, animator Émile Cohl worked in both France and the United States, and today French animators circulate from country to country and project to project as global employees. René Clair's earliest sound films were shot in the German Tobis-Klangfilm studios, and Paramount was simultaneously filming English and German versions of early European sound films in Paris. Even Louis Lumière's operators filmed and projected around the world, as Georges Méliès and Charles Pathé established production offices in Europe and North America. Defining the parameters of France's cinema poses immense challenges from the outset. Moreover, international coproductions have also played a vital role throughout French film history. French cinema has always been actively international in its scope and vision.

While "French cinema" may be a fluid or even slippery concept, it is nonetheless a highly functional term with relevant legal, aesthetic, and cultural definitions and meanings. National cinemas exist in intricate cultural systems and regularly appeal for state support, protection, and recognition as a vital art form and industry of national interest. Thus, national cinemas strive for pride and loyalty at home while they must simultaneously integrate themselves in global film and media systems and marketplaces. There is much at stake in establishing, maintaining, and marketing a strong film industry, and the French government, its filmmakers, and its audiences are all actively involved in their cinema's achievements and influence. This book investigates the various contexts for French film practice across the decades, providing examples from canonical and lesser-known representative productions alike, acknowledging that French national cinema is impossibly vast and filled with contradictions and paradoxes as well as some highly consistent traits and practices that lend it a surprising unity and a highly successful recognition factor. The label "French film" may have meant different things to different people across time. Famed for its often progressive and sensitive humanism, it can also include colonialist, racist, and sexist tendencies. French cinema has consistently connoted a certain level of narrative and stylistic ingenuity, skill, thematic resonance, and even sophistication.

French cinema is indeed unique and insightful for historians and filmmakers alike in that it has always involved an extensive array of viable modes of production simultaneously. In any given year, there is a healthy mix of classical studio productions alongside a vital *art et essai* independent art cinema, as well as avant-garde, animation, and documentary films, many made by niche producers, small teams, or individuals. No other national cinema has so steadily allowed for this sort of variety in production, distribution, and exhibition. Certainly, since World War II the regulation and advocacy by the Centre national du cinéma et de l'image animée (CNC) has been vital in preserving French cinema's heritage while promoting the wide range (*diversité*) of films produced in any given year. This volume necessarily limits itself to a condensed sample of companies, films, people, institutions, and cultural forces to present an overview of some of the most significant factors in what has made French narrative cinema so compelling from its very beginnings. As Christian Metz argues, film historians are like curators in an archive, writing to create their own imaginary archives, personal cinematheques to preserve the social memory of the films that matter most to them (12). *French Film History, 1895–1946* presents my survey of French cinema from its earliest days through World War II, complete with all the films that would be programmed in my imaginary cinematheque.

From Moving Images to Moving Photographs

While researchers throughout Europe were investigating perception, motion devices, and ways to visually record real events, Paris held a privileged position as a hub of scientific, social, and cultural experimentation. The city was host to multiple national and international expositions revealing new commercial, academic, and artistic accomplishments throughout the 1800s, leading cultural critic Walter Benjamin to designate Paris as the "capital of the 19th century." These varied exhibits and conferences, or *congrès*, attracted some of the world's most innovative researchers to share ideas and their latest developments in the industrial sciences and arts. European and North American entrepreneurs and scholars particularly contributed much to the achievements and outcomes of these events. It is important to note that the rise of new technologies, national programs, university research, and the Industrial Revolution were rapidly changing the realities of the nineteenth century, and advocates in the French republic lobbied to ensure that France remained central to as many new fields of inquiry as possible.

Photography became one of France's special fields. The camera obscura had taken on many forms and applications, but it was the physiognotrace, demonstrated by Gilles-Louis Chrétien at a Paris salon in 1797, that began a fad for reproducing portraits in profile. Chrétien's device allowed an artist to trace a subject's portrait onto a copper plate. The gadget made its way to the United States, where it was used to document the image of many important figures, including George Washington and Dolley Madison. British scientists experimented with the camera lucida, an aid for sketching intricate settings, and attempted to fix images chemically in camera obscuras. While many individuals were working on technologies of representation simultaneously, in 1816, Joseph Nicéphore Niépce recorded and fixed the first negative photographic images. He and his brother Claude pioneered many inventions, including what may have been the first internal combustion engine. Niépce initially worked as an individual inventor in his Burgundy home, where he adapted new optical devices and chemical techniques for engraving on various surfaces, including glass and treated paper. He eventually shared some of the details of his "heliography" with entrepreneur and inventor Louis Daguerre, whose promising diorama business had folded after declining interest and a devastating fire.

By 1829, Daguerre and Niépce formed a partnership, with Niépce making further strides toward shorter exposure times and sharper images. Daguerre built on Niépce's research and discoveries and forged advances in camera construction and optics. As Laurent Mannoni points out, the origins of photography and cinema are similar in that both were begun by researchers working in relative isolation who came very close to successful final products: "Then a 'newcomer' appeared in the inventor's laboratory, studied the problem, and found the technical or chemical detail which was needed for commercial exploitation of the process" (*Great Art* 191). Daguerre worked with Niépce's son Isadore to complete a reliable system for fixing a detailed photographic image on silver-plated copper sheets. They then sold all their scientific formulas and design specifications for the daguerreotype (and Daguerre's earlier dioramas) to the French government in return for lifelong annual pensions. The brand name ensured that Daguerre was perceived as the principal inventor of the process.

Thus, already in 1839, the notion of national interest in important visual inventions was coupled with the assignment of authorship and ownership. France had secured a national stake in the daguerreotype, with government officials helping promote its regional and global distribution. The daguerreotype took off with phenomenal success. Although the apparatus was quite expensive and required professional training to use, the images themselves were relatively cheap, with surprisingly high resolution. Each image produced was unique and did not allow further copies, a factor that ultimately limited its viability, but not before motivating frenetic international research activity surrounding the capturing and reproduction of images: "'Daguerreotypomania' gripped the whole of Europe and even the United States, from 1839 on" (Mannoni, *Great Art* 196). Photography would revolutionize how people saw the world, starting with one another.

France remained near the epicenter of many technical and entrepreneurial ventures tied to photography. When British researcher John Herschel made several key discoveries in fixing images, he and William Henry Fox Talbot communicated their methods immediately at the French Academy of Sciences in 1839. This presentation is credited with the first appearance of the word *photographie* in France. Herschel visited Daguerre that year to secure equipment, including one hundred unexposed plates, for his upcoming Royal Society expedition to Antarctica. Daguerreotypes were thus used for much more than portraiture. The collected research activity in England, Germany, and France resulted in a fascination with capturing and sharing photographic images, which became a major preoccupation of the nineteenth century. The Exposition Universelle of 1855 in Paris offered the first such gathering with a special photography exhibit. Photography's potential practical and commercial applications were immense. Parallel developments in the study of perception and motion quickly complemented this enthusiasm for the photorealistic still image.

Research on the study and replication of motion took many forms during the nineteenth century and often overlapped with popular entertainment and parlor games involving spectacles that combined new technologies with devices from magic acts. Networks of scientists and inquisitive inventors pursued a wild array of theories and practical avenues for rethinking how humans perceive the world and whether it might be possible to animate images to simulate motion. Researchers sought ways to slow down or freeze rapid actions photographically to study them more carefully. It is important to note that while some research was aimed at creating illusions of movement, central goals involved breaking down and recording human and animal locomotion for a better understanding of real-world behavior in time and space. As Alison McMahan points out, the pioneers of motion studies, including Étienne-Jules Marey and Eadweard Muybridge, initially sought to secure a visual record of motion that could not normally be perceived by the unaided human eye: "Scientists who specialized in motion studies were also interested in the movement of the planets, the flight of birds and the movement of air currents" ("Animation" 373). Such inquiries required recording the data for verification and repeated study, which led scientists toward adapting cutting-edge optical and photographic processes.

There were many motivating factors behind nineteenth-century motion studies. A variety of important human vision studies were undertaken in the 1820s by a cluster of scholars, including John A. Paris and Peter Mark Roget in England and Joseph Plateau in Belgium. Rapid advances in optics and techniques for the precise measurement of time and space motivated new modes of inquiry into perception and stroboscopic effects. One of the simpler, more immediate mechanisms used to illustrate our ability to merge two different successive images into a single, artificial construct was the spinning thaumatrope with portions of an image printed on each side. If there were a horse on one side and a rider sitting in mid-air on the other, a thaumatrope spun at an appropriate speed could produce the illusion of a man seated on a horse. Two colored objects could be merged into a third hue that was not physically present. What fascinated scientists about these synthetic images, which might place a bird in an empty cage or hair on a bald man's head, was the fact that although the mind knew there were two separate pictures, the perception system overrode that logic to present a convincing, unified image. This phenomenon seemed quite timely for nineteenth-century scientists interested in the mental and perceptual processes behind this sort of visual deception. By midcentury, stereoscopes exploited our ability to merge two static images into one for further entertainment and scientific effects.

In 1832, Joseph Plateau developed a more practical spinning device, named the phenakistoscope. The initial version consisted of a single cardboard disc with a series of twelve or more images printed in a circle, fanning out around the surface. In between each drawing is a slit so that the viewer would spin the disc, image side toward a mirror, and see the illusion of some repeated action, such as a dance, someone chopping wood, or a horse leaping a hurdle. Many of the characters and patterns on Plateau's wheel were designed by painter Jean-Baptiste Madou. Thanks to their detailed pictures, the phenakistoscope is credited as the first apparatus for presenting complex and convincing illusions of movement. The wheels often included sixteen drawings for fluid motion, which anticipated the eventual frame rate for silent cinema. Early historian Georges Potonniée helped ensure Plateau's significance, writing in 1928, "There is one precursor to the Cinématographe whose name should be written in gold letters at the beginning of cinema history, Belgian professor Joseph Plateau" (1).

Beyond its application for studying vision, the phenakistoscope became a model for the commercial application of subsequent motion machines and gadgets. Patented in 1833, phenakistoscopes were sold with packages of six replaceable discs beginning that year and enjoyed great success as a looping moving image toy. The simplest model had one disc, while another version included a second disc with slits, removing the need for a mirror. David Robinson, a scholar of early motion devices, proclaims that with this device, Plateau "devised the earliest form of moving picture" (8). At least Plateau's disc may be the first consumer version of a moving image apparatus that could be doubly marketed, selling it as a product and as batches of removable discs for subsequent new content. They were also sold under the name Fantoscope. Years later, French animator Émile Cohl acknowledged the significance of Plateau's invention: "Without animation we perhaps never would have had that incomparable invention, Lumière's Cinématographe. . . . Most of us owned a phenakistoscope . . . the cinema is right there" (301).

Following up closely on the heels of Plateau's spinning disc was the zoetrope, which provided a more stable illusion by placing a flexible strip of images inside its drum. The viewer spins the device and peers through a series of slots. Here, too, the "show" of moving images provides a short, repetitive attraction, although the linear series of drawings sometimes suggested more narrative action. As Nicolas Dulac and André Gaudreault observe, some viewers also doubled the number of strips seen at one time or intercut them to "edit" several cycles together (235–36). The sudden switch from a dancing girl to a leaping horse anticipates the sudden transformations in Georges Méliès's trick films. The zoetrope proved a very popular and profitable motion toy from the mid-1860s onward, and, as with the phenakistoscope, specialized companies sold the apparatus and varied sets of image strips.

During the 1860s and 1870s, a wide variety of devices were designed to allow for increasingly stable motion machines, including the ability to project zoetrope bands. Projection of images had been common in magic lantern shows since the 1660s. One of its key inventors, Christiaan Huygens, had spent time in France. He participated in the Académie des sciences in Paris in 1666 and even met Louis XIV. Magic lanterns were put to all sorts of uses, from scientific demonstrations to fantastic storytelling to occult evenings full of mysterious figures projected on various materials. The slide shows were colorfully hand-painted and often used several lenses to allow for fades and dissolves between images. As new research in photography, perception, and optics was accomplished in the nineteenth century, various magic lantern systems were often used to illustrate the results. Part of the point of generating moving pictures was their exhibition value outside the laboratory. One of the most important figures to link all these trends during the nineteenth century was Émile Reynaud.

Like many scientists of this era, Reynaud sought ways to synthesize the physical sciences and the arts. At age fourteen, Reynaud was an apprentice to a well-known Paris optician, Georges-Étienne Gaiffe, who was among the first to master the daguerreotype. Gaiffe taught the young Reynaud about precision optics, mechanical engineering, and photography. One of Gaiffe's many inventions, the electric metronome, was adapted during the 1880s for rapidly opening and closing apertures during series photography. After Gaiffe, Reynaud moved to the studios of a famed artist, Antoine Samuel Adam-Salomon, who was shifting from sculpting likenesses of famous people in metal medallions to photographic portraits of his contemporaries. Poet Alphonse de Lamartine, who had initially dismissed photography, publicly announced his change of mind after admiring Adam-Salomon's work: "Photography is . . . better than an art, it is a solar phenomenon in which the artist collaborates with the sun" (Lonjon 46).

These apprenticeships allowed Reynaud to launch his own photography service, where he specialized in botanical and scientific work. By taking hundreds of photographs of plants and flowers, some shot through microscopes, for Adolphe Focillon's science encyclopedia, Reynaud helped prove that photography could uncover minute details of the physical world. He also presented magic lantern lectures on photography and science. During his drive to represent the stages of plant growth, he reworked aspects of the phenakistiscope and the zoetrope, placing a series of mirrors in the center of a drum, with a strip of images facing them, for bright, stable illusions of motion from a series of images. Reynaud patented his praxinoscope in 1877, initially with twelve mirror faces and accompanying color lithograph images of entertaining short subjects and movements on flexible strips of paper.

The praxinoscope was an immediate hit. In 1878, Reynaud added a candle option for a brighter view of the action and a box attachment allowing the viewer to look through an opening with cut-out matte page to mimic a theatrical setting. Consumer models came with up to five different stage inserts. This praxinoscope-theater thus provided a scenographic context for the figure twirling, dancing, or leaping around and around in the mirror. Reynaud's invention won an honorable mention at the 1878 Exhibition Universelle in Paris and a slightly revised model won a silver medal at the Paris Industrial Exposition in 1879. Reynaud went on to sell 100,000 praxinoscopes as consumer toys with scientific applications. He was shifting from being a scientist to an entrepreneur to a showman. By 1880, at the Société française de photographie, he presented a new version equipped with twelve glass slides that were angled to reflect into a magic lantern device with an oxy-hydrogen light source, projecting them through a lens onto a screen. According to the society's write-up, "M. Reynaud commented that the effects would be still more beautiful if, in place of the hand-drawn images representing the different phases of a movement, it were possible to obtain them by means of photography. One would have a perfection of representation and exactness of movement" (Mannoni, *Great Art* 374). In 1882, Eadweard Muybridge used a projecting praxinoscope to present his photographic images; Reynaud's invention offered the best solution for presenting stable images with a convincing, fluid sense of movement (Lonjon 109–11).

Reynaud innovated his design further, abandoning the limitations of a zoetrope-like drum. He devised a new projection apparatus, the *théâtre optique*. The optical theater involved a series of painted glass or glycerine slides, sixty millimeters square, fixed in a flexible belt that was cranked in a continuous movement past a light source. The long strips were perforated so that sprockets could advance the images steadily as the belt was wound between large reels. As the slides passed the steady beam of light, each drawing was projected by a series of mirror facets rotating at the same speed, much like the core ring of mirrors in a praxinoscope, onto a fixed mirror, which then reflected them up through a lens into yet another angled mirror, bouncing them onto the projection screen.

Unlike later cinema projectors, Reynaud's contraption had no shutter mechanism. However, a separate magic lantern would project a static setting, such as a garden or beach, onto which the characters would be composited. Because the complex device had to be positioned directly in front of the screen, Reynaud back-projected his show, placing the audience on the other side to avoid obstructing their view. His patent stated that the images inserted in the malleable strip of slides could be hand-drawn, printed mechanically, or even obtained via photography. The optical theater could present a much longer linear action or narrative than the zoetrope or praxinosceope and more stable movement. Dulac and Gaudreault observe that although Reynaud's optical theater involved hundreds of still images, "paradoxically, for the viewer, there was now *only one image*" moving constantly on the screen: "Reynaud's apparatus thus went beyond mere gyration, beyond the mere thrill of seeing the strip repeat itself; narrative had taken over as the primary structuring

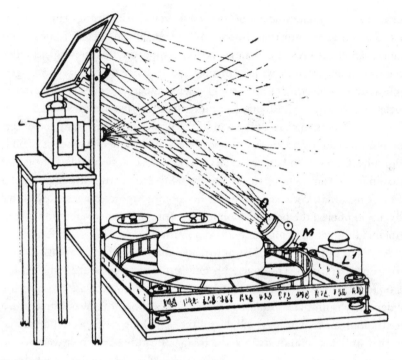

Optical Theater patent sketch (*La Nature*, 1878)

principle" (239). Reynaud's spectators experienced an additional thrill in that they witnessed the apparatus itself, with the inventor at the controls behind the screen turning the handles. As *La Nature* reported, "He resembles Captain Nemo at the helm of the Nautilus—20,000 leagues under his dreams" (Tchernia 5). For the premiere, the venue manager invited his friend Georges Méliès, who was then exploiting magic lantern slides in his own theatrical spectacles. Reynaud and Méliès met after the show and even discussed whether some photographic process might be possible to reduce the labor-intensive task of drawing hundreds of required slides. Both men were aware of Thomas Edison's experiments at the time, and Reynaud regularly considered new techniques and materials for belts and slides as his performances continued over the next few years.

While Reynaud's praxinoscopes were sold in a variety of French stores, the optical theater was a unique, one-of-a-kind, and rather cumbersome apparatus. To exploit it, Reynaud signed an exclusive contract with the Musée Grévin, a famous wax museum and venue for magic shows in Paris. Beginning in 1892, Reynaud presented programs throughout the day at the Grévin. The first line-up included three different subjects, alternating with other acts: *Poor Pierre* (*Pauvre Pierrot*) was made up of 500 drawings with a duration of ten minutes; *The Clown and His Dogs* (*Clown et ses chiens*) was composed of 300 drawn images and lasted roughly eight minutes, including lots of movement; and *A Good Beer* (*Un bon bock*) was a twelve-minute comedy with seven hundred slides in which a kitchen employee fools thirsty clients by drinking their beers when they are not looking. Reynaud would stop, pause, and reverse certain scenes to extend the show. For instance, the harlequin tormenting Pierrot may dance three times in a row, forward, backward, forward, from one set of drawings, a bit like the later Lumière *cinématographe* shows in which a wall could be knocked down, then shown leaping back up in place. These "illuminated pantomime" gags anticipated the lengths of later one-reel films and commercial cartoons. Reynaud offered a full show, including live musical accompaniment and hand-colored moving images for a paying audience. Hence, Lonjon provocatively titled his monograph *Emile Reynaud: The Real Inventor of the Cinema*. The Cinémathèque's Laurent Mannoni agrees: "Reynaud was not a 'precursor'; what he made was true cinema, both as spectacle and as 'inscription of movement'" (*Great Art* 386).

In 1894, scientist and photographer Étienne-Jules Marey mentioned Reynaud and his optical theater in a book on movement, suggesting that photographic images would greatly improve the effects (Mannoni, *Great Art* 382). That same year, famed photographers Auguste and Louis Lumière visited Reynaud at the Musée Grévin, returning several times and positioning themselves to watch Reynaud and his apparatus in action. They borrowed several elements from his complicated contraption, especially the flexible belt wound between two reels, an idea Reynaud gleaned from observing bicycle chains and sprockets. Reynaud tried to adapt his *théâtre optique* further after 1895 to compete with the popular Kinetoscope and Lumière Cinématographe showings, but he never managed to perfect his own photographic processes. Later in the 1890s, he did employ cinema cameras to record actions, including the popular comic pair Foottit and Chocolat performing their William Tell pantomime act in 1896. However, rather than projecting the film strips, he cut up the positive prints to trace and color them, much like later rotoscoping, for what he called "animated photo-paintings" (Auzel 94–95; Myrent and Langlois 199). By 1900, the audiences for Reynaud's performances had declined, overshadowed by the cinema, especially Lumière's actualities and Méliès's fantasies. Moreover, the Lumières filmed Foottit and Chocolat and their William Tell apple shooting routine in 1897, followed by Méliès and his own comical William Tell sketch, incorporating flashy stop-motion effects. The moving pictures built on and then surpassed Reynaud's accomplishments.

Reynaud nonetheless proves to be a key figure bringing together new technologies and new modes of marketing motion pictures. For many historians, Reynaud is the first real animator of moving images. It is estimated that 500,000 people attended his performances between 1892 and 1900 at the Musée Grévin, providing a lucrative model for the exploitation of motion pictures and repeated short subject screenings. Moreover, Reynaud was intricately entwined with the other pertinent researchers of his day. He even made use of pioneering fast exposure photography by Muybridge and Marey to ensure that his human and animal figures, including a galloping horse, moved correctly in his drawn slides (Sadoul, *Histoire* 14). Although Reynaud's life and goals had changed dramatically as he moved from the physical sciences and photography to becoming an entertainer, Marey, another active participant in the rise of French cinema, remained focused on scientific applications of serial photography, motion, and projection systems. His intended audience was always the scientific community, but he influenced cinema technology far into the future.

Initially, Marey was a physiologist who backed into serial photography in pursuit of research goals related to body movement, including muscles, nerves, and fluids. His 1859 thesis was on blood circulation, and he pioneered many new methods for observing and measuring the body's vital functions. For him, the living body was a machine that could be measured and explained thanks to the laws of physics and mechanical engineering. He brought precision tools usually used in industrial settings to bear on bodies in motion (Braun xvii). For Marey, blood flow was simply a matter of hydraulics, and the heart's pumping was a purely mechanical process. To measure subtle bodily movements and pressures, he devised methods for graphing his evidence visually. His first invention, a sphygmograph, measured the pulse and earned him an invitation to Napoleon III's court. He continued to search for new ways to observe, record, and transcribe moving muscles in living bodies. His inventions included the polygraph, which measured pulse and respiration simultaneously. Similarly, his myograph and cardiograph provided revolutionary graphic read-outs on muscle and heart movements in real time. His findings were regularly covered in the prestigious scientific journal *La Nature*, and the resulting devices were quickly adopted by the medical profession. He was fortunate enough to have access to laboratory space supported by his teaching fund from the prestigious Collège de France.

Marey's research team created tiny mechanisms to quantify and graph beating wing patterns among insects and birds. Early on, Marey believed that his experiments would one day lead to human flight. He was especially interested in documenting how wings generate air currents. His 1873 book *La Machine animale* (*The Animal Mechanism*) presented his findings for measuring normally unobservable phenomena in time. For instance, he placed devices on a horse's legs to record graphically its motion, when its feet left the ground, and for how long. He concluded that a horse's hooves all leave the ground at full gallop. This report motivated California governor Leland Stanford to engage Muybridge to provide definitive photographic proof, which Muybridge accomplished in 1878. As Marey quickly learned, however, such graphic records were scientifically valuable, but photographic records could provide more convincing visual evidence for those beyond the laboratory. Moreover, Marey and other scientists had faith that serial photography could teach artists much about real-world accuracy, especially for naturalistic paintings of animals and humans in action.

Marey not only followed the early stages of Muybridge's career before they met in 1881; he was also inspired by French astronomer Pierre Jules César Janssen's photographic revolver, invented to record the planet Venus passing between the Earth and the Sun during an eclipse. Janssen's expedition had traveled to Japan to record the 1874 event. Janssen returned to great fanfare and traveled widely to present the images he had captured on his revolving daguerreotype plate. One camera model allowed him to capture forty-eight impressions in seventy-two seconds, though the exposure times and lens produced rather soft images. Janssen demonstrated his photographic device to the French Academy of Sciences, was written up in *La Nature*, and gave illustrated talks at the Société de Géographie and at the Palais d'Industrie, where his photographic equipment was put on display (Mannoni, *Great Art* 302). Later, Méliès regularly lampooned such pretentious publicity-seeking scientists and their expeditions. However, it is worth noting that the large number of influential scientific and artistic societies, to say nothing of the French government's support for promising inventions and frequent expositions, fueled an interest in motion photography research and kept Paris at the center of new developments.

Prior to Janssen's revolver technique, previous French attempts at sequential image recording had used other methods, including those of Henry Du

Mont, a Belgian working in France, who patented a camera and projector in 1861 to reproduce "successive phases of movement," via treated glass dry plates, though it was not very practical (Frizot 38). Du Mont experimented with images of a dancer and a horse running on a beach. Similarly, Louis Arthur Ducos du Hauron patented an unusual device with several hundred tiny lenses exposing minuscule photos on a wet plate or a strip of photo-sensitive fabric wound between two cylinders. Mannoni asserts that "the essential principles on which present-day cinematography are based" were first defined by Du Mont and Ducos du Hauron (*Great Art* 252–53). Janssen created a more stable process with a single lens. These researchers were pursuing overlapping, clearly defined research agendas. Alan Williams applies the useful notion of bricolage, a sort of do-it-yourself set of combinations and makeshift processes, to explain the haphazard creation of cinema from various existing, disparate components (*Republic of Images* 9). Clearly, however, many of the key figures in this era were driven with very precise research and development plans, often with specific goals, sometimes with intended commercial applications that shifted over time or were synthesized with other new discoveries. These researchers and entrepreneurs shared their projects, devices, and findings at photography and industrial science expositions and in *La Nature*. Scientific inquiry, the marketplace, and the rise in urban entertainment options all helped drive the interrelated realms of photography, moving images, and visual culture.

Marey became the most important link between the worlds of scientific experimentation and the field of motion pictures. He reimagined Janssen's revolver design, publishing detailed specifications for his own camera-gun in 1882, which initially used a rotating dry plate disc capable of twelve exposures at a speed of 1/720th of a second. Marey's approach differed from Muybridge's battery of separate cameras firing in sequence to record images on wet plates. Muybridge copied his figures onto his zoopraxiscope projector to replicate the movement. Marey's single perspective and clear photographic evidence proved far superior. Marey "resolved the problems of inaccuracy inherent in Muybridge's system; it was measurably precise; it worked with unprecedented speed and produced the number of images needed for synthesis—the twelve images it made each second were enough to synthesize motion on a phenakistoscope" (Braun 61). Marey could visually document accurately birds in flight, horses trotting, and people leaping. He also filmed the first known photographic record of blood flowing through veins. Excited by the precise measurements and clarity of his images, Marey continued to upgrade his rifle gun with ever faster film stock and exposure times, incorporating more photographic options in his "chronophotography" research.

Marey hired Georges Demenÿ as an assistant, and together they formed a Physiological Station in the Bois de Boulogne on the edge of Paris. In addition to his interest in chronophotography and image projection, Demenÿ was devoted to the new concern over exercise and health. He helped bring physical education into the school curriculum in France and launched the new field of sports medicine. Their Physiological Station benefited from Marey's research money and support from the Minister of Public Education and the city of Paris. Importantly, a portion of their budget came from government interest in physical strength and fatigue involved in activities such as military maneuvers and agricultural labor. The history of cinema in France was funded in part by a growing concern over strength and efficiency in business, sports, and the military. Throughout the 1880s, Marey and Demenÿ completed hundreds of photographic experiments in their visual laboratory of physical movements.

By 1888, Marey had adapted his latest camera to expose a strip of paper film, recording twenty images per second. He also created another camera to record multiple exposures of an event and demonstrate his findings about

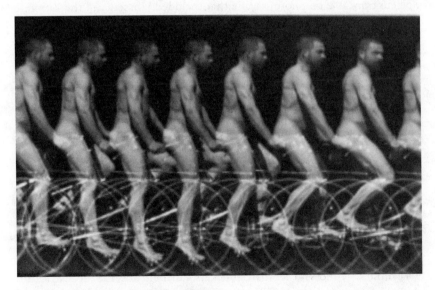

Marey bicycle (Cinémathèque Française)

human and animal locomotion to his sponsors. The resulting array of images allowed movement to be recorded in slightly blurred overlapping stages of fluid motion. As Mannoni observes, these images could be "somewhat surreal . . . showing the movement of a human being or an animal with a degree of abstraction worthy of the Futurists" (*Great Art* 338). The resulting photo-collages, including images of athletes leaping, naked men riding bicycles or trotting under heavy backpacks, provided valuable information on locomotion and muscle performance. They became abstract artworks in their own right. Furthermore, for some experiments, Marey photographed human subjects wearing black costumes with reflective metal strips affixed at strategic points to help measure muscle and bone movements, in what now look like motion capture suits.

As Braun concludes, Marey's research not only affected the nineteenth-century understanding of physical motion; it changed the social conceptions of the body. Marey and Demenÿ's research was accelerated by its applicability to multiple research agendas, including larger national ideological concerns and studies in human health and efficiency. For the 1889 Exposition Universelle in Paris, Marey, Reynaud, Thomas Edison, and the Lumière brothers all demonstrated their latest discoveries, further enhancing France's role as the world's showplace for the most important advances in photography and motion studies. Edison even attended a dinner sponsored by the Société francaise de photographie that included Janssen and the Lumière brothers. Before leaving France, Edison met with Marey, who showed Edison his projection device and introduced the American to the advantages of flexible celluloid over Edison's cylinder process. This meeting was "a pivotal point in Thomas Edison's motion picture experiments." As Edison acknowledged, "'I knew instantly that Marey had the right idea'" (Spehr 145).

Marey's laboratories were among the most advanced in the world. He could observe, record, and project scenes of moving humans and animals from many different angles, including cats and rabbits being dropped, upside down, to record their struggle to right themselves before hitting the ground. To examine flying insects, his team devised an apparatus capable of filming rapidly beating wings via exposures up to 1/25,000th of a second. By 1890, his team had created a camera with two reels, feeding a spool of sensitized film stock inserted in a larger band of paper. The patent sketch certainly resembles a later motion picture mechanism, though the flexible film is advanced via cylindrical rollers rather than sprockets. Furthermore, the "eccentric cam shaft" developed by Demenÿ to allow the film stock's stop-and-start action,

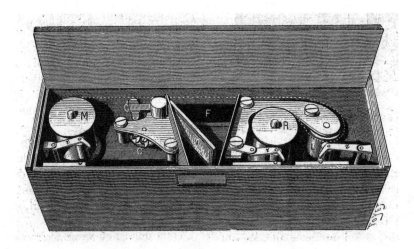

Marey 1890 camera patent (*La Nature*, 1890)

halting briefly before the aperture even as it was wound continuously between the two metal spool reels, became a crucial component for Thomas Armat and Charles Francis Jenkins's Vitascope in the United States.

Marey's chronophotography had multiple applications for the physical and applied sciences, as well as education. A professor from the National Institute for the Deaf raised the idea of using serial photographs to study the mechanics of speech with the goal of teaching deaf people to read lips and mimic speech. Demenÿ took on the challenge in 1891, recording his own face in close-up with Marey's camera as he spoke short phrases, "Je vous aime" and "Vive la France." He printed the twenty-four positive images around the edge of a glass disc attached to a lens with a magic lantern for projection, allowing the series of images to be shown, moving realistically, in a classroom. Demenÿ presented his device at the French Academy of Sciences in 1891, and it was soon hailed as a major breakthrough, "the optical equivalent of the phonograph" (Braun 177). In 1892, he patented this phonoscope projection system, and it was featured at the International Photography Exposition in Paris that year. Demenÿ was confident there would be a great demand for "living portraits" of important people. He and his rotating disc invention received attention from around the world. The clarity and function of Demenÿ's phonoscope helped make it an appealing attraction and potentially valuable in the eyes of teachers and scholars alike, though his attempts to commercialize the apparatus failed. Even with its largest disc of sixty images, a projected action on a phonoscope would only last four seconds before repeating.

Meanwhile, Marey's persistent fascination with flight led him to create a small wind tunnel to record smoke, providing visible evidence that air currents actually resembled water currents in many ways, exerting measurable force on bodies in motion. This work proved essential for international experiments in designing airplane wings and gliders. Marey communicated his findings widely and corresponded directly with US aeronautic pioneer Samuel Pierpont Langley. Moreover, Orville and Wilbur Wright read Marey's *Animal Mechanism*, and his work on birds inspired their plane designs (Braun 221–22). When Marey died in 1904, just months after the Wright brothers' successful flight, he was one of the world's most respected scientific figures. He had taught for more than fifty years at the Collège de France and had been awarded nearly every possible honor from French photographic, medical, and scientific communities. His freeze-frame illustrations and representations of overlapping figures in various phases of an action also inspired artists who found his "decompositions" of real time and fluid motion as poignant as they were beautiful: "Marey's work in chronophotography had a seminal influence on early twentieth-century abstract art" (Braun 277). Painter František Kupka even visited the Marey exhibit at the 1900 Exposition Universelle, and eventually many Cubists, Futurists, and Dadaists became fascinated with Marey's fragmentation of the visual world.

As president of the French Society for Photographers, Marey had been well acquainted with Auguste and Louis Lumière. He and Demenÿ had even begun using Lumière photographic materials, plates and then film stock, during the 1890s. Clearly, the cinema resulted from many varied interactions among a wide range of researchers. France's interconnected professional societies, government institutions, and scientific journals and expositions fueled collaboration and competition on a scale unprecedented anywhere else during the end of the nineteenth century. Marey was well situated at the nucleus of much of this activity. Next, the young Lumière brothers and their new generation of researchers and entrepreneurs built dramatically on the work of the pioneers of scientific inquiry and serial photography.

CHAPTER 2

Lumière, Méliès, and the Rise of Cinema in France

Lumière et Cie

Between 1895 and 1905, the Lumière company got the Cinématographe out of their laboratory and into the world, creating and distributing more than 1,400 motion pictures. It would take more than twenty hours to watch their entire output of fifty-second movies end to end. The Lumière catalog offers a stunning array of perspectives on the birth of the twentieth century, including scores of films shot in the Middle East and Africa, East Asia and the South Pacific, and North and South America. Thus, the scale and scope of the Lumières' cinematic output is staggering. Moreover, the many other significant, nonphotographic inventions by brothers Auguste Lumière (1862–1954) and Louis Lumière (1864–1948) warrant book-length studies themselves. The Lumières were at the forefront of a new sort of progressive industrialism, offering health insurance and other benefits and protections for their workers, with on-site nurseries and a savings plan to help employees in their retirement. They had faith that new technologies and enlightened capitalism could improve everyone's lives, and they were optimistic about science, the arts, and the new century.

Their father, Antoine Lumière, began as a painter but shifted over to the new field of photography in the 1860s, launching several very successful photographic portrait shops before settling in Lyon. He started with daguerreotypes before switching to wet plates. Once in Lyon, Antoine became immersed in progressive politics and scientific organizations of the region. His studio was among the first businesses to have electricity. He exploited its artificial lighting for his portraits, adding artistic touches that helped set his painterly photography apart from his competitors. Importantly, Antoine Lumière set up a photographic booth at the 1878 Exposition Universelle in Paris, which featured an electric sign and drew a great deal of attention and brisk business. From this point on, he became one of the best-known photographers in France. This new wealth and visibility, along with a direct train line between Paris and Lyon, allowed Lumière to interact regularly with top scholars and entrepreneurs. His sons were plunged into the family business early on. On their summer vacations at the beach, Auguste and Louis, in their early teens, set up a darkroom laboratory to take and develop tin-type images of tourists. Soon, when Antoine Lumière heard about an experimental dry gelatin silver bromide photographic process developed by Belgium's Désiré van Monckhoven that showed potential, he realized that this simpler technique could open photography to nonspecialists. If Lumière could master the process, he could sell photographic materials to the public, popularizing and democratizing what was still a highly professional vocation.

Initially, he could not match or improve on Monckhoven's experimental process. Frustrated, he turned the problem over to his inventive sons, Auguste and Louis, still in their teens. The brothers attended the radical Martinière School, "dedicated to teaching mathematics, the arts, and science with the goal of training students to go forth into society as progressive agents to build wealth for all of society" (Faucheux 38). Their curriculum stressed problem solving and preferred trial and error over set lesson plans. The whole institution was devoted to creativity and innovation. In 1881, at age seventeen, Louis devoted himself to evaluating Monckhoven's photographic process, ultimately surpassing it with a revolutionary formula that proved much more efficient than existing dry plates. Moreover, with the right infrastructure, the new plates could be mass produced. This discovery was the beginning of a lifetime of important inventions for the brothers. Throughout their lives, Louis and Auguste were nearly inseparable and they agreed early on to share all patents, regardless of which brother was lead inventor. They ultimately co-signed 350 patents in photography, chemistry, optics, and medical devices. Realizing the significance of their new process, Antoine bought a large plot of land for a factory to produce Lumière photographic materials. Clients could purchase a box of twelve glass plates to expose anywhere and develop later.

Louis continually updated their already popular line of dry glass plates, creating the Etiquette Bleue product line in 1885, named after the blue box label. The blue label brand lasted for sixty years and guaranteed the family's fortune. Much of the work of coating the plates and developing photographs was accomplished by women equipped with special lamps for the darkrooms.

Sister Jeanne Lumière also worked in the labs, contributing to research on new chemical formulas and product innovations. Their family business expanded quickly from just under 300,000 francs in 1886 to 2.7 million by 1892. In 1890 alone, the Lumières sold 350,000 glass plates. The family also spent lavishly on villas and property, as well as setting aside ample funding for continuing research and development and making contributions to social causes and employee benefits. They believed in the modern notion of vacation and travels, participating in new trends of leisure activity and mobility, which they chronicled with family photographs. Thanks to the Lumières, photographers were no longer limited to studio-bound portraits. They could become active participants in documenting social changes and modernization.

By 1894, Louis and Auguste were well aware of the motion and image experiments by Reynaud and Marey and had heard about the Edison company's progress in moving photographic images. In fact, Edison's rush to gain publicity had motivated him to present demonstrations and publish patent specifications and diagrams of his Kinetograph process among scientific groups and potential Kinetoscope customers alike (Spehr 379). Antoine Lumière lived part-time in Paris, where he saw one of the earliest demonstrations of the Edison Kinetoscope in spring 1894. In October he visited the first Kinetoscope parlor in Paris. This shop was owned by one of his business acquaintances who was already looking for cheaper alternative 35mm films to run in his Kinetoscopes. The shopkeeper gave Antoine a strip from Edison's *Barbershop* to take back to Lyon. Antoine explained to his son Louis and their chief engineer, Charles Moisson, that "Edison is selling this at crazy prices, and the agents want to make these films in France" (Mannoni, *Great Art* 422). Initially, the motivation for devising a working 35mm camera and a new film strip process sprung from a competitive challenge. However, Edison's business model still privileged selling machines for individual viewers. The Lumières quickly realized the larger potential in producing and exhibiting films to groups of paying customers.

Developing a viable motion picture camera, film stock, and projector became the top priority for the Lumière brothers. Antoine is famously credited with asking Louis to "get the images out of the box." Already in December 1894, the local *Lyon Républicain* newspaper announced proudly that Auguste and Louis Lumière were working on "a new sort of kinetograph, no less remarkable than that of Edison, and about which the local Lyonnais will be the first to hear" (Gautier and Lamotte 15). It is important to note that they had to do more than just build a projector. Flexible film stock was still very new to the Lumières, and at first they experimented with strips of photographic paper. Next, they bought celluloid from a US supplier, but they soon contracted with Victor Planchon to produce celluloid in France, forming a jointly owned company. Moisson and his team constructed an apparatus to cut the sheets of celluloid into 35mm strips and perforate them with round sprocket holes, while Louis worked on an emulsion that would adhere to the slick, bending material and be easy to develop and print. Louis managed to invent a stop-start mechanism so that the film could be moving constantly from its reel while also halting briefly in front of the camera's aperture for a clear, stable exposure. He was partly inspired by studying the precise movements of a sewing machine as it advanced and stitched thread. The camera and reversible projection components, from the claws to the cam shaft and rotating shutter, had to be delicate enough to run film through at a steady pace and tension, plus durable enough to work repeatedly outside the laboratory setting. The mechanism also had to be gentle on the film stock. Thanks to their clever claw mechanism, this projector could also be reversed, running the film backward.

On March 19, 1895, Louis conducted his first official test of the Cinématographe, setting up his camera in the street to record workers leaving the factory for their lunch break, *Workers Leaving the Factory* (*La Sortie de l'usine*). As historian Michel Faucheux states, "This first film reveals what will be the Cinématographe's true calling, to show movement, yes, but also to reproduce the surge of modern life" (97). At the same time, the Lumières revealed the new active role of women, who are very prominent among the factory employees. The shot of bustling workers provided a good test for resolution and contrast because their movements could be captured in several planes of depth and with a variety of lighting levels. Louis recorded the same action of workers leaving the factory several times that year to assess ongoing upgrades to the camera and film stock. The Cinématographe had an exposure rate of 1/50th of a second at fifteen, then sixteen, frames per second. Louis may have been the Cinématographe's chief engineer, but Auguste and other employees at Lumière helped with solving design challenges. Furthermore, Antoine did more than encourage his sons; he proudly spread the word in professional circles that the Lumières would soon surpass Edison's Kinetoscope.

Louis presented a screening of *Workers Leaving the Factory* and explained the Cinématographe at an industrial conference in Paris that spring. In

June 1895, he demonstrated his invention more fully, presenting eight films for the French Photographic Society meeting in Lyon, where he also filmed the members of the congress and later projected the moving pictures for them. The resulting *Photographic Society Arrives in Lyon* (*Débarquement du congrès de photographes à Lyon*) generated a startling impression on the participants. Throughout 1895, the Lumière brothers and Moisson continued improvements on the camera, emulsion, and projector, testing new versions on various small professional audiences. Their progress motivated a great deal of curiosity, and they turned down scores of requests to purchase the experimental Cinématographe equipment and films.

Thus, prior to the famed December 28, 1895, commercial premiere in Paris, an audience for the Cinématographe was already building and the Lumières were fielding all sorts of invitations. Moisson traveled to Belgium, projecting films for the Belgian photography association and even Prince Albert (later King Albert I), whose office wrote to Louis that the prince "was most impressed with your Cinématographe and is deeply interested in that remarkable invention" (Rittaud-Hutinet 49). Among other inquiries, the Eclair firm contacted Louis, but he explained, "we are currently unable to make any firm commitments regarding this device" (Rittaud-Hutinet 41). Thus, the Cinématographe was well understood by the Lumières to be an invention with a strong potential future. Their goal was to construct a dependable working model before deciding on an appropriate business plan to exploit their new product line.

The Lumières outsourced the construction of the wooden Cinématographe and its internal mechanism to Jules Carpentier, an engineer working near Paris. The existing letters exchanged between Louis Lumière and Carpentier reveal the extent to which the Cinématographe was an ongoing series of models with nearly constant upgrades and improvements. The two men met often but primarily communicated via a steady flurry of letters, often hand-illustrated. The new, rapid train service allowed them to keep in touch and respond to one another almost daily. They discussed everything from subtle variations on the shape of the tips of the claw mechanism to the solidity of the drive rods and even debated what sort of soft cloth worked best to line the bins that caught the film as it fell during projection. The Cinématographe had no take-up reel. Louis was clearly fascinated with every detail, enforcing rigorous construction standards. Carpentier's shop produced the first commercial Cinématographe and ultimately two hundred more over the next several years. Louis Lumière monitored, tested, and approved every aspect of the Cinématographe's development, including refinements to Planchon's production of their film stock.

Surprisingly, the famous premiere of the Cinématographe to a paying audience in Paris on December 28, 1895, was arranged by Antoine Lumière. Louis and Auguste stayed home in Lyon with their families. For the opening night, Méliès and the director of the Musée Grévin were present as well as the manager of the Folies Bergère. All three men separately offered large sums of money to Antoine for the rights to exploit the Cinématographe, but Antoine refused. The room he rented beneath the Grand Café contained nearly two hundred seats, and a fire marshal was present as well. The first screening of ten films sold only thirty-three tickets, but word spread quickly, audiences swelled, and soon shows were scheduled from 10 a.m. to 11 p.m. As many as three thousand people attended on some days, and crowd control became a problem. During spring 1896, the Lumières opened a second venue in Paris and another in Lyon. By June 1896, their screenings had generated an astonishing one million francs, and the Lumières helped Planchon build a new factory on the edge of Lyon to manufacture the nitrate film stock. In 1897, as the attendance for their shows started to decline, the Lumières began marketing more aggressively but also sold Cinématographes to other operators. Eventually they revised their sprocket holes from two to the more universal four per frame so their films could be shown in competing brands of projectors, and the Cinématographes they sold could combine Lumière and non-Lumière movies for their screenings. They profited from selling the apparatus and film stock as well as presenting their own shows.

It is difficult to overstate the significance and impact of the first commercial showings of the Cinématographe initially in France and as they spread around the world. As the write-up of the opening night presentation from the newspaper *Le Radical* reveals, the moving images proved awe inspiring:

> It is a new invention and certainly one of the most unusual things of our era. . . . For instance, there is the *scene of blacksmiths* [*Les Forgerons*]. One works the bellows and the smoke escapes the firebox, while the other takes the hot iron, pounds it on the anvil, then plunges it in the water, generating a large plume of white steam. . . . But the one that created the most excitement and enthusiasm was *Bathing at the Sea / La Baignade en mer*. The sea here is so true, so wavy, so shaded, so dynamic, while the bathers and divers who climb up on the pier, run across the deck, and dive headfirst are truly a wonder. (Banda and Moure 40)

Lumière pier (*Bathing at the Sea*)

This ecstatic review was fairly typical of the reactions. Audiences marveled at the mobile reflections on the water or glass surfaces, the wind in the leaves behind the baby's breakfast scene, the smoke blasting from a train, and all sorts of minor details in the background. One early commentator pondered whether audiences would ever look at flat theatrical sets in the same way again. Despite the lack of sound, movies in 1895 were already seen as potential competition with live theater.

The Lumières made the important decision to hire and train a cadre of young operators. The camera's hand crank and advancing system had some play in them, so early on Louis learned to pace himself, turning the handle evenly for steady tension. He also taught all his operators to hum the same tune and crank the film on the same beat as he did when filming or projecting. These cinematographers were dispatched around the world to record a diverse array of films, including views of exotic international locales, to expand offerings in their catalog. The notion that operators in Egypt, Moscow, Indochina, and Mexico were all humming the same French refrain as they recorded their films is as charming as it was practical. These young men acted as representatives of the Lumière company and even ambassadors for France itself. Often, before they could receive permits for their unheard-of presentations, the operators needed letters of introduction and even assurance from influential people in those foreign lands. The Lumière cinematographers routinely provided initial private screenings to princes, governors, industrialists, and mayors to gain support and permissions. By the end of 1896, the Cinématographe and its films had already been exhibited in many of the world's major cities.

One of the first Lumière operators, Félix Mesguich, was sent to the United States, Canada, and Russia, arranging his own itinerary and travel plans, toting the equipment, developing the film he shot, and usually projecting the

Lumière duel (*Pistol Duel*)

Lumière rickshaw shot of children (*Namo Village Panorama*)

shows as well. Alexandre Promio was also part of the first cadre of operators. He is credited with some of the most striking Lumière movies, including a mobile shot from a train arriving in Constantinople and the first films
of the Jaffa Gate in Jerusalem. He traveled across Europe, visiting everyone
from the Russian tsar to Sweden's king to the queen of Spain; he even filmed
Queen Victoria's funeral. Eventually he went to work for Pathé Frères.
Another operator who traveled far and wide was Gabriel Veyre, who took
the Cinématographe to North America, Mexico, Cuba, Japan, Indochina, and
beyond. Veyre shot the deceptively realistic reconstruction of *Pistol Duel* (*Duel
au pistolet*, 1896) in Mexico as well as the exhilarating film of laughing children
in rural Vietnam, shot from a rickshaw, *Namo Village Panorama* (*Le Village de
Namo: Panorame pris d'une chaise à porteurs*, 1900). While there were ultimately
1,422 titles issued in catalogs by the Lumières, many more films were created. The main office in Lyon decided which films would be reproduced and

distributed officially. Moreover, untold numbers of films shipped back to Lyon were lost in transit, including most of those shot by Veyre in Canada among indigenous people.

The Cinématographe had quickly become an important facet of the Lumière enterprise as they shifted from a profitable small-scale exhibition model to selling machines and mass-producing movies for international sales. While photographic products remained at the core of their business, their motion pictures put France at the heart of the new medium, cinema. For the 1900 Paris Exposition Universelle, which Richard Abel reminds us was intended "to celebrate the world's progress over the course of the past 100 years, and designed to prove France's domination, with Paris as the center of the universe," the Lumières projected films onto a gigantic screen (*Ciné* 1). They ran two shows each evening for months, replacing the line-up regularly, presenting 150 different movies to an eventual audience of 1.4 million people. The Cinématographe was more than a special attraction at this point—it was a sensational new cultural phenomenon.

Beyond launching successful technological and commercial practices, the Lumières established many aesthetic principles that subsequent filmmakers prized and followed. With a technologically limited maximum length of fifty seconds, the Cinématographe camera was often positioned to offer compelling glimpses of real-world actions from striking angles. Whether it was a train pulling into a station, a snowball fight in the street, or a string of workhorses lumbering across a field with a heavy load, Louis Lumière's camera and those of his operators typically framed the shot to capture movement from a diagonal set-up, exploiting a clear vanishing point to emphasize depth cues. By contrast, Edison's Kinetoscopes were restrained by their bulk and electricity and regularly recorded the action straight on, as if filming a stage set, with shallow playing space and frontal positioning. Assigning authorship to Lumière films raises interesting challenges. Although Louis did not shoot most Lumière films, his practical and aesthetic training of the operators, including instructions on appropriate topics, and his help curating the catalog place him in a unique creative role as an early sort of auteur director-producer-distributor.

The Lumière films may rightfully be compared with artistic photographs or even carefully composed paintings. Promio's *Unloading a Ship* (*Déchargement d'un navire*, 1996), for instance, recalls photos by Alfred Stieglitz and other pictorialists with its bursts of steam, varied light values, sharp diagonals, and evocative depth. Other striking pictorialist-style films include *Drawing out the*

Lumière loading ship (*Unloading a Ship*)

Coke (*Défournage du coke*, 1896) and *Workers Repairing an Asphalt Sidewalk* (*Ouvriers réparant un trottoir en bitume*, 1897). In fact, Jacques Aumont builds on Jean-Luc Godard's famous claim that Louis Lumière was equivalent to the last Impressionist painter, adding that "in Lumière's films, it is as if the air, water, and light had become palpable and eternally present" (24). Clearly, these views of daily life were as artistic as they were entertaining.

Louis Lumière's choice of subject matter and aesthetic composition, including a striking depth of field, helped bridge artisanal production with a modern fascination with industrialism. It is striking how many of the films feature new technical devices and inventions, such as moving sidewalks, elevated urban trains, steam ships, or factories in full swing. For instance, the shot taken while ascending the Eiffel Tower must have proven dizzying to early audiences (*Panorama pendant l'ascension de la Tour Eiffel*, 1897), and shots from moving boats and trains, such as the arrival by train in Lyon (*Panorama de*

Lumière sidewalk (*Workers Repairing Asphalt Sidewalk*)

l'arrivée en gare de Perrache pris du train, 1896), reveal shifting perspectives that seem to make buildings turn on their foundations. The cinema allowed new, fluid glances at the previously fixed world. The choice of subjects was also determined by the apparatus and the need for a strong light to expose the film stock properly. Thus, almost every Lumière film takes place outside, including domestic scenes like a baby's breakfast. Government officials are shown marching in fancy dress down exterior stairs rather than meandering through their palaces or in more intimate spaces. We never get to peek inside homes or offices, much less cathedrals or museums. Nonetheless, the subject matter of the films remains humanity itself, as if the Cinématographe is assessing the reality of their times or at least some public aspects of life. Though the initial operators were all young white men, the films display a shared desire to present people, rituals, landmarks, and simple slices of reality from as many corners of the globe as possible.

Lumière Eiffel Tower (*Ascending the Eiffel Tower*)

Louis Lumière often quipped that the Cinématographe brought the world to the world. Whether it was a shot of camels parading past the Sphinx and pyramids in an impressively framed image (*Les Pyramides*, 1897), a bustling open-air market in Martinique (*Fort de France, Marché*, 1902), or an unfortunate steer being hoisted aboard a ship in Tonkin Bay (*Embarquement d'un boeuf à bord d'un navire*, 1899), the Lumière operators produced significant records of people going about their lives. The Lumière operators participated in turn-of-the-century Europe's booming global exploration, but they also witnessed and preserved a new era of increased mobility for the wealthy in France, capturing instances of people traveling to the mountains and beaches and the Exposition Universelle in Paris. They visually documented a new European leisure class with unprecedented opportunities. In general, the Lumière catalog, which includes parades, dances, busy streets, bullfights, and bountiful harvests, projects an optimism about the human condition while fueling an earnest curiosity about people and their changing lives.

While much has been made about the functions of Lumière's films in documenting and even contributing to the spread of modernity, with cameras positioned in bustling city centers, they also demonstrated troubling aspects of colonialism. Gabriel Veyre created many movies set in Indochina in 1899, including shots set in vast coal mines, owned by French corporations, and a famous shot of a decimated couple smoking opium. One of his most striking compositions features two French women proudly tossing cheap *sapèque* coins to local children in what is now central Vietnam (*Indochinese Children Collecting Sapèques, Enfants Annamites ramassants des sapèques devant la pagode des dames*). The women are Blanche Doumer, wife of Paul Doumer, the governor-general of the colony and future president of France, and their daughter. The shot presents the elegantly dressed women tossing the coins

Lumière Indochina women (*Indochinese Children Collecting Sapèques*)

on the ground as if flinging seeds to chickens, as the poor children scurry about gathering the offerings, surely egged on by Veyre behind the camera. As Bertrand Tavernier explains in the DVD release commentary, it offers "a great comment about colonialism in fifty seconds." The Lumière operators staged, captured, and revealed a wide range of vital aspects of their era.

It is worth noting the surprising degree to which Louis took on the Cinématographe as a personal project, watching over every detail of its design, construction, and distribution, though he and his family did not necessarily settle into a long-term business model. During this same time, he was also busy experimenting with many other products, including color photography. By 1904, Louis presented his dazzling new Autochrome color photographs at the French Academy of Sciences to great acclaim, and by 1907, the Lumières were selling color plates. Autochromes revolutionized color photography and offered subtle variations in lighting that fit in with the Impressionist paintings of the era. As Faucheux puts it, at a time before Proust's *Remembrance of Things Past* or Albert Einstein's theories of relativity in space and time, and simultaneous with Bergson's rethinking of matter and memory, Louis Lumière was actively inventing unprecedented techniques that modulated temporality, allowing spectators to see the world in a whole new manner (210). The Autochrome proved highly popular with photographers and with scientists of all sorts who soon depended on this new tool for documenting, transmitting, or verifying data or observations. The Lumières produced and sold several million Autochrome plates, which remained a dominant color process up to the 1930s.

Louis Lumière went on to patent hundreds of other products, including a 360-degree Photorama device and an elegant fan-shaped loudspeaker. Meanwhile, Auguste began to specialize in medical research and development, thanks largely to his concern for victims of industrial and military injuries. Despite his lack of any academic medical degree, Auguste Lumière contributed many valuable health care patents and processes. He championed the use of X-ray machines for research and diagnosis, and the Lumières processed thousands of X-rays free of charge for wounded soldiers during World War I. Auguste also invented a new generation of bandages and vaccines, as well as modern diagnostic methods, all of which saved untold numbers of lives during the war and after. He made hundreds of important contributions to medical science, including new treatments for asthma, cancer, and tuberculosis. The Lumière brothers received the Legion of Honor and left their mark on many aspects of the twentieth century. As part of their ongoing legacy, the

Lumière Institute in Lyon still functions as a center for cinema preservation, research, and advocacy today.

Georges Méliès and Cinematic Spectacle

Popular magician and entertainer Georges Méliès had become instantly fascinated with the Cinématographe at its premiere in 1895. He saw immediate possibilities for incorporating moving pictures into his shows at the Robert-Houdin Theater. Frustrated that the Lumières initially refused to sell their device, he traveled to London to purchase an Animatographe projector from R. W. Paul in 1896, at the urging of his star performer and eventual second wife, Jehanne d'Alcy. Méliès, who had studied art and then learned magic and lightning sketch tactics in London, was already a well-known entertainer in Paris by 1896. At the Robert-Houdin Theater, where Méliès and his troupe performed tricks, magic acts, and other attractions, they began projecting Edison and British movies before Méliès started filming his own shorts. Among the Edison films they exhibited was *The Execution of Mary Queen of Scots* (1895), which included a trick effect for the beheading of the queen. Just before the ax hit, the kinetograph had stopped and the actress was replaced with a mannequin. Méliès already included many transformation and substitution tricks on stage via trap doors, magic lanterns, and mirrors, and he became intrigued with adapting his magic acts via new cinematic techniques for more dramatic illusions (Deslandes and Richard 419). Méliès and several associates managed to build a camera, reversing their projector's internal mechanisms. They purchased lenses from Eugene Krauss's company in Paris, which manufactured precision Zeiss lenses. The Lumières and Charles Pathé soon purchased Krauss's fast lenses for their equipment as well.

Méliès was well prepared to engage in the challenging business of early filmmaking. He had worked for his father's successful boot and shoe factory, learning mechanical and commercial practices. However, he preferred the artistic worlds of painting, satirical political caricatures, and live performance. Thanks to a sizable dowry from his first marriage and his share of the family business, Méliès moved to Paris and bought the floundering Robert-Houdin Theater. He quickly became a major figure in the city's entertainment and culture industry. He set up his own darkroom to master photography at the same time that he was managing and programming the demanding theater. He designed shows involving fanciful action that took advantage of his love of machinery and magic. For instance, in 1891, he staged a show about the misadventures of Nostradamus, involving a farcical series of illusions and encounters involving travels to the moon. He later adapted the premise for his famous film *A Trip to the Moon* (*Le Voyage dans la lune*, 1902). Constantly looking out for fresh attractions, he recognized both the potential value and the threat of new visual technologies.

As we know, Méliès had seen Émile Reynaud's projected optical theater at the Musée Grévin in 1892. While he was familiar with the praxinoscope, this new version, complete with sound effects and live music, proved promising for his theater. Méliès mentioned to Reynaud that they needed to investigate ways to mechanically reproduce the images rather than hand-paint them all. From that point on, Méliès began watching for other entertainment options and took a renewed interest in possible photographic solutions to the projection of moving images for his spectacles. It is also worth noting that he built most of his shows around his own performances. He not only wanted to record skits and magic acts; he looked forward to performing on the screen himself. Hence his great impatience to acquire a camera and projector once the Kinetoscope and Cinématographe became operational.

By 1896, Méliès was creating his own motion pictures. Initially, these films resembled the actualities of Lumière or staged acts of Edison and the British. However, he boldly decided to expand his offerings by building a glass-and-iron studio the size of his live-action theater on his property in Montreuil, on the eastern edge of Paris. He planned on a year-round schedule of film productions that could initially be integrated into his theatrical program. Clearly, Méliès had a completely different conception of cinema than did Louis Lumière. Méliès engaged his theater staff to build sets, design costumes, and perform for his staged films. His design for the building sprang from models of rooftop photography studios and even greenhouses. Yet he wanted his fictions to seem far from their studio setting in Paris. For instance, he created a rocking set to represent a ship reeling at sea for *Between Calais and Dover* (*Entre Calais et Douvres*, 1897). Fantasies and fictional re-creations would be his central topics. He also had his eye on marketing and controlling his product internationally from the beginning. He named his production and distribution company Star Film, in English, with the five-pointed star as his emblem. England and the United States were already his potential customers. To curb illegal duplications and protect his intellectual property, Méliès had the star punched in the opening of each official print as a sort of creative signature and guarantee of their validity and quality (Abel, *Red Rooster* 16).

During 1897, Méliès filmed several dramatic reenactments from the ongoing war between Turkey and Greece, including the action-packed *Surrender of Tournavos* (*La Prise de Tournavos*, 1897), while his more typical films involved tricks of bodies being transformed or diabolical figures comically appearing and disappearing. But his earliest output included subjects as varied as the exhibitionistic, "érotique" short *After the Ball* (*Après le bal*, 1897) with Jehanne D'Alcy undressing, the not-so-pious *Temptation of Saint Anthony* (*Tentation de Saint Antoine*, 1898), and the politically engaged series of eleven episodic films devoted to reproducing the controversial Dreyfus affair (1899). Furthermore, he innovated many variations on hybrid live and cinematic spectacles. For instance, he filmed the popular singer Paulus performing one of his standard hits, then Paulus would belt out the song, unseen in the wings at the popular Bataclan theater, while the audience watched him on screen seeming to sing in the silent movie version. Throughout his career, Méliès expanded cinematic options, synthesizing conventions from phonographs, photography, news illustrations, and caricature with modes from live performance.

To create the exotic mise-en-scène for his fantasies, Méliès made ready use of backdrops, which were also in common use by photographic portrait studios. He added sets with false perspectives, mirrors, and trap doors. He went far beyond simply filming live magic acts and tricks as if he were in his theater. From the start, he systematically exploited the stop-start potential of the camera combined with editing to cut out the substitutions and flash frames. André Gaudreault labels this construction of a narrative from strings of effects as "trickality" to distinguish it from mere "theatricality." Méliès carefully preplanned scenes with postproduction editing in mind: "'Every appearance, disappearance or substitution was of course done in the camera but was always re-cut in the laboratory on the negative'" (Gaudreault, "Theatricality" 42). A clear early instance of Méliès staging a film to allow for editing and matches on action can be seen in *A Nightmare* (*Le Cauchemar*, 1896), in which a fellow writhing in bed (Méliès) is suddenly visited by a series of characters magically appearing at the foot of the bed. The backdrop changes dramatically several times, while the position of the performers is precisely maintained throughout. In fact, Méliès displays fine performance skills, remaining in the correct position from effect to effect, guaranteeing a fluid flow of character gesture and feigned reactions. In *A Nightmare*, the man initially leans in to kiss a lovely young woman, who is then replaced by a male musician in blackface, then a Pierrot dances on his bed with a moon in the distance, which suddenly leaps forward to bite Méliès's hand, though he punches the moon back into the sky before awaking in the original set-up. He nearly tumbles out of bed in agitation, much like the later dream land

Blackface in Méliès (*A Nightmare*)

comics of Winsor McCay. This "one-take movie" includes seven shots and four backdrop changes in just over fifty seconds.

Unfortunately, many historical accounts reduce Méliès to a fellow stuck in the conventions of live theater. Even André Bazin dismisses him as a man "who saw film only as a way to perfect his theatrical marvels" (*What Is* [2009], 163). But Méliès was more than a stage showman adapting his live spectacles for a camera. His planning and staging of fantastic tricks advanced early cinema in profound ways. As Jay Telotte points out, "Méliès discovered in the properties of film technology a great potential for furthering his fantasy efforts, particularly in the mechanism's ability to create a whole new sense of time and space" (79).

Méliès invested more time and resources in his film productions, reducing the number of live shows at the Robert-Houdin Theater, which gradually became a movie venue. By the early 1900s, new audiences began stopping by in hopes of meeting the man they had seen on screens around France. Ever the showman, Méliès, one of the cinema's first stars, was even known to run the projector for the crowd. To liven up his movies, he often hired well-known dancers and acrobats from the Folies Bergère and other trendy establishments. According to Madeleine Malthête-Méliès, her grandfather was known for paying talent well. Average performers could earn twenty francs a day, which generally meant filming between 11 a.m. and 3 p.m., when the light was most even, and lunch was included (226). The talent moved readily between live performances during the evenings and motion picture work during the day.

As Star Films continued to grow, Méliès resisted industry trends of consolidation, despite tempting offers from Pathé and others to collaborate and share patents. All Méliès films were self-financed, which ultimately limited his ability to compete against a new generation of entrepreneurs and their corporations, especially as films grew longer and more expensive. Typically, Star Film had to sell one hundred prints before reaching a break-even point. Furthermore, a large portion of their clients were traveling fairgrounds exhibitors who could not afford the longest films, preferring short comedies and trick films such as *The Infernal Cauldron* (*Le Chaudron infernal*, 1903) or *Bob Kick, the Mischievous Kid* (*Bob Kick, l'enfant terrible*, 1903) over more serious fare such as *The Damnation of Faust* (*Faust aux enfers*, 1903), a multiscene melodrama.

Through all the challenges, Méliès remained personally involved in all the eventual 520 Star films, working with a steady crew, including technical assistant Lucien Roulos and camera operator Lucien Astaix. Méliès constantly reinvested funds in upgrading his studio, including digging a cellar for space below the stage and trap doors. He built a second, larger studio in 1907, allowing two scenes to be in production at the same time. Because of the layout of the property, actors often enter from the right, the courtyard side of the studio, and exit to the left, into the garden. Unlike the Robert-Houdin sets, backdrops were painted in a range of gray tones to allow the costumes to stand out more clearly. Moreover, the range of light grays allowed for color to be painted over the black-and-white prints and sold at a premium.

The hand-coloring of Star films was contracted with Élisabeth Thuillier, a former magic lantern painter. The most expensive coloring jobs included four separate colors. Business became so brisk that Thuillier eventually hired a staff of two hundred women. For individual prints, each worker would apply one color in an assembly-line shop that required two, three, or four women per print, depending on the variety of colors. Sales of colored films brought extra profit to Méliès, despite their extra cost. Color could add extra benefits, isolating the main character visually and guiding the audience's attention in a busy frame while it distracted viewers from noticing the substitution splices (Yumibe 72). Méliès historian Jacques Malthête points out that the first Star Film listed as available for purchase in color was *The Rajah's Dream* (*Le Rêve du Radjah ou la forêt enchantée*, 1900), though Thuillier later claimed she colored all the Méliès films from 1897 to 1912 (69). Assessing early color history is always difficult because most prints were lost or remain damaged, and some color effects were added much later for retrospectives, such as the 1929 Méliès Gala event in Paris. By 1903, the more efficient stencil process allowed another option for intricate color work as films became progressively longer. Nonetheless, regardless of whether one used the full hand-color method or a series of stencils, the dyes still had to be applied to every frame, once for each color used, on every print.

Méliès wrote clever commentary to be spoken by announcers during screenings to add humor and guide the viewer in some of the increasingly narrative films during the era before intertitles. In *A Trip to the Moon* and many others, the audience would be told the names of the characters and a number of plot points to help maintain their interest and focus their attention across the hectic array of performers. For instance, *The Impossible Voyage* (*Voyage à travers l'impossible*, 1904), which unfolds in forty tableaux, features a narrator identifying the chief explorer by name and explaining that one woman seen flailing her arms feels faint because she is too near the fumes from the molten metal. Later, the narration provides the voice of the train conductor announcing, "Everyone detrain, Jungfrau Station." In addition to the fanciful train, *The Impossible Voyage* ends with a spectacular fire aboard a submarine. Some films with elaborate costumes and busy sets, such as *The Palace of the Arabian Nights* (*Le Palais des mille et une nuits*, 1905), benefit from the narration to identify key characters in the crowd and explain their thoughts and actions. Thus, story information that might later be provided with variations in shot scale, continuity editing, and title cards was initially accomplished with staging, color, and spoken commentary.

Méliès was so significant in the new industry that in 1907, he wrote a lengthy assessment of his contributions to cinema for a photography journal. He labeled his work as belonging to the "transformation" genre and explained some of his trademark effects, warning that negative film strips would often rip when exposed seven or more times for in-camera superimpositions. He also noted the challenge of training actors to precisely replicate their gestures for multiple takes. This article has been called the first case of a filmmaker systematically detailing the processes and creative choices of his craft (Banda and Moure 95). Méliès emphasizes that staged fiction films

guarantee the cinema's future, as opposed to the more limited genres of actualities shot on location or scientific films. Narrative films with actors and
planned action, following a theatrical model, "have given the Cinématographe its immortality because subjects owing to the imagination are infinitely
variable and inexhaustible" (Méliès 101). Méliès was more than a practitioner
of a new sort of fiction film—he was an advocate and theorist as well.

The most popular Méliès transformation trick films were those involving
decapitations and multiple exposures. For his *Four Troublesome Heads* (*Un
homme de tête*, 1898), the onscreen Méliès pantomimes for the camera as if a
stage magician, but then he quickly removes his own head, places it on a table,
and repeats the gag two more times. Once he has three heads on the tables,
Méliès plays banjo and sings, accompanied by his severed heads. Heavy dark
cloth covers his head and body parts in the four different passes of the film
through the camera. Thanks to his technical training, Méliès also experimented with exposure times and even tricks of developing the film stock to
compensate for the multiple exposures and uneven lighting levels between
takes for stop-start filming and substitution editing. Another clever variation

Méliès in multiple exposures (*Four Troublesome Heads*)

on animated heads and multiple exposures can be seen in *The Mysterious Knight* (*Le Chevalier mystère*, 1899), in which Méliès sketches a woman's face on a chalk board, then pulls a live head off the surface and even skewers it on his sword. After chatting with her head, he magically conjures up the whole woman before she is reduced again to a head, returned to the chalk board, and erased.

The tricks in such films are nearly seamless with convincing interactions and even glances exchanged between Méliès and the assorted heads. Furthermore, he crawls under tables and waves his arms over the lively heads and body parts to prove there are no wires attached in these cinematic magic acts. Later examples include *The One-Man Band* (*L'Homme orchestre*, 1900), in which seven versions of Méliès play music together; *The Triple Conjurer and the Living Head* (*L'Illusioniste double et la tête vivante*, 1900), where he splits in two; and *The Terrible Turkish Executioner* (*Le Bourreau turc*, 1904), in which four men are decapitated, though their heads pop back out of a barrel and reattach to the bodies, allowing them to take revenge, cutting the executioner (Méliès) in two. One of the most impressive of these severed-head movies is *The Melomaniac* (*Le Mélomane*, 1903), in which Méliès tosses multiple copies of his own head up onto lines to serve as musical notes in a fast-paced and zany demonstration of his cinematic talents.

Méliès's famous *A Trip to the Moon*, along with later adventure films, including *The Impossible Voyage* and *The Conquest of the Pole* (*A la conquête du pôle*, 1912), helped solidify his reputation as a fanciful storyteller and satirist. *A Trip to the Moon* in particular can be read as a mockery of both colonialism and scientific pretensions. It thrust the world of science fiction into cinema. These elaborate longer narratives demonstrate how carefully Méliès staged action and composed his shots, often packing every corner of the screen with moving characters and impressive props. *A Trip to the Moon* took three months and 10,000 francs to make and was based in part on his earlier Robert-Houdin Nostradamus show and featured acrobats from the Folies Bergère as the Selenites. Méliès synthesized references to Jules Verne, H. G. Wells, and a host of other popular influences. Méliès belonged to a generation that grew up with Verne's *Extraordinary Voyages* and was well aware of Jacques Offenbach's operetta *Le Voyage dans la lune*.

A Trip to the Moon proved significant for Star Films right away. It was an immediate international success and continued to play well for several years. Edison managed to acquire a print and sold duplicated copies to Vitagraph. *A Trip to the Moon* thereby became a hit in the United States less than a month after its opening in Paris, but with no royalties for Méliès (Solomon 2). Méliès quickly sent his brother Gaston to the United States to set up a US branch of Star Films and protect their work from future trademark infringement. Soon, Méliès began filming each movie with two cameras so that a paper print could be sent to the United States to ensure copyright protection. His daughter, Georgette, often worked as one of the cinematographers. They also paid representatives in Spain and other nations to oversee sales and fight illegal reproductions. The excitement over *A Trip to the Moon* abroad firmly established Star Films as a global player in motion pictures.

A Trip to the Moon and the subsequent adventure satires expanded on themes, tricks, and humor from the Robert-Houdin spectacles, as well as Méliès's fascination with astronomy and exploration. These films about comically intrepid explorers, ridiculous encounters, and absurd luck foreground Méliès's arsenal of tricks, including substitution editing, shooting through fish tanks, and using miniatures. *The Impossible Voyage* proves an insightful example, with spinning cut-out factory wheels, a train lifted by dirigibles right into the mouth of the sun, a submarine with a cut-away side, and a composite shot through an aquarium. Méliès adventure films are visually imaginative and yet somewhat quaint, insulated, and studio-bound productions.

The Star Film catalog offered a wide range of film subjects and lengths, many of which exploited repeated plot points and recurring settings and even costumes. In addition to his long string of films with haunted rooms and disappearing women, Méliès returned regularly to fairy tales and well-known stories. He shot two Cinderella films, made elaborate versions of *Gulliver's Travels* and *Robinson Crusoe*, and even presents a biography of Joan of Arc (*Jeanne d'Arc*, 1900), which includes an accurate image of her childhood home, while her imprisonment, angelic visitations, and fiery execution show off his passion for rousing, cinematic spectacle. Beyond their fantastic effects, Star's films were also unusual in their persistent emphasis on representing women in a wide variety of roles. Méliès presented women as "active, professional figures capable of articulating new forms of engagement in the modern world," whether in earnest dramas or social parodies (Duckett 162).

In addition to selecting the topics and motifs, Méliès carefully sketched out the set designs and costumes for each project. Moreover, thanks to their intricate staging and realistic objects combined with painted backdrops, many Méliès films seem to engage overtly with the shifting modern spaces and new modes of representation at the heart of film production. For instance, *A Mix-*

Up in the Gallery (*Une chute de cinq étages*, 1906) establishes a photographic studio in his real film studio, offering "viewers a glimpse into the artificial film world" in a sort of *mise-en-abyme* narrative, mixing realism and artifice for dual rooftop and street sets (Jacobson 66). Méliès played the film's unhappy photographer. While new options for production, distribution, and exhibition, as well as technology, were in constant flux, Méliès remained fixed in his methods and economic model. His was an expensive, rather unwieldy mode of production. He insisted on writing, directing, and producing all his films himself, which sheltered Star Films from fresh ideas and caused him to lose good talent, who moved on to new opportunities with his competitors. While Lumière's trajectory proved less viable for the new studio system, Star Films provided many important blueprints that could be improved on by more highly capitalized companies and a new generation of filmmakers exploring innovative narrative techniques as well as mise-en-scène and editing strategies.

Gaumont promptly followed Méliès's model and built a new studio in 1905 in north Paris at Buttes-Chaumont, hiring many young cinema technicians and performers. Moreover, Pathé's chief of production, Ferdinand Zecca, early on began to direct fantasy films very similar to Méliès's titles. Zecca even hired away André Deed. The actor and acrobat had been performing for Méliès and could share his cinematic tricks with Pathé's technicians. Deed, just one actor among the troupe at Star films, received his own comic series with Pathé in 1906. Spaniard Segundo de Chomón, who worked briefly with Méliès, found Pathé more encouraging. He brought his new color stencil process and knowledge of stop-start filmmaking to their studio. Pathé's cofounder Claude Grivolas, an avid magician and cinema engineer in his own right, also tried to talk Méliès into partnering with the growing Pathé Frères, but Méliès insisted on remaining independent (Malthête-Méliès 275).

When his business began failing in 1911, Méliès was forced to relent and allow Pathé to provide financing for the final few Star Films, including *The Conquest of the Pole*, whose title reworks Pathé's slogan "A la Conquête du monde," and *Cinderella* (*Cendrillon ou la pantoufle merveilleuse*, 1912), which Zecca recut, to the horror of Méliès, and his last movie, *The Voyage of the Bourrichon Family* (*Le Voyage de la famille Bourrichon*, 1912), about a family in debt, fleeing their creditors. These final Méliès films are staged in tableau style with exaggerated gestures and theatrical backdrops, much as every other Star Film had been for the past fifteen years. In fact, the frenzied and frightened Bourrichon family seems to be escaping back into the world of Méliès's past. His

studio business was finished in 1913, and Méliès, in a gesture of anger echo-
ing that of Reynaud, burned many of his negatives and sold off his film prints,
shutting down Star Films. René Clair later declared that while Edison and
the Lumières may have invented the cinema, Méliès "created the fiction film
and the film of poetic freedom" (124).

CHAPTER 3

Pathé and Gaumont Create
a French Film Industry

Pathé Studios as Industrial Model

The Lumières and Méliès were among a large cadre of inventors, researchers, and entrepreneurs with interests in motion pictures during the 1890s. It was Charles Pathé and Léon Gaumont, however, who provided the most successful industrial models and helped establish many of the business and aesthetic practices that shaped cinema's expansion globally. In 1894, Charles Pathé began setting up phonograph parlors at fairgrounds and selling the devices in his store. He bought Edison phonographs, followed by British counterfeit versions. These players, with their three-minute wax cylinders, could accommodate up to twenty listeners at a time via acoustic tubes as earphones. Customers would pay to listen to popular music and famous voices. Business was so brisk that Pathé began selling the phonographs wholesale for others to exploit, and then profited by selling batches of new cylinders to those clients.

The resourceful Pathé even began recording his own cylinders, hiring local musicians to cut costs. He also had people read speeches or poetry, pretending to be various famous literary figures, actors, or politicians. In 1895, he arranged to purchase British versions of Edison's Kinetoscope, and long lines quickly formed at his store and fairground stalls. Soon the moving picture portion of Pathé's store took on a life of its own. Encouraged, Pathé and engineer Henri Joly patented their own "chronophotographic camera" in 1895, although their goal was still to make content for these single-viewer devices. Pathé sped up importing and selling Kinetoscopes, further expanding the market for the short films he bought, made, and sold.

Once the Lumière Cinématographe proved a hit, Pathé and his staff devised a projector, which went on sale during the summer of 1896, promising purchasers "a certain fortune within months of exploitation" (Mannoni, *Great Art* 434). Along with his brother Émile, Charles Pathé launched Pathé Frères for their joint businesses in phonographs and moving pictures. Their customers were primarily itinerant fairground show people. In 1897, Pathé was joined by Claude Grivolas and other investors to produce cameras, projectors, and films. They built their first studio space in 1897, opened a factory in Vincennes in 1901, and added a second studio in 1902. In 1904, they opened a third studio and constructed a massive factory in Joinville to manufacture film stock and process prints. They switched their business model in 1907, halting the outright sale of prints to shift to a rental system. This move marked the transition away from itinerant fairground and part-time exhibition in cafés and music halls toward more fixed, dedicated movie theaters.

Pathé Frères established distribution offices and partnerships throughout Europe and then in the United States, completely altering the industry as others followed suit and saw the financial benefits of short-term rentals. This new mode of distribution jump-started the nickelodeon boom. With the availability of more movies at lower upfront cost, cinemas could change their program several times a week to satisfy repeat customers and build a stable audience. By 1908, Pathé was selling up to five hundred projectors each month, equipping a large portion of the new cinemas opening across Europe and North America. Their factories could churn out 40,000 meters of film a day, roughly a quarter of which would be tinted or stenciled in color, thanks in part to a female workforce. As Richard Abel explains, "Their repetitive 'detail' work in splicing and coloring prints was probably quite similar to what they would have done in a textile factory" (*Ciné* 20).

The Pathé company soon provided more films to the United States than the entire Edison trust combined. Further, Pathé launched the first true newsreel service in 1909 and owned more than two hundred movie houses in France alone. They forged a new cinematic experience with their full catalog of film offerings and policies to standardize screenings. Pathé had indeed conquered the cinematic world as they rapidly industrialized an upstart entertainment medium into a vertically integrated system for production, distribution, and exhibition of mass-marketed motion pictures. Furthermore, Pathé Frères continued to upgrade their product line of film equipment, and their cameras and projectors were recognized as among the very best available. Once Gaumont adopted many of Pathé's strategies, French films easily dominated world markets.

Pathé's reputation for varied and high-quality motion pictures owed in part to the creativity and management skills of Ferdinand Zecca. Beginning in 1900, Zecca supervised the film production wing of the firm. He is credited with 250 films between 1900 and 1906 for Pathé, including dramas such as *Story of a Crime* (*Histoire d'un crime*, 1901), which features the prisoner's subjective vision as a split screen. Zecca staged popular Méliès-inspired fantasies. His adaptation of Faust, *The Devil's Seven Castles* (*Les Sept châteaux du diable*, 1903), included forty shots, fifteen different settings, and three hundred original costumes. As production expanded, Zecca served as a story person, director, and producer, assigning various genres and subjects, such as chase films, realistic melodramas, or historical reconstructions, to specific directors and assistants. For instance, Lucien Nonquet directed the rousing reconstruction of the recent *Potemkin* mutiny in Odessa harbor, *The Russian Revolution* (*La Révolution en Russie*, 1905), while Albert Capellani was assigned the fantasy *Aladdin and the Marvelous Lamp* (*Aladin ou la lampe merveilleuse*, 1906). *Aladdin*

Split-screen dream (*Story of a Crime*)

is a prime example of Pathé's quality and Capellani's innovative storytelling. Its compelling tale opens with a split-screen subjective vision. The film boasts detailed sets, fluid camera movements, spectacular tricks by Segundo de Chomón, and a diverse cast. It was available in brightly colored stencil prints. Capellani also specialized in short morality plays, such as *Tale of Passion* (*Drame passionnel*, 1906), in which a woman is seduced and abandoned, as her lover becomes engaged to a wealthy woman instead; the betrayed woman shoots him down in the church on his wedding day, in front of their love child, in a tale of passion, betrayal, and revenge.

Pathé faced a double challenge in their shift to renting prints. They had to promise and deliver a steady stream of motion pictures, and those films had to be of superior quality to earn brand loyalty from the new generation of nickelodeon owners and their audiences. Chase films became a sure-fire genre that could churn out relatively cheap but popular movies. *The Policeman's Little Run* (*La Course des sergents en ville*, Zecca, 1907) is a well-known example; its twenty-three shots were filmed mostly on location. A dog leaps onto a butcher shop counter and makes off with a leg of lamb, pursued by a gaggle of clumsy police officers in hot pursuit. The officers fall all over one another as they race through the neighborhood, disrupting everything in a series of comical disasters. Zecca even had a reproduction of a building front on the studio floor, shot from above, so the dog seems to run right up a building wall, with the police diligently crawling up behind him. The final section turns the action on its head, with the cornered dog chasing the bumbling cops back into their station. Chase movies could be shot cheaply and shown immediately anywhere in the world without the need of intertitles.

Pathé's early catalog included many colorful titles that sold well at the fairgrounds and in nickelodeons. For instance, *The Golden Beetle* (*Le Scarabée d'or*, Chomón, 1907) is an orientalist trick film involving an Egyptian sorcerer, beautiful exotic women, fountains, fireworks, and multiple exposures for layers of special effects. The hectic performances compete head to head with those of Méliès, while the optional stencil version shows off the Pathé color, making it largely a motion picture about colors and magical transitions. Color historian Joshua Yumibe points out that stencils expanded on the tinted lighting effects popular in live theatrical spectacles of the era, "creating dazzling trick effects that sculpt in depth," showcasing their striking designs as colorful attractions (93). Bold coloring, whether by stencils or tinting, gave extra value to any film and helped the young cinema participate in chromatic trends in modernist consumerism of the era. France's coloring work was also so far ahead of the rest of the world that even some US firms shipped their prints to Paris for color versions. At the center of French practice was Pathé.

Pathé was also actively integrating multishot narratives into its array of subjects, helping shift French cinema away from fairground attractions toward more developed story films. *A Narrow Escape* (*Le Médecin du château*, 1908) develops and reworks melodramatic and chase film formulas in a suspenseful film about a doctor who is lured away from home by a fake telegram sent by two robbers. This tale makes extensive use of parallel editing to alternate shots of the doctor's outing with the simultaneous attack on the wife and son by devious thieves back home. Pathé's film condenses the thirty shots of action down to essential events, with ellipses for sequences such as the doctor ordering his car to be brought around, and it anchors several shots with eyeline matches. Spatial arrangements are also meticulously established, both outside and within the physician's home. The combination of functional mise-en-scène, including understated acting, effective editing, and crisp camerawork, produced a convincing, fast-paced, and suspenseful story that obviously proved influential: *A Narrow Escape* was adapted by D. W. Griffith as *The Lonely Villa* the very next year. Cinema was already a global enterprise, and every producer was actively assessing the competition and rapidly adopting new narrative, technical, and industrial practices. By the end of its first decade of film production, Pathé had established itself as the most significant studio in the world. Its equipment, its business model, and its modes of filmmaking helped launch a successful, sustainable entertainment industry.

Léon Gaumont and Alice Guy Compete with Pathé

Léon Gaumont started out as an apprentice to Jules Carpentier in 1887, at age seventeen, a few years before Carpentier partnered with the Lumières. Fascinated with popular science and entertainment, Gaumont found a job with a photographic equipment company in 1893. Two years later, he bought the business, renaming it Léon Gaumont et cie., thanks to confident investors, including Gustave Eiffel. Gaumont also became friends with Georges Demenÿ and Auguste and Louis Lumière. He and Demenÿ entered into a brief partnership to market Demenÿ's 60mm camera, which operated thanks to rollers rather than sprocket holes, but it ultimately proved impractical. Soon, Alice Guy, age twenty-one, joined Gaumont as his personal secretary. She quickly took on increased responsibilities dealing with business clients, and in March 1895, she accompanied him to see one of the earliest Cinématographe demonstrations. With the success of the Lumière experiments, Gaumont's company began adding 35mm film equipment within the year. Their engineer, Leopold René Decaux, improved on Demenÿ's patents, launching a new line of cameras and projectors in 1896 and buying film stock from Lumière's partner, Victor Planchon. Meanwhile, Guy had become familiar with the new product lines, even shooting some 60mm scenes. Gaumont put her in charge of generating films to fuel interest in their cameras, projectors, and other equipment.

Guy was named head of production, perhaps the first such title in film history. In fact, Zecca had occasionally acted in early Guy productions at Gaumont. Guy's first film seems to have been a 60mm version of *The Cabbage-Patch Fairy* (*La Fée aux choux*) in 1896, which was reshot in 35mm in 1900 and expanded in 1902 as the satirical skit *Midwife to the Upper Class* (*Sage-femme de première classe*), complete with screaming babies harvested from a cabbage patch. Thanks to reliable equipment and Guy's line-up of movies, Gaumont and company quickly became a successful business venture and enjoyed a strong presence at the 1900 Exposition Universelle in Paris, where their powerful new projector won a prize. Gaumont and Pathé grew into dominant, competing companies simultaneously, while a host of other upstarts struggled to gain a foothold in the motion picture market.

Guy was a highly influential figure for early international cinema. Historian Jean-Pierre Jeancolas states boldly that she was indisputably the world's first professional director (*Histoire* 16). Guy and her camera operator, Anatole Thiberville, were responsible for hundreds of attractions, from her first one-shot *actualités*, staged performances, and comic gags, such as a man accidentally chugging absinthe straight up (*Wonderful Absinthe*, *La Bonne absinthe*, 1899), to chase scenes with dogs stealing sausages. Gradually, Guy adopted a more narrative model, plotting out longer fictional stories with clear comic or melodramatic resolutions, and situating them increasingly on real locations when possible. One of her greatest accomplishments was *The Birth, the Life and the Death of Christ* (*La Naissance, la vie et la mort du Christ*, 1906), codirected with Victorin-Hippolyte Jasset. This passion play is a series of twenty-five tableau scenes, mostly in single shots, from Christ's birth, through several miracles and major events, some including angels and special effects, leading up to the crucifixion and the epilogue of the Resurrection. It was sold in varying episodes and lengths up to the 600-meter total, motivating Pathé to counter with an updated and even longer version, *Life and Passion of Christ*

(*La Vie et la passion de Jésus Christ*, Nonguet and Zecca, 1907). One key distinction is that Guy's passion play concentrates more on the women surrounding Jesus than does the Pathé adaptation (Abel, *Ciné* 166).

Guy's cinema reveals efficient scene-to-scene structuring, whether in a long series of consecutive shot-sequence episodes or by organizing a more unified satirical comedy or family melodrama. For instance, her studio-bound *The Consequences of Feminism* (*Les Résultats du féminisme*, 1906) provides a broad farce on role reversals. Men play the homebodies, folding laundry, running errands, watching the children, and trying to get their wives to leave the bars to return home. Everyone is a caricature, with the men sporting flowers and strutting about, displaying excessively feminine gestures. The women move with brash confidence, flirting with the boys, drinking, barking orders, and threatening to fight one another, before the men rebel and return things to "normal." The sets are all highly artificial, including painted backdrops, and the action unfolds with comic gusto in a series of one-shot tableaux sequences.

By contrast, *On the Barricade* (*Sur la barricade*, 1907) presents a heartfelt melodrama that combines a theatrical domestic set with scenes shot in the streets. During a time of revolution, a mother sends her devoted son out for milk. He is caught up in a battle between government troops and a group of rebels blocking the street with a makeshift barricade. Captured, the boy begs to complete his errand for his mother and promises to return, which he does. Just before he is to be executed on the street, his mother wins his freedom. Here Guy's narrative alternates from tableau scene to tableau scene, relying on expressive, earnest acting to guide the audience's attention and allegiances. As Susan Hayward notes, Guy played a key role in launching early French film: "Many histories of French cinema have tended to adopt, repeat, accept the 'two trends' approach to its production as exemplified by the now famous Méliès-Lumière duopoly. This canonization of cinema into two styles (illusion and realism respectively) does not in fact hold true" (70). Guy introduced a narrative film tradition that helped synthesize the documentary-realist tradition of the Lumières with the fantasy of Méliès.

In addition to organizing production practices at the rapidly expanding Gaumont et cie., Guy was a key participant in some of the world's first successful synchronized sound motion pictures. By 1902, Gaumont had introduced an experimental sync-sound process known as Chronophone. A clever compressed air system helped amplify the mechanical sound from the recorded discs through the Gramophone's megaphones. The resulting films were known as *phonoscènes* of entertainers singing and performing to the

Felix Mayol in a phonoscène by Alice Guy (*The Trottins' Polka*)

camera, often with prerecorded background music. It was a dual system resulting in a 35mm print and a sound recording. During exhibition, the projectionist could slow or speed up the projector slightly to keep the image closely in synchronization with the audio player. Guy directed roughly one hundred *phonoscènes* between 1902 and 1906. She was responsible for rehearsing the actors to perfectly match their songs, and then filming them as they lip-synched and gestured in time to the music. Well-known popular entertainers of the era, including Dranem and Félix Mayol, performed some of their most famous musical numbers for her, often in elaborate settings resembling stage shows, shot straight-on with a fixed camera. Guy and her team also recorded exotic dancers and some speeches and theatrical scenes. Unfortunately, most of these dual-system *phonoscènes* are lost. There were only two Gaumont theaters in Paris, including the vast Palace, with the required equipment to offer Chronophone exhibition, but they were also presented in London and eventually in the United States.

The years 1906 and 1907 proved significant for French cinema's development. Guy's new husband, Herbert Blaché, was sent to New York to manage *phonoscènes* in English, leading Guy to quit her position and leave France in 1907. Her job was handed over to Louis Feuillade, while Guy created her own production company, Solax, renting out Gaumont studio space in New York to relaunch her career there. But Americans were also beginning to influence the French market more boldly. In early 1907, Vitagraph became the first US studio to open an office in Paris to help arrange imports of its films, including J. Stuart Blackton's popular and influential *The Haunted Hotel* (1907). Up until 1906, the domestic output was adequate for French exhibitors, with Pathé, Méliès, and Gaumont dominating the market and foreigners like Charles Urban forming Eclipse in France. However, the rapid expansion of cinemas in towns throughout France, during the French equivalent of the nickelodeon boom, required more titles among competing venues. By 1910, Edison, Biograph, and Selig had all opened offices in Paris and representatives of Lubin, Essanay, and Max Sennett soon followed. Before World War I, Americans accounted for up to one-third of the French box office.

French Comics

The most successful genre in France for Pathé, Gaumont, and other studios before World War I was certainly the one- and then two-reel comedy. Pathé dominated that market largely because they learned early on to market their comedies around recurring actors, including André Deed, Max Linder, and Charles Prince. For instance, in 1906, Pathé launched the Boireau series starring Deed as a consistently bumbling gent, sowing chaos everywhere. As Richard Abel observes, Deed's Boireau character comes right out of the popular music hall tradition, exploiting his stage training "as a grotesquely bewildered clown and a skillful practitioner of physical gags" (*Ciné* 228). In this first stint as Boireau, Deed made fourteen comic shorts from 1906 through 1908, then left to star in a string of Italian comedies as the similarly foolish Cretinetti, before returning to Pathé in 1912, and making nearly fifty more Boireau films by the end of the decade. Charles Pathé and his managers were very aware of their regional and global competition, and in an effort to maintain their standing, they steadily increased production budgets to remain competitive via high-quality storytelling and visual style. They paid top wages to hire and retain the best talent and crews. The negative cost of a Pathé production more than tripled between 1908 and 1912 for every meter of completed footage.

Pathé's biggest star before World War I was Max Linder, discovered by Zecca in 1905. At Pathé, Linder developed his persona as a dapper fellow prone to misjudging a situation, often entering a series of steadily accumulating physical gags and embarrassments. In his earliest films, he could comically struggle to ice skate, compete unsuccessfully with domineering mothers-in-law, be cruelly hypnotized, or just end up in a fix trying to cook for himself, all in broad farces that resembled slapstick routines crossed with comic strips. Repeatedly he gets into situations he cannot control, and it is no wonder that Charlie Chaplin called Linder his "professor." In one early movie, *Contagious Nervous Twitching* (*Un tic nerveux contagieux*, 1908), for instance, Max is afflicted with a pesky twitch, and as he wanders through town, people notice his bizarre gesticulations and adopt their own disruptive shuddering movements. Even a statue in the park begins to twitch. By 1909, Pathé capitalized on Linder's popularity by putting the name "Max" in all the titles, which often summarized the basic plots, such as Max takes a bath or Max goes on vacation, blurring the lines between performer and character.

When the prolific and popular Linder suffered a dangerous appendectomy near the end of 1910, he eventually appeared in a series of films to prove he had recovered, including *Max in Convalescence* (*Max en convalescence*, 1911), with his real family welcoming and caring for him at his real childhood home.

Max Linder and sister Marcelle (*Max in Convalescence*)

The series could be boldly creative, as in *Cordial Agreement* (*Entente cordiale*, 1912), where Linder's friend Harry Fragson takes advantage of Linder's hospitality in Paris and competes with Max for the attentions of the new maid, played by Stacia Napierkowska, a rising star in live theater and cinema. Eventually, the set itself bounces wildly as everyone dances to celebrate the union of Max and Stacia. Linder is generally credited with writing and directing his comedies, though typically he worked with codirectors, such as Louis Gasnier. He starred in nearly 150 titles, and his mode of production included few rehearsals and a great deal of improvisation on the set, thanks to his reliance on a core of clever fellow actors.

For *Max's Tragedy* (*Max et Jane veulent faire du théâtre*, 1911), the expressive Jane Renouardt performs opposite Linder. Initially, this young pair resents being set up on a blind date by their parents. Max and Jane disguise themselves as repulsive and behave rudely before recognizing their attraction to one another. However, the film suddenly cuts from the happy couple to their plight a few years later, as a poor drunken pair, coming to blows and dying in a miserable apartment. Suddenly, the camera pulls back to reveal they are now popular actors playing out this tragic scene on a theatrical stage for a

Max and Jane Renouardt perform (*Max's Tragedy*)

live audience. The impressive range of slapstick and dangerous action in *Max's Tragedy* demonstrates Linder's successful formula, including a wide range of slapstick and tragic elements, but the play within the film eerily anticipates Linder's ultimate real-life 1925 murder-suicide pact with his young wife.

Throughout the 1910s, the Max films had Linder repeatedly falling in and out of love and marriage and trying his hand at multiple tasks, from climbing snowy mountains to dueling and fighting bulls to looking for a job. Sometimes the films are in a sequence. For instance, in 1911, he made *Max's Divorce Case* (*Max se marie*), which is actually about his miserably embarrassing wedding party, followed a month later by *Max's Mother-in-Law* (*Max et sa belle-mère*), in which Max heads off to the mountains in an effort at a nice honeymoon with his new wife (Paulette Lorsy), only to find that her domineering mother insists on joining them. In fact, Max dates and marries a number of different women over the years in dramas that emphasize performance, social status, and humiliation. His comic persona worked well. By 1912, he was earning one million francs a year and traveling about Europe for premieres, further promoting himself and Pathé Studios. As Ginette Vincendeau points out, Linder may be considered the world's first film star: "He possessed all

Max in the snow (*Max's Mother-in-Law*)

the key attributes of stardom: immense fame, clout in the industry, wealth, and crucially, a recognizable and recognized identity" (*Stars*, 49). When he died in 1925, the *New York Times* labeled him one of the world's earliest film comedians.

Thus, while Pathé dominated the marketplace thanks to a wide range of business strategies, equipment sales, and film genres, the constant flow of comedies accounted for a large part of their box office and theater loyalty. Another prominent example is Charles Prince, a veteran performer in popular theater, who brought his burlesque physical comedy to Pathé's Rigadin series in 1909, eventually churning out an episode every week until 1914. While the scenarios and theatrical sets did not always show the imagination of Linder or other successful comedies, the Rigadins were another reliable product for Pathé, directed consistently by Georges Monca. The Rigadins also benefited from other Pathé actors, including Mistinguett, who appeared as "the lady doctor" and love interest. Such popular comic series gradually increased their narrative contexts and characterization as they shifted from one-reels to two during this transitional period of the early 1910s. Many new directors and performers learned their craft with gag-based comedies and chase films before moving to more melodramatic subjects.

At Gaumont, Louis Feuillade and Romeo Bosetti built on Alice Guy's models. They codirected *A Very Fine Lady* (*Une dame vraiment bien*, 1908), which follows a serial structure derived from comic strips as much as previous cinematic gag routines. An attractive woman crosses a neighborhood, distracting the men so badly that a steady string of accidents result, one even pastiching Lumière's *Waterer Watered*. Eventually, two gendarmes, equally impressed by her stunning beauty, cover her up and escort her safely home. Abel observes that "Gaumont was especially adept at turning this kind of comic film into social commentary." He argues that such films mock male desire while they simultaneously "endorse the cultural myth of the single, unattached woman's disruptive power," which must be tamed, here by the law (*Ciné* 219–20). As in the case of Guy's *Consequences of Feminism*, male order is first undercut and then reinstated.

French law, soldiers, and especially its police, repeatedly come under ridicule during this period. They are easy targets in Gaumont comedies. For instance, Bosetti's *The Long Arm of the Law* (*L'Agent a le bras long*, 1909) features an initially helpful gendarme with the amazing ability to stretch his arm out to bizarre, even perverse lengths as he points directions, uses his arm as a bridge for passing citizens, or reaches down chimneys to capture criminals.

Some of Bosetti's effects are manual, but many involve hidden editing tricks and some stop-motion animation in a chronological series of attractions that is typical of the sorts of clever short motion pictures that continue to satisfy the nickelodeon-era need for quick, effective content.

Jean Durand wrote and directed several highly creative comedies for Gaumont, including the Calino series, starring Clément Mégé in ridiculously ill-fitting clothes, and the Onésime films featuring the acrobatic Ernest Bourbon and Gaston Modot. In *Calino Wants to Be a Cowboy* (*Calino veut être cowboy*, 1911), Mégé plays a bumpkin in America, mimicking the cowboys around him, only to return home to his apartment in Paris, where his attempts at rope and pistol tricks wreak havoc. This sort of slapstick tale reveals the international context and awareness in early French movies. Georges Sadoul argues that Durand was one of France's most accomplished early filmmakers: his physical routines were copied by Mack Sennett and his editing inspired René Clair (*Histoire* 16). In a similar vein, *Calino Love Tamer* (*Calino dompteur par amour*, 1912) begins with a simple narrative set-up, as Calino pesters an attractive woman (played by Berthe Dagmar, Durand's wife), who tricks him into serving as a lion tamer at the fair. After Calino lets the lions loose, a raucous series of chase scenes ensues, with the lions chasing the circus staff and patrons around the city before wandering back to their cage at the end.

For another comic series at Gaumont, Durand directed Lucien Bataille, later famous for his split-head effect in Germaine Dulac's *Seashell and the Clergyman* (*La Coquille et le clergyman*, 1928). Here, Bataille played Zigoto, another inept dandy who gets into a series of scrapes, many involving modern technology and the changing cultural landscape. For instance, in *Zigoto's Outing with Friends* (*Zigoto entre des amis*, 1912), he destroys a new automobile; in *Zigoto Drives a Locomotive* (*Zigoto et la locomotive*, 1912), he offers to serve as engineer after a train's crew goes on strike, though he leads the locomotive off the tracks and destroys much of the local town, knocking workers off scaffolding and smashing through storefronts.

Durand's comedies make use of many medium shots (*plans américains*) mixed with more typical medium-long tableaux shots, but he also includes some intricate tracking shots. For Onésime, starring Ernest Bourbon, backed up by Gaston Modot, Durand alternates between conventional stage sets, real locations, and even Méliès-style trickery. In *Onésime Goes to Hell* (*Onésime aux enfers*, 1912), the poor Onésime gets the Devil to pay his bar tab but is then whisked away, lifted through the roof into the night sky, and spirited off to a cave-like Hell, surrounded by acrobatic evil spirits, including "Satan's Girls," who magically appear, transform, and disappear, before he awakes from a dream in the bar. Similarly, for *Onésime, Clockmaker* (*Onésime horloger*, 1912), the hapless hero learns that his rich uncle left him money, but he must wait twenty years until he perhaps has finally matured. Onésime concocts an intricate machine to speed up time, which leads to a series of fast-motion scenes in which he marries and has children who grow rapidly, as twenty years pass in the span of forty days (three minutes of screen time), and happily, he wins the inheritance though he has lost twenty years. *Onésime vs. Onésime* (1912) uses split-screen effects to allow Bourbon to interact with his double in a cluster of gags pitting the identical Onésimes against one another.

The highly cinematic Durand movies provide good examples for this transitional era exploiting clearly staged medium shots and mobile cameras, while retaining some static deep space shots in the style of a Lumière film. Thus, a wide range of French comedies from this era demonstrate a lively mix of innovation and consistency in a format that guaranteed solid box office returns and accounted for up to a third of the weekly releases at Gaumont and Pathé. It is also worth keeping in mind that in the early 1910s, films were still shown in an array of venues, including music halls, outdoor patios at cafés, and fairgrounds. Short attractions were still in high demand. However, as Jennifer Wild explains, the increase in large, specially designed movie theaters during the period from 1908 to 1916 normalized new, more immersive spectatorial practices, building on high art theatrical viewing conventions. Cinema's status was "uplifted," thanks to these prestigious, cathedral-like structures, including the massive Gaumont-Palace, that accompanied the ongoing shift to longer films and predictable programs (141–42).

Léonce Perret and Émile Cohl at Gaumont

One of the most influential of comic stars at Gaumont was Léonce Perret. As Abel explains, "If Gaumont consistently produced the most outrageous of the slapstick comedies in the *Onésime* series, the company also was responsible for the most sophisticated—Perret's *Léonce* series" (*Ciné* 417). Perret stars as a self-assured, wealthy fellow who cannot help pursuing beautiful women, though he also has a marvelous wife (Suzanne Grandais) at home. As with Max Linder, Perret blurs the line between his fictional and real personas. In *Léonce, Cinematographer* (*Léonce, Cinématographiste*, 1913), Perret even plays a movie director. In the earlier *Mariage par le cinématographe* (1911), Perret visited the Gaumont studios, which allows an occasion to reveal five different scenes being shot for five different genre films at once in a long tracking shot. Throughout his series, Léonce goes on vacations, has marital problems, and suffers from run-ins with various relatives, especially his mother-in-law. Ultimately, Perret made scores of Léonce films from 1912 into 1916, solidifying his fame and name recognition and closely following most aspects of Linder's formula. Perret also violated Gaumont's prohibition against including the talent's real names by adding title cards for himself as actor and director, as well as for Grandais, increasing their status.

While making the Léonce series, Perret also began directing and acting in serious dramas for Gaumont. One of Perret's most engaging cinematic three-reel short features, *The Mystery of the Kador Cliffs* (*Le Mystère des roches de Kador*, 1912), looks like a film from later in the 1910s, displaying many narrative innovations. An orphaned young woman named Suzanne (Grandais) is due to inherit a great fortune; however, her guardian, Fernand (Perret), heavily in debt, hopes to get that money for himself. Jealous and frustrated, he decides to eliminate her new beau, Jean (Émile Keppens). He will shoot Jean and drug Suzanne to make it look as if she were the guilty party, which should plunge her into madness, after which he can retain control of her

Screen therapy for Suzanne (*The Mystery of the Kador Cliffs*)

inheritance. After a rousing first act, with the young couple barely surviving their ordeal, Suzanne remains in a catatonic state of shock, and no one understands what happened. The second reel is devoted to a remarkable experiment to cure her by showing her a filmed reenactment of the events leading up to her trauma. After the shock of seeing the movie, Suzanne is jolted back to reality, allowing Jean and others to help investigate and eventually solve the case. This crime melodrama is a cinematic marvel for the era, with subtle camera movements reframing the action, many point-of-view shots, and matches on action that merge location shooting seamlessly with interior studio shots.

Perret followed *The Mystery of Kador Cliffs* with the technically polished nationalistic tale *The Child of Paris* (*L'Enfant de Paris*, 1913), Gaumont's first long film, running two hours in two parts. In *The Child of Paris*, an upper-class military man (Keppens) is sent to Casablanca, where his troops are overrun, and he is presumed dead. His wife dies of a broken spirit, leaving their daughter, Marie-Laure (Suzanne Privat), as a ward of their best friend, another officer who is quickly dispatched to another colonial crisis. The young girl ends up

The orphan Bosco is rewarded (*The Child of Paris*)

abducted and mistreated by a gang of thugs, then forced to work for a drunken cobbler until her father miraculously returns to Paris to lead a search. Bosco (Maurice Lagrenée), a humble orphaned cobbler's assistant, risks his life to rescue her, leading to an elaborate, suspenseful chase from Paris to Nice. By the end, a new bourgeois family is formed as the grateful father adopts the young man. For this Dickensian drama, Perret presents the lower classes as greedy, grimy, and scheming, and the only promise seems to be an upper-class patron to save them. The rather subtle acting styles reveal each character's class as well as personality.

Many historians have noted that Perret's visual style during this period rivals that of most any other director of the time, including D. W. Griffith. As Abel explains, "Perret's representational choices—deep-space tableaux, reverse-angle cutting, silhouetted figures, cut-in close shots, emblematic crosscuts, and subjective images within the frame—all serve to render his films' stories more intimate and psychological" (*Ciné* 342). While the location shooting is often evocative, with contiguous spaces cut efficiently together, the staging for interiors is equally inventive, often building frames within frames. For instance, in the cobbler's claustrophobic home, the camera pans left to reveal Marie-Laure's tiny closet of a room. Later in a grand villa in Nice, when Bosco breaks her door down to help her escape, the wall divides the room like a cut-away set, recalling the earlier prison-like rooms. Although the bulk of the shots are long tableaux, often as shot sequences, Perret reserves cut-ins to emphasize or isolate intimate actions. There is also striking use of depth for interior and exterior compositions, especially with several suspenseful shots where Marie-Laure on the inside peers out a window to gauge whether others are spying on her. Perret was one of Gaumont's great storytellers in the 1910s, and this five-part narrative unfolds like the chapters of a carefully constructed, highly cinematic adaptation of a novel.

Importantly, Gaumont also launched the career of animator Émile Cohl. In 1908, the caricaturist and graphic artist created *Fantasmagorie*, which is widely accepted as the first true animated motion picture. Cohl built his own animation stand, positioning the stop-motion Gaumont Chrono camera vertically above his drawings. He adapted his comic caricature aesthetic to the cinema, printing the negative to produce white figures on a dark background, mimicking chalk talks and lightning drawings. The stick-figure clown and rapid transformations in *Fantasmagorie* establish models for Cohl's ultimate series of films. His work features abstract spatial arrangements and minimally narrative comic set-ups, often including subjective visions rendered via

Two Cohl frames, seen through a microscope (*Merry Microbes*)

circular frames to simulate a dream or microscope field of vision. He added live-action sequences to introduce and motivate the animated portions in many of his films, including the satirical *The Merry Microbes* (*Les Joyeux microbes*, 1909) and *The Neo-Impressionist Painter* (*Le Peintre Néo-impressionniste*, 1910).

Although Cohl was a unique talent, he was also rather typical of filmmakers of his era in that he moved regularly from company to company, including Pathé, Eclipse, and Eclair, even traveling to the United States, where he introduced his techniques to American producers. There he began to adapt established, commercial newspaper comics for cinema. Later, back in France, Cohl exploited many modes of animation, from his trademark stick figures to cut-out paper puppets to tiny, pixelated objects. Cohl's fanciful visual style and unique mode of production provided for a personal style, making him the first real animation auteur. Cohl also inspired other cartoonists, including Winsor McCay, to help launch a whole new genre. During the 1910s, Cohl's films offered brief, spectacular attractions at a time when French studios were constantly on the lookout for new options in synthesizing experimental new visions with commercial modes of exploitation.

Pathé and Gaumont may have dominated the market, but a number of important production companies participated in the vast output of 1910s motion pictures in France. Talented cinema managers, engineers, and directors were in demand, and many individuals shifted quickly from company to company, sharing their expertise and looking for more independence and higher pay. Pathé's Henri Joly struck out on his own to help form Société Lux while Eclipse, an offshoot of British Urban Trading, managed to gain a foothold by marketing several successful film series that were distributed in the United States by George Kleine. Another company, Eclair, became a major player, thanks in part to its string of popular series featuring recurring characters. It launched the Nick Carter series based on the highly popular new American dime novels, as well as other genre films, including adventure films, westerns, and pirate movies. Eclair's most successful and influential series began in 1911 with the Zigomar films, which helped establish the exhibition practice of playing a number of episodes together to form a sequential program. While Eclair expanded into the US market as well, by 1914 and the arrival of World War I, its fortunes had faded. Throughout the 1910s, France continued as a source for top-quality film equipment, with an array of ongoing developments in film stock, projectors, and cameras, including the lightweight Debrie Parvo, which proved valuable on locations and allowed for excellent frame-by-frame exposures for animation and other effects.

The Film d'Art and Cultural Pretensions

While most of these smaller studios modeled themselves on prevailing trends in serial mystery thrillers or comedies, one alternative in French cinema was initiated by the Film d'Art company. Formed by a cluster of well-connected people in Parisian theater, including Henri Lavedan of the Académie Française and Charles le Bargy of the Comédie Française, Film d'Art's goal was to offer one-reel prestige dramas. It launched its company with the elegantly staged *The Assassination of the Duc de Guise* (*La Mort du duc de Guise*, 1908), presented with original music by composer Camille Saint-Saëns as well as elaborate sets based on the real location of the famous murder in the Château de Blois. Although some later historians dismissed this sort of "high art" intrusion, the Film d'Art mode enlivened French and international cinema in profound ways. Already in 1911, fellow filmmaker Victorin-Hippolyte Jasset credited Le Bargy and his "masterpiece" *The Assassination of the Duc de Guise* for a new set of mise-en-scène options, including acting: "Well-known artists acted by standing still instead of running around; they achieved an increasing intensity of effect." Moreover, he asserts, these high-cost, quality films motivated other French producers to strive for more dramatic and professional standards and influenced their American rivals: "[Film d'Art] opened the eyes of the American school, transformed it, and made that school what it is today" (Abel, *French Film* 56). Indeed, *Moving Picture World* immediately championed *The Assassination of the Duc de Guise* in 1909, with the reviewer proclaiming he had "never seen a better motion picture drama . . . the acting is superbly natural" (Harrison 200). As Tom Gunning points out, the Film d'Art catalog, "with its pedigree from established art forms, carried the mark of social respectability and therefore provoked imitation on the part of American production" (*D. W. Griffith* 172). The young, global film industry was surprisingly quick to respond to new innovations and competitors.

Film d'Art went on to produce many adaptations from literature and theater, such as *Carmen* (1910), *Macbeth* (1910), and *Camille* (*La Dame aux camélias*, 1912), starring Sarah Bernhardt. Other art film competitors, including Pathé's new division, the Société cinématographique des auteurs et gens de lettres (SCAGL), rose up to compete in this high culture niche. These French companies exploited the status of their performers at a time when the US Motion Picture Patents Company forcefully repressed the names of talent to keep costs down. The French star system proved to be a powerful draw in almost every genre of production, though the Film d'Art productions tended to be quite costly, and eventually their theatrical aesthetic, and especially their painted backdrops, appeared increasingly outdated in contrast to the more commercial narrative strategies of Gaumont, Pathé, and their US rivals. SCAGL, however, proved most resilient. They hired a cluster of top cinematographers and directors, and their facilities included a glass ceiling and wall for consistent natural light, with Sun arc lamps and Cooper Hewitt mercury vapor units for fill light. They even had a permanent pool for miniature scenes at sea and other special effects. These high-quality films spurred on narrative and stylistic innovations at competing studio facilities.

Among the more popular SCAGL films were the literary adaptations by Albert Capellani, who served as SCAGL's initial head of production. His early adaptation of Émile Zola's *L'Assommoir* (*Drink*, 1908) reduced the lengthy novel to three highly melodramatic sections. Capellani made creative use of off-screen cues, with characters coming in and out of the playing space, and in a scene of betrayal, he frames the guilty woman in a dark doorway deep in space while everyone else rushes to help the fallen protagonist in the foreground. He exploited mise-en-scène and plot ordering to generate strong, clear dramatic and moralizing effects, anticipating D. W. Griffith's manipulative narrator system. Capellani's reputation, as well as that of SCAGL, grew continually thanks to their high production values and prestigious literary topics.

In 1913, SCAGL released Capellani's four-hour version of *Les Misérables* in four episodes, one new installment each week for a month. The high-profile project adapting Victor Hugo's saga gained so much preproduction publicity that many top politicians of the day visited the sets. Capellani had a street in the Paris Marais neighborhood dressed for the era and another artificial set built in Vincennes for the battles on the barricades. Starring Henry Krauss as Jean Valjean, young Maria Fromet as Cosette, and Mistinguett as Éponine Thénardier, Capellani's *Les Misérables*, which he bragged was edited with the novel in their hands, became a major hit in France and abroad. It made a stir in the United States, where *Moving Picture World* celebrated its realistic settings with their "unwavering detail throughout" as well as Krauss's "majestic" acting, calling this groundbreaking twelve-reel movie "a masterpiece" (April 26, 1913, 362). *Les Misérables* was a triumphant success, prompting Capellani to continue with a string of heritage films, including a two-and-a-half-hour version of Zola's *Germinal* in 1913. For *Germinal*, Capellani took his cinematographer, Pierre Trimbach, on a research trip into a coal mine before they built the set for underground scenes, which ended up being fifty meters long. The film also boasted crowd scenes with 130 extras in period costuming. He followed up with rousing adaptations of the Alexandre Dumas novel *The Knight of the Red House* (*Le Chevalier de la maison rouge*, 1914) and Hugo's *Ninety-Three* (*Quatre-vingt-treize*, 1914, released by codirector André Antoine, 1921). His adaptations avoid excessive dialogue title cards, reducing explanatory titles to a minimum, yet they were praised for their faithfulness to the original storylines.

Capellani's style provides an excellent demonstration of French staging for the era, with long takes carefully choreographing action in depth, as well as a mix of locations and realistic set design, typically for a fixed camera position. For instance, early in *Germinal*, the hard-working Lantier (Krauss) meets his colleagues in a café for lunch. The nearly two-minute-long take begins as Lantier takes the suddenly empty seat at a table in the foreground right. As he reads his paper and pours his wine, a downtrodden fellow walks into the café. He works his way toward the camera, shaking his comrades' hands, before arriving center frame beside Lantier. The man produces a note that shows he has been fired for missing too much work when ill, which appears as an insert. The distraught man motions to the back of the room and the men step aside to reveal his sad wife and baby against the back wall. Lantier is motivated to take the man by the arm and head to the door on their way to appeal to his boss. Next they are shown petitioning the foreman in a real factory setting. This scene quickly establishes the humanity of the workers, the respect they feel for Lantier, and the cruelty of the workplace, all in a single shot with deep space staging. Soon Lantier also loses his job and must search for work, eventually becoming a coal miner, playing a major role in an extended strike, and enduring a series of melodramatic disasters. Capellani's combination of real locations and special effects offers a gripping adaptation, which *Moving Picture World* again labeled a masterpiece, "in the true sense of the word" (Bush 416). Capellani's Pathé films were heralded as technically and artistically polished, though some later historians dismissed these sorts of "quality" literary adaptations. Fortunately, new attention to the era and these films has revived Capellani's reputation. As Kristin Thompson observes, Capellani proves over and over that his films can be "more sophisticated, more engaging, and more polished" than contemporary movies by the more celebrated D. W. Griffith: "Nothing in Griffith's pre-war career comes close to *Les Misérables* or *Germinal*" ("Capellani").

Deep interior staging (*Germinal*)

Louis Feuillade and the Crime Serial

After 1910, new trends toward recurring characters and increasingly dramatic narratives, whether crime dramas, adventure tales, or comical melodramas, expanded the range of topics and lengths of French films. As Kristin Thompson and David Bordwell point out, a true serial carried a story line over several episodes and provided a transitional form between one-reelers and features: "Serials were usually action oriented, offering thrilling elements like master criminals, lost treasures, exotic locales, and daring rescues" (49). Among the most successful and influential serial directors was Louis Feuillade, who directed hundreds of films for Gaumont starting in 1906, often shooting well over sixty short movies in a single year. Feuillade was paid a bonus for delivering profitable films, and he readily exploited the latest fads in filmmaking as well as successful formulas. As Bordwell explains, "Feuillade unabashedly put on display all the clichés of popular narrative. There are dying mothers, orphaned children, saucy maids, benevolent American millionaires, henpecked husbands, seductive adventuresses, and cunningly disguised villains armed with poison, bombs, and the power to hypnotize innocents. If you want your movie to sell, he told one director, hire a child or a dog" (*Figures* 43). Feuillade continued to serve as artistic director for Gaumont. As a response to Pathé's *Perils of Pauline* and other new serial formats, Feuillade adapted *Fantômas*, serial novels launched in 1911 by Marcel Allain and Pierre Souvestre. The episodic film series and published stories proved remarkably timely and influential.

Fantômas was a chronological chain of tales pitting the resourceful Inspector Juve (Edmund Breon) and earnest journalist Fandor (Georges Melchior) against the devious master criminal Fantômas (René Navarre), who could rapidly change his appearance and identity like a chameleon. The title sequence even revealed Navarre, a veteran of scores of Feuillade shorts, in a number of disguises, glaring out at the audience, celebrating the talents of Fantômas the character and Navarre the actor simultaneously. Fantômas was regularly backed up by his accomplice, Lady Beltham (Renée Carl). The first installment, *Fantômas in the Shadow of the Guillotine*, establishes the clever strategies of Fantômas, who magically appears in a wealthy woman's room in a highly secure hotel and robs her, leaving only a blank calling card on which

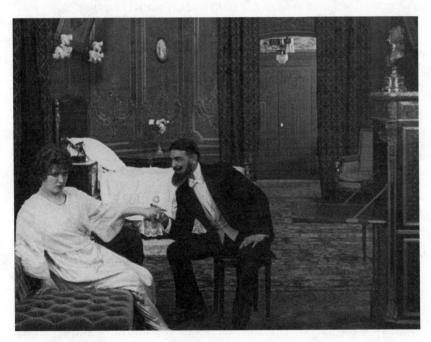

The charming thief (*Fantômas in the Shadow of the Guillotine*)

his name later appears thanks to invisible ink. This crime provokes great shock and fear from the victim and staff. Meanwhile, in an unrelated case, Inspector Juve is assigned to locate the missing Lord Beltham. Juve solves the crime and arrests Fantômas, but thanks to Lady Beltham, as well as a series of disguises and mistaken identities, Fantômas escapes prison and justice, opening the door for the next installment. As the series continues, Juve learns to disguise himself and exploit unconventional tactics in his struggle against his nemesis. Fantômas proves as charming as he is cruel, happily killing and maiming, blowing up buildings, smashing trains, and sending innocent men to the gallows in his place. No one is safe in his destructive path, and he seems to feel no empathy for any of his victims as his actions generate an ominous atmosphere in which the urban space becomes "a crime-filled arena" (Callahan, "Representations" 69).

Throughout the *Fantômas* series, Feuillade employs rather understated acting, deep space blocking of action, and locations to open up the settings beyond the studio artifice. The carefully balanced shot compositions, which are often quite crowded in some scenes, guide the spectator's attention from character to character and from one plane of action to another. Feuillade was exceptionally skilled at forging a functional, pictorial narrative space, making full use of depth and lateral and diagonal staging with sharp focus on all elements in the frame (Bordwell, *Figures* 55). Feuillade shot hundreds of shorts prior to *Fantômas*, but this and subsequent serials provided ample opportunity for him to develop his narrative and stylistic styles over an extended collection of interconnected episodes. Feuillade becomes a major auteur for later critics, thanks primarily to his serials.

Feuillade's next serial, *Les Vampires*, followed with ten episodes playing over a six-month period from fall 1915 to early summer 1916. This was a wartime production made under difficult conditions, and its success further encouraged expansion of the urban crime serial genre in France. Once again, there was a core of recurring characters, but also more lurid and intriguing titles such as "The Severed Head," "The Corpse's Escape," and "The Bloody Wedding." This time the protagonist, Philippe Guérande (Édouard Mathé), is something of a synthesis of Juve and Fandor. He is a crime journalist, eventually working with the former Vampire gang member Oscar Mazamette (Marcel Lévesque) against the diabolical and seductive Irma Vep (Musidora) and a shifting group of Vampire villains. Across the *Vampires* episodes, fantastically diabolical crimes and deceptions are committed, beautifully staged in realistic sets and on location. Guérande and Mazamette are repeatedly frustrated by the elusive Vampires and a rival band led by Juan-José Moréno (Fernand Herrmann).

Major players come and go in the chaotic plots, often woven together with busy intertitles, but a large part of the delight from this series stems from the unpredictability of the characters and the violence with which important characters can suddenly be eliminated. Irma Vep began to gain power and screen time after the third episode. A master of disguise, Vep turns up regularly, even as the string of male Vampire grand masters are killed off. She is first seen performing in the Howling Cat Cabaret and eventually plays a number of key villainous roles, including mixing deadly poisons, planting bombs, shooting a colleague under hypnotism, and committing larceny in her sleek black outfit. Vep's erotic appeal and unpredictability heightened her significance in Feuillade's rambling narrative. Further, Vep's shocking demise, as she is gunned down on her wedding day by Guérande's wife, Jane (Louise Lagrange), helped generate a great deal of commentary on the representation of the new woman in French crime films and, by extension, in French culture.

Irma Vep makes a bomb (*Les Vampires*)

Unsettling "new women" perform in Feuillade (*Les Vampires*)

Some of Feuillade's contemporaries attacked his popular brand of cinema, with Louis Delluc proving particularly cruel, but many Surrealists later embraced his characters and their sudden, often bizarre plot reversals. As Vicki Callahan puts it, "the uncanny provides the primary narrative drive for many episodes" (*Zones* 62). Moreover, Feuillade offered his contemporaries unsettling versions of urban settings and modern devices. His films engaged in complex ways with the *nouvelle femme*, who was simultaneously appealing and dangerous. Later, these serials found a second life thanks to Henri Langlois and the Cinémathèque Française, where André Bazin and Alain Resnais (among others) rediscovered Feuillade's work, celebrating *Fantômas* and *Les Vampires* as both skilled screen masterpieces and authentic popular art.

Judex, Feuillade's next series, was created with the help of novelist Arthur Bernède. They conjured up a central character, Jacques de Trémeuse (René Cresté), whose aristocratic father was ruined by a devious banker, Favraux (Louis Leubas). Henri, who adopts an alter ego as Judex, vows revenge. While Fantômas and the Vampires needed no backstory to justify their mysterious actions, Judex's vengeance is motivated and all-consuming. Judex manages

to fake Favraux's death, exposing his past deeds to Favraux's honest and innocent widowed daughter, Jacqueline. Judex also disrupts the evil subplots by
Diana Monti (Musidora) and her accomplice, Moralés. The central themes
include revenge, justice, and forgiveness, issues that permeate all the events
of this action-packed domestic melodrama.

During the thirteen-episode series, Judex, who lives in a fantastic modern
setting under the ruins of the old Château-Rouge, imprisons the supposedly
dead Favraux to taunt and punish the old banker. He watches over and protects Jacqueline and her young son, Jean, while he solves kidnappings and
foils repeated escapades by Diana Monti and Moralés. Judex even has a highly
trained pack of dogs. His character, complete with black hat and cape, was a
calculated cross between an avenging aristocrat, not unlike the Count of
Monte Cristo, and a modern Robin Hood. He also had a young sidekick, the
Licorice Kid. Clearly, Judex influenced subsequent popular culture figures,
anticipating many elements of Batman and other superheroes with dual identities. Feuillade's serials, including the stylish *Tih Minh* (1918), presented
engaging crime melodramas featuring rapid shifts of fortune and mistaken
identities and an array of entertaining minor character types, all shot with
stunning cinematography in evocative locations. Feuillade's reputation for
innovative narrative, cultural, and stylistic contributions to French filmmaking still owes largely to these finely made episodic films, but his ingenuity is
also on display in his hundreds of Gaumont shorts. As Bordwell concludes,
Feuillade may have "cast his lot with the mass audience," but in the process
he helped create "a cinema of subtle beauty" (*Figures* 43, 82). Feuillade died
in 1925, at age fifty-two, having helped shape the first quarter-century of
French film practice.

World War I and Its Aftermath

Despite the boom in adventure films, literary adaptations, and crime serials,
Max Linder remained the most celebrated figure in French cinema and an
international phenomenon when World War I broke out. With the declaration of war and a general mobilization in August 1914, the French film industry was quickly closed down. The assumption was that an intense but short
war would soon be won and things would return to normal. Linder publicly
declared his eagerness to serve and even rode to the front in his chauffeur-
driven limousine on official missions. However, his fragile health limited his
involvement, and he was apparently wounded as well. At one point, a French
newspaper even reported erroneously that Linder had been killed in action.

Though he survived, his physical and mental health were permanently strained. Fortunately for the furloughed Linder, during 1916, Essanay Studios in Chicago invited him to come make comedies for them after Charlie Chaplin left for another studio. Linder joined Essanay for only a few films before returning to France in 1917 when Pathé gradually resumed producing the Max series, which never regained its vitality.

Linder's suddenly uneven career path parallels the long rise and then rapid fall of French film dominance in the 1910s. By the end of the decade, the French industry was recovering, but it was no longer the uncontested global leader. World War I had brought an abrupt halt to the expansion of French cinema in general, and Pathé and Gaumont emerged greatly changed, adapting their industrial models for a new, more competitive international marketplace. Just prior to 1914, Pathé's Vincennes plant alone turned out 100 million meters of film stock a year. But the declaration of war meant an immediate stop to production as talent was called up, studio space requisitioned, and the manufacture of film stock prohibited because nitrate was reserved for munitions. Paper rations forced the many specialized film weeklies and magazines, including the trade paper *Ciné-Journal*, to condense or even curtail their business, further crippling French film culture.

In 1914, France's share of the global market dipped to 30 percent, and the declaration of war sent its output and international sales steadily lower. The arrival of World War I greatly aided US producers in particular, allowing their growing throng of independent studios to fill the gap left by declining French competition. Earlier, Thomas Edison had justified the Motion Picture Patents Company as a patriotic institution to counter the dominance of French cinema. Thanks to increased production capacity and weakened European studios, American filmmakers fully owned American screens, and soon they accounted for up to 90 percent of the wartime box office in England as well. In France, the market was controlled by the largest four distributors, Pathé, Gaumont, Aubert (with its many Italian connections), and Agence Générale Cinématographique (AGC), each pushing its productions and contracting with popular imports. Every distributor, exhibitor, and producer was crippled by the general mobilization. Despite shortages in electricity and rationed film stock, cinemas slowly began to reopen in 1915 as the industry successfully argued that entertainment was healthy for the war-weary populace. With domestic production at a near standstill, many of the movies shown were foreign, including Italy's impressive *Cabiria* (Pastrone, 1914), which ran for four months in Paris.

During the winter of 1915, the government launched a new department to document the war, the Section cinématographique de l'armée (SCA). This division of the War Ministry forged a collaboration with the major film studios to produce and distribute films to counter German propaganda, highlight the triumphs of the French military effort, and provide documentary evidence of the ongoing destruction of French territory. Pathé, Gaumont, Eclipse, and Eclair cooperated with the SCA, assigning staff to accompany military operations and creating collective national newsreels on a weekly basis, *The Annals of War* (*Annales de la Guerre*). Many of their films stand as striking documents on the daily routines of the soldiers marching, making camp, loading their cannons at Verdun, or reinforcing trenches in ghostly terrains. The newsreels reveal official staged events, such as Red Cross presentations, officers handing out medals, or proud pilots inspecting their airplanes. The SCA covered multiple perspectives on the war era, and their films offer rare archival evidence of the battlefronts and resulting devastation in many areas of Europe, as well as fascinating glimpses of the soldiers, technology, and military realities of the day.

French studios also turned out a regular line-up of patriotic and historical dramas, and many celebrity performers contributed to the cause. For instance, *French Heart* (*Coeur de Française*, 1916), directed by Gaston Leprieur, exploited a number of well-known actors from the prestigious Odéon Theater in a detective tale about German spies. Eclair's *French Mothers* (*Mères françaises*, Hervil and Mercanton, 1917) starred Sarah Bernhardt as a woman who loses her son and her husband in the war. One highly symbolic and powerful scene stages her with Joan of Arc's statue in front of the damaged cathedral at Reims. Typically, historians excuse or dismiss most of the "serious" films made in France during the war. Historian René Jeanne, writing in 1932, set that pattern, arguing that these wartime movies abandoned concerns for artistry in favor of cliché attempts at inspirational dramas on small budgets, shot under difficult circumstances. He argues that French cinema had to wait until 1917 to find a movie worth remembering (Jeanne194). Nonetheless, patriotic movies such as *French Mothers* exported well, even playing for fund-raising events in Canada and the United States.

Gradually, the gaps in commercial production did allow some fragile niche films by less conventional artists late in the war, including Germaine Dulac's first films, *Venus Victrix* (1917) and *Mysterious George* (*Géo le mystérieux*, 1917), which were produced by Dulac, her husband, Albert, and Irène Hillel-Erlanger and their company, Les Films DH. As Tami Williams points out, the war "created a momentary rupture from traditional social roles and offered an unprecedented experience of liberty and self-affirmation for many women" (51). Some gains were short-term, including the small studio founded by actresses Musidora and Stacia Napierkowska, but these ventures were encouraging for later women and avant-garde filmmakers. Nonetheless, it is worth underscoring the devastatingly rapid decline in French cinema's status, which went from being a national source of pride as the strongest national cinema in the world in 1914 to the despair of losing dominance globally and even domestically by 1918.

Even before the end of the war, as increasing numbers of US movies found their way to French screens, there were pressing calls for revitalizing France's domestic industry, reasserting its cultural capital. American westerns, comedies, and romances were immensely popular, and their fast-paced editing and seemingly casual style challenged many of the staging and acting norms of the most prestigious French commercial cinema. For some industry insiders, making any sort of domestic movie to counter the influx of Hollywood product was seen as a patriotic necessity, with some critics warning that France could become a cinematic colony of the United States. Preserving French cinema was a key component of the cultural imperative felt by French citizens during and after the war: "At stake in the Great War was France's cultural survival . . . a certain cultural identity that they believed was fundamentally opposed to the cultural identity of their German 'aggressors'" (Murphy 11). That the American allies were keeping the French audience entertained with Charlie Chaplin, Mack Sennett comedies, and westerns was appreciated by some, but their rapid dominance worried many in French film business and culture, including the influential Henri Diamant-Berger, publisher of *Le Film*.

The postwar period ushered in dramatic changes in the industrial structure and aesthetic directions for French cinema. Most of the French pioneers, including the Lumières, Méliès, Pathé, Gaumont, and Zecca, had been born in the 1860s, and the Great War left France and its cinema with radically different economic and cultural situations by 1918. During the war, top talent had been displaced, with younger film workers serving and dying in the military, while many established people moved temporarily or permanently to England, Italy, or the United States, where they helped fuel the booming studio system. For instance, Maurice Tourneur took over the US branch of Eclair in 1914, remaining in the United States until the late 1920s. Albert Capellani served briefly in an artillery unit on the front lines at age forty. He was dismissed for health issues at the end of 1914. In early 1915, Capellani left for the United States, where he was announced as "the man who directed *Les Misérables*" and hired by World Film Corporation, Mutual, and Metro before eventually forming his own studio in Hollywood, only returning to Paris in the late 1920s. Capellani's brother Paul, an actor, typified another option. He stayed in America only until the war ended, returning to work the rest of his career on stage and screen in France. Léonce Perret also worked in the United States, directing features for producer Harry Rapf in New Jersey from 1917 to 1921, returning with a patriotic vow to help France regain its cinematic place in the world. These talented émigrés contributed to the synthesis of French and American traits for new aesthetic and economic models after the war.

Even more significant were Charles Pathé's frequent voyages to the United States, where his company remained a key player in producing and distributing a wide range of movies, including animation. Pathé capitalized on its 28mm Pathéscope, or Kok, which exploited its new safety stock, for sales of projection equipment and films to the niche market of schools, museums, and home projection systems for the wealthy. By 1918, Pathé initiated a careful study of the conditions in France, concluding that French cinema should more closely follow the stylistic innovations he found in American movies. He encouraged shorter scenes with more systematic use of close-ups and more energetic editing. Diamant-Berger also promoted shifts in French practice in a 1919 series of *Le Film* articles outlining how to "save" French cinema. He pointed to directors of promise, including Abel Gance, Jacques Feyder, and Raymond Bernard: "We knew we had to rally a new generation if we were to recover from the mediocrity into which the French cinema had fallen" (Drazin 33). Amid all the changes, a new cohort of film enthusiasts entered film production and criticism. Some were motivated by the escapist and even therapeutic value they had found in moviegoing during the war, while others championed cinema as the newest modern art form, pure and simple. Cinema's potential as a mighty social force and cultural medium was suddenly very visible. French commercial cinema may have slumped because of the war, but the crisis led to a unique set of mechanisms that unleashed a wild array of impassioned proposals for rebuilding the national cinema, even if its period of global dominance never returned.

In the postwar French film industry, major changes, including decisions by Pathé and Gaumont to emphasize distribution and exhibition over production, brought new economic models to the foreground. Thus, although a handful of companies still dominated commercial cinema's releases, a less centralized production system opened the field to a wider variety of smaller studios, paving the way for a younger generation to enter French cinema as it was reshaping itself. Moreover, in 1917, the Ministry of the Interior established a commission to assess cinema's situation and recommend ways to stabilize the industry and enhance its artistic potential. The war had brought a national tax on all ticket sales, which continued, with the addition of local municipal taxes, which were determined by the Ministry of the Interior's commission. By 1919, conflicts over local and national control of content and censorship led to another commission, this one under the Ministry of Public Instruction and the Beaux Arts, which established guidelines for producers to earn a national visa for distribution. Producers were assured that local censor boards could not close down screenings, and the ministry charged a fee to each film to be evaluated for its exhibition visa. These arrangements set the stage for increasingly stable relations between the industry, local governments, and national ministries.

The devastation of the war, along with the postwar artistic and cultural upheavals, including Paris regaining its status as the artistic and cultural center for Europe, brought new debates about the future directions and even responsibilities for French cinema. As some older established figures were returning from abroad, they were confronted with a radically different set of concerns from young critics writing for a new generation of restless spectators. Postwar French cinema was not simply coming to terms with a changing marketplace; it was confronting the realities of American domination. Chaplin or "Charlot" comedies, the melodramatic blockbuster *The Cheat* (DeMille, 1915), and other popular genre films from adventure tales to westerns had won over French audiences and demonstrated the pressing need for alternatives in France's film offerings. The shifts in the realities of French production provided opportunities for new talent, including some daring production strategies, and increased calls for a vital, nationally specific French cinema. The unusual postwar conditions helped establish a French cinema that allowed and encouraged commercial studio films as well as smaller production models specializing in bold artistic experiments. This radical French model was being forged at a time when the Hollywood studio system was increasingly standardizing its practices, further consolidating the US film industry around set genres and stylistic conventions.

CHAPTER 4

French Production Practices
of the 1920s

Revitalizing Art and Industry

Toward a Renewal of Commercial French Cinema

By 1920, the French industry had indeed made fundamental changes. Charles Pathé reorganized his company, expanding its number of movie theaters and emphasizing distribution, especially of popular international films, to maximize profit and avoid risky investments in filmmaking. He sold off many divisions of his corporation, including the film stock factory at Vincennes. Gaumont followed suit, pulling back on film production and closing many foreign offices, while Eclair rented out their studio space to others, earning the bulk of their income from their successful line of production equipment. Richard Abel points out that with the cutbacks from the former studios, "the burden of French film production fell on a diverse group of smaller production companies and independent producers" (*French Cinema* 17). This cluster of often underfinanced companies, without their own state-of-the-art studio space, could scarcely compete with the onslaught of imports from American and German studios.

Nonetheless, several producers, including Louis Nalpas and Henri Diamant-Berger, financed a few big-budget films based on Hollywood's model, and Pathé and Gaumont regularly invested in such joint productions for high-profile projects. For instance, *The Three Musketeers* (*Les Trois mousquetaires*, 1920–21) was released in twelve one-hour episodes, produced by Diamant-Berger. Films like these highlighted specifically French themes, including historical reconstructions and adaptations of popular novels, to counter Hollywood genres. Many of the most spectacular commercial films were funded from a few big-name producers, with Pathé and Gaumont participating in projects they did not initiate, minimizing their financial exposure.

The relatively small market in France meant that the average feature film's budget was usually 10 percent that of a Hollywood movie, and the limited number of French screens meant that even modest films depended on international markets to break even.

Many advocates for a stronger national cinema emphasized this need for high-quality adaptations of famous French literature and folk tales, as well as shooting on real locations to emphasize France's striking landscapes and historical settings. Location shooting helped sidestep the weak studio situation and restricted some costs, but it also tended to privilege naturalist tales or historical dramas set in medieval or Renaissance locales. André Antoine provides a strong example of the realistic tendency. Long a major figure in French theater, having launched Thèâtre Libre in the 1880s, Antoine rejected theatrical conventions. Pathé's SCAGL initially hired him to complete Capellani's *Ninety-Three* (*Quatre-vingt-treize*, released in 1921); after this experience, he began adapting celebrated naturalist writers he had already staged in theater, including Émile Zola. Antoine was dedicated to opening up the stories in cinematic ways, including with great depth and camera mobility. He took his casts and crews out of the studio and into real places. For *Those Who Work at Sea* (*Travailleurs de la mer*, 1917), they filmed along the rugged Brittany coast; *The Swallow and the Titmouse* (*L'Hirondelle et la Mésange*, not released) was set on barges and canals in Belgium; *The Earth* (*La Terre*, 1921) was shot in the rich farmlands near Chartres; *The Girl from Arles* (*L'Arlesienne*, 1922) was filmed in the picturesque and swampy Camargue area, where the Rhône river meets the Mediterranean Sea. Antoine proclaimed that cinema must "abandon the studios to work in nature just as the Impressionist [painters] did," transporting the camera operators and equipment into real buildings and settings (Abel, *French Cinema* 96). For him, theater now offered an imitation of nature while cinema produced a living creation. Escaping the artifice of studio sets for locations and sunlight was essential for artistic realism.

Throughout his film career, Antoine emphasized painterly and photographic compositions, priding himself on breaking from representational traditions or static tableau staging. He also rehearsed his performers over and over to eliminate any "acting" clichés or mechanical gestures. He advocated a low-key, instinctive acting style and a carefully choreographed visual style that revealed the natural rhythm for characters performing daily routines in their usual milieu of these authentic locales. "Boats, trees, bridges, even people who are not directly engaged in the action, are often only partly in frame, as if to suggest that what the film registers is only a glimpse of what is there" (Chothia 183). Moreover, his actors often turn their backs on the camera, just as they had in his theatrical productions.

The Earth, based on a Zola novel, provides key examples of Antoine's strengths and challenges at constructing a casually paced realistic cinema. The story is structured around an aging landowner whose bickering children end up cheating him out of his property and money. There is an inserted doomed love plot concerning earnest young farmworker Jean (René Alexandre), who falls in love with the old fellow's kind, hardworking niece, Françoise (Germaine Rouer). Antoine often alternates between long shots and quick, inserted close-ups to ensure that no one misses the point or an emotional cue on an actor's face. Scenes regularly begin with the promise of deep playing space and leisurely long takes but are quickly broken down for maximum clarity. For instance, the scene where Françoise is nearly raped by her brother-in-law while resting in the fields begins with a two-shot before reducing the action to short emotional bursts. In the middle of the scene, after Françoise has run off crying, the brute of a man eats his usual lunch at

The vulnerable Françoise (*La Terre*)

his usual pace seated with his wife, while Jean stumbles on the traumatized Françoise nearby and has sex with her behind a pile of hay. The mix of an everyday rhythm of events along with high melodrama in the contested space of the family's various fields demonstrates Antoine's balance of narrative efficiency alongside spontaneity. Even his shot organization can be ambiguous, with few establishing shots. Spectators are often forced to position characters retroactively in relation to one another even though everyone seems to be in relatively contiguous places. Thus, Antoine works hard to explore the spatial and temporal options that cinema has to offer over the fixed theatrical stage.

Antoine helped provide some viable options for a realistic series of films based on French classics that emphasized France's landscapes. André Bazin later dismissed Antoine's theatrical realism: "Antoine might decorate the stage with real joints of meat but, unlike the cinema, he could not show a whole flock of sheep passing by" (*What Is Cinema?* [2009] 175). Yet, with *The Earth*, Antoine managed to include meandering sheep, cattle, and ducks in real settings. He ultimately walked away from filmmaking in 1921, however, leaving *The Swallow and the Titmouse* incomplete. As Abel points out, Antoine may not have managed to "transform the French cinema the same way that he had the French theater," as he and Charles Pathé had hoped, but he did manage to "articulate ideas and institute practices that were fundamental to the emergence of French realist film" (*French Cinema* 95). Antoine's films provide clear examples of the sort of higher-budget prestige pictures that producers such as Pathé, Gaumont, and Diamant-Berger saw as an avenue for a competitive French cinema.

Among the more popular productions of the early 1920s was Jacques Feyder's adaptation of Pierre Benoit's hit book *L'Atlantide* about colonial forces in North Africa. It was initially funded by a collection of sources before Louis Aubert stepped up to produce and distribute the film. Feyder opted to shoot on location in Algeria, which expanded the already high production costs. *L'Atlantide* (also released as *Lost Atlantis* and *Queen of Atlantis*, 1921) featured a cadre of colonial officers in the Sahara who seek a remote, mythical place and people, ruled over by the bizarre seductress Queen Antinea (Stacia Napierkowska). Feyder's two-hour, forty-minute film proudly remains close to the novel and includes a very long flashback in which lieutenant Saint-Avit (Georges Melchior) explains how he and the now missing Captain Morhange (Jean Angelo) encountered Antinea in an isolated valley, which was once the core of Atlantis. Only in the middle of the movie do we meet Antinea, who has her evil band of followers repeatedly capture European men for her to seduce, often driving them mad with frustrated desire. Finally, she has their dead bodies embalmed as golden statues and placed around her red marble room. Morhange proves to be her toughest conquest.

L'Atlantide is built around the destructive allure of the colony's alien cultural practices. The French officers are disoriented by smoking hashish and are introduced to mysterious rituals and potions. Its elaborate plot includes multiple flashbacks embedded in the primary flashback. L'Atlantide's mise-en-scène features elaborate costuming, ornate interiors, expressive acting, and evocative lighting, including many nighttime silhouettes in Antinea's lair. Most famously, the film boasts long sequences in the burning desert, including picturesque camel caravans and treacherous Berbers hiding high in the mountains, biding their time before they attack. The cliché dangers and attractions of North Africa are on full display.

Critic Louis Delluc was somewhat put off by the huge publicity campaign and extravagant costs but praised L'Atlantide for presenting an expansive scale and freedom of movement rarely seen in French cinema. He added, "There is a great actor in L'Atlantide, the desert sand" (Lherminier 130). This comment was partially sarcastic and aimed at the passive performance by the white Napierkowska as an unlikely North African seductress. Delluc's comment also reflects his constant search for *photogénie*, a dimension of the cinematic experience that transcends mere realism. Not only was L'Atlantide incredibly successful at the box office; it fueled a trend toward colonialist and orientalist genre films. Both the novel and the film "expressed the French fascination with people of color, profound unease with Europeans' place in Africa, and deep fears of the polluting effects of contact on European racial and personal identity" (Slavin 35). In fact, by the end of L'Atlantide, Saint-Avit, who had been deeply troubled by all he had seen in the desert, voluntarily returns there, "intoxicated" by his desire for Antinea and the irresistible allure of her barbarous, sadistic world. Feyder's adaptation and the many subsequent movies about Foreign Legion missions into the dangerous but tempting colonies became a reliable genre well into the sound era when some of these tales (including L'Atlantide) were remade.

With the immense success of L'Atlantide, Feyder became an influential model for commercial French cinema of the early 1920s. Next he adapted *Crainquebille* (*Coster Bill of Paris* in UK, 1923) from an Anatole France novella

Napierkowska as the exotic Antinea (*L'Atlantide*)

concerned with judicial injustice and social inequality. Thanks in part to impressive location cinematography by Léonce-Henri Burel, Feyder managed to anchor the tale in the streets and alleys of the Paris market district of Les Halles. Yet he retained internal narration from France's story, exploiting mental subjective images. *Crainquebille* follows an aging fruit and vegetable cart peddler, Jerome Crainquebille (Maurice de Féraudy), on his route, crossing paths with the poor Mouse (Jean Forest), a homeless boy who sells newspapers. However, an overzealous lout of a policeman arrests Crainquebille. During his trial scene, the simple old man's distress over the injustice is revealed via distorted images. Once he is released from jail, Crainquebille is shunned by his former customers and descends into drunkenness and poverty. Finally, the street urchin stops the desperate Crainquebille from his suicidal plunge into the Seine and takes him to safety in his makeshift home. Abel calls *Crainquebille* "probably the best of the 1920s realist films" (*French Cinema* 127), and its naturalistic performances and camerawork, inserting the actors into real neighborhoods, anchored Feyder's cinematic reputation.

The old peddler and Mouse (*Crainquebille*)

Feyder quickly moved on to another personal project, *Faces of Children* (*Visages d'enfants*, 1923–25), based on his own script. In 1917, Feyder had married actress Françoise Rosay, who had a minor role in *Crainquebille* and worked as assistant director for *Faces of Children*. She was now Jean Forest's godmother, because the young actor's mother had just died, and they hired him to play the unhappy boy in *Faces of Children* who also just lost a beloved mother. The story, shot on location in the Swiss Alps, revolves around the arrival of a new stepmother and the domestic challenges of harmoniously melding the new mother and her daughter, Arlette, in with the mourning Jean (Forest) and his little sister, Pierrette. This family melodrama unfurls at a leisurely pace with many parallels and contrasts helping organize the plot. For instance, while the father proposes to his next wife (Rachel Devirys), Jean visits his mother's grave. Arlette (Arlette Peyron) displaces the loss of her father onto her doll, while Jean's fetish object is his dead mother's dress. After establishing the tensions between all the family members, the final portion of the film pursues two rescues, first of Arlette, saved by her stepfather after an avalanche, and second of the suicidal Jean, rescued from a raging river by the stepmother.

A mostly realistic film, *Faces of Children* nonetheless inserts Impressionistic moments and several montages for subjective effects, as when Jean faints from emotion after his mother's funeral. This and other Feyder films proved quite engaging: "He strikes hard with his bracing realism built on strong psychological authenticity" (Beylie 94). For the avant-garde, Feyder was far too conventional, and some of the presentations of social rituals, such as the earnest funeral procession, are precisely the sorts of scenes the Surrealists later lampooned. Nonetheless, as Feyder proves with these films and his subsequent stylish silents, including the Impressionistic *Mother of Mine* (*Gribiche*, 1926) and *Carmen* (1926), he was a highly influential member of commercial French cinema. Later, he made the transition from silent to sound, championing the audio track's potential to bring special, powerful audio effects to the cinematic experience, which he called *phonogénie*, to parallel the concept *photogénie*, a term connoting a transcendent potential of the silent film image to evoke more than the concrete objects revealed in a shot. In 1977, the town of Epinay named a new school in his honor, Le Lycée Jacques Feyder, partly because he shot films near there and partly because of his sensitive treatment of children during his career.

Big-budget French films aimed at both a healthy domestic audience and international markets appeared regularly during the 1920s, and many continued to exploit specifically French settings and themes. One of the more action-packed and successful movies about France's heritage, *Miracle of the Wolves* (*Le Miracle des loups*, 1924), was directed by Raymond Bernard. Previously, Bernard had directed a number of films based on stories by his father, Tristan, a very popular playwright and novelist. *Miracle of the Wolves* was a novel by Henry Dupuy-Mazuel and the first project produced by the Société de Film Historiques, a company founded by Bernard, Dupuy-Mazuel, and several investors. The production boasted top acting talent, an original musical score written by Henri Rabaud, and set decor by Robert Mallet-Stevens. It was one of France's most expensive silent films. The tale romanticizes King Louis XI's very personal struggle to reunite France in the 1460s, battling the Duke of Burgundy and other feudal lords. Bernard, apparently at the urging of André Antoine, managed to situate as much of the action as possible in real historical settings, though for the final battle, the southern medieval city of Carcassonne stood in for the northern town of Beauvais. Its central plot involves Jeanne (Yvonne Sergyl), the ward of King Louis (Charles Dullin), who falls in love with a knight, Robert (Romuald Joubé) of the Burgundians. The couple is separated by their loyalties but are finally reunited after Jeanne, taking a strong feminist stance, leads the women in resisting the siege of Beauvais until the king's forces can arrive to save the day.

Beyond the exceptionally fine costuming, sets, and real locations, *Miracle of the Wolves* impressed 1920s audiences in France and beyond with the scale of its battle scenes. The initial battle of Montlhéry is shot with multiple cameras, including handheld, to reinforce the chaotic violence and confusion among the soldiers. In convincing scenes of gruesome hand-to-hand combat, Bernard turns the battlefield into a stunning if brutal flood of rousing images. Historical battles had rarely (if ever) been handled with such engaging and horrifying realism. Heads are smashed and bodies skewered in a hectic scene that lasts just over five minutes with an average shot length of under four seconds. The battle of Montlhéry ends with a draw but offers a sobering recreation of what in reality was also an indecisive and vicious event. A second major suspenseful sequence involves the king, menaced by Charles and his Burgundian accomplices, awaiting Jeanne to deliver a note that can save him. However, her party is ambushed in the snowy wilderness. Fleeing for her life from the enemy soldiers, she is suddenly trapped between the murderers and a pack of wolves emerging from the woods. As she falls to her knees praying, the wolves suddenly act like her trained dogs, defending her and killing most of the men pursuing her. The extended wolf attack is handled in a frenetic manner, as the wolves maul each of the men who killed Jeanne's father and betrayed the king. Great pains are taken to reveal the horror of the wild beasts biting into the seemingly helpless men in the snowy field.

Eventually Jeanne gets a second chance to the save the king and France itself during the epic siege of Beauvais. Shooting with four thousand extras, including three thousand soldiers loaned out by the government, Bernard used as many as fifteen cameras to cover various angles of the vast battle scenes. In addition to massive crowds of soldiers swarming across the fields and running about the ramparts, the action is reinforced with authentic weapons and huge clouds of smoke. During the climactic attack by the marauding forces of Burgundy on the barely defended walled city, Jeanne proves a mighty archer until she is nearly killed by mistake by her lover, Robert. The spectacular Beauvais siege occupies nearly the final third of the narrative. Thanks to its settings, stylistic flourishes, and unprecedented scale, *Miracle of the Wolves* set a new standard for quality heritage productions. The French president attended its premiere at the Paris Opera before it began its exclusive

The epic battle, staged at Carcassonne (*Miracle of the Wolves*)

three-month run in Paris. It conquered international markets, and for its US release, much was made of the producers' intentions of proving French equivalence with Hollywood's production values. Thus, despite the uneven industrial infrastructure in French cinema, many creative and influential commercial productions combined auteur touches with genre conventions to offer high-profile prestige products and foreground what were considered particularly French themes, styles, and settings.

French Criticism and Impressionist Cinema: Louis Delluc, Germaine Dulac, and Abel Gance

Even before the war ended, French filmmakers and critics were growing anxious about the future and debated the best paths forward. Art historian Élie Faure was typical, complaining that French films were burdened by the influence of theater and the novel, while American cinema, best represented by Charlie Chaplin to him, offered urgent alternatives. Furthermore, there were a host of popular film magazines and daily newspapers and specialized arts journal reviews advocating a cinematic renewal. Among the more influential figures was Louis Delluc. Initially a poet, Delluc became interested in cinema on meeting actress Ève Francis, who took him to see *The Cheat*. Delluc suddenly embraced Ricciotto Canudo's claim that cinema was indeed the newest art form, exploring the rhythms of time and space in ways that painting, music, theater, and literature could not. Delluc began writing insightful articles and reviews in *Le Film* and *Comoedia illustré*. He challenged film professionals as well as critics and audiences to demand more from cinema, "the fifth art." During the war, Delluc began France's first daily column on cinema in the popular *Paris-Midi*. He celebrated the best in US cinema while also arguing for a vigorous French response: "We can no longer film actors in front of painted backdrops" (Lherminier 202). He called for a radical revival of France's industry that did not simply try to mimic Hollywood or its genres. Delluc wanted a cinema displaying both popular and artistic form, worthy of his beloved France (Frodon 83). Nonetheless, Delluc's *Le Journal du Ciné-Club* featured a majority of Hollywood stars on its covers (Powrie and Rebillard 28). *The Cheat* initiated him into cinephilia, and Delluc strove to synthesize the two film worlds.

Delluc was part of a dynamic cluster of critics and filmmakers dedicated to revitalizing French film, offering lessons based on global film practice. He warned audiences to stay away from "bad" cinema and pointed out his favorite directors. He labeled the best filmmakers as *cinéastes*, people pushing cinema in important new directions. His favorite *cinéastes* were so varied as to include Chaplin, Max Sennett, Victor Sjöström, and Germaine Dulac, whose *Mad Souls* (*Ames de fous*, 1917) ran three and a half hours with no intertitles. Delluc also celebrated Marcel L'Herbier's *El Dorado* (1921), which, he claimed, resembled no other film the world had ever seen (Lherminier 208). He proposed the term *photogénie* to designate instances when cinema successfully exploited its unique abilities to transform real objects, altering the spectator's visual experience of the world. His friends Louis Aragon and Jean Epstein quickly adopted and adapted *photogénie* as a label to celebrate cinema's potential to energize human perception thanks to camerawork, editing, and mise-en-scène choices.

These filmmaker-critics agreed that the most modernist functions of "photogenic" cinema involved visual rhythm and spatial fluidity. "Suddenly one could apprehend aspects and dimensions of life that the human eye had never seen before and that remained beyond the grasp of ordinary perception and the traditional art forms. In other words, cinema was celebrated as the instrument of a new encounter with the world" (Dall'Asta 85). When a film worked well, even if only in certain sequences, it demonstrated this powerful quality, *photogénie,* which generated unique, transformative effects on the audience that were only possible in cinema. *Photogénie* allowed critics "to highlight the poetic movement of things in the world but also render the transmuted perceptions generated by contemporary urban life, namely speed, simultaneity, and multiple information" (Stam 36). Moments of *photogénie* were manifestations of cinema in its purest and most aesthetically powerful form.

The intense critical attention to cinematic techniques and strategies led to emphasis on how films expressed thoughts and moods. Even many commercial, realistic films began employing devices to signal mental states visually and avoid depending on explanatory intertitles or conventional acting gestures. Narrative films that experimented heavily with such perceptual and mental subjectivity soon became labeled Impressionist. A character recalling a long-lost love may see her face superimposed across the landscape, for instance, or a farmer's surprise at the hustle and bustle of a town could be communicated in a rapid montage of busy streets. Some critics praised films that offered impressionist tableaux, while Delluc considered L'Herbier's *Rose-France* (1919) "poetic impressionism" (Lherminier 120). Poetry and visual references were fine; literary models were not. In 1919, Canudo upgraded cinema anew, arguing it could now deliver the subconscious level of its characters, their subtle moods, and the very conditions of their souls (Canudo 494). By the end of the 1910s, French artists, poets, and critics alike underscored cinema's ability to transport the thoughts of characters directly to spectators around the world. The best in cinema owed little or nothing to live theater. Moreover, the term *Impressionist* created a significant link to French visual arts while emphasizing their differences from the competing modernist vogue of moody German Expressionism.

While Delluc sought out potential moments of *photogénie,* Germaine Dulac helped summarize Impressionism as a group style: "Impressionism made us see nature and its objects as elements concurrent with the action. A shadow, a light, a flower had, above all, a meaning as the reflection of a mental state or an emotional situation. . . . We experimented with making things move through the science of optics, tried to transform figures according to the logic of a state of mind" (Abel, *French Cinema* 280). Later, Georges Sadoul labeled French Impressionism a cinematic school with Delluc's *Fever* (*Fièvre,* 1920) as its first real film though others cite Gance's films of 1918 and 1919 as starting points. The Impressionist movement spanned much of the decade right up to 1929. However, it splintered somewhat after 1927, when more radical Surrealist trends pushed avant-garde practice further away from narrative.

Impressionist cinema was not totally opposed to realism, and these film-makers often worked on location, much as Impressionist painters had. Above all, however, Impressionists prized the ability of the cinematic apparatus to explore and communicate mental states and emotion. Dulac argued that it was ridiculous to place characters in a narrative situation without evoking their inner thoughts: "We need to strip away any element that is not personal" (Dulac, "Le Cinéma," 360). As David Bordwell explains, Impressionist film style regularly stressed the filmmaker's interpretation of the filmed material, but most often expressed the characters' psychological states via tactics "to denote subjective time, space, and rhythm." The style's goal is to render the director's and/or character's impression of an action or situation ("French Impressionist" 145–46). Scenes exploiting perceptual and mental subjective depth, including fantasies and memories, were regular features of the stories. The more flashbacks, distorting lenses, and frenetic montages a film included, the more "Impressionist" it became. Often such scenes were said to reveal *photogénie* in action and were highly prized in ciné-club screenings.

Delluc not only wrote about films; he encouraged open discussion and debate in the form of ciné-clubs, bringing critics, audiences, and filmmakers together. Local ciné-clubs across France became lively hubs for the aesthetic evaluation of current and past film practice. Spectators could gather, meet fellow cinephiles, and hone their critical skills. Special guests such as Delluc and Dulac turned theaters and casual projection spaces alike into cinema classrooms. Delluc wrote novels as well as criticism. Thanks in part to the unsettled nature of the era, he was also given a chance to enter into film production. Louis Nalpas at Film d'Art bought the rights to several of Delluc's books. Delluc codirected two of the resulting films, then worked out a script of his *Spanish Fiesta* (*La Fête espagnole*, 1920) for Dulac to direct, starring his wife, Ève Francis. The result featured location shooting, naturalistic acting, dance scenes to highlight bodies in motion, and themes critiquing the limited options available for women. Delluc continued, directing three more Impressionist films starring Francis, *The Fever* (*La Fièvre*, 1921), *The Woman from Nowhere* (*La Femme de nulle part*, 1922), and *The Flood* (*L'Inondation*, 1924). Always provocative, in January 1921 Delluc announced to an audience, "Ladies and gentlemen, the cinema does not yet exist" (Lherminier 203). Cinema to him was an ongoing experiment with the true artistic potential still some time off in the future. As a practicing critic, he praised the avant-garde but also Mack Sennett's "rhythm of images," and the joyous acrobatics of Douglas Fairbanks. Sennett and Fairbanks rejected the dreaded filmed theater of mediocre cinema. Delluc demanded dynamic impressions of life and highly cinematic flourishes that went beyond mere characterization or theme.

In his eagerness to overhaul film practice, Delluc synthesized many influences from the other arts, including symbolism, as he sought out unusual devices to narrate his own stories. With *Fever*, he concentrated all the action into a short span of time in a single evening in a rough Marseilles waterfront bar. Topinelli (Gaston Modot) and his wife, Sarah (Francis), run a cabaret. A group of sailors arrive, including Sarah's old lover Militis (Edmond Van Daële), who has an exotic new wife (Elena Sagrary in heavy "Asian" makeup). The seemingly hardened Sarah begins to reawaken and nostalgically dances with Militis. As the former lovers discuss running off together, the jealous Topinelli starts a brawl, killing Militis. By the end of *Fever*, Sarah is mistakenly arrested, and the nearly catatonic Asian woman, alone now in a sad, alien place, has become transfixed on a fake flower, a sign of disillusionment: "Delluc, like Griffith, makes use of flashbacks and multiple points of view to build the drama to a pitch of desire and aggression" (Andrew, *Mists* 40). Rather than staging a theatrical drama, Delluc opens up the flow of real time and space with subjective devices and iris shots of ships in the harbor. Dulac credits *Fever* with exceeding realism thanks to "a bit of dream that went beyond the dramatic line and rejoined the 'inexpressible' above its unambiguous images" (19). In other words, *photogénie* hovers over the action. *Fever* mixed naturalist imagery with Impressionistic narrative strategies, earning critical praise when it opened in 1921, only six weeks after the release of Delluc's *Ernoa's Way* (*Le Chemin d'Ernoa*), which he codirected with René Coiffard, starring Ève Francis.

Ernoa's Way, based on a rather convoluted Delluc script and set in Basque country, concerns a wealthy local man who adores a visiting American woman (Francis), who exploits his attentions to get him to protect her and her bank robber husband. Their story is intercut with that of another criminal on the run and two nice Spanish refugees caught up in all the deceptions. By the end, the rich man realizes his folly: he once cruelly dismissed the young Spanish woman. The man apologizes and takes her back to his home, with the suggestion of a romance. As with *Fever*, Delluc inserts tiny flashbacks as characters recall the past, as well as subjective flashforwards as they discuss the future. The film includes bouncy point-of-view shots taken from a car on dirt roads, all of which accumulate into Impressionist effects. *Ernoa's Way* was a quick, low-budget project shot on location, but its release was delayed, and it met an uneven reception.

Delluc's next film, *The Woman from Nowhere*, opens with an unknown lady (Francis) walking alone on a country road, returning after several decades to visit her former beautiful estate home, now owned by a family who have left most everything intact. The husband is about to leave town for two days, while his wife secretly awaits a visit from her lover. That night, the lover begs the young wife to run away with him, abandoning her husband and child. It becomes clear that the younger woman is in a romantic predicament similar to that once faced by the mysterious former tenant. Delluc exploits soft focus flashbacks for memories that further underscore the parallels between these women from different generations. The Francis character looms like a ghost from another world, meandering through the highly significant settings. Ève Francis became the leading performer of the Impressionist school, according to Sadoul (*Cinéma* 26). Furthermore, Francis helped with the script and served many functions on the production normally assigned to the assistant director. Her character initially warns the young mother to give up on her adventure and stay with her child. However, once she starts recalling how happy and amorous she once was, she changes her mind, urging the young

Ève Francis cautions the restless mother (*Woman from Nowhere*)

mother to follow love rather than duty, as she had long ago. Just as the wife prepares to run off with her dashing lover, the toddler chases behind her and the husband returns home early. She stays. With the family reunited, the Francis character feels the weight of her loneliness even more and wanders off, leaving an ambiguous open-ended tale of memory, love, and loss.

After *The Woman from Nowhere*, which was a financial failure, Delluc was physically weakened and deep in debt; soon he had to close his *Cinéa* journal, though he continued to publish scripts and write criticism whenever possible. One of the key critical voices of his era, Delluc was struggling to find a consistent audience. His final film, *The Flood*, an adaptation of a popular novel, came to him as a favor from Marcel L'Herbier. However, L'Herbier insisted that Ève Francis play the lead, even though she and Delluc had just gone through a bitter separation. Francis and Delluc finally agreed and traveled south to shoot on location near Mornas on the swelling Rhône. The story involves the return of Germaine (Francis) to her childhood home, looking for her father after many years away. Her mother had taken Germaine away as a child, much as in Delluc's previous film. The earnest, poor Germaine becomes attracted to the most eligible bachelor in town, Alban (Philippe Hériat), but suffers scorn from the local women. Tensions mount as she falls victim to a fever while the river, which was really overflowing, threatens the region. Her desperate father kills off Alban's girlfriend, pushing her off a bridge, to help Germaine's chances, hoping the flood will cover his crime. Ultimately, the murderous plan ruins the father but unites the suffering Germaine with Alban. Delluc relies on mental visions during Germaine's deadly fever and delivers the actual murder scene as a flashback with strikingly original shot compositions. *The Flood* showcased most of Delluc's Impressionistic cinematic traits but also employed local lighting and deep space to anchor it all in a concrete, realistic environment.

Unfortunately, the cold, rainy location shooting during November 1921 exacerbated Delluc's declining health. He died in March 1922 of tuberculosis right after completing *The Flood*, two months prior to its commercial release. Within ten days of his death, a ciné-club was organized to show all his films. René Clair attended and stated that Delluc's bold articles formed the very foundations for subsequent French film criticism. Louis Aragon, poet and Surrealist, declared that he liked Delluc's films because they feature characters "who desire each other for a whole hour until the people in the audience make their seats rattle" (Clair 19). Delluc's friend Léon Moussinac soon formed

Le Ciné-Club de France in his honor, preserving Delluc's notion of lively film debates between critics and spectators. Later, in 1936, the Prix Louis Delluc was inaugurated to reward one French film for its overall artistry and importance. As Sadoul concludes, "Delluc left behind a considerable body of critical work. But his cinematic work had barely reached its preface" (*Histoire* 171).

The rise of activist film criticism encouraged a wider range of possibilities in French film practice. The fragmented economics of the industry also provided new opportunities for ambitious young talent. Among the new generation of filmmakers to attract both critical and popular attention was the brash Abel Gance. A frustrated playwright, Gance began selling script ideas to Gaumont and Pathé when he was just twenty years old, including an adaptation of Honoré de Balzac's *The Red Inn* (*L'Auberge rouge*, 1910). He formed his own tiny company, Le Film Français, shooting on his own when possible. Already in 1912, Gance had published an article celebrating cinema as the sixth art form, a "wonderful synthesis of the movement of space and time," that was only getting started. He claimed that going forward, he would make money for his producers, just as Molière and Wagner had in their times (Abel, *French Film* 1:66–67). From that point on, Gance championed the exploration of new tactics for storytelling and worked hard to distinguish himself from his colleagues, selling his vision as modern and even prophetic. He peppered his declarations with references to the great minds in culture and inserted quotes in his films from the likes of Corneille and Baudelaire. Early on, Gance fought for ever longer, more expensive films, all of which cultivated comparisons with D. W. Griffith.

During the war, Gance was given directing assignments by Louis Nalpas at Film d'Art. His weak health kept him out of the military, and he was lucky enough to travel occasionally to London, where he caught up on recent American and international cinema. He was greatly impressed with the mood lighting of *The Cheat*, the melodramatic narrative and alternating montage of Griffith's epic *Birth of a Nation* (1915), and the vitality of Mack Sennett comedies. Confident in the cinema's potential to rival theater and even the novel, Gance launched ambitious projects with flashy visual effects and dynamic editing. Ever the showman, he began including a close-up of himself in the opening title sequences of all his films, beginning with *Right to Life* (*Le Droit à la vie*, 1917). His *Mater Dolorosa* (1917), produced by Film d'Art, proved to be a great box office success. It incorporated mental subjective images and flashbacks to reinforce characterization, all bolstered by Burel's camerawork.

The Tenth Symphony (*Le Dixième symphonie*, 1917) was a family melodrama that exploited Gance's trademark dissolves between close-ups and an emotional original musical score. However, for most historians, Gance's greatest accomplishments, helping forge new technical and exhibition strategies, were *J'accuse* (*I Accuse*, 1919), *La Roue* (*The Wheel*, 1923), and *Napoleon* (or *Napoléon vu par Abel Gance*, 1927). With these three films, Gance became a major figure for French cinema, straddling the boundary between commercial cinema and the avant-garde.

Gance's script and production budget for *J'accuse* depended on the approval of Charles Pathé, and Gance made a deal with the military's cinema unit, borrowing two thousand soldiers who were on leave from the front lines for several crowd scenes. In one of the most harrowing sequences, these soldiers lie dead on a field, in their real uniforms, then slowly rise up like zombies to confront those back on the home front who sent them into battle. According to Gance, always a master of melodrama, "They played the dead knowing that in all probability they'd be dead themselves before long. Within a few weeks of their return, 80 percent had been killed" (Brownlow 533). The soldiers even stand in a field, spelling out the opening title; they embody the angry taunt, "J'accuse."

The frame story involves a sensitive poet, Jean Diaz (Romuald Joubé), who has always been in love with Edith (Maryse Dauvray), who has inexplicably married a rich boor of a man, François (Séverin-Mars). At one point, François brutalizes Edith in a scene reminiscent of the searing attack on another Edith in DeMille's *The Cheat*. Once war is declared, the husband is sent to fight first, leaving time for the devoted Jean and love-starved Edith to begin a passionate affair. When François returns on leave to discover their relationship, he sends Edith off to live with his parents in Alsace, and the guilty Jean joins the military, where he eventually serves as the officer in charge of François's unit in the trenches. Amid the disastrous fighting and long periods of tension, both men develop a new respect for each other; their shared love for Edith brings them solace. However, Edith has been captured and sexually assaulted by the German soldiers. Eventually, she returns with a daughter, François is killed, and Jean goes mad, calling on the dead to rise up to confront the living for their profiteering and deceptions. The notion is that this shared public guilt will shock the survivors into living better lives, making the sacrifices of the war more tolerable. The original three-part version of *J'accuse* runs 166 minutes, taking its time to develop sympathy for Jean, Edith, and eventually the brutish François, who dies holding Jean's hand. Throughout, Edith is the only female love interest, so great amounts of screen time deal with male jealousy and frustration. By the end, Marie and her child, Angel, have been abandoned by the narrative, and Jean transforms into a Christ figure in the final image, dying for the sins and mistakes of others.

Stylistically, Gance works hard to avoid conventional camera set-ups or frontal tableau shots; he often strove to deliver impressions of actions and moods rather than full events. "The perceptual, emotional, and mental activity of the characters is presented not only in their behavior but also through camerawork, editing, and optical devices" (Bordwell, "French Impressionist" 221). There are even shared mental subjective fantasies, including an entire military unit "seeing" a mythical Gaul warrior leading them into a fierce battle. *J'accuse* allowed Gance to demonstrate a broad arsenal of visual effects, including many superimpositions, as in skeletons dancing over shots of men running off to battle, rapid montages to visualize Jean's nature poetry, and split screens and parallel editing for ironic, thematic contrasts. For instance, a scene of François assaulting Edith is alternated with Jean reading a poem to his bed-ridden mother.

Edith with the vicious François (*J'accuse*)

The imagery and symbolism in *J'accuse* were hard hitting, dividing critics about whether Gance pointed the way to the future of artistic, socially engaged French cinema or was dragging it on a bombastic tangent toward an overly literary and pretentious elitism. Delluc was among those who warned that Gance was losing track of the humanity in his characters as they became theatrical clichés, overwhelmed by the exaggerated stylistic flourishes (Lherminier 111). These tendencies, however, became the foundation of Gance's auteur style and returned even stronger in *La Roue*. With its release in spring 1919, not quite six months after the armistice, *J'accuse* created a huge stir as a timely and haunting cinematic experience, first in France and then throughout Europe. Accounts even mention women in the audiences fainting, especially by the end with the resurrection of the dead soldiers stumbling off to spy on their loved ones back home.

Gance recut prints and inserted new titles for specific national releases. *J'accuse* made a huge impression in England. In the United States, *J'accuse* initially premiered at the Strand in New York in 1921, sponsored by the American Legion, and summarized in its publicity with strangely inaccurate, patriotic terms: "Love of country, devotion of husband to wife, and forgiveness between men when death threatens." The American prints, distributed by United Artists, removed the adultery and sexual violence and inserted mention of the important contributions of US soldiers and a statement on world peace by President Warren G. Harding at the opening. *Variety* noted the film's grim, unrelenting atmosphere and "terribly real" representations of war. They also point out that the ending was changed in a very truncated version for the American market, with Jean cured, ready to live happily ever after with Edith (renamed Marie here) and her child. The length of *J'accuse*, and even its messages, may have varied from place to place, but the authorship of Gance, whose face appeared in the opening shot, was reinforced with every screening.

Encouraged by the popular and critical triumph of *J'accuse*, Gance launched an even more ambitious project, *La Roue*, which was initially shown in a special nearly nine-hour version of thirty-two reels divided into three separate screenings. It was eventually released in shorter versions, including a fourteen-reel, four-and-a-half-hour print. This is a tale of widowed train engineer Sisif (Séverin-Mars), who secretly rescues an orphaned toddler, Norma, from a train wreck. Sisif raises Norma alongside his young son, Elie, in a hovel of a house in the train yard. Strangely, none of Sisif's colleagues have apparently asked how he ended up with a new daughter after his wife died giving birth to Elie. Norma never seems to ask about her mother or the train crash. As the years pass, Sisif becomes extremely jealous of any attention to Norma (Ivy Close), especially from her adoring "brother" Elie (Gabriel de Gavron). Sisif, it turns out, is wracked with guilt for lusting after Norma. His boss, the wealthy Jacques de Hersan (Pierre Magnier), finally uncovers the family secrets and blackmails Sisif into allowing him to marry the disinterested Norma, who is more comfortable in her sensitive brother's company.

Norma is forced to marry de Hersan and leave town, while Elie and Sisif commiserate together, both loving Norma but promising never to mention her again. Eventually, the nearly blind and broken-down Sisif is sent to run a small train up and down Mont Blanc in the Alps. Elie, who builds and repairs violins, lives with him in a small cabin until he discovers that Norma is not his real sister, and they could have married. The miserable Norma, still oblivious to her origins, tracks them down, but the jealous brute Jacques follows her, fights with Elie, and throws him to his death from a cliff, though Elie fatally wounds Jacques before falling. Finally, Norma manages to comfort the distraught Sisif until he dies, his spirit wafting off over the mountains. Gance's story again revolves around male suffering, seemingly pitying the men for their impossible attractions to the one unfortunate woman in their world.

Many French critics celebrated *La Roue* as a major milestone for French cinema, invigorating storytelling with daring new options. Epstein found it equivalent to cinematic poetry, a visual symphony. Dulac observed that it was the treatment of objects rather than the storyline that made the movie special: "The emotion bursts forth not by the action or gestures, but by visual tones" ("Le Cinéma" 360). René Clair lamented Gance's excessively literary script, but he praised certain lyrical scenes, including Sisif's suicide attempt on a racing train. The plot was "odd" to him, but the imagery of "tracks, signals, puffs of steam, a mountain, snow, and clouds" created pure sensations (55). However, Delluc attacked *La Roue* for its third-rate literary pretensions, including citations of books and famous authors, from *Oedipus Rex* to Kipling and Baudelaire, as Gance proclaims himself the Walt Whitman of the screen (Lherminier 112). Critic Émile Vuillermoz concluded that *La Roue* was a mediocre melodrama, proving "Gance is a genius who is lacking in talent" (Abel, *French Film* 1:275).

Yet many artists embraced *La Roue* as a significant modernist work. Painter Fernand Léger praised *La Roue* for helping elevate the level of cinematic art, and Jean Cocteau boldly stated, "There is cinema before and after *La Roue* as

Gance in the title sequence (*La Roue*)

there is painting before and after Picasso" (Sadoul, *Dictionary* 321). Clearly, *La Roue* played a key role in exploring cinematic rhythm during the 1920s, as the opening reel with the train wreck demonstrates, with its audacious camerawork, dissolves, fragments of engines and rails, lack of establishing shots, and random characters running to and fro. *La Roue* displays a catalog of modernist cinematic options, many anticipating both Impressionist and soviet montage styles. The excitement over *La Roue*'s mix of subjective visions, rhythmic editing, and highly mobile camerawork helped insert Gance into a new pantheon of highly distinctive cineastes. While *La Roue* was shot mostly on location, with sets built along the train tracks near Nice and on cliffs and glaciers in the Alps, the settings are constantly manipulated to make the characters' emotions abundantly clear. As Jesse Matz points out, "*La Roue* does two things at once: it invents new techniques for filmic subjectivity and it tells the story of a train conductor subject to his machine. . . . The film also explores what it takes for human feeling to emerge from the filmic mechanism" (115). Clearly, Gance had managed to propel himself forward as a leading figure in French cinema of the 1920s and forced almost everyone to react to his new array of stylistic techniques and models of production, exhibition, and even authorship.

Germaine Dulac's career was less visible internationally than that of the self-promoting Gance, but her impact on 1920s and 1930s French film culture was extensive. Already in 1917, when Dulac premiered her first three films, Delluc wrote that she might soon eclipse Gance because her movies were more intimate, less intellectual, and displayed more inner harmony and concern for deep issues in real life (Lherminier 113). Dulac ended up directing twenty-five short, medium-length, and feature films before shifting over to sound in 1930. Beyond writing, directing, and producing, she wrote insightful criticism and served as an officer of the Société des auteurs de films, founded to promote and defend film directors. She was an early member of the CASA ciné-club (Le Club des amis du septième art). Throughout her life, she fought for artist's rights and women's rights, while championing cinema's educational role, especially via editorials and ciné-club debates. Dulac's role in French film culture is exceptional, and in 1936, she was a founding member of the Cinémathèque Française, which grew out of the ciné-club movement.

Though she married Albert Dulac, Germaine was bisexual and all her work emphasized rethinking social and gender constraints. She credited an actress, Stacia Napierkowska, with shifting her attention from theater to cinema. Dulac had been a theatrical critic, but during the war, she came to believe in the exciting potential of cinema for engaging with ethical and aesthetic issues. While Albert was serving in the war, Germaine formed a company, Les Films DH, with her female partner, Irène Hillel-Erlanger. They worked with Nalpas and Film d'Art for financing and distribution.

The Cigarette (*La Cigarette*, 1919) is a key demonstration of Dulac's drive to rework domestic melodrama to highlight women's new options in post–World War I France. The script was written by her close friend Jacques de Baroncelli (a.k.a. de Javon), the new artistic director of Film d'Art. He had confidence in cinema as a realistic, socially engaged medium. *The Cigarette's* story unfolds like another variation on *The Cheat*, although it subtly exploits aspects from comedy to undercut its melodramatic contexts. An older archaeologist, Pierre Guémande (Gabriel Signoret), has married the much younger Denise (Andrée Brabant). The husband's museum has just received a female Egyptian mummy, which initially keeps him quite distracted, until he notices that his wife is spending a great deal of time with a dashing young playboy, Maurice (Jules Raucourt). Pierre works constantly and is quite set in his ways, while young Denise dresses in the latest fashions, golfs, and dances. Feeling abandoned, Pierre brings the mummy into their home. He learns that this mummified Egyptian princess was unfaithful to her own, much older husband. The saddened old Egyptian prince, too weak to take his own life, devised a plan to have a number of his favorite cakes baked, one containing poison. Every day he was served a cake until the fateful day when chance determined his death.

Impressed by this tale, and identifying with the prince, Guémande poisons one of his many cigarettes with a syringe, in a scene worthy of one of Fantômas's criminal acts. Someday soon, he will succumb to the fatal cigarette. Denise, however, has figured out his plan and replaced all the cigarettes. She has been faithful all along, just craving a bit of recreation. The final scene in the existing version has the smiling Denise deliver a cigarette to Pierre in the garden and then boldly hold one to light for herself, comically defying her husband's earlier command that she never smoke. She is both a dutiful wife and a playful young woman: "In *The Cigarette*, Denise's liberty and modernity, which are shown to exist within a conventional marriage structure, remain entirely unreformed and unpunished" (Tami Williams, 93). Unlike Edith in *The Cheat*, Dulac's Denise does not have to be punished for her modern, independent behavior. Here, the husband is mocked rather than the wife, as Dulac presents "one of the most patently liberated women, if also one of the most distressed and suicide-driven male heroes, of her oeuvre" (Tami Williams 92).

Dulac followed *The Cigarette* with projects that increasingly explored mental anguish and female subjectivity. For *Death of the Sun* (*La Mort du soleil*, 1922), Dulac explained that she manipulated "technical acrobatics" to convey emotions and thought: "Certain methods, such as fade-outs, dissolves, superimpositions, mattes, irises, etc. had a suggestive value which was equivalent to musical signs" (Flitterman-Lewis 54). By the time she adapted the one-act "theater of silence" play *The Smiling Mme. Beudet* (*La Souriante Mme Beudet*, 1923), Dulac's style embedded many artificial devices, including soft focus and distorting mirror shots, within a bracketing location setting of contemporary small-town France. Exteriors were shot in Chartres. Madame Beudet was to become a sort of Everywoman, burying her passions and hopes under the constraints of middle-class society. The more restrained feminist themes of *The Cigarette* were pushed aside to foreground the predicament of a married woman trapped in a role she could not escape, even in her fantasies.

The Smiling Mme. Beudet pits an unhappy, seemingly average housewife (Germaine Dermoz) against her grotesque cloth merchant husband (Alexandre Arquillière). During one rather typical day, her husband receives tickets to a local presentation of *Faust*, but she refuses to go along. They have competing mental visions of the possible performance. Moreover, whenever Beudet feels frustrated with her, he holds an empty pistol to his head, sarcastically acting out a suicide. He is a pathetic ogre, regularly distorted by lenses. The resentful Mme. Beudet reads modern magazines and imagines a handsome tennis champion leaping off the page to throttle her husband. Increasingly alone and desperate, Mme. Beudet loads the pistol so that next time he pulls the trigger, he really will shoot himself. The next day, when he repeats his suicide prank, her anxious, ambiguous gestures disrupt his routine slightly. To his surprise, the gun goes off, missing him but hitting a vase near his wife. He completely misunderstands her motives and assumes she had loaded the pistol to shoot herself. In a bitterly ironic ending, he clutches her close as if he will now watch over her even more, as a Punch and Judy–style puppet show appears in the background, a commentary of their theatrics. Finally, the film ends with the Beudets meandering away up a gloomy street, greeted by a cheerful priest. As Tami Williams explains, the doubling of their resolved situation with marionettes followed by the exterior shot moves the movie firmly into parody. The characters are mere players in a larger system. Tradition marches on, and we can expect even fewer smiles in the future for Mme. Beudet (133).

Dulac's *Smiling Mme. Beudet* continued and deepened several of the tendencies in the Impressionists with its "subjective style of pictorialism to go beyond external action and evoke the psychic flow of the characters" (Bordwell, "French Impressionist" 222). The Impressionists were aware of their place in postwar film culture, and Dulac and her cohort were exposed to the latest Swedish and German Expressionist films, thanks in part to their ciné-clubs. Such international avant-garde trends motivated some of their distorted lenses and evocative lighting set-ups. By 1923, when *Smiling Mme. Beudet* appeared, Delluc, Gance, Dulac, Epstein, L'Herbier, and a cluster of Russian émigrés were opening up a rich new path for avant-garde narratives that would influence even commercial French film history far into the sound era.

Impressionist Test Cases, Marcel L'Herbier, and Films Albatros

Marcel L'Herbier quickly entered this lively artistic milieu. Like many of the other new post–World War I filmmakers, L'Herbier came to the cinema after establishing a reputation in theater and literature, and he cites *The Cheat* as a personal revelation and turning point. His close friend Musidora dragged him to see the film, which motivated him to join the army's cinematography unit during the war to learn the trade. Later, many of his films included plot points, shot compositions, and lighting set-ups that owe to *The Cheat*. After recovering from health issues related to his military service, L'Herbier's important financial and artistic connections helped him move into the hectic postwar French industry. In a partnership with the propaganda wing of the government, Gaumont produced his first feature, *Rose-France* (1919). However, the heavy-handed patriotic symbolism, intercut plot lines, and wild array of camera tricks divided critics and led to a dismal commercial release. But along with *J'accuse*, *Rose-France* is considered an important early Impressionist film. At the time, Delluc was among the small clique of critics saluting L'Herbier's bold visual style and rhythm. For his part, L'Herbier believed the cinema was the best artistic method for communicating human emotions in tempo with the radical new rhythms of the twentieth century.

L'Herbier's *Man of the Sea* (*L'Homme du large*, 1920), loosely based on a story by Honoré de Balzac, gained him new critical attention. It is a very structural family melodrama about Nolff, a Brittany fisherman (Roger Karl) obsessed with the sea, who tragically spoils his lazy son, Michel (Jaque Catelain), at the expense of his wife (Claire Prélia) and humble suffering daughter, Djenna (Marcelle Pradot). In his first film role, Charles Boyer plays a friend and bad influence for Michel. *Man of the Sea* is shot partly on location at the bleak, rugged coastline, and L'Herbier wanted to prove his adaptation could make the sea itself a central protagonist in a way Balzac never could. Most of the story is told in flashback, with the lonely, bitter father watching the ocean for a sign of hope. The story begins with Nolff as a young married man. Despite his attempts to raise his son to be just like him, Michel prefers the raucous bars to his father's isolation and hard work. Djenna struggles to care for her ill mother, as the women are all but ignored by the men. L'Herbier exploits alternating montages and split screens to contrast the dutiful daughter with the drunken son in this divided family. There are also superimpositions, symbolic insertions of the cross, plus irises and masks to alter the framing in Impressionistic ways.

Eventually the narrative builds toward a dizzying, chaotic bar fight, tinted deep red in the restored prints, in which Michel stabs a man in a squabble over a woman. The scene lurches from shot to shot, carefully building a barely unified space from close-ups and crowd scenes to simulate the confusion and excitement of Michel being carried away with emotion. To save him from years in prison, the father buys Michel's liberty with all his savings. By contrast, the neglected mother secretly entrusts all her money to Djenna before dying. The newly freed Michel steals the "sacred" money from Djenna, stabs her, and is caught by his father, who nearly kills him before pushing the wounded Michel out to sea in a small boat. The horrified Djenna heads to a convent in desperation, but one day she receives a letter from Michel, who has somehow survived and found redemption on the sea. She leaves the convent and informs her father, and the film ends close to where the plot began with the father shouting at the sea, impatient for his son's return. Critics looking to understand the new avant-garde impulses of French cinema quickly pointed to the poetic, rhythmic qualities of *Man of the Sea* and its unusual visual language, mixing subjective storytelling with concrete realism. However, before the Ministry of the Interior would grant a visa for distribution, several shots of violence and sexual contact had to be eliminated by L'Herbier and Gaumont (Leglise 64).

L'Herbier came from a rich artistic background. With each new film, his balance of literary ideas, visual rhythms, and cinematic experimentation proved more accomplished. He was strongly influenced by stylistic trends in European filmmaking, including Scandinavian lighting effects and Expressionist acting. *El Dorado*, which Richard Abel considers "the first masterwork" of the Impressionist era's narrative avant-garde (*French Film* 306), reveals a wide array of cinematic techniques to underscore subjective temporal and spatial effects, often in real-world locations. *El Dorado* exploited striking landscapes and ancient city street scenes as well as haunting interior sets and evocative studio lighting. For location shooting, they filmed in and around Granada, including key scenes in the Alhambra. L'Herbier's visual design was built around the psychological state of the protagonist Sibilla (Ève Francis), who sings in the raucous El Dorado nightclub. Now a popular performer, she was seduced and jilted by the wealthy Esteria (Georges Paulais), and lives above the cabaret with her sickly illegitimate son. Luckily, the miserable Sibilla meets Hedwick (Jaque Catelain), a young Scandinavian painter, and her melancholy condition makes her the perfect subject for his Impressionist paintings of the region. However, the increasingly bitter and desperate Sibilla stabs herself after Hedwick and his lover, the evil Esteria's daughter, promise to raise Sibilla's son as their own.

The film repeatedly exploits distorted imagery to reveal Sibilla's mental state, but Léon Gaumont famously cried out "Focus!" during an avant-premiere, forcing the stunned L'Herbier to explain that he and cinematographer

Sibilla and her son (*El Dorado*)

Georges Lucas worked very hard for those hazy effects and subjective point-of-view shots. Beyond the risky visual flourishes in *El Dorado*, L'Herbier wanted an Impressionistic musical accompaniment for this very personal drama. He commissioned a score by Marius-François Gaillard, which was composed in perfect synchronization with the final print. For the premiere at the Gaumont-Palace, a seventy-piece orchestra performed the symphonic score, which included some contrapuntal effects. L'Herbier edited the film knowing it would have a perfect accompaniment from the music, reinforcing double rhythmic registers to create an unprecedented performance in images and sounds. It was to be an emotional melodrama in the purest musical sense of the term. L'Herbier never thought of it as a silent movie. Fortunately, *El Dorado* was a huge success. L'Herbier's friend, fellow filmmaker Henri Fescourt, recalled years later that the premiere of *El Dorado* was one of the three most memorable events of the silent era, equivalent to the first screenings of *La Roue* and Sergei Eisenstein's *Battleship Potemkin* (1925) (Burch 71). Gaumont was so appreciative of the box office returns that he offered L'Herbier a generous new contract. However, in 1922, L'Herbier founded his independent studio, Cinégraphic, which allowed him to produce his own films and others, including Delluc's *The Flood*.

Along with Gance, Delluc, Dulac, and Epstein, L'Herbier promoted an avant-garde approach to revitalizing and purifying French narrative cinema, moving it away from the clichés of literature and theater. With *L'inhumaine* (*The Inhuman Woman*, 1924), L'Herbier boldly explored cinematic techniques, including camera speed, framing, and focus, for an increasingly Impressionistic cinema based in *photogénie*. In *L'inhumaine*, reality is never allowed to unfold for long on the screen without some device calling attention to the camera, the artificial settings, and manipulative narrative presence. L'Herbier and Pierre Mac Orlan, a novelist, singer, and critic, wrote the script together, hoping to foreground the latest in French decorative arts and cinematic invention. The production was largely dependent on the financial support of its star, opera singer and actress Georgette Leblanc as Claire Lescot. Leblanc was nearly thirty years older than her leading man, Jaque Catelain (Einar Norsen), but had a strong following and provided much of the extravagant production budget.

In many ways, *L'inhumaine* was a vanity project for L'Herbier and Leblanc. They hired an impressive array of contemporary figures from art and design for the production. Architect Robert Mallet-Stevens, known for his sleek, modern spaces, designed the exteriors, while Alberto Cavalcanti created interiors for Claire Lescot's vast home, and Fernand Léger was responsible for Einar Norsen's hypermodern laboratory. In addition, costumes and furnishings were designed by top jewelers, fashion houses, and even René Lalique. Mallet-Stevens was delighted to work on such a project. He complained that mainstream French cinema relied too heavily on decor of the distant past and only seemed interested in daring new art and architecture as a setting for debauchery, but by embracing modern art, cinema would triumph (5–6). Modernist composer Darius Milhaud was commissioned to write an original, highly percussive score, and several scenes were choreographed by Jean Börlin of the Ballets suédois. *L'inhumaine* still looks eccentric today and must have been quite a shock to 1920s audiences. The unsettling performances were part of the design scheme; the actors seemed closer to mannequins than humans, and the staff in Lescot's home wore smiling masks. L'Herbier mapped out a dynamic color scheme of tinted and toned footage that could pulsate with the percussive editing rhythm. *L'inhumaine* was labeled a symphony in color. During a climactic scene in the laboratory with its series of electrical explosions and gyrating ballet of machine parts in motion,

L'Herbier's brightly tinted images blasted the screen at their own rhythm, countering the beat of the music and reinforcing the disruptive montage effects. Some reviewers claimed they could almost hear the projector's light striking the screen during this spectacular, emotional sequence.

L'inhumaine's story follows a young engineer, Einar Norsen, as he tries to attract the attention of Claire Lescot, who exerts a bewitching power over an international batch of wealthy suitors, including the conniving Djorah de Nopur (Philippe Hériat in heavy "orientalist" makeup). Frustrated and insulted by her lack of attention, Einar fakes his death in a car accident, which finally makes the insensitive diva feel guilty and realize her very authentic feelings for Einar. When Claire Lescot decides to perform, despite just learning of Einar's death, the crowd arrives quite hostile, ready to disrupt her singing, but she ultimately calms them, winning everyone over to her side. Clearly, her voice is her most seductive power, which is a daring plot point for a silent movie. Many of Paris's most famous artists and intellectuals served as extras for this riotous theater scene, including Pablo Picasso, Erik Satie, and James

Einar and Claire in the lab (*L'inhumaine*)

Joyce. However, once enticed to Einar's home, Claire is shocked to discover he is alive. He demonstrates his wild collection of electrical equipment, including a bizarre television system that allows her to sing to the entire world and see her audience on a large monitor. Later, the evil Djorah, jealous of Einar's return, puts a poisonous snake in her flowers and later drops her stricken body at Einar's home. He quickly fires up his lab full of devices, reviving her in a sensational display of electrical jolts as his carefully choreographed staff leaps about in their shiny outfits in a Constructivist "symphony of work" to save her. *L'inhumaine* offers an early and striking sort of science fiction, taking advantage of new lighting units and dazzling technological devices. Clearly, L'Herbier and Cinégraphic intended *L'inhumaine* as a demonstration of all that was new and stylish in 1920s France. In fact, L'Herbier would be a member of the jury for the International Exhibition of Decorative and Industrial Modern Art in 1925, which helped launch Art Deco internationally. He thought cinema should be at the heart of contemporary French arts and culture.

L'inhumaine is embedded with a number of particularly Impressionistic scenes, and the cinematography offers highly unusual mobile perspectives that work alongside a radical new rhythm. For instance, the evening when Einar feels mocked and spurned at Claire's house, amid frenzied entertainment, there are rapid cuts to musicians and instruments, often out of focus, to show his increasingly panicky, delirious state. Once Einar vows to kill himself, he races off in his sports car. The chaotic driving montage, with distorting lenses warping the landscape and a shaking camera mounted in the car for perceptual points of view, sometimes in double exposure, alternate with static shots of Claire singing back home. Such "bravura editing sequences" compiled from tiny bits and pieces to present frenetic pacing in ultrafast montages capture a new sort of perceived space for the Impressionist film era (Guido 70). Many of L'Herbier's rapid-fire sequences make some later Soviet montage films look positively sluggish. He also incorporated many international art cinema traits into his array of avant-garde tactics, including words floating across the screen, distorting lenses, and mattes to vary the image's size and shape. Although the film draws on lively, experimental devices, the long melodramatic plot with minimally compelling characters made *L'inhumaine* a commercial and critical failure, even though it did play for a month during the famous Art Deco exhibition. *L'inhumaine* stands as one of L'Herbier's most interesting contributions and boasts some of the most impressive sets, shots, and sequences in French cinema. It still disorients viewers today.

Further Impressionist experiments appeared in some daring projects by Russian immigrants fleeing the Soviet revolution. Many major figures in Russian cinema already had strong ties with Pathé and Gaumont, and some of them formed the Société des Films Albatros in Paris in 1922. Among the new cadre of talent were producer Joseph Ermolieff, directors Alexandre Volkoff and Viktor Tourjansky, as well as the popular actors and married couple Ivan Mosjoukine and Nathalie Lissenko. Mosjoukine, who had been a matinee idol in Russia, was the subject for Lev Kuleshov's montage experiments. Kuleshov cut up old footage featuring Mosjoukine's intense glare to demonstrate the power of editing, the "Kuleshov effect." Mosjoukine was rebuilding his career in France. Initially Albatros relied on Russian talent and financing, but after 1923, the society became increasingly involved in coproductions, gradually collaborating with French directors, including René Clair, Feyder, and L'Herbier, and venturing into international distribution. Albatros productions became known for highly artistic production designs, mixing a wide array of influences, including Constructivism, Expressionism, and Impressionism. Its second feature, *Le Brasier ardent* (*The Burning Crucible*, 1923), was codirected by Volkoff and Mosjoukine, and although it was a financial failure, it proved aesthetically influential.

Mosjoukine's script is a tangled fantasy, exploiting a wide variety of sets, locations, and eccentric plot twists. *Le Brasier ardent* begins with a writhing woman's nightmare about the famous detective Zed (Mosjoukine). This opening horror montage reveals the woman, Elle (Nathalie Lissenko), trapped between two men; Mosjoukine is chained and being burned alive, and a demonic man (Nicolas Koline) is tormenting them both. Part Expressionist nightmare, part Symbolist drama, the opening dream shifts about constantly, allowing Mosjoukine to play an elegant gentleman, a benevolent bishop, and a beggar who stabs himself in the heart when the woman refuses his advances. The frantic woman awakes after what is essentially an avant-garde one-reeler prologue that condenses the central story points to follow, of a woman torn between two powerful men. Its disorienting rapid-fire editing, with an average shot length under three seconds, and location shifts, plus the multiple performances by Mosjoukine and Koline, who will turn out to be her husband, all establish Elle's confusion as she alternates between desire and repulsion, sacrifice and panic. As she awakens, she realizes her visions had been motivated by her reading of the real-life adventures and disguises of the famous detective Zed.

Elle and her husband (*Le Brasier ardent*)

The ultimate story of *Le Brasier ardent* revolves around Elle, who lives in an extravagant chateau with her foolish rich husband (Koline). Her bedroom is equipped with buttons and windows to satisfy her every desire. But the husband is suspicious when she does not want to move from Paris to South America with him. After comically chasing his wife across the city, he stumbles accidentally into a secret Seeker's Club of eccentric detectives, where he engages the real Zed to win back his wife's affections. Eventually, Elle falls in love with Zed, the dashing man of her dreams, forming a new family with him and his grandmother, thanks in part to her perceptive husband, who finally leaves France, alone but free. She has been passed on like an object from one man to another. As Abel writes, "*Le Brasier ardent* may begin in the cauldron of savage passion, but it ends on the couch of domestic inhibition and motherly love" (*French Cinema* 372).

Stylistically, *Le Brasier ardent* is a bit of a compromise. It incorporates some Impressionistic mental subjective flashbacks, as well as dissolves, camera tricks, and frenetic montages, but it also relies on comic slapstick setups that foreground Mosjoukine's acrobatic talents and range of performance skills. The moments of *photogénie* occur mostly in iris-framed close-ups, shared memories (including shots of the Paris Elle loves), and the rhythmic editing. But much of the action takes place in rather conventional locations, with only brief extravagant set pieces like the Seeker's Club with its trap doors, moving floors, and rooms full of suspended eyes and ears. Mosjoukine and set designer Alexandre Lochakoff incorporated many European influences, especially ornate flourishes that echo Fritz Lang's *Dr. Mabuse the Gambler* (1922). Thus, *Le Brasier ardent*'s achievements include forging synergies between the French avant-garde and German Expressionism (McCarron 223). Although the film was initially unpopular, its reputation has grown with time. Jean Renoir credits *Le Brasier ardent* with motivating him to become a filmmaker: "One day at the Coliseum I saw *Le Brasier ardent*. . . . The audience howled and whistled, shocked by a film so different from the usual pap. I was ecstatic. Finally, I had before me a good French film" (Bazin, *Jean Renoir* 151).

With *Kean* (Volkoff, 1924), Albatros once again capitalized on its lead actors' reputations within an Impressionistic tale built around performance. Based on a play by Alexandre Dumas, *Kean* examines the last few years in the life of British Shakespearean actor Edmund Kean and provides another opportunity for Mosjoukine to demonstrate his talents and for Lochakoff to reconstruct historically accurate settings. Volkoff's *Kean* is a much more conventional biopic and heritage film built around Kean's impossible love for the admiring Countess de Koefeld (Nathalie Lissenko) amid his declining health. In debt, Kean spends much of the film avoiding his creditors while upper-class women, including the adoring Anna Damby (Mary Odette), prefer him to the men in their privileged lives. The film's most famous scene, Kean's raucous dance in the Coaly Hold Tavern, serves as a showcase for Mosjoukine's athleticism as well as rhythmic, Impressionistic montage, with an average shot length well under two seconds for the sequence. Twice during the scene, Volkoff inserts shots of the countess in bed staring at a superimposed Kean in his Romeo costume, proving the actor is indeed obsessed with her approval. He dances furiously in his drunken stupor, rattling bottles and spinning on the same dolly with the camera so that the whole room seems to rotate in his dizzy state as he stares desperately into the camera before collapsing, exhausted and traumatized by visions of the countess riding off without him. *Kean* ends tragically after the actor's downward spiral of carousing and mental anguish over the countess's uneven attentions. He loses his public, his health, and his mind.

A fantasy shot, Mosjoukine and Lissenko (*Kean*)

More popular than *Le Brasier ardent*, *Kean* figured quickly within the canon of 1920s avant-garde narratives. Dulac gave a lecture in 1924, soon after *Kean's* release, arguing that silent cinema must strive to communicate via a specifically cinematic language. She showed the drunken dance scene and explained how it allows the audience to step into the action and the characters' minds: "For two minutes you watch a wild rhythm dance. You can see the wantonness in his eyes, in his gestures and his mouth. Pleasure at all costs! Once the exaltation has passed—sadness, emptiness, a long, static pose" (Abel, *French Film* 1:307). Delluc also championed *Le Brasier ardent* and *Kean*. Just before his death in 1924, Delluc celebrated Mosjoukine for helping push French cinema into the future.

Albatros occupied an influential place in French production in the 1920s. L'Herbier, despite losses on *L'inhumaine*, was able to continue filming by partnering with Albatros and Mosjoukine for *Feu Mathias Pascal* (*The Late Mathias Pascal/The Living Dead Man*, 1926). In this adaptation of Luigi Pirandello's novel, Mosjoukine plays Mathias Pascal, who is writing a mammoth study on personal freedom. He makes an unfortunate marriage, which comes with

Adrienne runs from two versions of Mathias (*Feu Mathias Pascal*)

a domineering mother-in-law. The young couple has a daughter, but all joy leaves their home as he takes a position in a cluttered, rat-infested library. Then his beloved mother and his ill child die on the same hectic night. Miserable, Mathias runs away to Monte Carlo, where he wins a record amount at the casinos, but as he returns home on a train, he reads a newspaper account reporting that a body has been found and it is Mathias, dead. Taking advantage of the mistaken identity of the dead man, Mathias pursues his liberty. He flees to Rome, adopts the name Adrien, and soon falls for his landlord's beautiful, kind daughter, Adrienne (Lois Moran). Eventually, after Mathias wins Adrienne away from her sinister fiancé, he realizes he cannot marry her. He is still married and has no legal identity; absolute freedom comes with its own costs. Distraught, he stages a fake suicide and returns home to find his wife remarried to a buffoon (Michel Simon in one of his first roles), which amuses and frees Mathias. After righting a few old wrongs, he visits his own grave and heads back on the train to marry Adrienne. Mosjoukine's performance is emotional and acrobatic. When Mathias's mind races, so does

L'Herbier's Impressionistic film style, and during one fantasy there are first two, then three Mosjoukines on the screen at once. Afterward, the actor credited L'Herbier for helping him move away from the theater-bound acting of his Russian films and toward a more modern performance style (L'Herbier 116).

The resulting mix of visual strategies in *Feu Mathias Pascal* and clever adaptation of Pirandello brought new praise for L'Herbier, and this Albatros-Cinégraphic coproduction proved highly popular. L'Herbier also wrote criticism and was an active member of a new international cinematographic lobbying organization set up to systematize job descriptions and protect artists' rights. In 1926, he petitioned the Nobel Committee to establish a prize for cinema. These dealings reinforced his significance among the new cadre of highly visible French filmmaker-critics working to guarantee a vibrant, sustainable national cinema. L'Herbier also took mainstream journalists to task if they dismissed or attacked the most modern of cinematic experiments. He saw himself as a participant in the ongoing revitalization of film culture and became an advocate for his colleagues, especially Dulac, the young Renoir, and Gance.

L'Argent (1928) was L'Herbier's last major silent film and another adaptation, this time transferring Émile Zola's fervently anticapitalist novel to present-day Paris. His version unfolds like an episodic novel as it follows the greedy financial shenanigans of dueling bankers Saccard (Pierre Alcover) and Alphonse Gundermann (Alfred Abel), as their deceitful plots ensnare others along the way, including the scheming Baroness Sandorf (Brigitte Helm). L'Herbier confessed that his personal frustrations with financing and his impatience with producers motivated him to take on this mammoth project. The coproduction financing with Société des Cinéromans allowed a vast cast, including a young Jules Berry and surrealist Antonin Artaud, spectacular sets, and cinematographer Jules Kruger, who often oversaw multiple camera setups. Throughout *L'Argent*, L'Herbier and his crew sought out highly mobile shot constructions, reinforcing the confusion and mental predicaments of the characters. The camera position often distorts the corrupt world of finance, including with very low sliding cameras at knee height, making everything seem a bit unnatural and off-kilter. The play of iris shots, circling cameras, superimpositions, and rapid montages catapult the potentially static world of business into a visually rich array of energetic scenes. The cinematographers' acrobatics captured the frenetic world of ruthless capitalism with a narratively motivated visual style. Grandiose locations

L'Herbier's floating camera (*L'Argent*)

included the Bourse (stock exchange) and the entire Place de l'Opéra, which was fitted with new lighting units for an all-night shoot. This attack on high finance required a very large budget.

L'Herbier, ever the showman, even commissioned Jean Dréville to make a movie about the production itself, *About L'Argent* (*Autour de L'Argent*, 1929). Dréville reveals the banks of artificial lights and huge spotlights needed to illuminate the vast studio spaces and exteriors. Parts of his documentary include montages of cameras recording the action from wild perches and homemade dollies. The initial two-hundred-minute print of *L'Argent* was edited down by the producer, to L'Herbier's horror, and met with uneven critical reception, though the box office managed to turn a profit despite the extravagant production cost. Several weeks after its premiere in December 1928, *The Jazz Singer* (Crosland, 1927) opened in Paris. L'Herbier was forced by this "thunderclap" to rethink cinematic art. Warner Bros., with *The Jazz Singer*, had "defrocked his Seventh Art," replacing his beloved, kinetic, and silent cinema with what he considered bad but popular filmed theater (L'Herbier 174). *L'Argent* was L'Herbier's last silent film, and while he had been working on *Feu Mathias Pascal* and planning *L'Argent*, Gance was undertaking on his own major opus, which would also complete his silent period, *Napoleon* (*Napoléon vu par Abel Gance*, 1927).

Napoleon

Between *La Roue* and *Napoleon*, Gance shot one of Max Linder's last comical shorts, *Help!* (*Au secours*, 1924), about Max's encounters in a haunted chateau, complete with distorting lenses, slow and fast motion sequences, and chaotic montages. Meanwhile, Gance was writing the script and gathering financing for his historical epic *Napoleon*, which was originally intended as the first of six chronological feature films. While the initial production of the first episode stretched for nearly two years, Gance famously continued to reedit its expansive footage over the decades. The film was released in various lengths by Gance and ever since, historians and archivists have struggled to reconstruct *Napoleon*, which has become an ongoing, almost mythic series of cinematic experiences. Gance originally shot 400,000 meters of film stock (roughly 290 hours of footage) for *Napoleon*, and his longest version ran more than 9 hours (Cuff 23). Gance also included the triple projector Polyvision system for the final sequence of Napoleon leading his army into Italy, which further complicated the film's exhibition. *Napoleon* was an extravagantly bold film on every level.

Gance wrote much of the screenplay for *Napoleon* on site in the Château de Fontainebleau to feel immersed in Napoleonic times. The script follows Napoleon from his youth in military school to his role defending the revolution to his early military accomplishments, fighting the British, defending Paris from the Royalists, and finally leading the Army of the Alps into Italy. The resulting episodic movie is built from a series of spectacular scenes, each with some dominant, experimental techniques. Much of the film was shot on location; the rest was reconstructed in the vast new Billancourt studios. Gance's creative team included a long list of top young talent, including Russian designers and architects, six assistant directors, and a cadre of camera operators.

First among the major sequences to establish Napoleon's personality, skills, and destiny is the snowball fight. Young Napoleon, already a hero to the working-class staff of his boarding school, cleverly leads an outnumbered cluster of boys against the larger team, who cheat, putting stones in their snowballs. Outraged, Napoleon launches a counteroffensive, and as the battle becomes increasingly hectic, Gance's camerawork mirrors the chaos, with swish pans and disorienting mobile cameras, some handheld, others strapped to the running operators' bodies or mounted on horses and sleds. These rapidly sweeping shots were cut down into dizzying montages and superimposed onto one another in nearly incomprehensible onslaughts of images that are punctuated by recurring images of a smiling young Bonaparte. The boy orchestrates everything. Despite this victory, young Napoleon is continually mistreated in school, and when his pet eagle is set free by the cruel boys, he fights them all in a wild melee, with pillow feathers flying and the screen divided into a grid for nine separate shots at once. This was the first instance of Polyvision in the movie, turning the screen into an experimental surface for multiple exposures to blur the overlapping time and space. The opening chapter uses extreme options in camera work and composition to reveal how Napoleon's suffering and determination prepare his path forward.

For the adult Napoleon, Gance hired Albert Dieudonné. In scene after scene, the brooding, independent Napoleon is aware of both the promise and the dangers of the revolution. Back in Corsica as a young lieutenant, he pushes for stronger ties with France and opposes the island's new bonds with England. As in school, Napoleon's powerful, wilting stare attests to the fire of his convictions and frightens or inspires those around him. Forced to flee Corsica for his life, Napoleon is tossed about at sea in a small sailboat during a terrible storm. His plight is intercut with the parallel "storm" in the Revolutionary Convention as Danton (Alexandre Koubitzky) and his faction cause a furor, denouncing their enemies and dividing the delegates. Gance builds the scene around a passage from Victor Hugo comparing the convention to a brutal wave, violently crashing bodies on reefs. A camera was even mounted on a specially designed pendulum swinging in and out precariously above the crowd, which went in and out of focus. As Paul Cuff points out, "The momentum of the swooping camera induces an astonishing sense of vertigo. . . . Conceptually the shot is also magnificently original: we are viewing the scene through the perspective of a metaphor!" (114). A guillotine is also superimposed ominously over the riotous moving images. By the sequence's close, the Reign of Terror has erupted into chaos and the lone Napoleon struggling to survive in his boat, a large French flag for his sail, is established as the only possible savior of the spirit of the revolution. Even his pet eagle returns to accompany him on his journey to save France.

The next stage in Napoleon's career reveals his military brilliance in the battle to free Toulon from the British thanks largely to his insistence on using modern artillery. Gance spent forty days on production in Toulon for this siege, which culminates in a stormy victory. The nighttime battles involved hundreds of extras and great amounts of munitions to generate smoke and explosions. Gance even inserts a few snowball shots to be sure the audience does not miss how young Napoleon's skills prepared him for this day. The raging battle is presented as a seemingly random mix of images of heroism, death, and destruction, of which only Napoleon seems capable of making sense. His risks pay off and he wins the battle. Yet even as his fame grows, Gance's Napoleon seems happiest watching from afar or standing alone surveying the land, in shots composed to mimic famous paintings of the romantic hero communing with nature. He ignores the adoring glances of women, too busy for personal relations, until he eventually meets his match in seductive Joséphine (Gina Manès) at a dizzying ball. Heterosexual desire is strangely downplayed in *Napoleon*, including Gance's own rather androgynous portrayal of Saint-Just.

Napoleon's fate is synchronized with that of Joséphine since both are ordered arrested on the same day and both are liberated with the end of the Reign of Terror and the execution of their accusers Saint-Just and Robespierre. Eventually, after Gance demonstrates the hurdles and sacrifices faced by Napoleon and the French people, a Royalist advance motivates Napoleon to accept the offer to defend Paris. Gance's long Reign of Terror and deliverance by Napoleon section culminates in the victims' ball, where the earnest hero of France meets Joséphine again amid a raucous celebration. A rapid flurry of images flash back to his previous encounters with her as he is finally struck by her qualities and decides to pursue her.

Napoleon's romantic period, including his personal campaign to win Joséphine away from her lover, is accompanied by soft focus and superimpositions of Joséphine's face on objects surrounding him. They marry, and he gains the army that will allow him to invade Italy. On his departure to the front, the morning after his wedding, he stops to visit the empty space of the convention hall, soberly surveying the room and perceiving mental subjective images of many ghosts of the revolution, including Danton and Robespierre, who ask Napoleon to serve as heir to their cause. Napoleon promises he will liberate repressed people throughout Europe and forge a universal republic. Empowered by his sacred mission, he races to his soldiers in the Alps, rapidly writing order after order in preparation for his battles to expand France's territory.

The final challenge for Gance's Napoleon is to take over the armies from their reluctant and incompetent officers, provide new support to their oppressed soldiers, and attack the enemy with newly energized forces and modern strategies. However, finances and the incredible length of his production forced Gance to reduce this last chapter. Napoleon's invasion of Italy is cut down to a few preparation scenes and representative shots of a town under siege. Yet Gance transformed this moment of Napoleon's personal and military success into an avant-garde reflection on his mythical status. Gance opened up the screen in an unprecedented manner. First, he shot some sequences with three synchronized Debrie cameras mounted on top of one another, carefully angled to take in a wide panoramic, triptych perspective. For the effect to work well, exhibitors would require three separate projectors as well as a special setup with three screens side by side. Gance also inserted other footage into the three panels, expanding his concept of cinema as visual metaphor. The gigantic lateral screen could suggest a broad unified landscape or a horizontal surface for radically discontinuous montages.

Although this final section is initially organized around various images of soldiers on the march, it soon transforms into an avant-garde spectacle. The left and right panels are sometimes the same but sometimes reversed mirror images of one another, while Napoleon or others occupy the central third of the image. As the momentum of battle and victory accelerate and Napoleon climbs to a mountain peak to look down on his victory and reflect on his rise to triumph, all temporal and spatial moorings disappear. Multiple layers of superimpositions represent the rush of Napoleon's thoughts and memories in one of the most frenetic of Impressionist scenes. Joséphine's face recurs along with the smoke of battle, maps, clouds, globes, soldiers, and eventually increasingly abstract images from the snowball fight, chalk calculations on blackboards, and his flapping eagle. Even in the unified wide shot compositions, audiences would always be aware of the visual glitch between the three projected images, though Cuff celebrates this technical problem: "I have found my every encounter with this 'parallax problem' deeply moving. The presence of the seams across Gance's huge canvas is the most marvelous evidence of workmanship," and Cuff compares it to brushstrokes on a painting (151). To this day, the all-too-rare theatrical presentations of the triptych incite pilgrimages from serious cinephiles seeking to experience the remarkable effects and aura of Gance's project.

By the end, the three prints are tinted blue, white, and red as the screens become the French flag and the cinematic images rush by, increasingly out of focus, until the visual fanfare plays out. *Napoleon* concludes with what amounts to a fifteen-minute experimental film, replacing the more linear presentation of the Italy campaign, to anchor Napoleon as embodying both the spirit of the revolution and modern France. While Gance's radical style did not necessarily inspire many imitations in subsequent French narrative cinema, which was about to confront the move to synchronized sound, the Polyvision did motivate Henri Chrétien to invent the widescreen anthropomorphic lens. Gance's *Napoleon*, which unraveled like a series of stunning attractions united by a fragmentary historical biography, may ultimately stand as a tribute more to Gance's vision than to Napoleon's legacy. Even the leftist critic Léon Moussinac, who warned that Gance had presented a Bonaparte for the fascists, wrote, "There isn't a single passage in the film without original technique" (Sadoul, *Dictionary* 237).

Although the extravagant stories and styles of L'Herbier and Gance proved highly influential, revealing the eccentricities possible in commercial French cinema of the 1920s, others during this wild decade pursued more radical avant-garde tactics, embracing a wide range of modernist artistic options, including Dada and Surrealism.

Poetic Impressionism and Jean Epstein

While L'Herbier, Delluc, Dulac, Gance, and Epstein have typically been grouped together by historians, they were all unique. As L'Herbier explains, "We did not share the same aesthetic. However, what did unite us was our searching for the famed cinematic specificity," *photogénie* (Burch 69). Their parallel experiments included critical essays as well as films and ended up shaping the trajectory of 1920s cinema.

Jean Epstein was raised on science and mathematics, but during his studies in Lyon, he and his sister Marie became obsessed with cinema. He claimed that seeing a William S. Hart western was like having a new world opened up to him. The young Epstein even met regularly with Auguste Lumière, who employed him to translate Polish and Russian medical articles. A poet as well, Epstein became a friend to Blaise Cendrars and Germaine Dulac, and he moved to Paris, working with Paul Laffitte, a cofounder of Film d'Art and now a publisher. Laffitte printed Epstein's film reviews and book, *Bonjour Cinéma*, and introduced him to Delluc. Epstein was hired as assistant director by Delluc for *Thunder* (*Le Tonnerre*, 1921) and also met L'Herbier: "Thus, before even starting his directing career, Epstein had rubbed shoulders with all the main representatives of the so-called French narrative avant-garde" (Wall-Romana 7).

With Gance and L'Herbier as mentors, the twenty-five-year-old Epstein soon codirected his first film, the educational biography *Pasteur* (1923); Louis Nalpas at Pathé then invited him to adapt a Balzac novel. The result, *The Red Inn* (*L'Auberge rouge*, 1923), featured a daring mix of styles, including a radical contrast of realism with Impressionism, complex mental subjective flashbacks, and internal narration. A dinner companion recounts a tale of murder from the past that turns out to be true and involves two visitors who happen to arrive that night at the inn. It uses two intertwined storylines from two different time periods. Epstein strove to create a drama in which the pace and effects respond directly to the psychological rhythm of the narration. The film also features many Expressionistic lighting setups complete with poignant shadows and pensive internal audiences listening to the narrator's tale.

Epstein claims to have written his next project, *The Faithful Heart* (*Coeur fidèle*, 1923), in the course of one night. This melodrama, based initially on a three-page scenario, was designed to allow Epstein to experiment further with impressionistic visual techniques. The close-up, which he believed was a key technique for expressing *photogénie*, would be central to his storytelling. Epstein shot some scenes on location in tough Marseille waterfront neighborhoods for realism but inserted symbolic touches, accelerated montage, and assorted camera tricks to display subjective, psychological depth. The story involves a young woman, Marie (Gina Manès), who works for cruel adoptive parents in a broken-down wharf bar. She is pestered by the young thug Little Paul (Edmond Van Daële) but secretly in love with Jean (Léon Mathot), a sensitive working-class fellow. After Paul drags Marie off to his hometown village and the distraught Jean learns she is gone, Epstein inserts what has become one of the signature sequences of Impressionism. Paul and Marie ride a merry-go-round at the village carnival. The mobile camera joins them on the spinning ride. Dizzying shots of the distressed Marie at the carnival are intercut with Jean trudging along a country road in pursuit of her. The rhythmic editing breaks the events down to flashes of people, gestures, and settings while keeping the chaotic actions tied to Marie and Jean's anxieties.

Eventually, Jean confronts Paul, who is armed with a knife, but Jean is unfairly arrested and sent to jail for one year. Upon his release, he finds work and rediscovers Marie, who lives with Paul and their child. He helps buy medicine for the sickly baby, forging a relationship with Marie's crippled young neighbor (Marie Epstein). During the second half of *The Faithful Heart*, Jean secretly visits Marie regularly until the suspicious Paul stumbles home to con-

Jean and Marie; an unsettling ending (*The Faithful Heart*)

front them, but the meek neighbor woman shoots the violent Paul with his own pistol. Finally, a melancholy epilogue alternates between a happy Marie on the merry-go-round with a glum-looking Jean, and the sad, crippled neighbor back home caring for the child. An abstract kaleidoscope shot merges with Marie and Jean as the words "for ever" from earlier in the film are superimposed over the final image of the couple. It is an unsettling resolution as the words reinforce both a sense of destiny and warning, and the narrator hints that the devoted neighbor may be a better match for Jean. He looks trapped and miserable throughout the final moments.

The Faithful Heart initially met with divided reviews and poor box office, in part because conventional critics considered it a rather tawdry melodrama with little real action. Epstein's tale is far from generic, however, and actually quite ironic on many levels, with Jean's faithfulness ultimately proving a burden. The 1920s ciné-clubs steadily improved the film's reputation and Dulac was an early defender, claiming to have trembled for hours after seeing it. Clair recommended *Faithful Heart* to anyone seeking to understand cinema's aesthetic potential: "It dates from tomorrow . . . composed for the joy of 'intelligent eyes.' . . . The lens turns in every direction, moves around objects and people, seeks the expressive image, the surprising camera angle" (Clair 70–71). Today, the stylish *Faithful Heart* helps illustrate *photogénie* with its superimpositions, pensive close-ups, frantic montages of body fragments, and visual sound cues to enhance the sensual impressions of the action and scenographic space. For instance, at one point the drunken Paul listens to street musicians and a complex series of superimpositions of sheet music and the spinning merry-go-round reflect his jumbled thoughts for a rhythmic musical montage. This sort of scene returns in Epstein's *The Fall of the House of Usher* (*La Chute de la maison Usher*, 1928). Modernist art critic Waldemar-George agreed that *Faithful Heart* pointed cinema in a new direction, making thoughts visual, concrete, and embodied (Daire 56).

Epstein's films and critical writing promoted a new *cinéma pur*. He, Dulac, and their colleagues praised film forms and rhythms that presented purely cinematic treatments of life, emphasizing movements and intense visual stimulation that could not exist in the other arts. The best of avant-garde cinema must surpass physical reality, visualizing ideas beyond language. Epstein argued that shots using *photogénie* could reveal the mobile aspects of the world and grant personality to inanimate objects as well as filmed people. Impressionism provided essential fuel to these strategies. Determined to remake French film practice for a new era, he eagerly presented lectures, churned out essays, and collected his writings in book compilations. Nonetheless, as Tom Gunning observes, Epstein has never gotten the sort of attention his career warrants: "To my mind Jean Epstein is not only the most original and most poetic silent filmmaker in France, surpassing impressive figures like Abel Gance, Jacques Feyder, Marcel L'Herbier and even Louis Feuillade; I also consider him one of the finest film theorists of the silent era" ("Preface" 13).

Driven by his passionate ideals, Epstein tried to keep filming constantly. He followed *Faithful Heart* with a documentary on Mount Etna, then a stylish adaptation of Alphonse Daudet's *La Belle Nivernaise* (1923), about a working-class family and their life on a river barge. After switching from Pathé to Albatros for a number of projects, he formed his own production house in 1926 before creating one of his most significant films, *The Three-Sided Mirror* (*La Glace à trois faces*, 1927). Epstein was devoted to demonstrating his faith in cinema's ability to present a new conception of temporality. For him, the present tense could only be understood as a personal psychological time, "time in us, our time," and cinema was the only means to represent this instantaneous experience that interested Henri Bergson, among others (Guido 40).

For his adaptation of this short story by Paul Morand, Epstein retained a three-chapter structure, each dedicated to a different female lover of a mysterious central man, plus a brief epilogue. After each tale, Epstein inserts sequences of the man leaving town hastily in his roadster and sending farewell notes to the women. The first woman, Pearl, runs from a restaurant weeping and explains to another man in a convoluted flashback that her lover is a tyrant with great power over her. The second woman, Athalia, is an exotic, androgynous sculptor who recounts how she met her latest lover, but she now admits that she finds him weak and fears she will tire of him quickly. The final young poor working woman Lucie pines for her lover, who often disappears for months on end. Even in her flashback, the lover seems to prefer looking at the young men swimming nearby over speaking with her. In the final section of *La Glace à trois faces*, the man drives away recklessly. He flies past danger signs and a cemetery in multilayered, jittery images, when a bird dives down from a wire, striking him between the eyes. Fragments of a crash are shown. Concluding titles announce that the narrating man ultimately discovered that his dead friend was the lover mentioned by all three women. The final words are "(Paul Morand)," leaving us to ponder whether the film is merging the author, narrator, and dead lover. A final shot reveals the man walking toward a three-faceted mirror, then disappearing, while the original short story concludes with the narrator realizing it is as if he has lost three friends rather than one.

La Glace à trois faces transforms the internal narrative structure of the original story, replacing conventional dialogue with every sort of Impressionist trick. As the women narrate their past encounters with the man, superimpositions, extreme soft-focus close-ups, flash pans, and disorienting editing confuse the time and space. We can never be sure which fellow is the listening friend. When the man drives madly away, the camera mounted on the car shakes wildly as multiple exposures and rapid montages express his careless abandon. Epstein offers a bewildering array of images and shards of several overlapping narratives. As Kristin Thompson writes, "Perhaps no other film of the Impressionist movement managed to create a plot that combines the subjective techniques that delve into character psychology with the presentation of events through fleeting impressions rather than linear causality. . . . *La Glace à trois faces* goes perhaps as far as any silent film does in

The reckless drive (*La Glace à trois faces*)

using challenging modernist tactics, frustrating the viewer with a lack of clarity about causes and traits" ("Ten Best Films of 1927"). Epstein's film was well received in art cinema circles but failed to generate much income. He dedicated his company's remaining funds to *The Fall of the House of Usher*.

The scenario reworked themes from Edgar Allan Poe's "Fall of the House of Usher" as well as "The Oval Portrait" and "Berenice," built around a married couple, Roderick (Jean Debucourt) and Madeleine Usher (Marguerite Gance), living in a decaying chateau surrounded by Expressionist marshes and forests. Luis Buñuel served as assistant director and Epstein's art director Pierre Kefer worked on the bizarre sets, while the camerawork by Georges Lucas and Hébert added haunting effects, manipulating film speeds and exposures. For the storytelling, Epstein again conflates the function of narrator and character, as a visiting friend (Charles Lamy) recounts his strange visit. This man is introduced in an ominous prologue that recalls that of *Nosferatu* (Murnau, 1922). The locals are stunned and fearful on hearing that the stranger wants a ride to see Usher. The house is presented as a vast, confus-

The stricken Madeleine Usher (*The Fall of the House of Usher*)

ing space, battered by constant blasts of wind. Roderick, like all the Usher
men before him, is painting a portrait of his wife. Gradually it becomes clear
to the visitor that this act is dangerous for both, as the husband becomes
increasingly obsessed with the painting itself, and his wife becomes weaker
the more he paints. Roderick also plays his guitar, and Epstein cuts in various nature images at varying shot lengths, producing a rhythmic series of
"pure cinema," as if each note played had a precise visual equivalent. *The Fall
of the House of Usher* allows Epstein to look back to Symbolism and its fascination with the senses, connecting them to cinematic Impressionism for a
visual symphony.

By the film's middle, Epstein brings all the extreme camerawork, mise-
en-scène, and editing tactics to a frenzy, melting time, space, and logic. As
Roderick paints, Madeleine droops ever more, weakened with each stroke
of his brush, with both figures shifting in and out of focus until she seems to
split in multiple exposure, eventually fainting in slow motion as the oblivious Roderick works at the canvas and the painting blinks, seemingly coming
alive. His madness accelerates, and the film's style becomes more eccentric.

Though the doctor and staff prepare Madeleine's coffin, Roderick, long interested in magnetic therapy, objects that she may not be dead. He vows to stay with her, but then they carry the body to their family tomb in a surreal procession full of superimpositions. During a stormy night, some time after her internment, the castle begins burning around Roderick, and he sees Madeleine return in her wedding dress, moving at a zombielike pace. Smoke and fire overwhelm their home, the painting burns, and the characters wander out into the gardens as the film stops. There is no attempt to narrativize the fantasy as Roderick's hallucination and no final bracketing scene of the narrator-visitor recounting his strange experiences to anyone. The story concludes without any conventional synthesis or closure.

The Fall of the House of Usher was championed by friends in the ciné-club and art house movements and subsequently became a landmark for 1920s avant-garde cinema. Cinémathèque founder Henri Langlois praised it as "the cinematic equivalent of Debussy" thanks to its rhythmic editing, mobile camera, superimpositions, and mannequin-like actors (Sadoul, *Dictionary* 63). However, it was a financial disaster. It premiered at Studio 28 in October 1928, just as Europe was beginning to come to grips with the pending arrival of synchronized sound cinema, derailing the avant-garde's ongoing search for visual equivalents to sound and music in French cinema. After this experimental period, Epstein chose a more naturalistic direction, with scripts and performances anchored in authenticity and shot on location. His nearly ethnographic *Land's End* (*Finis terrae*, 1929) featured nonprofessional locals from Ushant Island off the Brittany coast as actors. Epstein explored new sorts of *photogénie*, combining authentic treatments of the sea and nature with dizzying sequences of delirium when one character becomes ill and infected. The silent, documentary-like *Finis terrae* was completed in 1928 and premiered in 1929, offering a sharp contrast to the studio-bound, theater-based sound films just beginning to conquer Europe.

Renoir during the 1920s

Jean Renoir, like many of his contemporaries, displayed a number of artistic influences as he sought narrative paths that skirted the commercial cinema. He could self-finance some of his early film experiments with his own production company, thanks to his family's wealth, which allowed him a unique trajectory as he strove to create a consistent and successful personal style. Renoir took up filmmaking to participate in this lively new art form and to launch his wife, Catherine Hessling, as a star. Hessling had been Auguste

Renoir's model, and Jean often frames and lights her in a painterly fashion, but he also allows her to emphasize her dance background, communicating thoughts and emotions in very physical, even eccentric performances. Their shift into cinema got the young couple away from their struggling business selling pottery. Beyond Hessling, Renoir worked with a recurring crew members, including cinematographer Jean Bachelet. Filmmaking was always a creative, cooperative group effort for Renoir.

For his first feature, *Whirlpool of Fate* (*La Fille de l'eau*, 1925), Renoir constructs a naturalistic melodrama that nonetheless exploits perceptual and mental subjectivity. Family and friends helped out, including brother Pierre Renoir as assistant director and actor, and the film was shot on family friend Paul Cézanne's property in Fontainebleau forest and Gaumont studios, among other spots. This tale of a young woman, Gudule (Hessling), begins on her father's barge, with many shots that must have influenced Jean Vigo for his barge movie a few years later. When the father drowns, the poor girl flees her drunken uncle's advances and endures a series of encounters before being noticed and saved by the sensitive, wealthy Georges. During one stormy night, while she is forced to sleep in the woods, Gudule falls ill and hallucinates. Her nightmare incorporates multiple Impressionist tricks and techniques, including montages, reverse movement, slow motion, and selective focus; it all culminates in a double-exposure sequence of her riding across the sky on a white horse with Georges. Although *Whirlwind of Fate* did not find distribution, Jean Tédesco, who ran the art house Vieux-Colombier, began screening the dream sequence as part of his show. Tédesco and the young producer Pierre Braunberger encouraged Renoir and Hessling to launch another feature project.

Their film *Nana* (1926) was designed to foreground Hessling's physical appeal. Playing Zola's Nana, she drives every man crazy from her first musical theater performance. Throughout, all the men and the camera concentrate on Nana's every gesture, from her initial climb up the ladder on stage right to her death throes with smallpox. This was a big-budget coproduction shot in Paris and Berlin, with Germany's Werner Krauss playing Count Muffat. Renoir credits Krauss with mentoring him through many directing challenges. The elaborate art design was by Claude Autant-Lara, who also performed Fauchery's role. Renoir's adaptation offered an unconventional take on the story, undercutting the usual naturalism with broad comedy. One central concept was that his Nana should be more like a marionette than a person, as she leads man after man to humiliation and financial disaster before

Hessling's melodramatic performance (*Nana*)

dying miserably herself. Renoir and his assistant Pierre Lestringuez worked for a synthesis between faster-paced American comedies and Zola's old-world themes; Expressionist moments and nods to Impressionism, especially during Nana's dying delirium, also contribute to a lively jumble of styles and caricatures. In the end, the film was a financial failure, and Renoir had to sell more of his father's paintings to cover the losses. During *Nana*, Renoir cemented a valuable friendship with the Braunberger, who helped him continue with new projects.

With some leftover film stock from *Nana*, Renoir and Hessling next filmed a bizarre short, *Charleston Parade* (1927), featuring "the black Chaplin," Johnny Hudgins. His character arrives from Africa in a strange flying sphere, landing in a devastated Europe, where he meets the last person living in Paris, played by Hessling. She is intrigued with this visitor, performing a wild, seductive Charleston in the streets, which excites her strange pet gorilla. The visitor, who appears in full minstrel attire, is thrilled to rediscover this old dance, apparently long forgotten by his own people. Renoir's surreal science fiction and colonialist satire resorts to a variety of techniques, including fast

Hessling confronts Hudgins (*Charleston*)

and slow motion, but its sense of humor is unsettling, offering "clever reversals of gender, race, and colonial fantasies" (Kern 112). As André Bazin
observes, "the thin and whimsical scenario is little more than a pretext for
an incoherent but charming exhibition of Catherine Hessling" (*Jean Renoir* 17).
Charleston Parade was never fully completed or shown commercially, but it
contains a free, eccentric style that reveals Renoir's desire to engage with
multiple artistic influences, and in many ways, it provides a skit-like reversal
of René Clair's *The Crazy Ray / At 3:25* (*Paris qui dort*, 1925) in which a few people
arrive to find everyone in Paris frozen in place.

Next, Renoir, Hessling, and Tédesco created a fanciful tragedy, *The Little
Match Girl* (*La Petite Marchande d'allumettes*, 1928), part of which was filmed in
a makeshift studio above Tédesco's theater. *The Little Match Girl* completes
the initial period of Renoir's cinema, "a phase marked by his enthusiasm for
tricks and by the dominance of the woman-child," and it was his last film
with Hessling (Sesonske 43). A loose adaptation of Hans Christian Andersen,
with a healthy nod to Chaplin's *Gold Rush* (1925), *The Little Match Girl* follows
the last miserable night of Karen's life, as she is sent out in a terrible snowstorm

to sell her pathetic matchbooks. She sees others enjoying their lives, beds down in an alley, and after an elaborate hallucination, freezes to death. The film is restricted to Karen's vision, and when she peers in frosty windows to watch people having fun, "powerful emotions are expressed through the economical means of simply alternating optical view-point shots and reactions shots; no words and very few gestures are necessary" (Bordwell, "French Impressionist" 193). Karen's hallucinations allow opportunities for more Impressionist visions and camera tricks. She drops into a toy store, filled with life-size dolls, and a young man she observed earlier returns as a toy soldier; the village policeman now is transformed into a jack in the box, but Death comes to claim her. This film failed to make money but became a regular attraction at ciné-clubs and art houses over the years. Bazin found it an important project combining conflicting tendencies: "The source of the still radiant charm of this little film is apparent today: it is the very realism of Renoir's fantasy" (*Jean Renoir*, 18).

Clearly, the exploration of film style and new narrative strategies dominated much of the most significant filmmaking of 1920s France, especially the Impressionist projects. As Impressionism waned and additional impulses, economic realities, and theories influenced French filmmakers, its legacy proved both immediate and long-term. As David Bordwell writes, Impressionism had a profound effect on film theory and criticism but also on film practice, influencing Soviet montage, and motivating subjective dream sequences and flashbacks in mainstream cinema ever after: "The French Impressionist movement has bequeathed us a permanent desire to explore certain artistic possibilities of that enigma, *photogénie*" ("French Impressionist" 258–59).

Avant-Garde Practice: From Dada to Surrealism

Given the vast array of cinematic experimentation during the 1920s, it can be difficult and even misleading to insert narrow aesthetic labels or place hard barriers between different films, trends, or art movements. There was a second avant-garde period beyond Impressionism, but it is also part of a creative jumble of modernist impulses and practices, a series of films reacting to one another in hectic and productive ways that overtly countered commercial norms. The 1920s were the height of silent experimentation in France, with many personal and small group modes of production, often synthesizing ideas from other arts and social sciences in efforts to build more radical and sometimes "purer" forms of cinematic expression. Nearly every avant-garde film was made by or in collaboration with a painter or other artist, but they were not trying to transfer conventional painterly attributes to the screen. Instead, they sought to explore and exploit the visual aspects specific to cinema. Paris was the bustling center for such experimentation in *cinéma pur*, drawing on international figures of the avant-garde from many competing camps. Often their aesthetic concepts and creative alliances were fluid and shifting.

Dada's Tristan Tzara moved from Switzerland to Paris in 1920, having made contact with Francis Picabia, Jean Cocteau, André Breton, and Man Ray. Tzara acted as a sort of trigger for many in the French literary and art world to pounce on public performance as a new option. His provocative events combined satiric theater, dance, nonsensical poetry ("Anti-dadism is a disease. . . . But the real dadas are against DADA"), unusual musical performances, including "Jean Cocteau and his Parisian Jazz-band," abstract photography, and eventually moving pictures (Rasula, *Destruction* 175–76). Dada cinema, along with other avant-garde projects of the era, fought aggressively to forge kinetic art in opposition to the other static arts. Dada filmmaking incorporated the new break-neck chaotic rhythms possible in cinema with its discontinuous, rapid montage editing and alienating superimpositions, consciously confronting and outpacing the traditional plastic arts.

Man Ray was one of many artists who migrated to Paris in the early 1920s. One of his specialties was the "rayograph" photogram, fixed images made without a camera by setting small found objects on photographic paper in the darkroom, then exposing the sheet to light. The result transforms the real-world items into hauntingly beautiful compositions, forging art from ready-made products such as light bulbs, beads, or combs, expanding on the concepts of his friend Marcel Duchamp. Man Ray bragged that he was committing crimes against photography. For Tzara's 1923 "Soirée of the Bearded Heart" Dada event, Man Ray was given a movie camera and some leftover film stock and invited to make a short film with almost no warning. Like many visual artists, he was intrigued with the kinetic potential of cinema. The result was *Return to Reason* (*Le Retour à raison*, 1923), a film that historian Jean Mitry credits with helping launch the drive toward cinematic purity of this second French avant-garde (*Histoire III* 344). By laying out salt and springs and pins on long strips of unexposed film, he created a moving rayography from the shapes pulsating on the screen during projection. These segments were juxtaposed randomly with nighttime shots of lights on a merry-go-round,

Man Ray's rayography (*Return to Reason*)

rolls of paper, a twisting mobile, and his girlfriend Kiki de Montparnasse's naked torso, in a loose multimedia collage. Kiki, an artist and model, actively collaborated with Man Ray throughout his Dada and Surreal period.

Another American, Dudley Murphy, came to Paris to join the avant-garde. His goal was to create "visual symphony" films. Murphy teamed up with artist Fernand Léger to make *Ballet mécanique* (1924), and George Antheil worked up a musical and sound accompaniment, including machine noises, sirens, revving engines, and metallic banging. The resulting film owes to many artistic impulses, from Constructivism and Cubism to Dada and pure cinema. Moreover, Léger's montages of whirling machine parts continued the fascination with mechanical rhythms he had exploited for L'Herbier's *L'inhumaine* laboratory scenes. Cinema's potential to break up real-world objects and make inanimate objects and fragments of images pulsate on a screen fueled his interest in *Ballet mécanique*: "For Léger, machine culture introduced a vivacity and color into everyday life: in contrast to the drab hues of modern clothing, the street staked its animated claim, eked out in a 'medley of neckties'" (Rasula, *Acrobatic* 88). Léger was intrigued with representing the contemporary world via real objects, claiming he was more inspired by department store windows than art museums. While Léger is credited with the film's eventual form, *Ballet mécanique* was indeed collaborative. Most of the images, and especially the distorted, kaleidoscopic sequences, were filmed by Murphy, while Man Ray shot some dizzying bits of footage, and a smiling Kiki appears, as well as Katherine Murphy. The film can be divided into nine segments, each with a dominant visual theme, but overall, its abstract form challenges our perception and underlines the ways cinema and modern technology change our visual and lived experience (Thompson and Bordwell 373–78). *Ballet mécanique* also engages with Cubism's goal of simultaneously presenting multiple fragments from various times, spaces, and vantage points, while offering a new sort of *photogénie* in its treatment of everyday objects.

Léger argued at the time that "as long as film is based on fiction or the theater, it will be nothing" (Clair 20). He called for moving beyond conventions of human performance or "acting." Instead, his film is composed of mirror shots and montages of machine parts, pan lids, and whisks; a washer woman climbing several steps multiple times in a loop; and a headline about a stolen necklace, abstracted into letters and numbers. Léger and camera can be seen reflected in a shiny pendulum ball, and tinted triangles and circles punctuate the film. Along with other artists and critics of the time, Léger advocated cine-plasticity, manipulating filmic techniques to create new modes of movement, perception, and spectatorship. For many, this sort of visual onslaught, bombarding the viewer with perceptual stimulation thanks to mechanically reproduced images, was a key trait of modernity. *Ballet mécanique* proved to be a major player in the avant-garde scene, premiering without a score in fall 1924. Antheil's musical accompaniment was completed the next year, but it could vary from performance to performance. At one screening, ten pianos banged out the score for the film. *Ballet mécanique* is still regularly screened at museums around the world as an exemplary avant-garde kinetic experiment. Whether it should be interpreted as an ominous warning about inhuman aspects of mechanical mass production or a joyous celebration of the machine age is still debated.

Man Ray also helped Marcel Duchamp produce the amusing and mesmerizing *Anémic Cinéma* (1926), a film that combines written words printed on spinning discs and rotating spirals that resemble kinetic mobiles made of paper rings. The discs include clever nonsensical puns and tongue twisters, such as "Esquivons les ecchymoses des esquimaux aux mots exquis" and "Avez vous déja mis la moelle de l'épée dans le poêle de l'aimée?" The authorship is ascribed to Duchamp's feminine alter ego Rrose Sélavy, which sounds like "Eros is life." *Anémic Cinéma* played alongside other "pure" cinema experiments, including Henri Chomette's *Five Minutes of Pure Cinema* (*Cinq minutes de cinéma pur*, 1926) at the Studio des Ursulines. Armand Tallier had just opened the three-hundred-seat Ursulines to specialize in programs balancing prewar French films with avant-garde shorts and new foreign features. Meanwhile Tédesco's Vieux-Colombier championed a wide variety of international experimental narratives, documentaries, and avant-garde films, such as Jean Grémillon's aptly named *La Photogénie mécanique* (1924) and Dimitri Kirsanoff's *Menilmontant*, starring his wife, Nadia Sibirskaïa (1926). By 1928, the art house Studio 28 opened as well. These cinemas hosted ciné-clubs, advocated for alternative film practice, and provided vital, high-profile opportunities for filmmakers and savvy audiences alike. The proliferation of film journals and art houses helped guarantee that Paris was the epicenter of avant-garde film culture.

For Francis Picabia's controversial Dada (or, as he claimed, "instantanist") ballet, *Relâche* (*No Performance*), in December 1924, René Clair shot a short introductory scene, with Picabia and musician Erik Satie hopping about in slow motion and firing a World War I–era cannon toward the camera. For the ballet's entr'acte, the rest of Clair's film was presented, along with Satie's meticulously timed musical accompaniment. Some in the crew apparently tried to keep the audience from sitting to watch the film, explaining that they were to leave and let the film show to an empty room. The *Entr'acte* portion starts out with fragments of rooftops at oblique angles, shots of balloon-head dolls, a ballerina shot from below, boxing gloves, pixelated matches, and other seemingly random shots before anchoring itself somewhat with two more men on a rooftop, this time Duchamp and Man Ray, playing chess until bursts of water and a superimposed paper boat disrupt their game. The mockery of ballet and cinematic voyeurism continues until the dancer is revealed to be a woman in a beard, and Ballet suédois director Jean Börlin shoots at a carnival egg in an impossible space, thanks to a montage effect worthy of Lev Kuleshov. But next Börlin is shot by Picabia. His fall launches the second half of the film, organized loosely around a Dada funeral procession that turns into a series of chases, including cars, trains, rollercoasters, and airplanes, in a dizzying display of cinematic representations of movement.

Clair explores slow motion, fast motion, montage, graphic matches, and superimpositions, as did many avant-garde filmmakers of the era, looking for ways to distort reality and create their own unique rhythms. The aggressive yet playful antics continually surprise and defy narrative or logical connections. A variety of challenging formal strategies undercut the film's unity and repeatedly acknowledge its artificially constructed nature. After the collage of shots of the hearse breaking free in a parody of chase films, and upside-down shots recalling the film's opening, Börlin's coffin tumbles away from the hearse, but he leaps out. Playing the magician, he makes everyone disappear. Finally, he bursts through the paper *fin* intertitle in slow motion, only to be kicked back through in reverse by producer Rolf de Maré, in a fitting conclusion to the Dada event. *Entr'acte* ultimately serves as an exemplary assault on film language and a collective exercise foregrounding the free-wheeling potential of avant-garde film practice, proving rhythmic movement is at the heart of Clair's cinema: "Clair's personal sensibility comes out through his inimitable way of treating cinema as dance" (Andrew, *Mists* 57).

While Dada was a loose collection of interventions and artworks, Surrealism was a more focused movement with a nucleus in Paris, led by André Breton. He initially wrote a rambling manifesto that includes praise of Sigmund Freud and the new attention to dreams. For Breton and other Surrealists, one goal was to replicate the undirected free play of thought and fantasy, celebrating the superior reality of dreams over the limitations of the rational mind. The rapid, chaotic rhythms and dizzying power of superimpositions, transformations, and displacements in cinema became the perfect means for approaching the frenetic pace and free flow of imagination. Cinema could help Surrealists go beyond the boundaries and conventions of language, while it moved beyond the purely formal experimentation of abstract and Dada toward dream logic and eroticism. Montage allowed absurd juxtapositions that mirrored the condensation and displacement of Freudian theory. Some Surrealists even claimed that motion pictures were invented so people could finally reproduce their dreams. Editing and camera tricks allowed cinema to deliver disjunctive bits of narrative more directly than the visual or language arts. Surreal cinema was proudly irrational, tapping into and replicating the hidden, repressed currents of the unconscious and "psychic automatism in its pure state" (Breton 26).

In the cultural context that privileged playful and illogical fragments of stories and disorienting styles, a surprising number of unique projects were accomplished in 1920s France. René Clair's fanciful *The Crazy Ray* mixed together influences from high art, Dada, Guillaume Apollinaire, and Alfred

Flirting on the Eiffel Tower (*The Crazy Ray*)

Jarry, as well as Mack Sennett comedies, to reinvigorate French comedy. Clair actually shot *The Crazy Ray* before *Entr'acte*, but it was released later. Henri Diamant-Berger produced this fun romp of an early science fiction movie. Clair edited *The Crazy Ray* like all his early films, placing the work print on a sheet of glass in front of a light bulb, looking through a magnifying glass, and cutting the film with scissors. *The Crazy Ray* demonstrates the audacity of the twenty-five-year-old Clair's vision of moving the cinema forward while paying tribute to its lively past. The story involves, first, a guard (Henri Rollan), atop the Eiffel Tower, who is puzzled that there are no visitors this day, and second, a group of five people who land at the airport to discover that everyone else in town is seemingly frozen in place. Paris is indeed asleep. The curious "survivors," including only one woman (Madeleine Rodrigue), team up to investigate, but they also profit from the situation, invading fancy restaurants, pocketing bank notes, and driving flashy cars. One businessman discovers his wife frozen in a compromising position with her lover. They also put money in the hand of a suicidal man, steal a pearl necklace for a woman, and pinch a watch from an escaping thief. The portable camera follows them as they meander about the Eiffel Tower, gambling away fortunes and fighting for the woman's attention, in a comic scene with fast motion, until they pick up a voice on the radio pleading for help.

The six characters in search of a cause discover the young woman (Myla Seller) behind the radio broadcast. She explains that her mad scientist father has a ray that has frozen the city. The ray did not reach as high as the top of the Eiffel Tower or the incoming airplane, hence they were all spared. Clair reveals the ray's actions via animation. The group confronts the baffled scientist (Charles Martinelli), who appears unaware of the trouble his machine has caused. Martinelli's scientist seems to have stepped right out of a Méliès movie. He sets about recalculating how to reverse the process and pulls the big lever, reawakening the city. However, the group has trouble readjusting and are arrested for continuing their free-wheeling antics and thefts. The police think they are crazy for claiming Paris has been asleep for days. By the end, they are freed by the confused officers; the pilot (Albert Préjean) flies off again, and the guard and the scientist's daughter return to the Eiffel Tower, where he discovers a leftover diamond ring and slips it on her finger. They kiss, locked up together on the tower for the night for an abrupt happy ending. The cinematic inventiveness, comical spirit, and chaotic stop-start rhythms of The Crazy Ray were expanded on throughout Clair's career in silent and then sound film.

One of the more controversial Surreal films of the era resulted from the quarrelsome collaboration between Germaine Dulac and Antonin Artaud, The Seashell and the Clergyman, which premiered at the Ursulines to an unruly crowd in February 1928. Artaud carefully wrote down the scenario, and Dulac adapted it as precisely as possible. The problems in their creative vision and disagreement over authorship and Artaud's claims of betrayal seem to have begun before the premiere, when The Seashell and the Clergyman was referred to in advance as a dream by Artaud, filmed by Dulac. Artaud resented Dulac's reducing and simplifying his script and its comparison to a dream. He argued that it was an exercise in bringing hidden aspects of the human soul to the surface. She defended her adaptation, claiming to have followed Artaud's structure faithfully, only adding stylistic flourishes for a pure visual experience. Dulac did build in experimental camerawork plus disorienting superimpositions and editing to generate Impressionistic and boldly surreal cinematic rhythms (see Tami Williams 145–47). Artaud and Dulac wanted to go far beyond the surface-level limitations of conventional cinema.

While most of the story fragments in The Seashell and the Clergyman deal with conflicts between a pompous officer with a large sword (Lucien Bataille)

The unhinged priest (*The Seashell and the Clergyman*)

and an unhinged clergyman (Alex Allin), most of the action seems motivated by the clergyman's desire for the officer's resistant wife (Genica Athanasiou) and jealous disgust toward the officer. The clergyman pursues the woman through streets and across fields and even in the church, where he rips her top off next to the confessional. Analyses of *The Seashell and the Clergyman* often emphasize its Freudian aspects. Artaud wrote the script for his former lover, Athanasiou, and had intended to play the clergyman himself. Frustrated desire, displacement, and condensation seem to be dominant aspects of the text, and the recurring motifs of humiliating encounters may be tied to Artaud's own fantasies and obsessions. Psychoanalytic readings have emphasized the fetishism of the shells and fragile glass vessels and the boat sailing in his hands, and the clergyman's alternation between wanting to possess or strangle the woman. Feminist critiques reinforce how Dulac's adaptation somewhat undercut Artaud's aggressive voyeurism and gender construction by giving the woman more agency, resisting her role as a passive object of desire. As Susan Hayward explains, "Patriarchal power is revealed for what it does to female desire. Female subjectivity demonstrates what it will not tolerate" (111).

Artaud reacted violently to Dulac's imagery, and their collaboration provides more evidence of the difficulties in isolating artistic movements and production trends of this era, which could blend symbolist, psychoanalytic, and Surrealist impulses. Some of its contemporaries found it too narrative; others thought it too formal, built on pure cinema rhythms rather than Surreal principles. Heated disagreements about interpretations of *The Seashell and the Clergyman* have been complicated over the years in part because even the order of the reels remains controversial. Some influential prints reversed the second and third reels, ending with the woman contained in a glass orb instead of the clergyman drinking from the seashell. For some, the notion that chance mistakes in the assembly and presentation of *The Seashell and the Clergyman* altered the sequence seemed fitting in the radical context of 1920s Surrealism. In any case, thanks to museum screenings, *The Seashell and the Clergyman* became one of the canonical avant-garde films representing 1920s French cinema, and Dulac's international reputation still rests partly on this joint project, even though she continued working on experimental films about dance, nature, and visual music and then expanded on feminist themes with the arrival of sound. By contrast, sound disrupted Artaud's hopes for film as a distinct art form: "Discouraged with cinema, he returned to his experimental theater, to the spontaneity and ritual it provided" (Andrew, *Mists* 141).

Another significant project of the era, Man Ray's *ciné-poème Emak-Bakia* (1927), owes to Dada, Surrealism, Constructivism, and other artistic impulses, as well as Man Ray's own dreams and aesthetic trajectory. Seemingly incoherent and arbitrary, Man Ray's recurring motifs and stylistic devices gradually lend a unity to the onslaught of tricks and themes displayed. The title refers to the villa owned by his sponsors in Basque country, which means "Leave me alone." Man Ray foregrounds the camera as apparatus, including out-of-focus and underexposed shots and distorting filters, as well as rayographs, superimpositions, pixilation, and jarring montages. While the purer Dada films emphasized juxtaposition over storytelling, *Emak-Bakia* was structured along a more subjective Freudian dream logic. *Emak-Bakia* also remains fixed on acknowledging the medium of cinema and its peculiar relations to vision. Opening with an eye superimposed on a camera lens, it ends with a portrait of Kiki de Montparnasse with painted eyelids. While some Surrealists complained that it lacked sufficient narrative elements, there are many purposeful links between motifs and sequences in this personal experiment.

Kiki (*Emak-Bakia*)

One of the few films that successfully synthesized Dada and Surrealism, Man Ray's *The Starfish* (*L'Étoile de mer*, 1928), offers a "dream vision" inspired by snippets from Robert Desnos's poetry. *Starfish* presents two heterosexual couples (Kiki, first with André de la Rivière, then with Desnos) and stages of their relationships through a distorting lens. It seems simultaneously to critique and reinforce male voyeurism. For instance, it cuts from an intertitle about the beauty of women's teeth to a shot of a Kiki's legs. The film also hints at male attempts to trap and possess women and their images. One poetic intertitle, "If the flowers were in glass," is followed by starfish in jars and Kiki lying in her bed behind a clouded glass filter. Inserted shots of train tracks, ships, and a factory, suggesting a possible trip, disrupt the developments between the woman and men, but the film ultimately questions the sincerity of the woman. Kiki is last seen in a shot that combines the word "belle" and a shattered pane of glass between her and the camera. Man Ray thus integrates bits and pieces of a narrative, principally involving a metaphorical male journey of desire and frustration toward and away from the elusive woman figure. As with *Emak-Bakia*, *The Starfish* premiered at Studio des Ursulines. In 1929, Tallier paired Man Ray's *Mysteries of the Chateau of Dice* (*Les Mystères du château du Dé*), in which masked figures frolic in a fancy chateau, with *An Andalusian Dog* in a private avant-premiere for Surrealists at Ursulines.

Surrealists were drawn to cinema because it was a young and popular medium without the historical baggage and conventions of the established arts. André Breton loved to wander in and out of cinemas, catching part of one movie, then dropping in for a few scenes from another and so forth, creating a unique filmic collage in his mind. Luis Buñuel, who helped Epstein on *Fall of the House of Usher*, found the opportunity to make a film of his own, thanks to support from his mother back in Spain. His friend Salvador Dalí convinced him to let him work on the project, which he claimed to have sketched out on the inside lid of a shoe box. Their collaboration resulted in *An Andalusian Dog*, and the brash pair bragged to the press that they were producing something completely new in the history of the cinema. Their methods included tossing random ideas to one another, retaining those they both found surprising and irrational, modeling their radical compilation of images and actions on the automatic writing of Surrealist poets (E. King 20). They were intent on inserting some favorite, provocative personal imagery. Buñuel wanted a slit eyeball, Dalí called for ants emerging from a hand and dead donkeys. Despite the unusual process, they carefully typed out a scenario to guide the production. Buñuel rented a studio space in Billancourt for a two-week shoot and hired Pierre Batcheff, known for his good looks and portrayals of sensitive young men, and comic star Simone Mareuil. It is likely that Batcheff also contributed many comic bits, including parodies of his previous roles and star persona (Powrie and Rebillard 145). The resulting seventeen-minute, three-hundred-shot film was initially accompanied by refrains from Wagner's *Tristan und Isolde* and two Argentinian tangos that Buñuel played on records at the screenings. Eventually the music was added for sound prints, continuing inconclusively over black leader at the end in surreal fashion.

An Andalusian Dog follows its own erratic and creative trajectory, and the actors were often quite puzzled about what they were being asked to do and why. Georges Sadoul warns that "any synopsis of this film would be necessarily meaningless since the power of the film depends on its succession of surrealistic images" (*Dictionary* 390). The film advances by way of digressions and false starts, even including two seemingly separate beginnings. First, in the prologue, Buñuel looks up to a cloud passing through the moon, which motivates his passing a razor through the eye of a woman (actually a cow's eye). Then, "eight years later," a man on a bicycle apparently goes to visit the same woman but falls over. There are no narrative connections between the two initial scenes. Buñuel liked to argue that nothing in the film was symbolic of anything. For him, every interpretation was just a subjective reaction rather than an informed analysis. Moreover, the film consistently, if unsystematically, overturned narrative, generic, gender, and technical conventions, generating a highly eccentric string of shots and scenes that obeyed dream logic rather than cinematic norms. Chance also mattered; if a shot were accidentally edited in upside down, it stayed upside down. *An Andalusian Dog* was a radical endeavor on every level. As the young director Jean Vigo warned, "Beware the dog, it bites" (Sadoul, *Dictionary* 391).

Throughout *An Andalusian Dog*, Buñuel and Dalí exploit and refer to as many cinematic techniques as possible. The scene of Batcheff riding his bicy-

Messan clutches the severed hand (*An Andalusian Dog*)

cle wearing a suit overlaid with frilly women's clothing and a striped box becomes part of a superimposition as he pedals right into his own process shot, then topples over in the street. When Mareuil seems to hear him coming and looks disgustedly out the window, there is a continuity error as the second shot of him lying in the street has been flipped, acknowledging the artifice of the usual eyeline match. Somehow the man appears up to her room, where the woman's intense gaze seems to animate the tie from the striped box. However, after the ants appear in the man's hand and a series of graphic matches, there is a shot down onto an androgynous figure (Fano Messan) in the street below, poking a severed hand, which a police officer awards her, in the striped box. This seems to be a play on "I give you this hand in marriage," since she clutches it lovingly. However, as the curious crowd is dispersed, Messan remains in the street until being knocked over by a car in a scene that again muddles continuity. Her hands are in obviously different positions in various shots. Thus, from the beginning, the loose sequence of actions break norms for cinematic camera position, editing, and comprehension.

The death of the androgynous figure seems to motivate an unhealthy desire in the man. Batcheff pursues Mareuil, and rubs her breasts and buttocks in a Freudian scene of displaced and condensed body parts until she breaks free and defends herself with the tennis racket. The man pulls on ropes stringing together boards that resemble headstones, two young monks, including Dalí, and pianos laden with dead donkeys. Dalí apparently personally ripped out the donkeys' eyes for the scene, which reinforces the mutilation and castration themes that permeate *An Andalusian Dog*. As the horrified woman makes a break for the door, the directors again go out of their way to point out the film's artifice since she catches his ant-infected hand in the door, which is opening outward in both shots. The absurd titles announcing time could easily be rearranged throughout the film without helping or hindering any narrative functions. In fact, another man who resembles Batcheff appears, angrily sending him to the corner, and this single action is interrupted by a title card declaring "sixteen years earlier." The confrontation continues until Batcheff magically transforms two books into pistols and shoots the man, who falls dead in a field next to a naked woman in a match on action to preserve the continuity of movement while substituting a new space.

The final section of *An Andalusian Dog* tags together scenes that hint at melodramatic plot points, and Batcheff continues to harass Mareuil until she simply walks out the door in defiance. The spatial arrangements again change as she is no longer in an urban apartment but at a beach. She is suddenly joined by a happy man, and the pair comes upon the smashed striped box and discarded clothes from earlier. However, "in the springtime" they are shown buried in the sand and motionless, with the later published script explaining that they are blinded and being eaten by swarms of insects.

An Andalusian Dog not only built on the contexts of the avant-garde and Surrealism to disrupt narrative and cinematic conventions; it overturned audience expectations in casting. Batcheff's persistent pursuit of Mareuil contrasts with his earlier earnest and romantic roles, while Mareuil's performance, including being groped naked, breaks decisively from her usual funny, wholesome portrayals. Critics and theorists have continually struggled to nail down specific influences and meanings in a film that constantly struggles to avoid or even mocks such attempts. As troubling and controversial as it was, *An Andalusian Dog* was immediately acknowledged as significant. After several high-profile private premieres, it screened exclusively at Studio 28 for months, even playing alongside American comedies. It was also highly prized at ciné-clubs throughout Europe, and the film's success ensured that Buñuel and Dalí were quickly welcomed into the Surrealist group as prized members. Furthermore, this was a transitional time when sound films were opening alongside silent films, as theaters began to remodel for sound movies and producers delayed productions to add music tracks. There was a decline in available French film products, and for some, *An Andalusian Dog* offered a startling culmination of 1920s silent avant-garde practice as everyone was forced to rethink where French cinema was headed next.

Transitions from Silent to Sync-Sound Cinema

Two of the more significant movies marking the close of the silent era were René Clair's *The Italian Straw Hat* (*Un chapeau de paille d'Italie*, 1928) and *The Passion of Joan of Arc* (*La Passion de Jeanne d'Arc*, Dreyer, 1928). Both films reveal the richness of late 1920s French cinema. After Clair directed several avant-garde and light comedies, Alexandre Kamenka of Albatros offered him the adaptation of the popular nineteenth-century farce by Eugène Labiche and Marc Michel. Unlike many drawing-room theatrical adaptations, *The Italian Straw Hat* offered plenty of cinematic potential, with chases across Paris and fast-paced physical comedy. Working with designer Lazare Meerson and the Albatros production team, as well as cinematographer Maurice Desfassiaux, Clair updated the setting to 1895 in a caricature of the Lumière era. He condensed the play drastically, replacing verbal humor with visual gags, and secured a top cast, including Albert Préjean, to turn the theatrical farce into a major filmed satire and one of the great commercial and critical successes of the decade.

The Italian Straw Hat follows Fadinard (Préjean) on his wedding day, but his horse happens to devour the expensive new hat of a married woman, Anaïs (Olga Tschechowa), who is secretly meeting her lover, Lieutenant Tavernier (Geymond Vital) in the bushes of the Bois de Vincennes. The angry couple insists that Fadinard immediately locate an identical hat so that her husband does not suspect some hanky panky. From that point, Fadinard's day ricochets back and forth from trying to pull off his very bourgeois wedding, which includes keeping his naive bride Helen (Marise Maia) out of the mess, while trying to placate the increasingly frantic Tavernier and locate a new hat. Clair populates the story with a comical array of eccentric characters, each with their own humorous ticks and challenges, from lost gloves and irritating dresses to tight shoes and unruly collars. Moreover, Anaïs and Tavernier occupy Fadinard's apartment, threatening to destroy all the furniture, while the groom struggles to keep his wedding on track, in what amounts to two interlaced comic films. Once the cuckolded husband enters the fray and the wedding guests return to the apartment as well, all the major couples and players collide in a rousing climax. The fast pace owes as much to the original farce as to French and American slapstick comedies. By the end, an uneasy order is restored to most of the characters, with a resolution filled with irony and lingering suspicions, and the relieved newlyweds head to bed.

Clair follows the trends of some late 1920s films by dramatically reducing the intertitles in *Italian Straw Hat*, relying on mise-en-scène, editing, and physical gags to communicate character traits and predicaments. His fixed camera allowed the performers to set the rhythm as they rushed about the sets. But while the film builds on many generic situations right out of a Max Linder comedy, with characters hiding behind doors, threats of duels, and riotous physical humor, it also inserts Surreal touches in its staging and editing. For instance, when Fadinard and Tavernier argue in his apartment, Anaïs faints about the room like a giant rag doll, and when Fadinard accidentally tells Anaïs's husband why he needs the hat, Clair cuts to a 1910-era tableau-style restaging of the scene. Throughout the film, Clair regularly employs unexpected angles, such as bird's-eye vertical shots onto the bustling heads of the wedding preparations, mental subjective shots as the flustered Fardinard imagines Tavernier ripping up his apartment, and visual cues for sounds and music. These strategies open up the stage play. A touch of avant-garde and faith in 1920s *photogénie* permeate *The Italian Straw Hat*, which became a popular and critical hit, representing the vibrant high quality of late French silents to global markets. Clair's final silent films were a poetic short dedicated to the Eiffel Tower (*Tour*, 1928) and another adapted play, *Two Timid Souls* (*Les Deux timides*, 1928), which proved anew to critics and the public alike that Clair was one of the most engaging young directors working in 1920s France. *Two Timid Souls* featured Pierre Batcheff, solidifying his status as one of France's top young romantic stars.

While Clair cleverly minimized intertitles in his late silent films, Carl Dreyer placed dialogue titles and close-up speaking faces at the center of his *Passion of Joan of Arc*. Sound cinema was already beginning to shake up the US industry and divide European filmmakers, many fearing that synchronized sound would lead back to excessively literary and theatrical models, to say nothing of limiting camera mobility, which some saw as a distinctively European trait. Sound would also put smaller national cinemas at a disadvantage on the global marketplace. The Danish Dreyer, however, hoped to make his next film in sound. He managed to interest the Société Générale des Films, producers of Gance's *Napoleon*, in another auteurist super-production. These would be the two most expensive French films of the decade, but it was not yet possible to film *The Passion of Joan of Arc* with sound, although Dreyer required his actors to speak their actual dialogue, as if it were recorded.

Joan of Arc has been the subject of motion pictures from Méliès on, and many of the films, including another 1928 version by Marco de Gastyne, tended to be big-budget productions celebrating nationalism and spirituality. Dreyer took a more radical approach. Early on, he worked with Joseph Delteil, who had recently published an award-winning Joan of Arc biographical novel. Then Dreyer turned to the actual record of Joan's trial. The film even opens with images of the archival transcripts being opened and displayed. The historical Joan had been captured after leading the French troops to victory and was put on trial for heresy in Rouen by a council of pro-British religious figures, backed by the military. She was executed in 1431. Dreyer and medievalist Pierre Champillion eventually condensed the twenty-nine interrogations down to five sequences. Dreyer hired a young stage actress, Maria Falconetti, to play the demanding role of Joan, and another stage actor, Eugene Silvain, as her lead tormentor, Bishop Cauchon. Other significant actors included Antonin Artaud as the kindly monk Massieu and

Michel Simon playing Jean Lemaître. Typecasting was part of Dreyer's arsenal, but he harbored a real belief in the actors' need to discover and express the inner truth of their characters, especially via subtle facial cues. Delivering the *photogénie* potential of the close-up was almost a spiritual mission to him. "The face is the mirror to the soul," he argued; the human face is a land one never tires of exploring (Bordwell, *Films* 22).

For the visual style, Dreyer worked with designers Hermann Warm and Jean Hugo, who built elaborate sets with moving walls, while Valentine Hugo designed costumes and Rudolf Maté was cinematographer. *The Passion of Joan of Arc* proved a key example of European international style, owing to German Expressionism, Soviet montage, and French Impressionism, as well as evocative Scandinavian mise-en-scène and camerawork. All these influences merge during the montage scene of Joan confronted with the tools of torture intercut with the menacing faces around her, the impression of which overwhelms her until she faints. As Paul Schrader writes, "The faces of Joan's inquisitors are genuinely oppressive, and part of Joan's fear and trembling comes from the Expressionist tradition: an innocent female victim trapped and terrorized by ghastly demonic distorted faces" (122). The wealth of artistic contexts in France enriched the creative options for this European production team: "Perhaps only in Paris of the late 1920s could Carl Dreyer's vision of Jeanne d'Arc have taken exactly the form it did," thanks largely to the intense avant-garde activity on all artistic fronts (Bordwell, *Filmguide* 13). Ironically, Dreyer's visual treatment boldly renewed the religious themes in substantial ways. Joan had only recently been granted sainthood, so her life, faith, and legacy were receiving renewed attention. Furthermore, unlike most late 1920s movies, Dreyer's *Passion of Joan of Arc* was not released with color tinting, so its pure black and white also lent increased spiritual weight to its representation of this courageous and holy peasant girl's last hours.

Dreyer's film begins with Joan brought before religious leaders and surrounded by soldiers, all male, all older. From the first shot of Joan's interrogation in what seems to be an endlessly long narrow room, Maté's cinematography provides an unsettling variety of angles, shot scales, and camera movements. The audience, like the young Joan, is disoriented by the unconventional manner in which the action unfolds. For one thing, close-ups dominate, but they also isolate characters from their narrative space. During Joan's first statement to the court, she swears to tell the truth, but a high-angle close-up is followed by a low-angle close-up, breaking screen direction, and the eyelines of other characters can rarely be judged as correct or incorrect.

It is often unclear where she is looking and whom she is addressing: "The sense of figures hovering in a gravityless space is exacerbated by manipulations of camera angle which cut figures free of the ground" (Bordwell, *Films* 68). On a scene-to-scene level too, *The Passion of Joan of Arc* surprises us, as Dreyer's film establishes a unique rhythm all its own.

The five interrogations alternate between Joan being brought to the judges or the judges coming to her chambers. Dreyer filmed the script in chronological order, so the exasperation of the court officials and the building fear and exhaustion on Joan's face accumulate from scene to scene, despite the fragmentary stop-and-go plot construction. Given the known outcome and execution, there is a fatalistic tone to every conversation, with each player seemingly aware of his role in her ultimate destruction. The paternalistic judges pretend to want to spare Joan, and after the logic of their arguments and appeals to Scripture do not sway her to repent, a visit to the torture chamber causes her to temporarily relent. She quickly recants her confession and reasserts her beliefs and defiance in the name of God and country. The final act, in which Joan struggles to accept her fate while the crowds gather in recognition of her righteousness, finally explodes as the people react with outrage at her conviction and burning. Dreyer builds a new level of horror and tension as the soldiers' chaotic violence plays out on the bodies of the people, and hers goes up in flames, with doves flying above. This passion play concludes in a shocking display of military repression and cruelty in which weapons, fire, and smoke confront the crowds until the final image of a cross, flames, and the empty top of the stake lends a solemn final image to wrap up Joan's earthly battle, though the end titles promise her soul was protected as it rose to Heaven. Nonetheless, the film concludes suddenly with a shockingly bleak indictment of the guilty parties, as if Dreyer wanted to find an equivalent to Eisenstein's slaughter and "remember" scene ending *Strike* (1925).

Dreyer's unusual choices in visual style and narrative structure, rejecting any psychological realism, force the audience to scan the image and concentrate on Joan's ordeal and the frustration of the surrounding characters. Time and space are abstract, with scenographic depth often undercut. The flat lighting, sparse props, and skewed angles make it difficult to tell how much space there is between characters and the walls in the background, generating what David Bordwell labels "an eccentric space" (*Films* 67). Rapid cutting and numerous intertitles confound any easy comprehension of spatial and temporal relations. The pacing, shot composition, and performance style all

Dreyer's eccentric framing (*The Passion of Joan of Arc*)

seem designed to disconcert the viewer, forcing us to dwell on Joan's face and her lonely moral and physical predicament. The audience is aligned with and gains genuine allegiance for the traumatized, trapped Joan despite the radical visual style. As Jean Cocteau famously declared, *"Jeanne d'Arc* seems like an historical document from an era in which the cinema didn't exist" (Sadoul, *Dictionary* 276). Dreyer inserts Joan in an exotic, troubling place that demands all her strength to remain sane and coherent, while he challenges the audience to become embedded in her demanding experience.

The Passion of Joan of Arc premiered in Copenhagen and had a successful opening. However, in France there were objections and threats of censorship. Officials from the Catholic Church demanded the producers cut the scene of Joan being bled. There were concerns that Joan's story, which was of such immense cultural importance, should not be written and directed by a foreigner, especially a foreigner who was raised Lutheran (Larson 58). The production company and distributor, fearing more censorship and already reeling from the expense of Gance's *Napoleon*, recut the film without Dreyer's input. However, that version performed so poorly that in 1929, the original print finally played to critical acclaim, although by then it was hardly commercially viable as a silent film, even released with a synchronized music track. It was initially banned outright in England for its harsh anti-British stance. The fate of *The Passion of Joan of Arc* was thus quite uneven, with the original Danish and German copies apparently destroyed or lost. Thus, Dreyer's movie existed in a bewildering array of censored prints, and a complete version was thought lost until the 1981 discovery of a nitrate print with original Danish intertitles in a Norwegian mental institution.

The unique experiment that is *The Passion of Joan of Arc* continues to inspire research and influence art cinema, with its haunting beauty and groundbreaking narrative. As Bordwell observes, "It is one of the most bizarre, perceptually difficult films ever made" (*Films* 66). *The Passion of Joan of Arc*, one of the aesthetic triumphs of late silent French cinema, should also remind us just how collaborative and international "French" film was. However, the arrival of sound motion pictures would bring an end to certain sorts of film practice and challenge many theoretical assumptions and manifestos. After all, what sort of synchronized sounds should accompany a scene such as Joan's death, to say nothing of actors clamoring about the Eiffel Tower, superimposed shots in a triptych of Napoleon's victories, or Madame Beudet imagining a handsome tennis player leaping from the page of a magazine? It would be up to many of these same filmmakers to explore the limits and potential of sound film technology while pursuing their ongoing experimentation with film art.

Beyond the burst of wildly diverse, creative productions during the late silent period, the end of the 1920s also saw cinema achieve a new national significance. Previously, French cinema fell under the umbrella of the Ministry of the Interior for enforcing censorship and other regulations. In 1928, Édouard Herriot, minister of Public Instruction and the Beaux-Arts, announced a new commission to protect and control the cinema, securing its place in French culture, while confronting foreign competition. The commission established categories for "French national cinema" based on each production's percentage of native French talent and its locations. With the arrival of sound and other shifts in global film industries, the government wanted to guide and guarantee French interests. Documentaries could not include more than one-third of their footage from outside France, for instance (Leglise 69). For feature films to be in the top category of 100 percent French, the studio, director, writers, technical and assistant directors, and cinematographers must all be French, with all interiors and exteriors shot on French territory. Foreign actors could not occupy more than 25 percent of the major roles. The second tier of productions required a 50 percent threshold for all major creative positions, with at least half of the production taking place in France (Montebello 20–21).

In addition to protecting and stabilizing France's film economy and workforce, Herriot's commission recognized the cultural value and quality of France's cinema. For the first time, France was officially elevating its cinema to the same cultural status as its theater and fine arts. The commission acknowledged the cinema's power to disseminate French culture at home and abroad and recognized that "quality cinema" represented "national quality" (Montebello 21). Moreover, the Herriot commission led to new laws prohibiting local and regional censors to block the screening of any film granted a visa for exhibition. Approved films were deemed in the national interest and guaranteed the right of distribution throughout France, which protected producers and exhibitors alike, making them equivalent to legitimate theater. Municipalities could not enforce arbitrary censorship codes; their only role was to enforce safety regulations (Leglise 70). The recognition and support of French cinema's quality and cultural value became a central concern for the government during the transition from silent to sound cinema. France's dedication to enhancing the status of French film shaped its policies and expectations for its national cinema from that point on.

CHAPTER 5

Early 1930s French Cinema

The Transition to Sound

The Challenges of Synchronized Sound in France

Alice Guy had directed scores of *phonoscène* sound shorts at Gaumont by 1905, and French entrepreneurs had consistently helped drive the development of new technologies, including widescreen formats, but there was little investment in synchronized sound processes in 1920s France. Léon Gaumont personally oversaw some sound research in his firm, including using anamorphic lenses for better optical recording tracks. Nonetheless, US, German, and Dutch electronics and radio companies pursued the most successful research and applications, so that initially the invention and diffusion of sound cinema came primarily from outside. Sound's arrival revealed anew how the French industry's decentralized structure left it vulnerable to global companies. German and American companies built new sound stages on French soil, and their sound equipment was installed in French theaters. Most important, the sound film cartel, Western Electric, RCA, and Tobis-Klangfilm, received substantial royalty fees for sound films produced in France. Thus, the coming of sound rattled the French cinema on many fronts, forcing economic, technological, narrative, and stylistic changes. Yet these radical challenges paved the way for a rich array of production options and some of the most stunning films in history.

In 1929, French film production declined dramatically as companies lost export markets for silent films and looked for facilities to add soundtracks to their projects. It is worth noting that feature film production was already relatively low during the late 1920s. For the five years prior, France released an average of seventy-two movies, with only fifty-two features in 1929, which was fewer than some major studios in Hollywood. Daring French films were often made by small production companies patching together funding from a few sources, including distributors and even theater owners, and it was rare that a movie generated substantial profits. Thus, banks and large investors did not have a strong stake in preserving or updating the film industry in France, as they did in the United States, where studios allied with big banks for expansion into sound. Furthermore, upgrading the French industry with new equipment was complicated by the fact that smaller companies were in charge of much of the production, postproduction, and exhibition, each pursuing their own financing schemes. Without secure funding from large financial institutions or vertically integrated studios, France could not support long-term production schedules and planning. The production sector relied on a range of funding sources for each project, including bank loans and industry partners, but small firms risked bankruptcy with every new project. The conversion to sound, which created a major upheaval in every national cinema, was particularly difficult for France.

Surprisingly, France's overall economic situation was actually quite impressive in 1930. The franc was solid, in contrast to the dollar, and unemployment was low, even after the country had accommodated two million immigrants in the previous decade. Automobile production was robust, and France had the world's third-largest steel industry. Its literary and artistic reputation continued to rise, as international writers and artists flocked to Paris as France exported modernist literary, artistic, and design trends. French radio was booming, helping expand the reach of popular songs and entertainers, many of whom soon found second careers in sound movies. Further, France's political standing appeared solid. Backed by the world's largest army, France's hold on its vast colonies seemed assured. Cinema, however, was particularly fragile: "During these years . . . (1928–1932), French cinema found itself shaken to its foundations. Humiliated, its very existence threatened, as it was seemingly being taken hostage by a technical and artistic revolution that came from outside its borders" (Billard, *L'Age classique* 12). One reason that silent French cinema had supported such a wide range of stories, styles, and even lengths of films had been the variety of exhibition outlets. The financial burden of converting to sound prohibited many of those smaller cinemas from adopting new equipment. The larger palaces in Paris and other major cities found funding first, creating stark divisions between big urban cinemas, neighborhood or specialty houses, and small-town theaters. High profits from American and French sound films were concentrated in the biggest,

most expensive venues, changing the exhibition landscape and distribution patterns over the formative years of 1929 to 1932. Every small cinema
struggled to survive, converting to sound if and when it could.

Prior to the arrival of the first synchronized sound films in Paris, there
was already anxiety among film critics and filmmakers. Much of French cinema's reputation in the 1920s rested on escaping literary and theatrical conventions. Sound cinema seemed to point straight back toward those influences and restrictions. An early alert came from Alexandre Arnoux, editor
for the influential film journal *Pour Vous*, who had seen several sound films
in London and warned of the "tyranny of words and noise." Yet he acknowledged that no one in commercial cinema could remain on the sidelines: "We
may wonder whether speech does not rob expression of more elements than
it brings with it. . . . We are present at a death or a birth, no one can yet tell
which" (Clair 129). Soon, however, one of the more influential and positive
examples of sound's potential for Europeans arrived in London: *The Broadway Melody* (Beaumont, 1929). Even more than *The Jazz Singer* (Crosland, 1927),
The Broadway Melody generated excitement and served as a model for creative sound strategies that surpassed filmed theater.

René Clair and Marcel Pagnol, among many others, traveled to London
to see and hear *The Broadway Melody* for themselves. Clair called it amazing
and marveled at the fluid camerawork and evocative acting, praising the
scene when Bessie Love, in medium close-up, looks offscreen with anguish
as we hear a car driving away. He concludes that Love could be more expressive as an actress with sound than she was in silent cinema (Clair 138). Pagnol, France's most popular playwright, concurred, praising *The Broadway
Melody* and sound's ability to enhance the emotional power of a script: "Pagnol claimed that talking film's capacity to capture the subtlest of nuances of
dialogue or appearance, those that would go unnoticed at a live stage production, instantly overcame the limitations of both theatre and silent film"
(Bowles, *Marcel Pagnol* 51).

The battle lines were quickly drawn for and against the incursion of talking pictures. Critics as well as industry professionals considered the arrival
of sound as a major break from previous practice. Whether sound cinema
was positive or negative depended on their own contexts. Bernard Natan,
head of the newly reformulated Pathé-Natan, announced, "The discovery of
sound film has reduced everything to zero" (O'Brien, *Cinema's Conversion* 47).
The shift to sound did not destroy all connections to the past, as the popular
arts and performance conventions continued to shape synchronized sound.

However, disruptive changes were being dictated from beyond the existing narrative and business models. It was uncertain whether France's mix of small production studios, independent auteurs, and various exhibition circuits could protect "French cinema" from German, British, and US competition.

The revised Pathé became a major force in the conversion to sound. In 1929, Bernard Natan, a Romanian immigrant, provided an important game plan, merging his profitable film stock and production company with Pathé, which had steadily been selling off assets and shrinking its overhead. Charles Pathé remained on the Pathé-Natan board of directors. Natan's new sound studios in Montmartre (now the La femis film school) and Joinville were constructed as state-of-the-art sound stages that could be rented out by others. But their competitors Gaumont-Franco-Film-Aubert (GFFA) also invested in new sound studios, while the French division of Germany's Tobis bought and converted Eclair-Menschen studios in Épinay-sur-Seine. But Pathé-Natan diversified further. It soon owned fifty-six first-run sound cinemas and began expanding into live entertainment for ancillary profits in record sales and radio, following the example of Warner Bros. Natan's goal was to build a cluster of ventures that provided synergy and economic efficiency under the umbrella of the Pathé-Natan brand. His expansion was funded by the Bauer and Marchal bank, and for the first part of the 1930s, Pathé-Natan led the French industry, producing more films than any other studio and selling film stock for image and optical sound recording to most of the nation's producers. Already in 1929, Pathé-Nathan produced *The Three Masks (Les Trois masques*, Hugon) in London's Twickenham Studios while its own RCA-equipped sound stages were under construction. *The Three Masks* is often called the "first 100% talking French film," despite being filmed in England. Some of its Paris critics attacked it as evidence of all the possible pitfalls of shooting in sync sound, including static cameras and performances in theatrical-style sets, but it was the first of Pathé-Natan's sixty sound films of the early 1930s.

As France geared up for sound, producers added music tracks to silent films then in production, such as *The Queen's Necklace (Le Collier de la reine*, 1929), so they would be able to play in the few sound-equipped cinemas as well as all the silent houses. *Miss Europe (Prix de beauté*, 1930), produced by a small German company, directed by the Italian Augusto Genina from a script by René Clair, and starring the American Louise Brooks, is typical of efforts to graft sound onto a globally marketable project. Another early transnational production was Braunberger-Richebé's *The Road Is Fine (La Route est belle,*

1930), shot in London by Robert Florey, the young French director who had just made *The Cocoanuts* (1929) with the Marx Brothers. Directors and technicians with any experience in sound were in high demand and fueled a wide array of projects exploiting sync-sound dialogue and music. Moreover, the coming of sound brought new audiences in the doors, creating a boom in ticket sales. While cinema only represented one-third of the entertainment business in the early 1920s, by 1929, movie ticket sales surpassed the receipts for all live theatrical venues in Paris. Sound cinema took a toll on attendance at legitimate theater and music halls and became the nation's chief form of entertainment by the 1930s (Montebello 11). Between 1929 and 1930, box office income skyrocketed for wired cinemas, encouraging rapid investment by small and large studios alike.

As more sound stages went online and more cinemas remodeled for sound, observers warned that France could not simply buy its way to a stable, Hollywood-style studio system. Indeed, only a few studios accounted for most of the investment in sound cinema, but when the Depression and international competition began to catch up with overly optimistic projections, it became clear they were woefully underfunded. Pathé-Natan in particular expanded by buying up many financially interrelated companies, but each entity brought new debt obligations, compounding the need for ever-increasing revenues. Natan was working energetically to rebuild his company in the image of the old vertically integrated Pathé. A visionary, he even bought the rights to Henri Chrétien's widescreen Hypogonar process and invested in research for television technology. However, as the Depression worsened and the profits from box office, studio rentals, and film stock sales proved inadequate, Pathé-Natan began to flounder, and its board and bankers blamed Natan personally.

GFFA grew at a similarly remarkable rate between 1927 and 1930, propelled by the high profits of its first sound films, but executives soon realized their expansion was undercapitalized. It was one thing to buy up a string of movie palaces; it was quite another to cover the costs of upgrading them. Large palaces could cost more than $20,000 each to remodel and equip for sound. In 1930, the six-thousand-seat Gaumont-Palace was closed for thirteen months for renovations as Gaumont installed its own brand of sound equipment. Within a year, Gaumont wired ninety-four theaters. The expenditures for Pathé and Gaumont, both of which tried to retain their pre–World War I status, were unsustainable without a steady increase in box office revenues and generous lines of credit from banks. Despite the studios' efforts, the overall rate of conversion remained low. By the end of 1932, roughly half of all French cinemas still showed silent films only, but none had been produced in the previous two years, forcing a crisis for many smaller and rural cinemas. Gaumont and Pathé offered older silent classics to these theaters, often in *format réduit* 17.5mm prints and at rental fees far below those of a new movie, all of which limited the content for hundreds of small cinemas and reduced the distribution income for the studios. Moreover, most new French sound films were aimed at the domestic market and French-speaking colonies due to the lack of funds for multiple-language versions. Lucrative export markets were often out of reach and increasingly dominated by American and German titles.

France's lack of a centralized industry group to organize the technological adoption of sound provided another challenge. The US studios had standardized their process early on with the 1927 Big Five Agreement, selecting sound-on-film so they could all move forward together with compatible equipment. France still had an array of sound companies with various competing sound-on-disc and sound-on-film options. However, Gaumont quickly made sure its sound projector met the foreign standards, though Tobis-Klangfilm tried to control all of Europe, suing for patent infringement to slow its competition. Finally, during the summer of 1930, the major sound companies Western Electric, RCA, and Tobis-Klangfilm met to forge international agreements. As Charles O'Brien points out, the resulting Paris Sound-Film Peace Treaty "stipulated that film-sound technologies be 'interchangeable' so that a film produced by any of the Paris Treaty's parties could be recorded and shown using any patented equipment" (*Cinema's Conversion* 19). In the process, they divided up regions and national cinemas among them, so while Canada and the Soviet Union were the terrain of Western Electric and RCA, for instance, Scandinavia and Switzerland belonged to Tobis-Klangfilm. They all wanted to be active in the valuable French market, so France was named an open zone for all three companies.

Once the agreements were in place, most French sound equipment firms had to close or become allied with the big companies and their processes. Some cinemas had already been wired during 1929 with early, often doomed systems, such as Mélovox and its sound-on-disc process, which ended up costing those theater owners dearly. The divide between major studio-owned cinemas and small chain exhibitors deepened. A number of silent films that had not yet been released due to the arrival of sound were upgraded with synchronized sound effects and music tracks. Some of these *films sonores* included clever musical interventions, but their reliance on intertitles rather than dialogue provided an unwelcome compromise to many critics and audiences. Even high-quality silents such as Julien Duvivier's *Au Bonheur des dames* (1930) failed to find the audiences they deserved. The different formats, uneven sound quality, and misleading advertising hurt independent cinemas and taught moviegoers to seek the safer studio products in the first-run palaces. Box office dollars went increasingly to the largest studios, distributors, and theater chains, further hurting domestic films and neighborhood houses.

Initially, German and American competition proved overwhelming. The giant German studio UFA regularly hired French personnel, shooting many French-language films in Germany. Tobis built a sound studio in Paris in 1929 and opened Film Sonor distribution offices there. Later that year, MGM began producing French, German, and Italian versions of their films. In 1930, Paramount invested $200 million in France, buying up and converting Gaumont's studio in Joinville, and shooting multiple-language versions of its films to play throughout Europe, sometimes in fourteen different languages, including Russian and Norwegian. In its first year, Paramount turned out one hundred features and fifty shorts, leading *La Cinématographie francaise* to announce, with a mix of pride and shame, that Paramount's output had helped establish Paris as the center of sound film production in Europe. For the 1932 season, Paramount completed two new "French" feature films each month. By the end of that year, however, improved dubbing practices reduced the need for costly multiple-language versions, and soon subtitles brought further savings, cutting costs from as much as $40,000 for a multiple-language version down to $2,500 per subtitled film (Montebello 9).

Multiple-language productions brought international cooperation and competition among partners. One interesting example was the German French coproduction of dual-language versions of *The Man Who Killed* (*L'Homme qui assassina*) by Terra-Filmkunst and Braunberger-Richébé. The German adaptation of the well-known French novel and play became *Der Mann, der den Mord beging* (1931), made by Curtis Bernhardt, starring Conrad Veidt and Trude von Molo. Meanwhile, the French version (1931), also shot mostly in Germany, was directed by Jean Tarride, starring Jean Angelo and Marie Bell. Both versions premiered the same week in January 1931, but the French film was codirected by Bernhardt, further complicating its authorship and nationality. The French press, including *Pour Vous* and *Ciné-Miroir*, emphasized the story's French roots.

Meanwhile, the French industry, burdened with the costs of rapid sound conversion and facing a tough learning curve in their mode of production, appealed to the government to decrease its high box office taxes, but no action was taken to help protect the domestic industry. An average cinema could expect to pay taxes on its income of 35 percent or more, thanks to a combination of state and municipal fees (Crisp, *Classic* 18). Some small-town theater owners went on strike to protest local regulations and taxes. For producers, sound required costly musical talent and performance rights, scriptwriters and adaptation fees, extra film stock for optical sound recording, and increased postproduction labor and time. Major stars demanded ever-larger salaries. The changing marketplace was full of hurdles.

Even Gaumont could not long survive these new business conditions. Despite its sales of sound equipment, chains of newly wired cinemas, popular sound newsreels, and state-of-the-art studios in the Buttes Chaumont neighborhood and Nice, Gaumont was quickly hobbled by the Depression's deepening effects. In 1934, GFFA stock value dropped so far that it was forced to sell off many of its assets, and by 1936 the conglomerate sank into bankruptcy, followed closely by the failure of Pathé-Natan. Natan and the Bauer et Marchal bank had become increasingly reckless in pinning their hopes on each new venture to help cover the other debt-ridden divisions of Pathé-Natan. Amid a string of unrelated high-profile national financial scandals, stockholders blamed the flamboyant Natan and his complicated schemes. He was eventually convicted of fraud and condemned to prison in 1938 for skimming profits and hiding debts. Natan had also become a target of the extreme right and antisemitic critics, including Maurice Bardèche and Robert Brasillach, whose film history book, originally published in 1935, blamed most of France's cinema problems on immigrants and Jews. They attacked Natan, Pierre Braunberger, Jacques Haïk, and Adolphe Osso, the four largest producers at the time, claiming they siphoned off funds, bankrupting the formerly strong "French" film industry (350–51).

The industry was indeed rather fragile, but for other reasons than poor management. Many investors and banks became increasingly wary: "One in three films failed to break even; at times, over a third of the active companies were going bankrupt each year" (Crisp, *Classic* 40). Moreover, the hope that sound could help resurrect Pathé and Gaumont as vertically integrated equivalents to the major Hollywood studios was soon crushed. Despite the output from Pathé and Gaumont, the bulk of French films of the 1930s were made by small production companies and often distributed by tiny ventures as well: "During the 1930s, 285 small firms made only one film apiece, and dozens more managed to produce only a few each" (Thompson and Bordwell 260). For instance, the Harry Baur vehicle *A Man and His Woman* (*Un homme en or*, Dréville, 1934), was coproduced by two companies, AV Films, which only made two movies, and Roger Ferdinand, which produced four, including Renoir's *Chotard et Cie* (1933). Companies came and went. The result was "an anarchic multiplicity of small under-capitalized production companies with no permanent production facilities, or staff and no structural connection to the distribution or exhibition sectors" (Crisp, "Business" 119). In between these small studios and the various theater chains were scores of minor distributors trying to get their few contracted movies per year onto screens, which decreased their negotiating power and the eventual box office returns for their small studio partners. The decentralized film industry had many financial and practical problems, but the worsening Depression reduced its audience, with a nearly 20 percent drop in ticket sales between 1932 and 1935.

Alternative Early Sound: Avant-Garde and Animation

In the meantime, a new range of options opened up for talent during the transitional years of the early 1930s. Some French directors learned sound techniques by directing French versions of American and German films either at the studios in France or abroad. For instance, Claude Autant-Lara, who had recently used Henri Chrétien's widescreen lens for *Build a Fire* (*Construire un feu*, 1928/30), directed French versions of several Buster Keaton and Douglas Fairbanks Jr. projects in Hollywood for MGM and Warner Bros. Other French workers, hired by Paramount, learned the new processes right in Paris. Multiple-language shooting, whether in Hollywood, London, Berlin, or Paris, was initially viewed as a financial necessity, and it brought many international figures and styles together, but it also muddied the waters about authorship and national styles: "The notion that it is possible to make several versions of the same film, like a piece of clothing in different colors, was and still is abhorrent to the critic, historian, or auteur" (Vincendeau, "Hollywood Babel" 217). Yet the exchange of technical and aesthetic knowledge brought new insights and influences that lasted longer than the practice of multiple-language filmmaking itself.

Several filmmakers pursued hybrid options during this transition from silent to sound. Germaine Dulac made a series of silent short films to be shown along with synchronized records, including songs by realist singers

Constantini approaches the Seine (*Those Women Who Worry*)

Fréhel and Damia about working-class women and prostitutes facing grim options. These social-realist musical "clips" provide a sort of triple feminist intervention with the voice of a famous female performer, an actress personifying the singer's character, and Dulac's cinematic discourse, mixing the worlds of popular music and naturalist film practice in a novel combination of song and moving images. For instance, during the first part of *Those Women Who Worry* (*Celles qui s'en font*, 1928), Lilian Constantini drinks, observes other happier women, and meanders the streets as Fréhel sings "all alone." Part of the time, Constantini appears to be singing the lyrics or talking to herself. In the second section, she plays another, more distraught woman. Scenes of her wandering Paris are intercut with Impressionistic memories of being left by a man, which apparently motivates her to drown herself in the Seine. Dulac labeled these shorts "*impressions cinégraphiques.*"

Luis Buñuel, with script assistance from Salvador Dalí, provided another experimental early sound film with the provocative *The Golden Age* (*L'Age d'or*, 1930), financed by the Vicomte de Noailles, a patron of Surrealism and devotee of Sade. Shot mostly silent, with postsynchronized music, sound effects,

and some dialogue, plus intertitles for the narrator's interventions, *L'Age d'or*
exploited audiovisual counterpoint. Initially granted an exhibition permit
based on the statement that the film was the fantasy of a madman, *L'Age d'or*
opened at the Studio 28 in Paris in fall 1930. However, an attack by an antisemitic fascist gang prompted the police and censors to demand cuts of two of
the most offensive and sacrilegious scenes, and eventually they banned it outright. A manifesto distributed at some shows proclaimed that the film
attacks "this rotting society that is trying to prolong its existence artificially
through priests and policemen."

As with *An Andalusian Dog*, frustrated desire permeates the dream imagery and partly justifies the plot's illogical construction. The woman (Lya Lys)
is first seen being sexually assaulted in the mud by the man (Gaston Modot).
A violent satire, *L'Age d'or* is playfully edited to provide impossible geogra-
phies and metaphorical juxtapositions, including motifs from Buñuel's and
Dalí's auteurist arsenals. Rome seems to be founded on mud and excrement,

Lya Lys (*L'Age d'or*)

modern advertising photos come alive erotically, the gamekeeper shoots his son, and Lys sucks the toe of a statue in her parents' elegant garden. Furthermore, Modot's disruption of a fancy party by slapping Lys's mother, the Marquise, motivates Lys to escape into the garden to make out with him during a concert. As Lys and Modot interact, a female voice announces the joy of having killed one's children, while his face explodes with blood. By the end, titles announce a criminal, sadistic orgy, claiming the worst offender was the Duc de Blangis, but it is a Christ look-alike who walks out the castle door. The final image, accompanied by festive music, is a cross bearing women's scalps. Christianity, patriotism, class, and family were all targets of *L'Age d'or*, which mixed sadism, Freudian symbolism, and Surreal dream work into a very male vision of cinematic revolt that rethinks story logic as well as sound-to-image relations.

The Vicomte de Noailles also produced Jean Cocteau's first film, *Blood of a Poet* (*Le Sang d'un poète*), in 1930, although the problematic reception for *L'Age d'or* delayed its release until 1932. An "intensely personal" film, *"Blood of a Poet* established the dream and psychodrama genres as central to experimental cinema," and inserted figures and motifs already present in Cocteau's poetry and artwork (Thompson and Bordwell 292). While Cocteau claimed to be opposed to Surrrealism, *Blood of the Poet* was based on the free play of creative, preconscious thought and incorporated many visual devices seen in earlier avant-garde films, including a mouth in a hand and eyes painted on a face. Cocteau summarized the project as a cinematic poem exploring the poet's inner self. The film is somewhat anchored around an erotic gaze onto the handsome young poet (Enrique Rivero) and his very acrobatic performance. As with *L'Age d'or*, there are intertitles in *Blood of the Poet*, but the soundtrack and disembodied voices lend a dream-like aura to the fanciful, concrete world unfolding in a series of four sequences. Characters also seem to defy gravity. Cocteau uses a vertical camera for some shots with the wall and ceiling sets placed on the studio floor, recalling early trick films. He clearly enjoys exploring the options of disjunctive editing, moving cameras, subjective points of view, and the potential for alternating sound and silence, as he pursues his trademark artistic preoccupations, including blood, sacrifice, and melancholy young men. Near the end, a black angel comes for a boy killed in a snowball fight, and Cocteau exploits negative imagery for the magical moment of transformation. When *Blood of a Poet* was finally released in early 1932, some artists objected, calling it "counterfeit" Surrealism, but the film proved influential in art houses and museums. In general, personal

The melancholy poet (*Blood of the Poet*)

avant-garde projects such as those by Dulac, Buñuel, and Cocteau were rare as independent French filmmakers struggled to adapt their ideas and practice to the expensive and cumbersome world of sound.

Another side effect of France's production system built around smaller studios and independent producers was the lack of support for a domestic animation industry. Sound only complicated the issue. During the 1920s, a few animated sequences appeared in avant-garde films, but most animators made a living from advertising. After World War I, Lortac (Robert Collard) and O'Galop (Marius Rossillon) set up what may have been Europe's first animation studio. Their company Publi-Ciné created commercials into the 1920s for clients such as Nicolas wine stores, Nestlé, and Citroën automobiles. By the 1930s, a cluster of individual animation auteurs worked independently on short films, often still relying on advertising contracts. Many artist-animators were emigrés who moved to Paris for the arts community and support. The Russian stop-motion filmmaker Ladislas Starewicz and his daughter Irene made a series of sound shorts, including five Duffy the Mascot films between 1933 and 1936. Their major work of the decade was the feature *The Tale of the*

The trickster fox (*Tale of the Fox*)

Fox (*Le Roman de renard*), initially completed in 1937 for Germany's UFA, then released in France in 1941. Credited as the first-ever stop-motion feature film, *The Tale of the Fox* is an adaptation of the medieval Renard cycle about a trickster fox. The Starewicz version animates beastly figures performing biting social satire. Walt Disney initially considered making his own version of the tale, but he feared that a feature film about the thieving, rapacious villain would have to be tamed too much for American audiences. Documentary filmmaker Jean Painlevé also produced and codirected a short stop-motion film, *Blue Beard* (*La Barbe bleue*, 1936), along with animator René Bertrand and music by Maurice Jaubert. Their tale, filmed in vibrant Gasparcolor, also included violence far beyond cartoon norms.

Russian Alexandre Alexeieff and American Claire Parker set up a tiny production house where they created one of the most unique modes of production, the pinscreen, to animate shadows from one million tiny pins. Alexeieff would work on one side of the screen and Parker on the other, moving pins in and out to cast an array of gradations from dim white to near black, for a blurry, Expressionistic result. *Night on Bald Mountain* (*Une nuit sur le mont chauve*, 1933) was a personal, nightmarish vision to accompany the Rimsky-Korsakov version of Mussorgsky's score, complete with tumbling demons, phantom horses, and a sad boy's visions. Alexeieff and Parker also made commercials to keep their venture sustainable. Another immigrant, the Eastern European Berthold Bartosch, who had assisted Lotte Reiniger with her silhouette film *The Adventures of Prince Achmed* (1926), moved to Paris, set up his own little workspace in the Vieux-Colombier Theater, and experimented with eccentric animation tactics for *The Idea* (*L'Idée*, 1932). Bartosch's film adapts a political allegory about a naked female figure sent into the world to support the working class against exploitation. It involves a host of abstract techniques and a haunting soundtrack composed by Arthur Honegger. *The Idea* was never commercially released, proving yet again that the high art aspirations of many animators in France did not fit with the commercial realities of the era.

England's Anthony Gross and American Hector Hoppin established a microstudio, HG Animat, in Paris. Their *Joie de vivre* (1934) uses two-dimensional cel animation with a synchronized soundtrack, without dialogue, for a rather sexist romp featuring a working-class fellow pursuing two graceful female characters across the countryside and into a train station before they all ride happily off into the sky on his bicycle. The women's loose dresses are constantly flying up, and they even take a break to swim in the nude. Despite these varied attempts to launch viable animation projects in France, Betty Boop, Mickey Mouse, Warner Bros., and Silly Symphony cartoons provided nonstop competition. Hollywood cartoons were inexpensive for exhibitors and arrived on a guaranteed schedule, often playing with popular American sound features. One niche studio that made some commercial inroads in France was Paul Grimault and André Sarrut's Les Gémeaux, formed in 1936 to counter the dominance of US animation. However, their optimistic plans never materialized, and most of their output in the 1930s involved advertisements and title sequences. No one established a sustainable studio model for animation during 1930s France.

Live-Action versus Filmed Theater

Unfortunately, some fears that live-action narrative cinema would become more regressive and static under sound's restrictions were coming true: "The tyranny of bad theater would be felt on every level, from the scriptwriter to the producer and director to the theater owner" (Courtade 9). In 1931, even Louis Lumière warned that sound films were retreating toward filmed the-

ater, sacrificing deep space and realistic exterior settings for scenes full of dialogue (*Pour Vous*, January 22, 1931, 2). Many early sound directors had worked
in cinema since the 1910s, including Louis Mercanton, Léonce Perret, and
Henri Diamant-Berger. Sound technology fit easily with their former traditional staging and theatrical acting gestures. The magazine *Pour Vous* repeatedly lamented the absence of films set on location and in nature. Admittedly, many run-of-the-mill productions and multiple-language films did fall
into an efficient studio-bound, canned theater aesthetic, opportunistically
aiming at a domestic audience anxious to hear French spoken and sung on
the screen. In 1931, Osso Films launched a high-profile adaptation of Edmond
Rostand's *L'Aiglon* (*The Eaglet*, Tourjansky), which was shot and released in
French and German versions. It became a target for critics complaining that
sound cinema could slip into subgenre absorbed by theater. Such films were
straying far from the cinematic purity of the 1920s and completely lacking in
photogénie (Smoodin, "Paris"). Typical of this tendency were the many movies adapted from plays, such as those by the popular and prolific Louis Verneuil. For instance, Verneuil's play *My Cousin from Warsaw* (*Ma Cousine de Var-
sovie*, Boese, 1931) was made into a dialogue-centered tale of a banker who
wants to write an opera, while his wife just wants to be left alone with her
lover. It is mostly staged in two- and three-shot conversations in interior sets.
German director Carl Boese nonetheless inserts an Impressionistic scene with
a racing car to add a touch of cinephilia amid the static scenes built around
rapid dialogue, exotic accents, and piano playing. Sixteen titles by Verneuil
were filmed between 1931 and 1935 in France, and his well-made filmed plays
punctuated with musical interludes were also adapted by German, British,
and American studios.

However, as Ginette Vincendeau observes, while "the word-driven nature
of filmed theatre permeated all classical French cinema, across filmmakers
and genres," France's theatrical traditions should not be seen solely as a limiting force ("Forms" 143). A number of early sound films incorporated lively
aspects of musical theater, including operettas to counter static sync-sound
dialogue scenes. Such interludes included actors singing their lines, often shot
silent to allow for more camera and character movement; the prerecorded
music was then used on the soundtrack. For instance, the 1931 romantic comedy *I'll Be Alone after Midnight* (*Je serai seule après minuit*, de Baroncelli) revives
an Albert Jean play about a socialite named Monique (Mireille Perrey) who
decides to get revenge on her unfaithful husband by committing adultery
with a random man. The movie opens with a short, animated sequence of

Cupid shooting arrows. Most of the film's dialogue is sung, including Monique's song about men's sexual appetites. Policemen kill time while singing about their crossword puzzles and one of Monique's many suitors, a black jazz musician, "speaks" via squawks on his saxophone. While static tableau shots dominate in *I'll Be Alone after Midnight*, de Baroncelli opens the space with some back-projected taxi scenes and cut-ins to sources of sounds, such as horns and telephones. When Monique panics and tries to run away from all the men she has attracted to her home, nondiegetic music covers a whirling montage of chaotic images of the chase in a scene right out of a 1920s slapstick comedy. Innovative strategies and theoretical goals begun during the 1920s were being adapted for the new era of sound cinema, as many filmmakers sought to synthesize theatrical and cinematic narrative strategies.

One clever alternative was Duvivier's adaptation of the top-selling novel *David Golder* by Irène Némirovsky, a young author who was later deported and killed at Auschwitz, ultimately becoming famous for her posthumous *Suite française*. Critics at the time heralded Duvivier's *David Golder* (1931) as one of France's first sound masterpieces. Legendary actor Harry Baur plays Golder, a sacrificial Jewish father figure who is exploited financially by his greedy wife and daughter until his weak heart gives out. As his friend announces, "It is the fate of all men: We work ourselves to death so our wives can get rich." Némirovsky's father was a major banker; she knew well the world of casinos, champagne, and extravagant jewels inhabited by the socialite daughter Joyce Golder (Jackie Monnier). Eventually, the aging Golder realizes his wife has long deceived him, Joyce was not really his daughter, and his life's work has been pointless. Exhausted and ill, he manages to secure a final contract with the Soviets before dying on the return trip amid a heavy fog on a steamer. While David Golder is sympathetically portrayed as an overworked, devoted father negotiating the cutthroat world of global oil and investments, caricatures of other Jews around him reinforce dangerous antisemitic stereotypes. Visually innovative, *David Golder* benefits from luxurious sets and costumes as well as expressive lighting setups. *Pour Vous* found the adaptation "faithful and respectful" but complained that the episodic narrative had a certain slowness, "in the German manner" (January 22, 1931, 8). Nonetheless, Duvivier's direction, including location scenes, dialogue spoken offscreen, and highly mobile camerawork regularly reframing the action, helps him avoid the relative stasis of many early sound films.

A second influential Duvivier, *Allo Berlin? Ici Paris!* (1932), which was an RKO and Tobis coproduction, retains spinning cameras, split screens, and

Harry Baur as the devoted father (*David Golder*)

rapid montages. Duvivier anchors the story in the world of modern sounds, with the central characters, male switchboard operators in Germany and female operators in France, meeting over the telephone and falling in love based on their voices. Duvivier alternates scenes between the two nations, with Erich (Wolfgang Klein) and his fellow worker friends speaking mostly German, while his French love interest Lily (Josette Day) can translate German. The romantic comedy's plot is built around the difficulty of their physically meeting, but the soundtrack foregrounds audio gags, with lots of snoring, percussive photo flashes, and singing, including comical choruses and realist French songs. When Lily visits Germany as a translator, the romance is resolved thanks to a nightclub where every table has a telephone. It is a movie about the ways new telecommunications are changing human relations ("Allo Shanghai," "I love you"). This French pre-screwball comedy proved influential and even includes an erotic moment with Lily undressing behind a hung sheet in a scene that returns in *It Happened One Night* (Capra, 1934). During this era, a wide variety of filmmakers as different as Dulac and

The French switchboard women (*Allo Berlin? Ici Paris!*)

Duvivier worked to blend the freedom of their silent film practice with the challenges of synchronized sound, without resorting to the filmed theater norms or tableau compositions that burdened many other productions.

René Clair as Test Case

The coming of sound had made many critics and filmmakers leery of the necessary financial and stylistic restrictions. René Clair, whose silent films had displayed radically innovative camerawork and editing, boldly rethought his film practice to update his personal style with a synchronized soundtrack. He was quite public in his declarations that the visual experimentation and expressive strengths of silent French cinema should not be sacrificed and that soundtracks need not slavishly serve the image. Shots of people standing and delivering dialogue should be reduced to a minimum. His earlier films had always been shown with live accompaniment for great effect; now he continued to shoot silent when possible and added a wild soundtrack to comment on the action and impose a new sense of rhythm. Tobis was looking for French content to produce in their new studio, so they hired Clair to shoot

Under the Roofs of Paris (*Sous les toits de Paris*, 1930). Initially Clair and his crew found the soundstage a strangely quiet, even solemn space where only actors and musicians were allowed to make noise. Yet there were advantages to shooting a prestige production for Tobis. Lazare Meerson designed street sets, a courtyard, and other exteriors inside the soundstage, often working from photographs of specific buildings in Paris that were redrawn and positioned in condensed combinations for a city at once authentic and fanciful (Flinn 42). The big sensation, however, was Clair's sound strategy, which built the music and sound effects in from the beginning as part of the overall narrative structure. The dialogue in *Under the Roofs of Paris* is just one mode of signification among many.

A former songwriter himself, Clair selected an existing tune to serve as a central motivating factor for the film. The main character of *Under the Roofs of Paris*, Albert (Albert Préjean), sells sheet music in the streets, where he meets and falls for Pola (Pola Illéry). Albert tries to protect Pola from the bully Fred (Gaston Modot) in their working-class neighborhood, but when Albert is arrested for unknowingly hiding some stolen loot, Pola ends up falling in love with Albert's best friend, Louis (Edmond Gréville). After Albert is found innocent and released, he realizes Louis and Pola belong together, and he returns to the street where he began, selling sheet music. Throughout, Clair reduced the actors' speech to a minimum, often replacing dialogue with sound effects in a strategy that fits the calls by theorists, including S. M. Eisenstein, to generate sound-to-image montage rather than realistic fidelity.

There are only about a hundred spoken phrases in *Under the Roofs of Paris*, with sound effects, mime-like acting, and other mise-en-scène strategies communicating the characters' emotions and intentions more than dialogue. Charles O'Brien points out that of 127 early sound films he tested, *Under the Roofs of Paris* had the fewest shots with sync-sound dialogue and the most action shots, for a quick average shot length of nine seconds ("*Sous les toits*" 121). Noises, music, and words punctuate the action and generate lively rhythms between image and sound. For instance, an early scuffle between Albert and a pickpocket begins with dialogue, but then nondiegetic music replaces their voices and the silent filming allows a variety of camera positions and editing options. Later, Albert tries to seduce Pola, whispering repeatedly into her ear, but all we hear is silence except for her repeated "no." Clair replaces diegetic sounds with other noises, diegetic or otherwise. We may see a man playing an accordion but hear something quite different, and when Fred and his gang attack Albert in an alley, their mouths can be seen moving, punches are thrown, and bodies fall hard to the ground, yet the only sounds are from a shrieking train rolling past. Clair was interested in the power and novelty of offscreen sound; he was inspired by early sound cartoons that exploited music and sound effects in artificial, comical ways, without relying on dialogue.

Surprisingly, the initial Paris premiere of *Under the Roofs of Paris* met with weak reviews and no subsequent rentals. In an era of "100% talking pictures," Clair's minimal dialogue seemed inappropriate to many. By contrast, its Berlin premiere was spectacular, launching the film's international success and motivating a rerelease in France. This deceptively simple tale, with its leisurely, anecdotal pace, became one of the signature films of the era, rapidly increasing the reputations of Clair and the Tobis sound process. As France's first international sync-sound hit, *Under the Roofs of Paris* inspired the young generation of filmmakers just entering French sound cinema and proved to producers that sound cinema could help promote and sell popular songs as well as star performers.

Pola says "no" (*Under the Roofs of Paris*)

With the triumph of *Under the Roofs of Paris*, Clair quickly launched a new project, adapting an old comic play, *Le Million* (1931). This farce revolved around the race to find a stolen jacket with a lottery ticket inside, and in many ways, it mirrored the fast-paced plot and search in *The Italian Straw Hat*. Clair reworked this wordy, literary text as an operetta. The music was written by a twenty-eight-year-old composer, Georges Van Parys, who believed that cinema could revolutionize the use and distribution of popular music. Beyond the sung dialogue and embedded songs, the script only included a few spoken words, and Clair left the words up to the lead actors to lend a more spontaneous rhythm to their performances. The sets were designed by Meerson and had to include space for the orchestra and offscreen choirs just behind the camera. Clair sought to mix fantasy with everyday naturalism. The plot is told in flashback, beginning with a clever camera movement past models of Paris rooftops built in front of a painted city backdrop and ending on the set for a raucous celebration. The revelers invite their curious neighbors, observing through the roof's skylight, to sit back and listen to the marvelous

The police station (*Le Million*)

tale of what happened that day. As with *Under the Roofs of Paris*, Clair's narrative eventually circles back to this opening setting, bracketing the film with a strong termination effect.

Le Million recounts how struggling artist Michel (René Lefèvre) and his conniving roommate Prosper (Jean-Louis Allibert), hounded by creditors, discover they have bought a winning lottery ticket. Michel is semi-engaged to Béatrice (Annabella), a dancer across the hall, and his eventual happiness depends on claiming his prize to seal the marriage. However, the ticket is in Michel's jacket, which Béatrice unknowingly gave to a fleeing criminal, Granpère Tulipe (Paul Ollivier), who then sells it to an opera singer looking for an authentic Bohemian costume. Pursuits include the police following Tulipe, who also tries to recover the jacket, as well as Michel and Prosper separately chasing after the ticket. Many paths cross in a series of near misses and misunderstandings. Michel even gets arrested at one point, in a plot twist similar to that of *Under the Roofs of Paris*. Once freed, he ends up on the opera stage with Béatrice, hiding behind the props as the show unfolds. While the singers belt out their romantic lyrics, the young couple becomes reconciled behind them, responding emotionally to each sung line.

During the course of the film, Clair comically and creatively foregrounds the artifice of sound cinema. For instance, when Prosper drops a vase, a musical flourish replaces the crash. A slap in the face is also signaled with music, and anyone can suddenly begin to perform in a chorus commenting on the action. During a battle for the jacket, the rushing men are accompanied by nondiegetic crowd noises, as if they were outdoors in a rugby match. Mundane conversations are eliminated or replaced with songs to deliver essential plot information. Eventually, the mercurial Tulipe returns the jacket and ticket in the nick of time, as a favor to Béatrice. The story catches up with the flashback's beginning, with everyone, including the surreal fellow in a bowler hat and boxer shorts, dancing through Michel's studio.

Clair and Tobis had another hit on their hands, as *Le Million* opened quickly in multiple language versions. It premiered in Paris in April 1931 and was already playing in London and New York by June. Critics consistently proclaimed Clair's musical comedy to be the most artistic sound film so far. *Ciné-Magazine* attests that Clair "stuns us with his capacity for invention and his true understanding of a comic style that is specifically French, yet belongs to him alone" (Billard, *Le Mystère* 175). The *New York Times* declared *Le Million* "scintillating entertainment . . . splendidly filmed" (Hall 37). *Le Million* was so popular in the United States that Sam Goldwyn and others tried to

get Clair to move to Hollywood. The fanciful *Le Million* managed to trans-
pose aspects of the purely cinematic visual rhythm, including dance-like cho-
reography and pulsating montages, into a playful synthesis with a creative
soundtrack. Voices were exploited as much for tone and pacing as for delivering story information. Clair's experimentation also paralleled modern
Brechtian strategies, helping win over hold-out fans of silent cinema and high
art critics alike.

Clair conceived of his next Tobis film, *Freedom Is Ours* (*À nous la liberté*, 1931),
when he was walking through a pleasant field and noted a grim line of factories nearby. This juxtaposition led him to build a scenario based on the
oppositions between freedom and imprisonment, nature and social confinement. The overall plot involves the ironic plight of two friends who escape
prison only to create and suffer from prison-like factory settings. Clair worked
quickly with many of the same crew members to create a joyous, comic fantasy with a political point. This third Tobis feature premiered just seven
months after *Le Million*, in December 1931. *À nous la liberté* was another huge
success, though several conservative nations, including Italy and Hungary,
initially banned the film, fearing it could stir up class conflict. *À nous la liberté* fully reinforced Clair's reputation as a master of sound comedy, and Charlie Chaplin later lifted many of its elements directly for his *Modern Times*
(1936). Clair forgave Chaplin, claiming he was honored by the homage, and
he refused to press charges.

À nous la liberté allowed Clair once again to mix clever sound devices with
a fast-paced farce. Louis (Raymond Cordy) and Émile (Henri Marchand) are
in prison for minor thefts and collaborate on an escape plan. The prison's
rhythms are determined by music. Inmates on an assembly line sing in chorus, and the limited dialogue is clearly not recorded in the setting. Cellmates
Louis and Émile quietly sing about freedom as they saw through their bars.
When they break out of their cell, only Louis manages to make it over the
final wall. Later, after robbing a store, Louis launches a career selling phonographs. Eventually he becomes a wealthy industrialist with a spoiled wife
and a huge Art Deco factory producing record players. His workers are organized rigidly, like prisoners. Meanwhile, poor, timid Émile is finally set free,
only to be rearrested for vagrancy. From his cell he hears what he thinks is
the lovely singing voice of the young woman Jeanne (Rolla France) living
across from the jail. The voice is actually from her phonograph record; she
works for Louis. No sound is authentic in this film. Émile escapes and
stumbles into a job in Louis's big factory, ultimately disrupting the efficient

Émile and Louis at the factory (*À nous la liberté*)

operations before reuniting with Louis and reminding him about the joys of living freely. By the end, the two take off anew, as a homosocial couple, singing for coins and rejecting the world of business and family responsibilities, but not before Louis's company allows automation to liberate the workers, creating a happy utopia for all.

Despite the comic action, *À nous la liberté* also explores more serious cultural issues, including Jeanne's sexual harassment by superiors at the factory, blackmail, the assembly line's dismal effects on workers, and the fascist links between school, business, and the police. The scene of money floating down on the crowd of greedy officials during a pompous ceremony recalls the extreme satire of *Entr'acte. Crazy Ray*, with its anarchy and mockery of money, is recalled here as well. Polite society and its repressive rules are continuously ridiculed in this pre–Popular Front social satire. Beyond its critical and box office successes, *À nous la liberté* earned the audience prize at the first Venice Film Festival (prior to being banned in Italy), and Lazare Meerson was nominated for an Academy Award in Art Direction. No foreign film had ever been nominated for a major Oscar before. Reviewers regularly compared Clair to

Ernst Lubitsch and Charlie Chaplin. He was hailed as a great comic director and one of the most important artistic figures in sound cinema.

These three films were followed quickly with *July 14* (*14 juillet*, 1933), also centered around raucous music and sound effects. However, *July 14,* with its love-triangle storyline, seemed out of step with a rapidly changing Europe, where social problems and fears over the rise of fascism were becoming much more pressing. Clair decided to shift away from escapist musical comedies. He offered Tobis a more relevant scenario, *The Last Dictator,* but it was rejected. His next proposal, *The Last Billionaire* (*Le Dernier milliardaire*, 1934), was also refused, although Pathé-Natan picked it up. Its caricatures outraged people on both the extreme right and the left, and it provoked a riot in the theater on opening night. *The Last Billionaire* was a major flop, something Pathé-Natan could ill afford at that point. The studio stopped bankrolling any more films that year.

Disappointed with *The Last Billionaire*'s reception, Clair decided to accept invitations to work in Hollywood, where Groucho Marx and others waited to meet the French comic genius. Clair followed his friend Rudolph Maté, who had also moved to Hollywood. As always, the creative give-and-take between Hollywood and France was complicated. The bulk of France's films came increasingly from small companies and auteur directors and writers who saw Hollywood studios as the enemy, seducing their audiences and stealing their talent. Meanwhile, French newspapers and magazines were obsessed with the lives of Hollywood stars and big-name producers, even as they printed editorials urging their readers to support France's film industry. But some American films proved inspiring for French critics. For instance, in the context of increased economic and political troubles in France, *Pour Vous* argued that King Vidor's *Our Daily Bread* (1934) should serve as a model for a more realistic, socially conscious cinema in France. One of their suggestions was to look to native French sources, including more adaptations of Émile Zola, whose stories are "commercial, dramatic, and socially engaged" (Andrew, *Mists* 199). The balance between following some of Hollywood's strategies while retaining French ideals and content was an ongoing struggle. American and French cinema continued to respond to one another in productive and surprising ways throughout the 1930s.

Jean Renoir's Transition to Sound

Jean Renoir's last three silent films included the rowdy military comedy *The Sad Sack* (*Tire au flanc*, 1928) and two big-budget commercial assignments, *The Tournament* (*Le Tournoi*, 1928), highlighting the magnificent medieval city of Carcassonne, and *Le Bled* (1929), designed to demonstrate the Algerian colony's natural beauty and potential for tourism and investment. All three films display impressive shot composition, with highly mobile cameras to explore the real and exotic settings, although the stories were far removed from social reality. Renoir was anxious to select his own projects and move into sound. He approached Pierre Braunberger, who had produced *Tire au flanc*, and his partner, Roger Richebé, with a proposal to adapt the Georges de La Fouchardière novel *La Chienne* (*The Bitch*, 1931). They had just refurbished their Billancourt studio for sound. However, *La Chienne* looked risky, and they suggested a more modest production that would allow Renoir to learn sound techniques.

Renoir chose to adapt a 1910 farce, *Baby's Laxative* (*On purge bébé*, 1931) as his transitional film. A porcelain manufacturer, Follavoine (Jacques Louvigny), is hoping to secure a contract with the French army for his new unbreakable chamber pots. The military figure in charge of the choice, M. Chouilloux

Satire by Michel Simon and Marguerite Pierry (*On purge bébé*)

(Michel Simon), arrives to test the pots, but Mme. Follavoine (Marguerite Pierry) keeps interrupting, concerned over their young son's constipation. The comedy is broad. The rebellious, "natural" wife clomps around in curlers and a bathrobe toting a slop bucket, ridiculing her overly snobbish husband and trying to get their son to drink his laxative. When put to the test, the pots explode, smashing into pieces, and the woman lets slip that she knows that Chouilloux's wife is unfaithful, which shocks the poor military man into accidentally tossing down the glass full of laxative himself. Once his wife and her lover (Fernandel) arrive to face the accusations, much more than the military contract is ruined.

The production of *On purge bébé* was completely limited to interiors in the Billancourt soundstage. The set was built in a circular pattern around the microphone. Renoir controls the rhythm with character movement, but he also reframes and dollies, shifting the camera from one end of the room to the other when possible. In many ways, his first sound film anticipates early television dramas that learn to adapt to their restrictions. Fortunately, the relatively quiet Debrie sync-sound camera allowed more flexibility than booths or heavily blimped cameras. Renoir filmed *On purge bébé* in six days, with many long takes, followed by six days in postproduction. The average shot length was an impressive twenty-six seconds, among the longest in Charles O'Brien's study of early sound production (*Cinema's* 192). The sound engineer, Joseph de Bretagne, taught Renoir to seek clarity as well as authenticity. Both men opposed postsynchronization and nondiegetic music, preferring direct sound for faithful, naturalistic recording. No music was used in *On purge bébé*, only dialogue and sound effects, including the famous flushing toilet, recorded in a real studio bathroom. For Renoir, the toilet sound functioned in the same way as a musical flourish. The film opened as soon as it was completed, quickly earning five times its cost in the first run, which encouraged Braunberger and Richébé to approve Renoir's *La Chienne* project.

During the early sound period, when budgets included so many new expenses, producers tended to prefer adapting existing plays and novels rather than take a chance on original scripts. Eager to put his own stamp on *La Chienne*, Renoir chose to continue exploring location shooting, direct sound, deep space, and natural, even spontaneous performance styles. *La Chienne* ushered in a cinematic realism that Renoir continued to develop throughout the 1930s. *La Chienne* was also devised as a vehicle for Michel Simon, who plays Maurice Legrand, a clumsy, repressed clerk. He is mocked by everyone, including his penny-pinching wife, who still mourns her late first husband, lost in World War I. Legrand's one pleasure is painting, a hobby his wife detests. One night he rescues a young woman named Lulu (Janie Marèse) from her pimp boyfriend, Dédé (Georges Flamant). Gradually the smitten Legrand manages to steal a bit of money and put Lulu up in an apartment where he can also hide his paintings. However, Lulu continues to see Dédé on the side, and they sell off Legrand's pictures, pretending Lulu is the artist.

Finally, the wife's "dead" first husband resurfaces, liberating Legrand from his marriage, but Legrand also discovers Lulu has been cheating on him with Dédé. Legrand stabs her in a fit of jealous rage, as a street singer and violin player preoccupy everyone outside with their love song. Dédé is condemned for the crime, and the pathetic Legrand wanders off. The epilogue reveals him as a tramp years later, running into his wife's old soldier husband, who has left her again. The two vagabonds team up and receive a nice handout in front of an art gallery that has just sold Legrand's self-portrait.

Renoir's ironic ending is a bit more ambiguous than that of Clair's *À nous la liberté*, where the two men head off playfully into the countryside, but both

Renoir's deep staging (*La Chienne*)

movies end with their protagonists rejecting bourgeois norms and morality. Furthermore, Renoir's *La Chienne* mocks the world of art critics and galleries, a sphere he and his father knew well. Another self-conscious device is the movie's bracketing puppet show announcing violently that this is neither a comedy nor a tragedy and there is no moral lesson to be learned here. Renoir reworked the novel, revealing that each of the characters had their reasons, their actions were determined by their contexts. His narrative does not caricature or judge any of the figures too harshly, except for the shrewish wife.

Stylistically, *La Chienne* paves the way for Renoir's subsequent film practice. He includes deep space shots, including neighbors visible across the courtyard while Legrand paints and argues with his wife in the foreground. Renoir tracks alongside actors walking down the street having conversations in real time. For instance, the first night when Legrand meets Lulu, the actors walk and talk, moving in and out of the lighting provided by streetlamps, a practice copied later by New Wave filmmakers. Furthermore, there is a dizzying dance sequence in which the camera dodges back and forth and bobs up and down as Dédé manipulates Lulu into seducing a rich client. Few sync-sound sequences like these exist elsewhere in 1931 France. Renoir and his crew worked to open up the playing space, shooting on location in the rain and in noisy city streets and pairing camera movements with direct sound when possible, in the studio sets. Marketed as a mature crime drama, *La Chienne* found a large audience, although in the United States *Variety* warned that its many crimes and bedroom scenes kept it from being family fare. *La Chienne* received unsettling press for another reason. During the production, Flamant and Marèse became lovers. He bought a fancy car, much like the one his character drives in the movie. Just after filming ended, he took Marèse on vacation in southern France but lost control of his car, killing her, and casting a sad pall over the postproduction and premiere. *La Chienne* was remade by Fritz Lang in Hollywood as *Scarlet Street* (1945).

Renoir's next four films, shot over two years, allowed him to continue exploring narrative and stylistic options. For *Night at the Crossroads* (*La Nuit du carrefour*, 1932), a low-budget adaptation of a Georges Simenon detective story featuring Inspector Maigret, Renoir shot all exteriors on location and mostly at night, including during rain and bleak winter fog. He continued to insist on direct sound, and often the sound levels are strikingly uneven, especially when several actors speak in the same shot. But the sound and camerawork lend a heightened physical realism to this cinematic adaptation. "Right from the credits sequence, the spectator-listener is overwhelmed with backfiring motorcycles, the scorching sound of a blowtorch breaking open a safe, the sharp bangs of guns and the tooting of car horns" (Marie, "Invention" 60). In addition, some of the key clues for Maigret (Pierre Renoir) come in the form of musical refrains and nervous voices in this *policier* featuring stolen diamonds, speeding cars, and murder. Jacques Becker worked as an assistant, and a number of the actors were friends and nonprofessionals, including Jean Mitry. The evocative settings and daring cinematography with extreme low-key lighting, deep space, and cluttered frames, anticipate both film noir and Italian neorealism. Every character is guilty of something, especially the fascinating femme fatale, Else (Winna Winifried). The opening lines from *La Chienne*, that Lulu is always sincere yet lies all the time, could also be applied to the seductive Else. However, Renoir's adaptation was judged rather incoherent, with portions of the script not filmed or lost in the lab, leading critics to consider it a poor *policier* in terms of plot but an excellent primer for presenting criminal settings and ominous atmosphere.

Renoir released seven films between 1931 and 1934. *Boudu Saved from Drowning (Boudu sauvé des eaux*, 1932) was based on another play and coproduced by Michel Simon. Simon played the free-wheeling tramp Boudu, who leaps into the Seine but is saved by a bourgeois merchant. The merchant tries to rehabilitate the tramp, who ends up disrupting the household and defying their attempts to tame the noble savage. After winning the lottery and marrying the maid, Boudu overturns a boat and all expectations, floating off alone, rejecting his wealth and wife to return to his homeless lifestyle. The women's roles remain more caricatured than in Renoir's previous films, with Simon's physical presence dominating the film. While less polished than Clair's *À nous la liberté*, *Boudu Saved from Drowning* pokes broad fun at class pretensions and celebrates personal freedom and anarchy, mixing theatrical performances, clever sound strategies, and location shooting to reinforce the gulf between the characters' worlds. It also contains a number of what Martin O'Shaughnessy labels Renoir's signature shots, combining staging in depth, embedded frames, and camera mobility ("Shooting" 19). While the press was quite divided on *Boudu Saved from Drowning*, and many mentioned Renoir's rough, inconsistent style, the film played well to audiences hungry for domestic sound films.

Renoir continued with a more famous property, *Madame Bovary* (1934), which was the only film ever produced by a company associated with the publisher Gallimard. France was in a rare situation with many small, undercapitalized companies turning out the bulk of French features in the 1930s.

Some of these producers managed to figure out how to survive on rather limited domestic returns, and others made only one or two films before failing. For instance, after *Boudu Saved from Drowning*, Michel Simon never produced another movie. Nearly three hundred French features were produced by such one-time producers. During 1932 and 1933, the trade press increasingly called attention to the drop in studio productions and the rise in unemployment in the industry. The existing sound studios increasingly rented out their space at rock-bottom prices, often with delayed payment plans, undercutting their business models. For his part, Renoir continued on a path toward location shooting combined with studio interiors when necessary. His rather casual production style often led to clashes with producers, as in *Madame Bovary*, which had to be cut in half for its release. *Madame Bovary*'s premiere also came at a time of violent demonstrations over political and economic scandals, further reducing its box office potential.

Renoir's next feature, *Toni* (1935), marked a decisive turning point in his career and in French sound cinema. Coproduced by Pierre Gaut and Marcel Pagnol, most of *Toni* was shot in a rustic town on the Mediterranean coast.

Toni seeks a room (*Toni*)

The locations and loose, anecdotal story based on a real crime of passion motivated Renoir to develop a realism far removed from literary or theatrical models. A relative newcomer from Pagnol's troupe, Charles Blavette, played Toni, an Italian migrant laborer who rents a room from Marie (Jenny Hélia) and quickly becomes her lover. However, the restless Toni falls for another woman, Josefa (Celia Montalván), who marries a brute instead, leaving Toni to enter a reluctant marriage with Marie. Ultimately, Josefa kills her cruel husband and Toni sacrifices himself, taking the blame. Trying to flee, he is shot and falls dead along the railway tracks where he arrived at the beginning. Another wave of poor, naive immigrants descend from the latest train, hoping for better lives.

The bittersweet *Toni* features a large ensemble cast. The dialogue is peppered with everyday expressions, delivered in authentic regional accents, but the visual style signaled a maturing of Renoir's filmmaking. In his drive to mirror documentary strategies, he often films actors from behind as they speak, with diegetic noises reinforcing the authenticity of the space. Long takes and oblique angles resemble homages to Lumière, and cameras track along the roads or perch on cliffs in the quarry as if trying to capture some real action already unfolding. Renoir's shot compositions are often packed with bodies organized to emphasize multiple planes of action. Many of his trademark tactics are on display here in this very empathetic narrative about working-class communities and especially women's limited social options. A young Luchino Visconti worked as an assistant director and was strongly influenced by Renoir's mode of production. The arrival of sound allowed Renoir to engage more fully with characterization, while his camerawork and soundtracks complemented each other, generating an impressive and ultimately influential auteur style that matured as the decade continued.

New Theatrical Influences: Marcel Pagnol and Sacha Guitry

Renoir's aesthetic choices in *Toni* ran counter to the studio-bound practice of much of early 1930s French cinema and pleased critics looking for new options. Even mainstream film magazines were asking, "Don't you miss exteriors?" and saying, "Cinema must escape theater!" While many voices pleaded for more cinematic sound productions, theatrical models remained deeply entwined with filming conventions, and sound studio recording techniques established for music and radio shows shaped how sync-sound scenes were staged. Sound engineers from radio were in keen demand, especially if they had experience with remote recording. Cinema became increasingly

attractive to theatrical performers now that sound had arrived. Dubbing foreign films into French also became a steady source of work for actors with
voice training, especially those who spoke several languages. The Depression hurt live theater quickly, driving actors, singers, dancers, writers, designers, and directors to find work in the movies. Among those migrating to
cinema were two of the most popular figures in French theater: Marcel Pagnol and Sacha Guitry. Despite their separate trajectories, both helped recon-
cile creatively the two worlds of stage and screen.

While Pagnol was of Renoir's generation, he had never been associated
with the French avant-garde. He grew up in Marseille and was proud of
his Provençal culture and region. After moving to Paris, he sought out and
befriended playwrights, including André Antoine, and wrote several mod-
estly successful plays. Then in 1928, Pagnol's smash-hit *Topaze* launched his
career and pointed him toward popular domestic melodramas. His next play,
Marius, staged in 1929, fully established his narrative world, filled with comical families torn between tradition and modernity, forced to confront gender conflicts. While French theater regularly privileged formal language,
Pagnol gathered actors from the Marseille region to speak with authentic dia-
lects and local expressions. This play was also a major success.

Pagnol rose to fame in theater just as sound cinema was taking hold in
France, and he quickly shifted from stage to screen, arguing publicly that
sound cinema made both live theater and silent cinema obsolete. He wrote
forceful essays on motion pictures, even coining the phrase *cinématurgie*,
arguing that the best cinema involved creatively updating theatrical principles. The camera, microphone, and editing all liberated the stage play and
script. Fortunately for Pagnol, Paramount's Robert Kane took an immediate interest in adapting *Marius*. However, Pagnol was opposed to the Hollywood studio models that minimized the role of the screenwriter, and he
demanded an unprecedented amount of control and a higher percentage of
profits. After Paramount agreed to his conditions, Pagnol announced proudly
that an American studio was finally producing a truly "French" film. Ultimately, *Marius* became one of the most prestigious films produced by Paramount in France.

Alexander Korda directed *Marius* (1931), working closely with Pagnol on
planning the shooting script, and he retained Pagnol's main actors from the
theatrical production. Thanks to its stage and screen successes, *Marius* became
the first installment of a popular trilogy, followed by *Fanny* (Allégret, 1932)
and *César* (Pagnol, 1936). The family melodrama follows Marius (Pierre

Marius confronts Fanny and Panisse (*Marius*)

Fresnay), who is frustrated at helping his demanding father, César (Raimu), run their bar on the harbor in Marseille. Marius dreams of the life of a sailor, and at the end of the first film, he abandons his devoted girlfriend, Fanny (Orane Demazis), to travel the world. In *Fanny*, it turns out that Marius had left Fanny pregnant. César's wealthy old widower friend Panisse (Fernand Charpin) agrees to marry her and raise her child as his own. When Marius comes home and discovers that he has a son, Césariot, and Fanny is married to old Panisse, there is a confrontation in which César charges Marius with having treated Fanny poorly in the past, behaving like a selfish dog. Panisse has become Césariot's true, loving father. Crushed, Marius leaves home a second time. For the epilogue, *César*, Pagnol directed the tale of Marius returning years later. Fanny confesses to a grown Césariot that Panisse, now dead, was not his biological father. Reconciled, Fanny and Marius may finally marry, bringing everything full circle. In its review, *Pour Vous* praised the final installment for its high quality and marvelous acting, concluding that Pagnol provided an immense contribution to French cinema with his trilogy.

Thanks to the popularity of *Marius*, *Fanny*, and other projects, Pagnol formed his own production company in 1934, complete with a studio and film processing facility in Marseille. He also bought a portable sound recording truck for location shooting. Freed from having to send rushes to Paris for processing, Pagnol became self-sufficient in Marseille, where he helped make southern France a viable hub for film production. His reliance on a steady stream of local culture, cuisine, and populist (often sexist) sentiment has motivated some to label his folksy output as *pagnolade*. Though comically mocked by the narrative, César always knows best, as his caricatured performance of the father reinforces patriarchy and paternity at every turn. As Ginette Vincendeau observes, "The mechanics of desire, repression, and economics that propel the narrative along are practically spelt out by the dialogue" ("Name" 11). The films generate great empathy toward Fanny's plight in a repressive, sexist society, but the older men display the best parenting and survival skills. *Marius* initiated Pagnol's formula for nostalgic, melodramatic, and moralizing fictional worlds: "It was truly a harbinger of a kind of realism that would become crucial to French cinema soon enough, realism spiked with Pagnol's inimitable poetic dialogue" (Andrew, *Mists* 98). Pagnol was also clever at asserting his authorship, overshadowing directors Korda and Allégret in the publicity campaigns.

Throughout the trilogy and in subsequent Pagnol films, everyone's gestures are exaggerated, in a sort of hybrid of theatrical and cinematic styles, with the actors often striking and holding poses as if on stage and waiting to make sure they have everyone's attention for a laugh or a tear. For instance, in the first film, Marius leans dramatically in to listen as Fanny flirts with old Panisse, in a scene right out of burlesque comedy, while later Fanny swoons, overcome with grief, cleverly distracting César as she sacrifices her own happiness to cover for Marius sailing away. The performances owe much to boulevard theater traditions, while the serious themes, including unexpected pregnancies and false fathers, countered the puritanical norms of 1930s Hollywood. Pagnol and his directors exploited synchronized sound and mood music to lift the action off the stage and into the realm of sound cinema. These movies were much more dialogue-centered than those by Clair or Renoir, yet their regional accents and rapid-fire banter were a large part of their attraction. Pagnol productions also established many stereotypes of

César scolds Marius and Fanny (*Fanny*)

southern France for the screen, including "a more relaxed leisurely lifestyle, not to mention an accent and vocabulary which lend color and humor to any narrative. Southerners are more volatile. . . . Their emotions are never far from the surface" (Crisp, *Genre* 59).

Marius, Fanny, and *César* all generated huge profits. Each was at the top of the list of best movies for their year, and they played on and on in second-run houses. The trilogy's *pagnolade* proved incredibly popular. *Fanny,* which cost under two million francs, earned nineteen million in its first run alone. The films' posters by Albert Dubout helped anchor these iconic Pagnol characters firmly in the cultural imagination. Globally the trilogy was a hit, not only during the 1930s but during subsequent rereleases over the decades and up to today, shaping the cultural myths of southern France. Pagnol's subsequent southern films and novels included *Angèle* (1934), another tale about a woman seduced and abandoned, and adaptations of Jean Giono's tales of Provence such as *Harvest* (*Regain,* Pagnol, 1937), about the rebirth of an abandoned village, and *The Baker's Wife* (*La Femme du boulanger,* 1938). In the latter, a young wife (Ginette Leclerc) runs off with a handsome farmhand, abandoning her older, dull husband (Raimu) and his bakery, before returning home, to everyone's relief. Pagnol celebrated family, rural life, and southern culture and traditions, while simultaneously revealing the comic absurdity behind social conventions, authority figures, and self-serving definitions of virtue. With his string of hits and personal mode of production, Pagnol provided a highly profitable and sustainable model for 1930s French cinema and beyond. Moreover, his Marseille studio proved especially valuable during the 1940s and the Occupation. Being situated far from Paris brought unexpected advantages beyond the authenticity of an alternative, regional perspective.

While Pagnol made a bold move into cinema just as his theatrical career took off, Sacha Guitry was already a major established theatrical force when sound arrived. Guitry wrote his first play in 1902, followed by more than 120 more titles, and he performed in many of them as well. He had no interest in silent cinema, and early sound films seemed only to verify his views on the medium's limitations. Regularly disappointed by the initial filmed versions of his plays, such as the Raimu vehicle *Black and White* (*Le Blanc et le noir*, Allégret and Florey, 1931), in 1932, he presented a talk, "For Theater, Against Cinema." Guitry's opinion mattered. He was the most popular playwright in France (some said in all of Europe), specializing in boulevard comedies and historical dramas. Even during the depths of the Depression, from 1930 to 1934, when live theater was suffering, eighteen different plays by Guitry were staged in Paris alone. However, in 1935, when Guitry heard that Warner Bros. was planning a movie on Louis Pasteur, his new young wife, actress Jacqueline Delubac, convinced the fifty-year-old Guitry to adapt and direct his own 1919 play *Pasteur* for the screen. He ended up performing as the title character and narrator, just as his father had in the play. Working with producer and codirector Fernand Rivers, Guitry followed *Pasteur* quickly with *Good Luck* (*Bonne chance!*, 1935), his first original screenplay, starring Delubac and himself. A lively romantic romp, *Good Luck* echoes their real lives. Guitry plays an older man, providing fatherly guidance and companionship for the younger Delubac's character, which leads to them jumping into bed and marriage. While the film is dialogue-heavy, it inserts brief exterior scenes of the pair climbing into airplanes and sporty cars, as Guitry overtly signals that he is breaking free of the physical limits of his theatrical productions.

Guitry appreciated the vast reach of cinema, which allowed him to expand his auteur status to new audiences. He was billed as the star actor, author, and director. He entered cinema with a rare burst of productivity. *Pasteur* and *Good Luck* actually premiered on the same day in Paris in September 1935, and Guitry directed nine more feature films over the next four years, in addition to writing new plays. He began to use storytelling and sound strategies that were not possible on a stage. For *The Story of a Cheat* (*Le Roman d'un tricheur*, 1936), he devised a sort of one-man show, as the central character recounts his life, narrating over flashbacks and even supplying the voices for other characters who are seen but not heard. He thought of the movie as a sort of documentary version of his only novel, *Memoirs of a Cheat*, published the year before. The opening title sequence is justly famous for Guitry's voice-over introduction of the key crew members and actors.

The narrative unfolds from Guitry's character's perspective, sitting in a café, writing his memoirs to the accompaniment of Adolphe Borchard's whimsical music. The first flashback shows how the character cheated death as a boy, the only survivor of an extended rural family that was wiped out by poisonous mushrooms. From then on, the chronological flashbacks follow his life from a series of early service jobs and gambling triumphs and failures to complex romantic relationships, including attractions to a young man as well as multiple women over his lifetime. Two other actors play the

Guitry writing the memoir (*Story of a Cheat*)

younger versions of Guitry's character, and Delubac appears as a gambling accomplice and temporary wife. Except for several discussions at the café, and a song by realist singer Fréhel, the entire film is shot silent, with Guitry filling in commentary, providing voice-over narration to accompany a montage of his life. Guitry thus pulled off a movie that was shot like a silent and yet was 100 percent talkie.

The Story of a Cheat displays Guitry's many talents, but it also reveals his desire to combine intermedial influences. Reviews foregrounded his multiple roles and disguises and argued that it was both good literature and good cinema. There are scenes that remind one of silent comedies, including soldiers marching forward and backward, but also the inclusion of a café-concert song, "And That's Why," by Fréhel: "Although the sequence as a whole is meant to be comic, Fréhel's appearance connotes lost sexuality, intense emotion, a generalized nostalgia, and a sense of community" (Conway, *Chanteuse* 97). Filmed mostly in high key light with a very professional polish throughout, *The Story of a Cheat* was a huge international success. Guitry's bold move of writing, directing, acting, and even speaking for the other characters was celebrated as a risky novelty act, and the *New York Times* found the result "a witty, impudent, and morally subversive show which everyone should see" (September 27, 1938: 25). Guitry and his team continued at a hectic pace, following *Story of a Cheat* with two more features that opened in November and December 1936, before completing *The Pearls of the Crown* (*Les Perles de la couronne*) in early 1937, codirected by Christian-Jaque.

The Pearls of the Crown provided another occasion for Guitry and his fellow actors to play a wide range of characters. The tale involves three different international teams simultaneously pursuing a mythical cluster of seven pearls as they change hands through history. Guitry as narrator Jean Martin excitedly tells Françoise Martin (Delubac) the amazing tale he has just learned about the four enormous pearls on the British queen's crown. He instructs her to close her eyes and imagine the events he will narrate. Simultaneously, a British official tells his version to the queen in English, and an Italian narrates the story of the pearls to the pope. There are three accounts in three languages that overlap and diverge, beginning with events in the sixteenth century when seven giant pearls are found, assembled into a necklace for Catherine de' Medici and then stolen and partly lost across time. Four of the pear-shaped pearls grace the British crown. The stories continue to the present day when the three men meet up in their search for the latest news on the lost pearls. The key actors play multiple roles. Guitry appears as four

Arletty as an African queen (*Pearls of the Crown*)

figures; Delubac plays three, including Marie Stuart and Joséphine. A host of famous performers join in the lavish production, including Jean-Louis Barrault as a young Napoleon and Arletty as an Abyssinian queen, perversely performing in blackface and body paint. *The Pearls of the Crown* relies mostly on carefully staged interior scenes, heavy with dialogue, and only occasional exteriors to open up the space with farcical chases and historical settings. Guitry's voice-over regularly comments on and replaces action in another self-conscious performance. At one point, Guitry/Jean Martin even says that if he can locate one of the lost pearls, he might make a film about it, further blurring the lines between his persona and the characters. The Martins locate the final pearl, but Jean clumsily drops it overboard into the ocean, suddenly ending the movie.

Pearls of the Crown was the fourth biggest hit that year, and France was not alone in celebrating Guitry's talents. When it opened in the United States in 1938, the *New York Times* review was titled "Sacha the Great." Guitry's reputation continued to grow with a steady stream of films, including *Désiré* (1937) with Delubac and Arletty, in which he personally addresses the audience and introduces the players from a photo album. *Quadrille* (1938) opens with "l'auteur" Guitry at his desk, pen in hand, ever the great performer and genius behind another polished tale in which his character becomes romantically involved with two women, played by Delubac and Gaby Morlay. Guitry became a powerhouse of 1930s French cinema, writing and directing twelve features between 1935 and 1939. His dialogue-packed, highly polished farces were popular but remained rather insulated from other cinematic trends and political realities of the decade. Ultimately, Guitry's self-centered stance and disregard for social engagement cost him dearly with critics and audiences by the time of the Occupation and Liberation in the 1940s.

Jean Vigo's Poetic Anarchy

One of the renegade young directors of the early 1930s who helped reshape French film practice in surprising ways was Jean Vigo. Vigo's father was a well-known political radical who died mysteriously in prison soon after being arrested, when Jean was only twelve years old. Physically frail, Vigo read film journals, including articles by Delluc and Epstein on *photogénie*, often while recuperating in a sanitarium. Early on, he decided to pursue a career in cinema. In his twenties, and newly married to Elizabeth Lezinska, a fellow patient, Vigo managed to pull together support to produce his first film, a short experimental documentary, *À propos de Nice* (1930). Dziga Vertov's brother Boris Kaufman operated the camera and collaborated with Vigo, who learned his craft as they worked together. The movie is organized around a series of themes and contrasts pitting the casinos and beaches of Nice, populated by idle tourists, against the narrow old city of the working-class residents. Vigo and Kaufman mock the seemingly doomed upper classes and their rituals, comparing them to mannequins, grotesque carnival figures, and cemetery statues. Praised for its quirky camera work, trick effects, and montages, *À propos de Nice* was distributed briefly in 1931. His second shorter documentary, *Taris* (1931), offers a somewhat tongue-in-cheek tribute to the star swimmer Jean Taris. It also allowed Vigo to learn underwater filming, which he exploited more fully in *L'Atalante* (1934). *Taris* was a commissioned project from Germaine Dulac via Gaumont (GFFA). She appreciated Vigo's ironic vision, and when he began a ciné-club in Nice, Dulac was one of his first guests.

Though Vigo and his wife were ill and poor, they pursued his career and found Jacques-Louis Nounez, who was willing to help produce *Zero for Conduct* (*Zéro de conduite*, 1933), a low-budget, medium-length film based on Vigo's

experiences growing up in various boarding schools. The producer struck a
deal with GFFA for access to modest studio facilities during Christmas holidays, when the space was in low demand. Kaufman again served as cinematographer. Occasionally he and other crew members stepped in to help direct
when Vigo became too weak. The process was rushed and often chaotic, both
in the studio and on location, and the crew was often forced to shoot scenes
in one take (Temple, 54). There are many casually framed shots with uneven
lighting levels and a jarring mix of performance styles. Maurice Jaubert's
musical score helped lend unity and compensate for the minimal dialogue.
Much of the free-wheeling lyricism ascribed to the film can be credited to
the creative soundtrack. Vigo's plot often veers off in unexpected directions,
and some scenes halt abruptly, as *Zero for Conduct* leaps from one of its eight
sequences to the next.

Zero for Conduct opens with boys returning to their boarding school after
a vacation. A new teacher, Huguet (Jean Dasté), is joining the staff, and this
hapless dreamer amuses the rebellious students and frustrates the other fac-
ulty throughout. The students smoke and roughhouse when they can, while
the bored Huguet imitates Chaplin at recess and doodles during class, which
suddenly becomes an animated shot. During a recreational walk through
town, Huguet forgets his duties and students, as everyone wanders off in their
own directions. The teachers are all cruel, and their clueless principal is
played by a bearded little person (Delphin), whose size and voice are more
childlike than the students. Tabard, a sensitive boy who troubles the administrators as a possible homosexual, surprises everyone by insulting the teachers and siding with the tough rebellious kids. The night before a school ceremony, the boys declare war and turn their dorm into a frenetic battleground,
with pillow feathers flying in slow motion in a delirious parade, and their
supervisor tied and propped up like an unfortunate crucifix. On the day of
the school's celebration for local officials, a mix of mannequins and officials
in the audience are assaulted by Tabard and his co-conspirators, who throw
debris on them from the rooftops and scramble off to freedom.

Georges Sadoul hailed *Zero for Conduct* as one of the great masterpieces of
French cinema, whose poetry, psychological depth, and anarchy influenced
generations of directors (*Dictionary*, 430). But *Zero for Conduct* divided contemporary critics and was banned for its attack on the French educational
system. Vigo's film was one of eleven movies censored outright in 1933, earning a cult status among his followers and defenders, some of whom interpreted it as an allegory about the corrupt government. *Zero for Conduct* was

finally released after World War II and became one of the standards of the
ciné-club circuit, along with Vigo's subsequent feature, *L'Atalante*. Nounez
took another chance on Vigo and obtained the rights to *L'Atalante*, a script
by Jean Guinée about newlyweds on a barge who break up and then reunite.
The project seemed safe and commercial since Jean Gabin and Madeleine
Renaud had recently starred in another barge movie, *La Belle Marinière*
(Lachman, 1932), a picturesque melodrama about a skipper and his frustrated
young wife. Much of the *Zero for Conduct* crew remained for *L'Atalante*, bolstered by better sound technicians and professional actors Dita Parlo and
Michel Simon, along with Jean Dasté and Louis Lefebvre. Although *L'Atalante*
proved an exceptional auteur production in many ways, it also fit some low-
budget economic norms of 1930s production, with a small-time, independent
producer negotiating with the struggling Gaumont for deals on studio space,
film stock, and distribution. However, this feature, shot mostly on location,
also foregrounds Vigo's surreal tendencies, anarchist spirit, and love of improvisation. Despite the difficult conditions and rushed eleven-week shooting
schedule, *L'Atalante* offers a lyrical style with some of the most striking images
of 1930s French cinema, extending the spirit of *photogénie* from the 1920s.

    Vigo's film begins with the wedding of Juliette (Parlo) and Jean (Dasté) in
her tiny village, which is quickly followed by a hectic departure, during which
she is brought on board like a sack of grain. From the first disjointed images
of the Atalante barge, Vigo evokes an alien, dreamlike atmosphere, with
stunning images of Juliette in her wedding gown, clusters of cats attacking
Jean, and Père Jules (Michel Simon) serenading her with his accordion. Vigo
inserts jarring shots to disrupt spatial continuity, but he also includes long
takes with great depth. However, from the start the story concentrates on
how Jean's repetitive job disappoints and disorients Juliette. She quickly tires
of the demanding work and isolation but is amused by the advances of a traveling peddler on shore. Tempted to see Paris beyond its mundane docks,
Juliette sneaks out on her own to peek in the stylish shop windows. Jean
refuses to wait. Alone, Juliette discovers quickly that the city provides brutal challenges. During her absence, Vigo cuts back and forth between the
struggling Juliette seeking work during Depression-era France and the clueless Jean, who gradually sinks into a despondent state. He nearly drowns himself hoping to see her image underwater. To reveal the husband and wife's
trauma and longing, Vigo presents an erotic alternating montage dissolving
from Juliette restless in her bed to Jean writhing in his. Finally, Père Jules
seeks out Juliette and literally hauls her back to the barge, where the reunited

Superimposed Juliette and Jean (*L'Atalante*)

couple embraces and rolls happily on the floor once again. Despite the cheerful resolution, *L'Atalante* underscored the tough social conditions of the era,
when every worker was vulnerable to unemployment and pleasure was fragile and temporary.

Vigo's meandering scene-to-scene construction provided opportunities for
powerful performance pieces. For instance, when Juliette visits Jules in his
room full of memorabilia, the crusty sailor puts on quite a show of his odd,
collected objects, including his friend's pickled hands and his own tattooed
body, as he mumbles incoherently. Later, a depressed Jean makes a mad dash
down an empty beach to the water's edge in a shot resembling a Surrealist
painting. This scene later inspired François Truffaut's ending for *The 400 Blows*
(*Les Quatre cents coups*, 1959). Yet Juliette, Vigo's first and last female character, ends up as the heart of the film, befuddling and inspiring the three
eccentric men with her independent spirit and curiosity. *L'Atalante* was
well received, and reviews emphasized the film's poetic nature and authenticity, with its evocative imagery, melancholy atmosphere, and haunting
music by Jaubert. The disorienting glimpses of riverbanks, docks, and back-

Vigo's poetic use of location (*L'Atalante*)

sides of cities present a realist vision rarely seen in mainstream cinema. Art historian Elie Faure, writing for *Pour Vous*, emphasized the poetic imagery of *L'Atalante*, claiming it reminded him of the "fugitive shadows" of Rembrandt, and its shots of water and landscape recalled Corot's paintings (Salles Gomes, 186). Other reviews repeatedly celebrated Vigo's magical, poetic vision. Many historians point to *L'Atalante* as the beginning of the Poetic Realism tendency in 1930s French cinema.

Unfortunately, the exhausting production schedule and damp conditions weakened Vigo. He died just after the Paris premiere of *L'Atalante*. In his short career, he completed fewer than three hours of cinema, far less than Guitry turned out in a year, but he proved more influential than most filmmakers of his era. Ironically, on the day before Vigo died, *Mon Ciné* concluded its review of *L'Atalante* with the hope that Vigo would soon make another film, strengthened by experience. His death startled many of his supporters and led to appeals for the release of *Zero for Conduct* as a tribute. In the 1940s, French filmmakers and critics rediscovered Vigo. Screenwriter Pierre Bost even argued that the dead director had pointed them toward the future: "The path that Vigo would have taken is the path that French cinema can still take. Where French cinema will go, Jean Vigo will already have been" (Temple 147). Vigo's status has continued to rise, and since 1951, the Prix Jean Vigo has been awarded every year to promising new works.

Populist Realism and 1930s Genre Cinema

The Depression began relatively slowly in France but gradually rattled much of the economy. French businesses began to lose markets abroad, which led to fewer investments in manufacturing at home. Most French workers were employed in smaller-scale factories and enterprises, which were most vulnerable to these new economic conditions. Ironically, within cinema, the chaotic economic and technological conditions of sound provided a highly innovative environment for parts of France's film industry: "Paradoxically, despite (or possibly because of) vertical disintegration, endemic bankruptcies, and many short-lived new upstarts, cinema was the fastest growing French industry in the 1930s, growing 5.3 percent annually, while industries overall shrank 1.6 percent" (Bakker 50). Furthermore, motion pictures remained thematically pertinent during the volatile Depression era by featuring stories that acknowledged the precarious position of the average person. Popular films regularly satirized the naively optimistic and insensitive bourgeoisie. A growing pessimism is credited with motivating a new cluster of socially engaged melodramas and crime films, many built around gender and ethnic battle lines, including a number of popular movies fascinated with the contradictions of France's colonial territories.

The arrival of sound brought a wave of popular music and voices into French cinema, but there was nothing in Depression-era France to parallel Hollywood's luxurious, escapist musical comedies. Instead, as Kelley Conway points out, bleak songs and realist singers, descendants of café-concerts and music hall traditions, dominated 1930s French musical numbers. Women singers, including Mistinguett and Fréhel, built their careers on a mix of nostalgia for better days long gone and sadness over the misery and disappointment of their lives today (Conway, *Chanteuse* 4–9). The songs themselves, whether in backstage musicals or inserted in bar and dance hall scenes, were typically tied to gritty working-class environments populated by small-time hoods and women living on the fringes of decent society. Sad ballads by and about desperate women regularly establish the milieu, comment on the action, and even motivate the characters in early 1930s films such as *Song of the Streets* (*Dans les rues*, Trivas, 1933) or two films by Louis Valray, *La Belle de nuit* (1934) and *Thirteen Days of Love* (*Escale*, 1935). Live realist music in seedy bars and records played in grim hotel rooms are common in crime melodramas of the era.

Music and a tough working-class milieu are also central to *Lilac* (*Coeur de Lilas*, Litvak, 1932), a tale about the street-savvy Lilas (Marcelle Romée) driven to murder and the undercover detective (André Luguet) who tracks her down but falls for her. Jean Gabin plays a local tough guy who loves her as well. The émigré director Anatole Litvak filmed on location, when possible, to preserve the sense of place. Portions of *Lilac* are shot silent with sound effects added later, keeping sync-sound dialogue to a minimum to allow for mobile camerawork and flashy montages. Even Litvak's studio-bound shots often include props looming in the foreground for naturalistic, cluttered frames, reinforced by sounds from the surrounding environment. When the men fight over Lilas in the bar, for instance, most of the action is offscreen, revealed by shadows and the sound of blows struck and breaking glass. Music was one of the movie's selling points, with Gabin aggressively belting out "The Rubber Kid" in a dance hall for a sexually aggressive duet with Fréhel: "The street

Romée backed by shadows of a fight (*Coeur de Lilas*)

'produced' Fréhel, and, in turn, Fréhel brings the street to *Coeur de Lilas* and to the spectators through her songs and her persona" (Conway, *Chanteuse* 104). Music and song provide important diversions in this crime drama; even a young Fernandel sings a lively song. When Lilas decides to turn herself in for murder, a raucous wedding party swirls around her, and as she runs to the police, superimposed Impressionist visions haunt her. Reviewers celebrated the film's visual and psychological realism. Sadly, Romée ended her own life by leaping into the Seine later that year, just as her career was taking off.

Marc Allégret's *Zouzou* (1934) was a significant backstage musical starring African American star Josephine Baker as Zouzou alongside her "twin brother" Jean (Gabin). The plot, in which working-class Zouzou goes from entertaining the other women in the laundry to helping save a musical show when the star leaves, parallels Baker's own rags-to-riches life. Initially, both Zouzou and Jean sing spontaneously for fun until he tricks her into displaying her talents for the desperate producers: "Her dance, in which she imitates the head-bobbing movement of a chicken, walks on all fours, and does the Charles-

Jean, Zouzou, and Claire (*Zouzou*)

ton, reproduces the combination of sensuality, animality, jazz, and primitivism that Baker symbolized for French audiences" (Conway, *Chanteuse* 142). Eventually, Jean finds love, but with a white French laundress, Claire (Yvette Lebon). Zouzou's performance guarantees her success but not romantic happiness. Allégret's mise-en-scène mixes realistic settings with Busby Berkeley–style musical numbers incorporating high camera angles and impossible stage sets to display the exotic Zouzou, who even appears on stage in a large bird cage. Baker returns as an outsider from the colonies dropped into Parisian society for the fantasy musical *Princess Tam Tam* (Gréville, 1935). She performs extravagant numbers once again, including showing the chorus girls how to dance "la Conga," before ending up back in her own land with her own people. *Zouzou* and *Princess Tam Tam* reinforced Baker's star persona as well as many colonialist themes of 1930s French cinema in which exotic women fascinate white men but then leave that space one way or another. It is thus another site "where discourses on national identity, imperialism and cultural assimilation unfold" (Bey-Rozet, "Casbah" 108).

Other popular genre films, especially family melodramas and *policier* detective films, built an empathy for everyday people struggling for happiness in an unforgiving world. For instance, Jean Benoît-Lévy and Marie Epstein both experimented in documentary before collaborating on several highly influential movies based on child-rearing, including *Children of Montmartre* (*La Maternelle*, 1933). This sensitive tale, based on an award-winning novel, was particularly timely during the Depression. The main character, an upper-class educated young woman named Rose (Madeleine Renaud), is rejected by her fiancé after her father loses their fortune and commits suicide. Rose drops out of her elegant world, taking a modest maid position in a nursery school, where she bonds with the poor children and adopts a street walker's troubled daughter. Ultimately, she is rewarded by marrying the nice schoolmaster. The grim realities of the children's lives and Rose's newly formed family reinforce a moralizing message that France must take care of its children, and modern women must make sacrifices and do their part. Benoît-Lévy and Epstein concentrated the action into cramped spaces, reinforcing the claustrophobia of the poor characters' living and working environments, which also worked well in the limitations of studio sound recording. Location shooting is used for one scene when the distraught young girl attempts to drown herself in the harbor after imagining Rose abandoning her for the principal, seen as a subjective Impressionist vision in the water. *La Maternelle* was incredibly successful in France and abroad and motivated

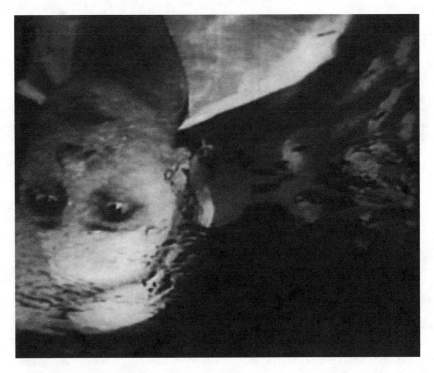

Girl's suicidal vision (*La Maternelle*)

open discussions about child welfare and women's roles and representations in cinema and society.

Many French films of the early 1930s included woman-centered melodramas confronting social inequality and melodramatic marital predicaments. Two examples in particular reveal the differences in tone and content from their Hollywood competition. *Dainah the Cross-Breed/Mulatto* (*Daïnah la métisse*, Grémillon, 1931) and *Whirlpool* (*Remous*, Gréville, 1935) confront issues that mainstream cinema typically skirted. Financial difficulties at Gaumont forced Grémillon and Charles Spaak, who adapted the novel, to reduce *Dainah* to fifty minutes for release as a *moyen métrage* rather than a conventional feature. Dainah (Laurence Clavius) is mixed race, while her husband, Smith (Habib Benglia), is black; both defy colonialist stereotypes of the era, with their perfect French diction and elegant clothes. While traveling on a luxury ocean liner, Dainah boldly flirts with other men, while her husband, a skilled magician, looks on. However, Dainah also attracts the attention of a

Dainah's exotic mask (*Daïnah la métisse*)

white machinist on the boat, Michaux (Charles Vanel), who tries to rape her one night and attacks and throws her overboard the next. Her husband takes revenge, striking Michaux, sending him crashing to his death in the engine room. Clavius and Benglia form a unique couple for the era, and Grémillon's camera foregrounds the intensity of their performances, including Dainah's exhibitionistic dancing and Clavius's magic act during a wild masked ball. The white passengers are mostly portrayed as ridiculous in contrast to the glamorous black couple. *Daïanah la métisse* is a boldly stylish film with Art Deco sets and a soundtrack that allows diegetic sounds to drown out dialogue, anchoring the characters in their noisy environment. The short format and daring plot, including its rare representation of race and sexuality, limited the film's initial distribution.

Whirlpool explores a different sort of unconventional marriage. The wealthy Jeanne (Jeanne Boitel) and Henri Saint-Clair (Jean Galland) begin a sexually charged, fairy-tale honeymoon in a string of luxury hotels, but a car accident renders him slightly disabled and completely impotent. Henri goes back to designing a huge dam project, while Jeanne tries to remain supportive, but she is clearly frustrated with separate beds and an evening kiss on the forehead. As she starts to socialize again, she begins an affair with her best friend's boyfriend, Robert (Maurice Maillot), a handsome rugby player. Nondiegetic inserts of rushing water punctuate the drama, and Albert Sendrey's highly melodramatic music reminds the audience repeatedly of the emotional stakes involved. Once Robert's girlfriend informs Henri about the affair, Henri silently confronts Robert. Their exchange of gazes communicates the passion, shame, and betrayal. Henri returns home to shoot himself, even after Jeanne swears that he is the only man she will ever love. Finally, the widowed Jeanne sends the lovesick Robert away as she stands peering lovingly at Henri's legacy, the dam project. Edmond Gréville was determined to retain as much stylistic freedom from the silent era as possible. One of only two films produced by H. O. Films, *Whirlpool* displays elaborate camerawork and editing, including Impressionistic effects, richly upholstered settings, and an elegant mise-en-scène meant to compete directly with Hollywood. But *Whirlpool* also featured headstrong, modern young women who drive around Paris independently, though they are still frustrated by their unsatisfying romances.

Another woman-centered drama, *Ladies Lake* (*Lac aux dames*, Allégret, 1934), was based on a novel by popular Austrian writer Vicki Baum, with dia-

Henri confronts Robert (*Whirlpool*)

logue from prestigious writer Colette and some input from the famed André Gide. It was the only film produced by Philippe de Rothschild, who hoped to free the cinema "from its servitude to the stage" and exploit natural locations (Andrew, *Mists* 190). At a summer lake resort, Jean-Pierre Aumont's character, Eric, arrives to teach swimming and attracts the attention of all the young women. Colette lends many witty conversations that foreground the women's desire and agency. Eric and several women team up to help his gold-digger friend Anika (Ila Mecséry) escape the police, but not before Anika spends some time reminiscing and cuddling topless with Eric. Eventually, after suffering a nasty, nearly fatal infection, Eric ends up with a wealthy young woman rather than the more sensual and natural Puck (Simone Simon) who rescued him from drowning and also loves him. Puck remains a nymph-like poetic force right up to the end, when she rows herself home.

At a time when Hollywood's Production Code drastically restricted content, *Lac aux dames* flaunted the personal and sexual freedom among these women. The handsome Aumont, featured in provocative poses for the advertising campaign, also helped attract audiences. The film can even be seen playing at a cinema in *Whirlpool* near Robert's apartment. This prestige

Simone Simon and Jean-Pierre Aumont (*Lac aux dames*)

production, distributed by Tobis, became a major critical and box office success, boosting the careers of Aumont and Simon as well as providing another high-profile example of the artistry of French sound cinema. Quality, contemporary melodramas that presented complex, modern women became a large part of the output in 1930s France. *Lac aux dames* proved significant; the *Pour Vous* review regretted that the film ended when it did, just as the audience was getting attached to these fascinating young people (May 28, 1934, 5).

As sound cinema progressed, Duvivier continued to be influential in French genre production. After releasing nineteen silent features, he directed eighteen sound films during the 1930s, often with a recurring team. Duvivier worked with a variety of producers from project to project, including coproductions through Films d'Art, La Société Générale de Cinématographie, and Francex. In 1937, after several major successes, he signed a one-year contract with MGM in Hollywood but found the production process too regimented, despite the generous budgets and large crews, and he returned to France until the war. Duvivier preferred the French system, with increased creative freedom and collaboration and less input from producers. After returning, he continued to experiment with sound mixing and compositing techniques, and he shot on location when possible, including in North Africa and Canada. Thematically, his films fit the French penchant for realistic dramas without redemptive happy endings. Life is tough for his doomed characters, especially the men, who repeatedly fail to achieve success because they are typically drawn to elusive or selfish women. A harsh misogyny permeates his work, and he created some of the more memorable femmes fatales of the period. He helped shape the image of the dominant male star of the decade, Jean Gabin, and the trajectory of French noir melodramas.

Four of Duvivier's sound films, *The Red Head* (*Poil de carotte*, 1932), *A Man's Head* (*La Tête d'un homme*, 1933), *Maria Chapdelaine* (1934), and *La Bandera* (1935), proved his versatility and professional craft as well as some of his recurring sexist stereotypes. For *Poil de carotte*, Harry Baur plays the ineffectual father, M. Lepic. His shrewish, controlling wife (Catherine Fonteney) rules the house and mistreats their rambunctious red-haired son François (Robert Lynen), while spoiling his older brother and sister. The resentful François struggles to earn his distracted father's attention, ignoring those who do care about him. By the end, the father saves François from hanging himself and they bond over their shared dislike for Mme. Lepic. Although the bulk of the action is anchored in realistic rural settings, Duvivier inserts several fantastic touches to present François's fears and nightmares, including two phantom

The last-minute rescue (*Poil de carotte*)

versions of the boy who debate suicide as the real François sleeps. *Poil de carotte* confronts dark themes not normally associated with children in family melo-dramas, and only the father and son find a somewhat happy ending. The mother has become a pathetic loner, and her daughter seems destined to follow in her mother's unhappy shoes. Duvivier's male protagonists thrive when they stand together and reject the women in their lives.

A Man's Head is a clever adaptation of Georges Simenon's novel. The story involves a rather forceful performance by Harry Baur as Inspector Maigret, who methodically pursues the killer of an elderly woman, recognizing before others that the accused, Heurtin (Alexandre Rignault), is being framed by the real murderer, a mysterious immigrant, Radek (Valéry Inkijinoff). Radek had overheard the dandy Willy (Gaston Jacquet) mentioning casually in a bar that he would pay handsomely if someone bumped off his wealthy aunt. The plot is quickly put in action by the deceptive Radek. It turns out Radek, who may be terminally ill, has been secretly obsessed with Willy's happy, care-free life and jealous of his girlfriend, Edna (Gina Manès). His muddled motives recall those of Dostoevsky's cynical Raskolnikov. Ultimately, the man's guilt is revealed, and he runs madly through the streets before being hit by a bus. In his last words, he confesses, taking credit for what he keeps claiming was a perfect crime.

To reinforce the pathetic milieu, Duvivier added a realist singer neighbor, played by Damia. She repeatedly sings a mournful song that fascinates and torments Radek, who only meets her near the end when he is attacking Edna in his room. As Kelley Conway observes, Damia's presence helps establish the urban environment of *A Man's Head*, bringing into relief "the bleak existences lived out in cheap, furnished rooms" (*Chanteuse* 156). Duvivier's sound strategies throughout *A Man's Head* include long scenes with voice-off as well as haunting offscreen music, singing, and shrieking. The detailed mise-en-scène and camerawork, with long tracking and traveling shots but also claustrophobic close-ups and some clever back projection, built an ominous atmosphere: "Duvivier, along with his production designer Georges Wakhévitch and cinematographer Armand Thirard, creates a succession of teeming, vibrant spaces in and around Montparnasse that prefigure the Poetic Realist aesthetic and early Hollywood *noir*" (McCann 62–63).

For *Maria Chapdelaine*, Duvivier adapted a Canadian novel and brought new attention to his stars, Madeleine Renaud, Jean Gabin, and Jean-Pierre Aumont. Shot partly on location in Canada, *Maria Chapdelaine* incorporates rugged landscapes with multiple special effects, including back projection, superimpositions, and spinning cameras. Most impressive are the sound strategies that link disparate places and the inclusion of folk songs to signal the cultural ties between old and new worlds. Duvivier evokes the isolation and camaraderie of the hard-working farmers and lumberjacks in this popular melodrama about a beautiful young woman (Renaud) in love with a wandering trapper, François (Gabin). After François freezes to death trying to visit her for Christmas, she sacrifices her chance at independence or happiness by marrying the dull farmer next door (Aumont). French reviews praised Duvivier's earnest adaptation and sensitive treatment of the harsher aspects of nature, family, and religion.

Next, Duvivier teamed up with Charles Spaak to adapt a novel by Pierre Mac Orlan, *La Bandera*. Though portions of *La Bandera* were shot at the Pathé-Natan studios, exotic exteriors were filmed in Spain and Morocco. Gabin returns to star as Pierre Gilieth. In the first scene, which Dudley Andrew points out could stand in as a prologue for poetic realism as a whole, the camera opens on an intricate set of Paris, revealing Pierre bumping into a tipsy couple and leaving blood-stained handprints on her white dress (*Mists* 253).

Pierre's precise crime remains a mystery. He flees to Barcelona with no money. Desperate, he joins their Foreign Legion, becoming part of a close-knit band of misfits headed to North Africa, though one of the recruits is secretly a detective (Robert Le Vigan) on Pierre's tail. In the colonies, missing France and fearing arrest, Gabin's character begins to crack. During one bar fight, the camera sways back and forth, meandering through the free-for-all, reinforcing the drunken chaos. Pierre's only consolation is the Berber dancer Aischa (Annabella, in exotic costume and makeup). The couple marries, exchanging tattoos and blood in an erotic intercultural union. Happiness is short-lived, however, as the Javert-like detective closes in and enemy fighters stage an offensive. The final battle leaves Pierre dead, Aischa in shock, and the detective regretful. As Ginette Vincendeau points out, Gabin's character "goes from skulking man-on-the-run to proud military hero in the process of restoring his identity as a good Frenchman, ready to give up his life for the *patrie*" (*Stars* 68).

By this point in his career, most of Gabin's roles featured scenes where he could display explosive rage and then sacrificial endings. As André Bazin observes, the public would not want to see Gabin as a happy family man at the conclusion of his movies (*What* 2:176). Moreover, Gabin was routinely featured in dramatic close-ups at least as often as his glamorous female costars. His brooding working-class heroes dominated their story and the screen. *La Bandera* fuels Gabin's star trajectory but also raised troubling cultural issues, including its rampant sexism and colonialist perspective. All the women are engaged in prostitution while the hypermasculine Pierre's initial crime remains unexplained, which allows our continued allegiance for this man on the run. Meanwhile, the North African enemy remains a menacing off-screen threat, vicious and unknowable. The novel and film partly celebrate Spain's fascist mission, with the movie even dedicated to Franco, whose government provided material support during filming. As Dudley Andrew writes, "A common myth of spiritual regeneration in Africa here joins the film's disturbing ideology of brotherhood in the Foreign Legion, where pasts are forgotten, and the future belongs to those who give the orders, in this case Francisco Franco ("Praying Mantis" 233). *La Bandera* thus becomes a powerful example of colonialist myth-making in 1930s French cinema, as it propelled the careers of Gabin, Annabella, and Duvivier forward.

As the Depression deepened in the early 1930s, the French box office and investments in production lagged. Between 1931 and 1935, there was a roughly 20 percent decline in ticket sales and a parallel decrease in the number of features released. Members of the government regularly staged inquiries and commissions to assess and stabilize the industry, including new versions in 1932 and 1933 under the Ministries of Finance and Beaux-Arts. Initially Henri Clerc proposed a national credit agency for more responsible funding for film productions, a cause continued in 1935 by Maurice Petsch and his commission. The Petsch report proposed more public-private controls. Ultimately Guy de Carmoy was put in charge of another finance inquiry, and his 1936 report called for a central committee for the industry. A Centre National de Cinéma was also proposed in various forms and definitions. However, suspicious members of the industry, newly concerned with talk of nationalizing portions of the system under the Popular Front, formed the Confédération générale du cinéma in 1936 as a sort of lobbying and administrative hub, defusing the government's interventions. As Colin Crisp concludes, the late 1930s were a period when "both state and industry recognized the need for a set of routinized working practices, incorporated either in legislation or in an agreed professional code, but neither state nor industry could manage to agree on them . . . or impose them" (*Classic* 38). In 1937, the Ministry of National Education made another attempt at organizing the chaotic film industry. This new commission, led by Jean-Michel Renaitour, wanted to control everything from tax evasion and false reporting of ticket sales to foreign competition, more consistent film stock production, new options for loans, and again, a national cinema center (Leglise 181–82). All these attempts to reorganize the sector shared one goal, "to give the national film industry the means to produce high quality films" (Montebello 21). Renaitour's proposals, which were published in a document titled *Where Is French Cinema Headed (Où va le cinéma français?)*, were not adopted, and French film production continued most of its frustratingly disorderly modes of production, distribution, and exhibition.

The cinema was widely seen as prestigious yet in a new crisis by the mid-1930s. Even mainstream newspapers urged people to "save our cinema" by attending more French films. Unemployed technicians, directors, and actors demonstrated in the streets. Problems were compounded with Hitler's rise to power in 1933, which motivated a new wave of professional film immigrants from Germany and beyond to seek work and safety in France: "On the one hand, foreign talent could help to forge a distinctively European alternative to Hollywood's sound output, but on the other, it threatened to dilute nationally specific cultural and working practices" (Phillips 108). In May 1934, members of the film community crisscrossed Paris in a series of protests to condemn the ongoing "invasion" by foreign film workers and argue for the preservation of "Frenchness" in France's cinema. A number of union groups were formed and strengthened, many working more closely with the communist-run CGT umbrella union. A new Confédération générale de l'industrie cinématographique expanded to include workers in seven syndicates, including divisions for directors, cinematographers, editors, designers, sound engineers, film musicians, and production personnel. Director André Berthomieu led the organization along with Duvivier and Renoir. Thanks to their lobbying, the government began to deny automatic work visas for foreign cinema talent settling in France. Nonetheless, up to 50 percent of French film workers remained unemployed or underemployed during the mid-1930s.

Another indicator of the faltering health of the industry by 1935 was the declining number of new, first-time directors, which was half that of the previous few years. Increasingly, cinemas offered double bills at lower ticket prices, which forced budgets even lower and made it harder to compete with American production values. Moreover, the industry never had a centralized system for distribution or exhibition. While run, zone, clearance distribution, and exhibition patterns operated loosely in most large cities, helping first-run movies earn more in the larger downtown houses before moving to smaller, cheaper neighborhood cinemas, business in smaller towns could be chaotic and less profitable. Many small houses closed. Between 1930 and 1933, 355 cinemas had gone bankrupt, and the few new theaters built were in Paris and other major cities (Leglise 99). Even in 1937, five hundred of France's four thousand theaters, mostly in rural areas, still lacked sync sound, so they generated no box office revenue for recent films.

Crises in the film industry were not the only problems. Unemployment, economic stagnation, and corporate scandals led to massive social unrest, violent demonstrations, and crippling strikes. French politics were extremely fractured, with an energized array of leftists facing off against a staunch, increasingly vocal right wing, emboldened by fascist gains in Spain, Germany, and Italy. Those neighbors cut back on granting visas to French films to protect their own industries, further reducing France's exports. In 1933, Spain was France's biggest customer; by 1936, Franco's government completely banned new French films. Thus, while filmmakers had begun the decade struggling to adapt to the economic, aesthetic, and technical challenges brought by sound, by the mid-1930s, financial crises coupled with forces outside the industry and beyond France's borders presented new hurdles. Yet

French cinema's output remained relatively robust in terms of its variety of subjects and stylistic options, preserving its artistic reputation. Throughout this turbulent decade with its political upheavals, underfinanced small producers, and decentralized industry, French cinema generated some of the most exciting films in the world. As Colin Crisp points out, rather than wondering how such a great variety of movies could be made despite such conditions, perhaps the correct assumption is that these cinematic triumphs were made precisely because of all the diverse economic, technical, and aesthetic systems at play during classical-era French film (*Classic* xiv, 91). Thus, despite ongoing challenges, French movies were recognized at home and globally as among the most creative in the world. No other national cinema in Europe could make the same claim throughout the 1930s.

Reynaud's Pierrot (Cinémathèque Française)

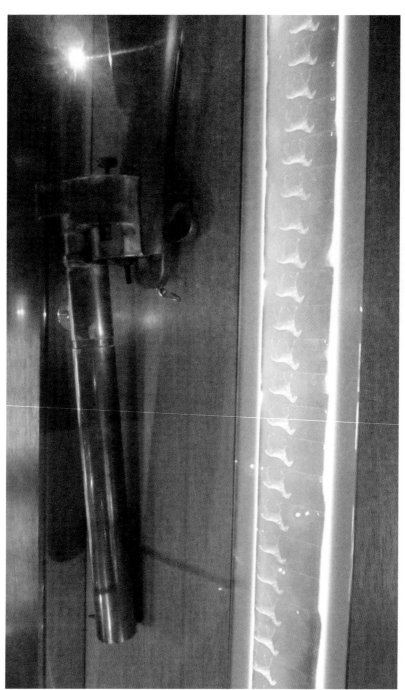

Marey gun camera (Collection Musée Lumière, photo by the author)

Submarine fire (*The Impossible Voyage*)

Méliès travelers land on the sun (*The Impossible Voyage*)

Joan's vision (*Joan of Arc*)

Joan's death (*Joan of Arc*)

Aladdin's dream (*Aladdin and the Marvelous Lamp*)

The genie appears (*Aladdin and the Marvelous Lamp*)

Einar in a Cavalcanti interior (*L'Inhumaine*)

The triptych as horizontal montage (*Napoleon*)

CHAPTER 6

Late 1930s French Cinema

Innovative Style, Politics, and Poetic Realism

Popular Front Tales

Despite ongoing economic and political problems, French cinema had reached a relatively stable stage by the mid-1930s. The film industry had managed to cobble together a highly workable array of tactics, institutions, and policies that allowed for commercial, often star-driven genre films and more auteurist independent productions. The apprenticeship of French film professionals, during which they actively tested sound strategies and synthesized intermedial influences from theater, the music hall, silent cinema, and literature, had all but ended and a more a classical cinema was in place by mid-decade. Historian Pierre Billard argues that around 1935, films such as Jacques Feyder's *Carnival in Flanders* (*La Kermesse héroïque*), in which a town full of women defuse the threat from an invading army by seducing them individually while their own men hide in fear, was representative of a new plateau of professionalism in French production (*L'Age* 77–78). It is worth noting that though it was popular at the time, Feyder's film was later attacked as defeatist, encouraging collaboration with the enemy.

By 1935, mainstream and auteur cinema alike were garnering renewed attention globally, signaling a new classical stage of well-crafted features. Clearly, France's production norms were not as standardized as those in Hollywood, but they were becoming more consistent across genres and directors. However, the best of French cinema, in the eyes of French critics of the era, were films with clear cinephilic touches, including Impressionistic dreams or visions, rapid montages, clever camerawork, creative sound-to-image interplay, and daring set designs or impressive location shooting. A French film, it was thought, should still connect to the spirit of *photogénie* and the artistic impulses of the past. Nonetheless, while the industry thrived, with the number of French films increasing to over 140 features for each of the years 1935 through 1938, American films dominated at the box office, earning half of the receipts in the late 1930s. French cinema was impressive on many levels yet remained in constant competition for its own screens.

In 1935, new grassroots efforts in France helped pull competing leftists together into a Popular Front coalition, and in 1936, a leftist alliance of communists, socialists, and radical socialists took power, led by Léon Blum as France's first socialist (and Jewish) prime minister. His government included several women in prominent positions at a time when women still could not vote. Blum delivered social reforms aimed at helping the lower and middle classes. Central goals included modernizing the economy with increased state intervention in banking, industry, and agriculture. The forty-hour work week was put in place, along with higher minimum wages and paid holidays, although inflation cut into immediate gains for many workers. With the new government, two rival unions for film technicians and artisans entered into agreements with the leftist labor confederation, the Confédération Générale du Travail (CGT), which lobbied with the studios for standardized rules in the film industry. For instance, workers could be required to work ten-hour days on film productions when necessary, but over the course of the year, they must not average more than forty hours a week (Leglise 142). The Popular Front, which many saw as France's equivalent to the New Deal in the United States, empowered the working class and provided optimism during dark economic and political times. However, the Popular Front was short-lived and never particularly unified. By 1938, after several dramatic shifts in government, it had ended. Its significance for cinema was nonetheless quite real, giving increased recognition to the unions. It also motivated important political documentaries and fiction films touching on working-class camaraderie, though few movies of the era dared offer utopian visions or optimistic happy endings. Even celebrations of working-class unity could become cautionary tales, adhering to an underlying cynicism and the conventions of 1930s French realist literature and filmmaking.

One of the first French films to embody working-class concerns explicitly was Jean Renoir and Jacques Prévert's *The Crime of Monsieur Lange* (*Le Crime de Monsieur Lange*, 1936). Their tale, based on an idea by designer Jean Castanier, is told in flashback at a small inn near the French–Belgian border. A couple has just checked in, and the locals realize that the man, Lange (René Lefèvre), is wanted by the police. While Lange sleeps, his protective companion, Valentine (Florelle), explains how they got there. Lange worked writ-ing popular *Arizona Jim* western tales for the unscrupulous swindler Batala (Jules Berry) in a small publishing house, set in a working-class courtyard next to Valentine's laundry business. Batala swindles everyone, even exploit-ing his mistress, Edith (Sylvia Bataille), to sleep with his creditors. The deliv-ery boy Charles (Maurice Baquet) is in love with a laundress Estelle (Nadia Sibirskaïa), but while he recuperates from a bicycle accident, Batala rapes Estelle in his office. However, when the corrupt Batala's legal problems pile up, he leaves town and supposedly dies in a train wreck. In reality, he took on the identity of a priest killed in the crash to escape his debts. Meanwhile, Estelle realizes she is pregnant. With Batala assumed dead, the workers form a cooperative to sustain their jobs and relaunch Lange's profitable series of *Arizona Jim* western magazines. The community pulls together. Valentine finally seduces the timid Lange and, to the delight of the neighborhood, Estelle and Charles end up together following the stillbirth of her child. Just when all is going well and there is talk of an *Arizona Jim* movie deal, Batala returns in his priest robes, hoping to reclaim his now flourishing business. Lange, acting decisively, like one of his western heroes, shoots Batala. As the dying boss ironically calls for a real priest, a friendly creditor drives Lange and Valentine to the border hotel in the dead of night, which brings the plot full circle. The men there, won over by Valentine's tale, allow the couple to flee into Belgium. Sometimes, killing a boss is justified.

Produced by Obéron, *The Crime of Monsieur Lange* involved members of the politically engaged October Group and featured a highly realistic studio set designed by Jean Castanier that reinforced the sense of spatial contiguity and working-class unity. The sets allowed the camera to establish playing spaces with deep planes of action. At other times, as in Lange's physical preparation to kill Batala, it could crane up and down and pan around the courtyard revealing and concealing events. André Bazin's summary of Renoir's sceno-graphic space even included a diagram to emphasize the extent to which *The Crime of Monsieur Lange* allowed him to explore the possibilities of both deep space and concentric camera mobility (*Jean Renoir* 46). The courtyard's work-places and residences allow a wide array of framing options, but doorways, hallways, and windows are particularly significant for the mise-en-scène and blocking of actors.

One of the more striking examples of Renoir's staging can be seen on the night that Batala first leaves: the camera in the dark courtyard seems to search for the voice we hear, which is Valentine singing a realist song about street

walkers. Florelle was a well-known music hall singer and here she is allowed
to dominate the scene with her bold and erotic musical interlude. A few
moments later, Batala's death is announced on the radio, with the camera
wandering about the courtyard, past various windows before returning to
Valentine and Lange in bed, where Valentine brushes off the death and redi-
rects Lange toward her very alive body: "Valentine is a revolutionary figure.
She actively chooses and wins her man, refusing to be defined by her sexual
past" (O'Shaughnessy, *Jean Renoir* 109). Valentine has both feet on the ground,
in contrast to Lange and his fantasy world of cowboys and comic books. As
Kelley Conway explains, "For Valentine, prostitution is the life she left behind
for better things: economic stability, autonomy, and the love of Lange" (*Chanteuse* 126). With *The Crime of Monsieur Lange*, Renoir and Prévert remain sensitive to the difficult plight of women but also provide options for their resistance and success.

Renoir's film delivers a fast-paced, almost giddy attack on crooked bosses
and racist colonialists, countering their ruthless, immoral values with a ring-

Valentine seduces Lange (*The Crime of Monsieur Longe*)

ing endorsement of working-class camaraderie and cooperation. Dudley Andrew and Steven Unger position *The Crime of Monsieur Lange* at the forefront of the cultural battles over representation and the Popular Front: "Featuring urban laborers in their fight against exploitation and corruption, this film contrives the solution of its social drama by invoking the power of popular art itself" (209). Yet the male-dominated violence and racial and gender stereotypes in Lange's *Arizona Jim* tales complicate the film's perspectives. *The Crime of Monsieur Lange*'s utopian vision for a new community built around cooperative labor and gender equality and respect is tempered with its ambiguous conclusion. Admittedly, Valentine acts as the omniscient narrator and Lange's defense attorney for a jury of working-class men, winning his acquittal and freedom. However, the couple must abandon their homes, their businesses, and their friends. French cynicism wins out even in the Popular Front, with the wind lashing the couple as they struggle alone across the wet sand. Renoir does not return to the courtyard, laundry, or printing press to end on a positive note or reassure us of the cooperative's survival. The legacy of Lange, Valentine, and the post-Batala community is left unresolved.

Estelle, Charles, and deep space (*The Crime of Monsieur Longe*)

Still, as the review for the leftist journal *Entre Nous* announced, "This film points out that we are all working in Batala's print shop—let's open the door!" Although the movie did well in France, its central theme, that murder may be justified for political and ideological reasons, prevented its release in the United States and other markets until years later.

Renoir's visible political commitment continued as he became one of the key figures in the radical collective project *Life Is Ours* (*La Vie est à nous*, 1936), produced by the French Communist Party (PCF, Parti communiste français) to boost its candidates for upcoming elections. This unique film directly confronts French political and economic realities, warning against the super-rich and their ties to the rise of fascism throughout Europe. Its mix of documentary and fiction modes and Brechtian sound strategies, including replacing Hitler's and Mussolini's voices with barking dogs and explosions, or laying circus music over footage of marching French fascists, make *Life Is Ours* an unusually clever and confrontational propaganda film: "It is the first militant left-wing film made in France" (Sadoul, *Dictionary* 403). *Life Is Ours* provides a provocative call for class unity in the face of ongoing social oppression. Everyone involved in the project worked for free, including October Group members and actors Jean Dasté, Nadia Sibirskaïa, Gaston Modot, directors Jacques Becker and Jean-Paul Le Chanois, editor Marguerite Renoir, and many others. The movie was featured at political meetings and rallies where the audience was introduced to a new journal, *Ciné-Liberté*, launched by Renoir and Germaine Dulac. *Ciné-Liberté*'s goals included democratizing film production and distribution and encouraging political debate at ciné-clubs.

The Crime of Monsieur Lange and *Life Is Ours*, as well as Renoir's political activity alongside Louis Aragon and the October Group, helped establish him as an outspoken advocate for the left in the face of the rise of fascism: "No other filmmaker of the period compared even remotely with Renoir in the public visibility of his stance as supporter of the Popular Front" (Buchsbaum, *Cinéma* 161). *Life Is Ours* enjoyed a relatively short life span, largely because it featured contemporary politicians then running for office, and it never received a commercial release permit. Only after the rediscovery of a complete print in 1969, at the peak of the post-1968 revolutionary fervor in France, did the film receive renewed critical attention. Renoir was suddenly recognized for making political films and exploring radical modes of signification in cinema decades before May 1968. *Life Is Ours* proved anew that he was continually experimenting in story and style rather than settling into any fixed pattern of a single auteurist stance during the 1930s. A handful of other Popu-

lar Front–era documentary and fiction films addressed the rising concerns
over class divisions and a mix of working-class impatience and successes. Le
Chanois directed a bold, documentary-style narrative, *The Time of Cherries*
(*Le Temps des cerises*, 1938), shot mostly on location in Paris and designed to
confront the increasing gentrification of the city at the expense of displaced
residents. The only feature by Les Films Populaires and produced by the PCF,
The Time of Cherries, with October Group actors Gaston Modot and Jean Dasté
and music by Joseph Kosma, defied commercial aesthetic norms and only
played in limited release: "A tough film, relegated to union halls and anonymous *cinémas du quartier*, it challenged the urbanity—and apathy—of . . .
films pretending to depict Paris" (Andrew and Ungar 243).

Duvivier's popular realist *They Were Five* (*La Belle équipe*, 1936) captures the
conflicting moods of the Popular Front era. Five unemployed friends, Charles
(Charles Vanel), Jean (Jean Gabin), Jacques (Charles Dorat), Tintin (Raymond
Aimos), and Mario (Rafael Medina), who is on the run from the police for
his antifascist work in Spain, live in a rundown Paris apartment until they
all win the lottery with a shared ticket. Jean convinces his four friends to pool

Charles resists Gina's demands (*La Belle équipe*)

their portions and become their own bosses rather than pursuing individual whims. They buy an old inn on an idyllic riverbank outside the city and set about building a restaurant. Early on, Jean warns his comrades that women are fine but only for the "short term." Women should never come between the men and their cooperative venture. The five men bond over their project, and at a party Gabin belts out a happy song about a Sunday stroll on the water's edge for their guests. However, even before they can open their inn, problems arise, including the arrival of the seductive Gina (Viviane Romance), the ex-wife of Charles, wanting her share of his money. Jacques runs off to Canada to avoid the temptation of Mario's girlfriend. Mario is expelled from France, Jean begins a secret affair with Gina, and Tintin falls off the roof and dies, leaving only Jean and Charles and the circling femme fatale, Gina. Finally, a heated disagreement over Gina leads rather inexplicably to Jean shooting Charles. As Jean is about to be led to jail, he laments that their dream project was too beautiful to work. Reviews praised Duvivier's mise-en-scène but were uncertain about the themes: is working-class unity possible or just a fantasy?

La Belle équipe is a stylish male melodrama. Duvivier's mobile camera tracks, pans, and reframes, fluidly following the action and revealing characters embedded in their environments. However, while the story begins as a celebration of the men's confidence and hard work, it devolves into another fatalistic Duvivier tale of human frailty and treacherous women. Initial audiences rejected its overly dramatic and tragic ending, leading the producers to release a second, recut version with a new resolution in which Jean and Charles team up against Gina, sending her packing and successfully launching their restaurant, Chez Nous, together. Duvivier and Spaak regretted the changes, but *La Belle équipe* became much more popular with its happy ending and Gabin smiling and dancing. Later, critics have read both endings against the Popular Front itself, one brutally fatalistic, the other naively optimistic.

Duvivier next worked with Spaak on a Maurice Chevalier project, *The Man of the Hour* (*L'Homme du jour*, 1937), and he had an immense success with *Christine* (*Un carnet de bal*, 1937), an episodic tale of a wealthy widow, Christine (Marie Bell), searching out the men she met twenty years ago at a dance as she tries to assess what she may have missed during her unhappy married life. This highly popular melodrama featured a star-studded cast, including Louis Jouvet, Françoise Rosay, Raimu, and Fernandel, as well as original music by Maurice Jaubert. *Un carnet de bal* won the Mussolini Cup at the Venice Film Festival in 1937. Duvivier's version of another popular North African book, *Pépé le moko* (1937), brought him his greatest triumph, synthesizing many of his themes with the star persona of Jean Gabin, all in a Poetic Realist format.

Poetic Realism and Late 1930s French Cinema

The label "Poetic Realism" gradually became associated with a cluster of dark and poignant psychological crime melodramas. During the early 1930s, critics pointed out the special, evocative realism of movies such as Jean Grémillon's *Little Lise* (*La Petite Lise*, 1930) and Pierre Chenal's adaptations *Street without a Name* (*La Rue sans nom*, 1934) and *Crime and Punishment* (1935), as well as striking design elements in films by Vigo, Renoir, and others. An expressive naturalism tinged with lyrical or poetic aspects was prized as an extension of the beloved *photogénie* and seemed to defy the limitations of mainstream, studio-bound cinema. By the end of the decade, technical and aesthetic trends tended toward increasingly dark French noir films, influenced in part by popular crime literature, increasingly grim political conditions, and faster film stocks for low-key lighting setups. What became known as Poetic Realist style also owed to ongoing syntheses of international styles, Expressionist touches, Impressionist sequences, and montage as well as some Surreal elements and symbolism. Writers, designers, actors, cinematographers, and directors all brought aspects of silent French and European production into the emotion-packed Poetic Realist sound dramas that anticipated and inspired American film noir of the 1940s.

Many of the canonical Poetic Realist films concentrate on the challenges for working-class men as they struggle to find a fair and safe route through a daunting world. The Popular Front fueled some of the recurring themes of hope mixed with frustration. Movies as different as *L'Atalante*, *La Maternelle*, and *The Crime of Monsieur Lange* helped lay the groundwork for innovative uses of locations and sets as well as increasingly expressive audiovisual styles. Moreover, women's roles in Poetic Realism displayed a keen awareness of sexual exploitation and limited social options. The status of French women of the interwar era still lagged far behind the recurring promise of equality and equity for women. These fictional worlds were dominated by a sense of cruel fate. Social realities and human frailty spelled doom for lasting romance or a just future, much less feminist ideals. Poetic Realism's characters, men and women, are trapped economically, culturally, physically, and ultimately psychologically. As Jean-Pierre Jeancolas points out, Poetic Realist films were also "conjugated in the present tense . . . their heroes dance to the music of their time: René Lefèvre, Jean, Gabin, Charles Vanel, and Jules Berry were contemporaries, even next of kin, of the viewers" ("Beneath" 78). These thematic and stylistic traits as well as aspects of noir fiction of the era permeated much of French genre filmmaking throughout the decade.

In addition to being influenced by new forms of realism, many French films of the 1930s presented colonialist topics told from romanticized European perspectives. In 1931, the Paris Colonial Exposition attracted millions of visitors and encouraged fanciful engagement with the colonial images and tales throughout the decade, even as aspects of France's empire were already crumbling. The novel *Pépé le Moko*, published that year, was adapted by Julien Duvivier, Jacques Constant, and Henri Jeanson in 1937 and shot primarily on artificial sets in Paris. It featured clichéd stereotypes of Algeria and its residents. For this noir thriller, Duvivier again relied on Jean Gabin for his central character and hired a cast of veteran actors, including Marcel Dalio playing an Arab. Pépé, a wanted bank robber living in hiding in the labyrinthine Casbah area of Algiers, must remain in the old town *quartier* or risk certain arrest. A visiting inspector, Janvier (Philippe Richard), turns up the heat on the local police to capture the elusive Pépé. A vacationing French woman, Gaby (Mireille Balin), also arrives and captivates Pépé, causing him to lose focus and his hard edge, as the pair flirt and reminisce about Paris.

Pépé's main lover, Inès (Line Noro), tries to protect him from this risky temptation, but Gaby's presence fuels his frustration over being stuck in Algiers. Tania, a sad surrogate mother-figure played by Fréhel, reinforces his misery and nostalgia by singing her own realist song, "Where Is It, Then?," about her lost youth and missed opportunities. Meanwhile the Arab inspector Slimane (Lucas Gridoux) plays cat and mouse with Pépé, waiting for a chance to tempt him into the open, using Gaby as bait. Indeed, Pépé dares to run to the port in search of Gaby before she sails off, but the jealous Inès informs Slimane. Pépé is arrested and then stabs himself with a hidden knife, falling on the iron fence separating their fates, as the oblivious Gaby looks longingly over his head toward the Casbah on the hill and the tooting ocean liner drowns out his cries. Inès realizes the folly of her actions and in typical Poetic Realist fashion, everyone loses by the end. Happiness and escape are impossible to attain.

Pépé le Moko was influenced by American gangster films and remade in Hollywood as *Algiers* (Cromwell, 1938), and it inspired subsequent films noirs

Trapped at the gate (*Pépé le Moko*)

and *Casablanca* (Curtiz, 1942). Duvivier's film fits the "man on the run" formula common to Poetic Realism, in which fleeing men undertake "a desperate journey toward death, where *femmes fatales* are generally waiting to deal the death blow" (Burch and Sellier 128). *Pépé le Moko*'s production design includes heavy cast shadows, harshly angled camera setups, and a claustrophobic narrative space built to reinforce the geographic and mental mazes trapping all the characters. The average shot length is a fast-paced four seconds, and the production team bragged that they shot and edited the film in an "American fashion." Duvivier also exploits distorted composite shots, as seen in Pépé's mad march toward the port, which recalls Gabin's race through the snow in *Maria Chapdelaine*.

Pépé le Moko allows Gabin to display his trademark acting range, including romantic conversations, joyful singing, fits of anger, and eventual self-sacrifice and suicide. Pépé's vulnerable masculinity dominates the story, and it is said that when he dies there will be three thousand widows at this funeral. Yet in colonial cinema fashion, the only woman he wants is Gaby, the elegant, white Parisian. By contrast, the devoted but hot-blooded Inès, in heavy

Mireille Balin and French noir (*Pépé le Moko*)

makeup, loose-fitting clothes, and unkempt hair, shifts suddenly from his concerned lover into a treacherous Arab *femme fatale*. Meanwhile, Pépé represents French masculinity of the Poetic Realist era; he is both tough and vulnerable. Ginette Vincendeau points out that Gabin, as the "good-bad boy" worker-criminal, displays a rare authenticity, even in this melodramatic French noir film: "The defining traits of poetic realism can be traced in the inner qualities of Gabin's characters from the 1930s, such as alienation, helplessness, assertive masculinity, and romanticism. It is in Duvivier's corpus that these qualities are best exemplified" (*Pépé* 79). Duvivier's technical and narrative contributions were highly significant for the global prestige of French cinema, especially in helping shape French crime melodramas and Poetic Realism, to say nothing of the Gabin's ongoing star status.

Mireille Balin teamed up with Gabin again for Grémillon's *Lady Killer* (*Gueule d'amour*, 1937). This time, her character Madeleine frustrates Gabin's character Lucien (a.k.a. Lady Killer) much more deliberately, playing with his emotions and driving him toward a violent outburst. *Lady Killer* was adapted by Charles Spaak from a novel by André Beucler and shot in UFA's

Berlin studio and on picturesque locations in France. The opening anchors the story in the southern city of Orange and includes heavy Provençal accents for the locals, adding a sense of authenticity to what is otherwise a very polished, mainstream movie. Once again Gabin plays a ladies' man, here a proud military figure, Lucien Bourrache, who is wrapping up his duty in the cavalry and adored by every woman he meets. However, as he tires of women pursuing him, he meets the elegant and elusive Madeleine while on leave in Cannes. He soon drops everything to pursue her in Paris, where he finds a low-level job in a print shop to survive. Lucien grows increasingly anxious and isolated, like an overwrought, frustrated young lover. Madeleine only spends an occasional night with him, while continuing to live with her wealthy protector.

Rejected and haunted by her memory, Lucien returns to the Orange area to open his own bistro and gas station. He learns his old friend René (René Lefèvre) has finally found happiness with a woman, a vacationing Parisienne, who turns out to be Madeleine. When Madeleine comes to see Lucien and shifts from apologies to mockery, Lucien finally unleashes his pent-up

René and Lucien (*Lady Killer*)

temper. The exaggerated performances of Balin sneering at her prey, and a shaky Gabin ordering her to leave, build to a troubling, illogical climax with him frantically strangling her in his bistro. Lucien runs to René to confess, and René, who may love Lucien most of all, offers him a train ticket for North Africa, sending him off with a hug and a kiss. The resolution, with a nearly catatonic Lucien escaping justice but heading into an unclear future—perhaps he will flee to North Africa or join the foreign legion—completes another cynical, melodramatic treatment of class and sexual tensions set in a stylish cinematic world. As Geneviève Sellier explains, *Lady Killer* has many elements common with 1930s dramas, including a femme fatale breaking up close male friendships and a murder that plunges the man into an internal hell worse than death (21). *Lady Killer* marked the beginning of a highly successful series of popular films from Grémillon, who became one of France's most respected directors going into the Occupation.

Marcel Carné also turned out impressive emotional crime dramas, anchoring his working-class male heroes and doomed young women in an unforgiving, keenly metaphorical environment. He helped solidify Poetic Realism of the late 1930s. Carné was just thirty years old when he directed *Jenny* (1936), which began his collaboration with writer Jacques Prévert. *Jenny* is a highly melodramatic tale foregrounding the divisions between a mother dependent on men and prostitution and her modern daughter enjoying a whole new world of options. Carné and Prévert next teamed up for a surreal, satiric comedy, *Bizarre, Bizarre (Drôle de drame*, 1937), featuring major stars, including Françoise Rosay, Michel Simon, and Louis Jouvet, a clever soundtrack by Maurice Jaubert, and inventive settings by Alexandre Trauner. But it was the sequence of three films released over thirteen months—*Port of Shadows (Quai des brumes*, 1938), *Hôtel du Nord* (1938), and *Daybreak (Le Jour se lève*, 1939)—that mark the culmination and then abrupt demise of Poetic Realism.

Quai des brumes was based on a Mac Orlan novel that appealed to Gabin, Carné, and Prévert alike. Initially signing with UFA, Carné and his team, including Trauner and famed German cinematographer Eugen Schüfftan, shot at the Pathé Joinville Studios and on location in Le Havre. This noir melodrama involves a deserter, Jean (Gabin), who meets a young woman, Nelly (Michèle Morgan), in the backroom of a run-down dive near the waterfront. The cynical Jean mistakenly assumes she is a prostitute. Prévert's poetic word play dominates the dialogue. The doomed pair fall in love and an artist's suicide allows Jean to adopt the dead man's identity. His devotion allows Nelly to feel safe and happy for the first time in her life. However,

Jean and Nelly, on the run (*Quai des brumes*)

Nelly's lecherous guardian Zabel (Michel Simon) and the jealous local gang-ster Lucien (Pierre Brasseur) disrupt their dreams of leaving France together. Jean, unjustly accused of killing the artist, ends up a murderer anyway, beat-ing the brutal Zabel to death while rescuing Nelly from his grasp. Then Jean is gunned down in the street by Lucien, ironically in front of a travel agency, just before he can flee on a ship to South America. By the end, Jean dies in Nelly's arms, mid-kiss, leaving her devastated and alone, trapped in Le Havre, while his lost dog runs madly about town looking for his master.

To further the impact of the tragic plot, which is full of fatalistic twists and betrayals, the film's visual style reinforces the sense of foreboding via low-key lighting, evocative shadows, misty wharves, and narrow, wet streets. The mix of bleak locations, distorting lenses, and claustrophobic sets estab-lishes an exemplary Poetic Realist environment. The actors are constantly framed and hemmed in by doorways, windows, and gloomy skylines, and even the pathetic bar where Jean and Nelly meet is perched on a sad little point of land: "The visual darkness of *Quai des brumes* is unprecedented in French commercial cinema" (Turk 104). The *New York Times* also concentrated on the film's pessimism, claiming it offers "a story that is no story at all, but is a sad philosophy, a conjuration of mood, with a conclusion that simply shrugs its shoulders in the gloom and murmurs 'Such is life'" (October 30, 1939). With its Expressionistic sets, bravura performances, and Jaubert's tragic music, *Quai des brumes* was a critical and popular triumph. It became the most successful French film of 1938 and won the Louis Delluc Prize. *Quai des brumes* delivered a stylish hit for Gabin while helping Morgan's stardom globally.

Next Carné quickly turned out another high-quality adaptation complete with evocative studio sets, including a replica of the Paris Canal Saint-Martin *quartier*. For *Hôtel du Nord*, Carné retained Trauner and Jaubert; Jean Aurenche and Henri Jeanson adapted the novel into a screenplay. He also assembled a cast of major stars, including Arletty, Annabella, Louis Jouvet, and Jean-Pierre Aumont. *Hôtel du Nord* centers on a lower-class hotel and its varied residents, which allows for a rather complex, even splintered narrative. One day during a first communion celebration, a troubled couple, Renée (Anabella) and Pierre (Aumont), check in with plans to commit double suicide. In another room, the prostitute Raymonde (Arletty) prepares to hit the streets for her

Doomed lovers Renée and Pierre (*Hôtel du Nord*)

pimp boyfriend Edmond (Jouvet). The desperate young couple stares out of their window toward the canal in a shot mirroring that of the doomed Jean and Nelly in *Quai des brumes*. Renée's intended suicide is all the more pathetic since she is in love with Pierre, but this is the most romantic idea she can muster because life has apparently been so cruel to both of them. The coward Pierre shoots her first, then loses his nerve and runs away. Renée barely survives and stays with the supportive hotel community while the captured Pierre is sent to prison.

Hôtel du Nord confronts the daunting array of challenges to personal and romantic happiness among the underclass. Throughout, a number of couples form and disband, including a gay tenant, Adrien (François Périer), who entertains men in his room. Renée flees to Egypt briefly with Edmond but soon returns to the hotel to wait for Pierre, who had shot her. Amid Bastille Day fireworks and music, Edmond is gunned down in his hotel room for past offenses and Renée and the newly freed Pierre walk off, climbing the steps again to try to renew their lives together. The dialogue includes everyday expressions and slang, helping anchor the performances in a Poetic Realist milieu, synthesizing the natural and stylized. Arletty in particular, sporting a black eye from Edmond's violence at one point, personifies this mix of populist realism and heavy symbolism. Darkness dominates most scenes; every character has something to hide and regularly casts a heavy shadow. Another success for Carné, *Hôtel du Nord* was filmed during frightening days for France, with increasing military threats from Germany and a string of concessions from the floundering French government. During production, a number of technicians were called up for military service, and even Aumont received a draft notice just before *Hôtel du Nord*'s December 1938 premiere.

Thanks to the lingering economic and political crises and scandals of 1930s France and the rise of fascism in Germany, Italy, and Spain, the moody Poetic Realist films were perceived as both symptoms and products of their pessimistic era. Following *Hôtel du Nord*, Prévert returned to team up with Carné, Trauner, and Jaubert for *Le Jour se lève*, another Gabin vehicle. *Le Jour se lève* became the most celebrated film of Poetic Realism and also marked its abrupt conclusion. André Bazin, one of the film's early champions, argued that it was perfect: "The realism of *Le Jour se lève* is as rigorous as that of a poem" (*Cinema from the Liberation* 12), while Thompson and Bordwell consider Gabin's portrayal of the doomed François "the ultimate hero of Poetic Realism" (266). *Le Jour se lève* opens and ends with deaths, including another of Gabin's trademark suicide performances. The film project was based on a three-page

François in his room (*Le Jour se lève*)

summary by Carné's neighbor, Jacques Viot. Carné was intrigued by the plot structure; he claimed he had never thought of a movie that began at the end and worked its way back to the beginning, like a confession, although that storytelling strategy mirrors Clair's *Le Million*, Renoir's *Crime of Monsieur Lange*, and several Guitry movies (Carné 121).

Le Jour se lève's opening title explains that a man has committed a murder and is recalling how he got in this predicament. Then in the first scene, François (Gabin) can be heard behind his apartment door yelling in anger. A gun is fired, and Valentin (Jules Berry) emerges and tumbles down the circular staircase. François barricades himself in his room, which is in the end corner on the top floor of the last building on the street. During the long night, he remembers how he came to be here in a series of three flashbacks, each interrupted by scenes of the police firing in his window and preparing for an assault as a large crowd gathers below to lend him moral support. In the first flashback, the amiable François works in a factory, where he meets a young flower shop employee named Françoise (Jacqueline Laurent). The fumes from his sand blasting prophetically kill the flowers she is trying to deliver.

He pursues Françoise, but she is under the spell of the older Valentin, who performs in a dog act with his mistress, Clara (Arletty). At that evening's show, Françoise leaves with Valentin and the disappointed François is seduced by the abandoned Clara. The second flashback reveals that François is now Clara's lover, keeping her in an apartment across the street. But he soon redis-covers Françoise, who gives him hope for a better life. Things get bleaker in each return to the present with the police moving ever closer, as he peers despondently out his smashed window at the rising sun. The final flashback, set entirely in his room, loops back to his shooting of Valentin and then meets up with the present, as he commits suicide just as the police lob tear gas into his room at dawn. While François dies, poor Françoise is lying delirious across the street, cared for by Clara, their own futures grim and uncertain. Unlike *The Crime of Monsieur Lange*, there is no chance for escape or help from one's community in this post–Popular Front world.

Le Jour se lève's resolution, with François dead and both women trauma-tized, ensures the story's fatalistic thematic unity and sustains Gabin's star persona: "With every Gabin film the cinema rewinds the infernal machine of his destiny—just as in *Le Jour se lève*, that night, as on every night, he winds up the alarm clock whose ironic and cruel ringing will sound at daybreak the hour of his death" (Bazin, *What* 2:177). Furthermore, as Maureen Turim points out, the death is ultimately irrational and pointless because François had won what he supposedly wanted—the love and devotion of Françoise. There is no real need to kill Valentin. François has simply unraveled, break-ing down over Valentin's boastful taunts (Turim 73). François suffers from some unexplained inner demons. This tragic tale of impossible love among the mirrored couples of François/Françoise and François/Clara is told with an Expressionistic mise-en-scène that repeatedly reinforces its mix of real-ism and poetic artifice. Symbolic objects abound, from the worn teddy bear with one happy eye and one sad eye and broken mirrors to the gaudy brooches offered by Valentin. Trauner's sets suggest the decline of this working-class neighborhood, which seems to be crumbling around François. They actually built a confining little four-walled room to enhance Gabin's sense of entrap-ment during the filming. All the while, Jaubert's compositions reinforce Fran-çois's downward spiraling condition.

With *Quai des brumes* and *Le Jour se lève*, Carné completed his important Poetic Realist cycle. As Bazin concludes, "Since they were not only impor-tant films but an imaginary universe unto themselves—destiny's geometri-cal space where the man of 1939 complacently recognized the will of the

gods—*Quai des brumes* and *Le Jour se lève* appear to us today as the idealization of a cinematographic paradise lost" (*Liberation to the New Wave* 86). Contemporary critics were not as quick to see *Le Jour se lève* in the same class as
Quai des brumes. Its status only took off after World War II, when André Bazin
and other new critics helped revive its reputation.

Late 1930s French Film Culture and Jean Renoir

Despite the initial challenges of the coming of sound and the rise of a newly
stable classical French cinema, 1930s ciné-clubs continued to champion past
and recent films of merit and encourage serious aesthetic and ideological analyses. *Pour Vous*, which catered to popular and industry audiences, continued
to include historical pieces and lament the rapid loss of silent film history.
Journalist Lucienne Escoubé wrote an influential call-to-arms essay for *Pour
Vous* on March 31, 1932, pleading for the conservation of France's cinematic
heritage. Books and the other arts last forever, she points out, but movies can
only be seen if someone saves, protects, and screens them (Escoubé 3). Her
appeal for a national *cinémathèque* encouraged young Henri Langlois. Already
a collector of film journals and memorabilia, Langlois sought advice on film
preservation from historian and cinephile Jean Mitry. Next, Langlois and
Georges Franju began Le Cercle du Cinéma ciné-club, setting the groundwork for a *cinémathèque* and engaging with friends and industry insiders to
form a repository modeled on the Museum of Modern Art and the British
Film Institute.

Langlois and Franju launched their fledgling Cinémathèque Française in
September 1936 with a collection of several hundred prints, initially bankrolled by Paul-Auguste Harlé, publisher of *La Cinématographie Française*.
Alexandre Kamenka eagerly donated the Albatros archives, and Pierre Braunberger provided prints from his productions. Germaine Dulac was also a
founding member. She contributed copies of her films and introduced Langlois to Jean Epstein, Jean Renoir, and officials at Pathé and Gaumont. Dulac
not only opened doors for Langlois and Franju; she served on the Cinémathèque's initial board of directors. Their shared mission was ambitious
and optimistic, dedicated to preserving and exhibiting avant-garde and mainstream cinema alike as well as gathering film-related materials, including
scripts, promotional items, journals, and magazines.

Initially, before the Cinémathèque had any official space, Langlois, still
only twenty-one years old, stockpiled donated and purchased 35mm film
reels, most on flammable nitrate stock, in his apartment's large bathroom.

Major names in the field, including Marcel L'Herbier, Jean Painlevé, Man Ray, and Ferdinand Zecca, signed on as founding members. Georges Méliès provided a space to store prints safely on his property. Within several months, the nonprofit Cinémathèque Française collected thousands of reels and established a budget to expand its holdings. Pathé arranged to donate copies of their latest newsreels week after week. Thus, a wide range of material quickly accumulated, some carefully sought out, such as their first purchase, Epstein's *Fall of the House of Usher*, while others were rescued from neglect in warehouses, deposited by filmmakers or producers, or even swapped among other collections and international *cinémathèques*. Langlois saved and hid the negative for Renoir's *A Day in the Country* during the Occupation and secretly safeguarded assorted prints left by fleeing Germans on their way through France, including Hans Richter. In 1939, the Cinémathèque Français took over the competing Les Amis de la Cinémathèque Nationale, consolidating their holdings and gaining more authority and funding as a state institution. This stronger Cinémathèque Française, with screenings in the prestigious Chaillot Palace, also helped ensure that Paris remained one of the world's centers for film history and exhibition. Today, the Cinémathèque Française continues to occupy a pivotal place in film culture as a center for the preservation, education, and advocacy of French and global cinema.

As one of France's most visible auteurs, Jean Renoir participated in the rise of France's global reputation for high-quality film culture, which had systematically been cultivated over the years by ciné-clubs and journals. A founding member of the Cinémathèque, he figured prominently at many public events, and he was referred to as the "genius director of the left" in the popular press. Renoir was also recognized by the president as a Chevalier de la Légion d'honneur, making him a major cinematic figure in the eyes of the government and its cultural arts ministry. Throughout the decade, Renoir churned out a steady stream of movies that combine some degrees of theatricality with an earnest cinematic naturalism. These films can appear lyrical, social, or Poetic Realist simultaneously. Moreover, almost all of his fifteen features were made with different production companies, further demonstrating the fractured, independent, and creative nature of film production during 1930s France. The second half of the decade brought a new consistency to some aspects of Renoir's stories and styles amid a rich variety of projects.

In what seemed like a surprising shift after *The Crime of Monsieur Lange* and *Life Is Ours*, Renoir next chose to adapt a Guy de Maupassant short story,

A Day in the Country (*Une partie de campagne*), for producer Pierre Braunberger. It was shot entirely on location during the summer of 1936 with Renoir's nephew Claude as cinematographer. Although the film was initially left incomplete, owing in part to delays from long stretches of bad weather, *A Day in the Country* was finally released in a forty-minute version with only minor revisions in 1946. Joseph Kosma's score helped unify the tone, providing a wistful perspective on the action.

Set in 1860, the film depicts a caricatured bourgeois Parisian family, including their lively daughter, Henriette (Sylvia Bataille), and their bumbling clerk, Anatole (Paul Temps), who arrive at an inn on a riverbank run by Renoir's character, Poulain. The delicate Henriette has been promised in matrimony to the foolish Anatole. Two local young men, the playful Rodolphe (Jacques Brunius) and sincere Henri (Georges D'Arnoux), talk the mother and daughter into separate river excursions. Rodolphe comically seduces the mother while Henri and Henriette share a more bittersweet and ambiguous sexual encounter. Renoir's trademark direct sound, deep space, Impressionistic camerawork, and contrasting acting styles are all on display in *A Day in*

Henriette on a swing (*A Day in the Country*)

the Country, which mixes farce and heartfelt melodrama. Renoir's gentle humanism and sensitivity to the plight of women come through with the representation of Henriette, who succumbs reluctantly to Henri's advances. The pair immediately seems stricken by their moment of passion. A final coda reveals that years later, Henri has returned to this romantic spot only to discover that Henriette and her husband, Anatole, are also visiting. After Henriette admits she thinks of their encounter every night, the central characters sadly part company. She has shifted from the delighted young woman on a swing to a regretful person, a tear in her eye. This somewhat anticlimactic ending became a recurring termination device for Renoir. His films often end with characters going their separate ways. Kosma's somber music also lends a poignancy to the closing images of the river.

Renoir had left *A Day in the Country* unfinished to move on to his adaptation with Charles Spaak of Maxim Gorky's *The Lower Depths* (*Les bas-fonds*, 1936), produced by Alexandre Kamenka of Albatros. Jean Gabin plays the petty thief Pepel, initially robbing, then befriending a downwardly mobile baron (Louis Jouvet). Both men end up in the same flophouse, where Pepel is involved with Vassilissa (Suzy Prim), the wife of Kostylev (Vladimir Sokoloff), the slimy boss and owner, but Pepel realizes he is actually more in love with her sister Natacha (Junie Astor). Defending the vulnerable Natacha, Pepel attacks Kostylev, and then the local men join in to help beat and kill the corrupt man. Only Pepel goes to prison, however, thanks to false claims by the jealous Vassilissa. Eventually he is freed and runs off with the faithful Natacha, wandering down a country road in an ending much more hopeful than that of *The Crime of Monsieur Lange*. Moreover, the baron seems to have found happiness living among this community of welcoming social outcasts. For Brett Bowles, *The Lower Depths* becomes an embodiment of Popular Front concerns as it "dramatizes the misery, revolt, and liberation of the proletariat from an oppressive society ruled by corrupt bureaucrats and greedy hypocritical petty bourgeois" ("Renoir" 398). Ultimately, *The Lower Depths* offered an engaged and somewhat optimistic Popular Front–era parable.

Beyond the humanist themes of class consciousness mixed with the male search for a helpful, worthy mate, *The Lower Depths* demonstrates Renoir's ongoing exploration of options in presenting narrative space, often tracking and panning rather than following routine editing patterns. He inserted many heavy shadows and Poetic Realist effects to link the characters' plights to their environment. Furthermore, what some critics see as a clash of acting styles is the result of Renoir's desire to find the appropriate performance for each character based on what best suits that actor. He believed everyone need not simply act in harmony and unison. Despite an uneven reception, *The Lower Depths* received the first Louis Delluc Award and furthered the reputations of both Renoir and Gabin; the latter told *Pour Vous* that he only accepts roles he likes, "and if I *like* it, I *feel* it" (September 24, 1936, 11). Gabin starred in two more Renoir films before the decade was out.

Renoir's subsequent feature, *Grand Illusion* (*La Grande Illusion*, 1937), solidified his reputation internationally and became his greatest critical and box office success. It also proved to many that French film production had reached a new artistic level. A war film that never shows combat, *Grand Illusion* was also a personal saga. Renoir had served as a pilot during World War I, and after an injury he was assigned to an observation wing of the air force, flying vulnerable Caudron planes on reconnaissance missions. He lost many friends in battle. The idea for the film began in 1934 when Renoir ran into a former comrade who had been shot down repeatedly but escaped his captors each time, including once from a prison in a fortified castle. Renoir brought on Carl Koch, husband of Lotte Reiniger, to advise. Koch had served in a German artillery unit in the Champagne region, where Renoir regularly flew. As soldiers they were on opposing sides; now they were close friends.

For their screenplay, Renoir, Koch, and Spaak sought to avoid the clichés of other World War I films, such as trench warfare, brutish enemies, and heroic victories. Eliminating battle scenes helped avoid glamorizing war and kept the budget low. They gradually organized the story around various modes of camaraderie in which class (rather than nationality) divided people, but their treatment preserved a sense of comic absurdity. Even the rather vague title was only added late in production. *Grand Illusion* was clearly a product of its era, with Popular Front and Poetic Realist touches mixed with Renoir's own wartime experiences and pacifist values. Produced by a first-time company, RAC (Réalisation d'art Cinématographique), *Grand Illusion* proves anew that a decentralized, undercapitalized production system could generate highly ambitious, artistic results.

Renoir's script shifted from the tale of heroic escapes by aviator Maréchal (Jean Gabin) to a looser story built from a series of anecdotal scenes. The story begins when aristocratic officer de Boeldieu (Pierre Fresnay) insists that Maréchal help obtain more detailed reconnaissance photographs. The plot abruptly cuts to the pretentious German ace pilot von Rauffenstein (Erich von Stroheim) announcing to his soldiers that he just shot down a plane. Maréchal soon arrives with a broken arm alongside the unscathed de Boeldieu. Repeatedly, *Grand Illusion* employs ellipses between scenes, challenging the audience to fill in temporal and spatial gaps, as Maréchal and de Boeldieu are transferred ever deeper into Germany's network of prisoner of war camps. Along the way, they meet the amiable and generous prisoner Rosenthal (Marcel Dalio). The three men come from different worlds. Rosenthal is wealthy and Jewish, Maréchal is a former factory engineer, and de Boeldieu comes from a long aristocratic lineage, yet they share a sense of personal if not always patriotic duty. A soldier's job is to fight, and to do that, they must escape. Eventually, they are moved to a bleak, remote castle, run by the wounded and bitter von Rauffenstein. Once there, Maréchal and Rosenthal devise a daring escape plan, but de Boeldieu sacrifices himself, creating a diversion that forces von Rauffenstein to shoot him.

The old-world order is doomed, and the future belongs to the union of workers and benevolent capitalists. The two escapees take refuge with a widowed German farm woman, Elsa (Dita Parlo), and her daughter, Lotte, but once healed and strengthened, the men push on toward home. In the end, they barely make it across the Swiss border, surviving thanks to a German

von Rauffenstein, de Boeldieu, and Maréchal (*Grand Illusion*)

officer who tells his patrol not to fire on Maréchal and Rosenthal trudging uphill through the deep snow. Once again, a Renoir film closes with two people wandering into an uncertain future rather than achieving a complete termination effect. Maréchal and Rosenthal may or may not return to their units to continue fighting the war. Maréchal may or may not return as promised to Elsa and her daughter when it all ends.

Grand Illusion reveals Renoir's mature visual style. He systematically experiments with longer takes and deep space to provide a sense of spontaneity, often framing clusters of characters in a shot, allowing relatively free movement. For instance, as Maréchal joins the prisoners at the first camp, they explain about their tunneling operation and Cartier (Julien Carette) descends for his shift digging under the barracks. The camera meanders around the room with bodies coming in and out of the frame as they mill about the room, chatting with Maréchal, while Cartier struggles underground. The other prisoners become distracted, learning that someone was shot trying to escape, and they fail to notice Cartier's alarm signal immediately. The suspense unfurls at a leisurely pace with the camera casually allowing us to follow the action. Cartier's near death also introduces Rosenthal's generosity as he pops into the frame to revive Cartier with fine cognac. The scene mixes a number of emotions, unfolding in a seemingly spontaneous fashion.

Later, when the prisoners stage a ridiculous musical show, many dressed in women's costumes, Maréchal interrupts to announce that the French army has taken a town from the Germans and the performers and audience erupt into a defiant rendition of "La Marseillaise." The camera circles the room, several Germans are seen looking concerned, and finally there is a leap to a distressed-looking Maréchal in a solitary confinement cell digging at the wall with a spoon. This shot sequence lasts one minute as a concerned guard enters and Maréchal makes a mad dash out the door, but the camera remains in the cell, waiting patiently until the guards carry the poor prisoner back in, dumping him on his bed. Again, an ellipsis between scenes and a bold camera choice provide a clever solution for presenting the action. This sequence of musical defiance and German retribution influenced the script for *Casablanca*, though *Casablanca*'s "Marseillaise" scene unfolds in thirty shots edited in conventional continuity fashion rather than employing a roving camera and long takes. Marguerite Renoir's editing in *Grand Illusion* preserves a sense of real time and space in individual scenes, while the plot structure creates ambiguity about how much time is passing between scenes.

There is a great deal of thematic ambivalence in *Grand Illusion*, especially for a film about class divisions being more significant than nationality. *Grand Illusion* ultimately generates empathy for everyone, including von Rauffenstein, who only shoots de Boeldieu when forced by duty, recognizing as well that their era has come to an end. Yet the film's allegiance may be strongest for the humble, working-class values of Maréchal and Elsa, who celebrate a touching Christmas together, as the sympathetic Rosenthal looks on from the sidelines. In every scene, Renoir embeds these psychologically complex characters in an evocative mise-en-scène and reinforces the realism with deep space, long takes, and evocative mobile framing, including recurring tilts, pans, and arcing movements. After Maréchal and Rosenthal escape the castle, for example, the roving camera allows us to rediscover them casually hiding in broad daylight in a cold ditch along a road. When they take refuge with Elsa and her daughter in their farmhouse, the camerawork seems to document their movements naturally, even as doorways, windows, and empty tables are used to comment on their relations. Their visit peaks when

Rosenthal calls to Maréchal (*Grand Illusion*)

Rosenthal informs Elsa of their imminent departure, then throws open the window to reveal a sad, resigned Maréchal waiting outside.

Many of these shots recall the staging choices in *A Day in the Country* and *The Crime of Monsieur Lange*. As André Bazin points out, Renoir's realism owed much to his camera work, which never separated the center of dramatic interest from the setting in which it was inserted ("Réalisme" 44). Furthermore, Renoir's visual style and narrative strategies richly complicate the overarching temporal and spatial details. How long do the fugitives spend at Elsa's farm? How far are they from Swiss border? Renoir destabilizes gender boundaries as well as temporal and geographic markers. As Martin O'Shaughnessy points out, *Grand Illusion*'s men are pulled out of the manly pursuit of war and plunged into a passive, unsettling world of domestic routines, male bonding, and cross-dressing performances (*Jean Renoir* 131). Not only is this a war film in which we see no war; it is a war film in which men play a wider range of roles than in a conventional genre film, and the men's goals only partly organize the narrative.

The immediate reception for *Grand Illusion* was universally positive, and it was the top movie that year at the French box office. *Pour Vous* praised it for being both artistic and straightforward and providing an ending that occurred naturally without seeming preordained (June 17, 1937, 5). After its triumphant summer opening in Paris, *Grand Illusion* was rereleased throughout France for Armistice Day, November 11, 1937, and was voted film of the year by the French press. *Grand Illusion* was named the best foreign film in many polls abroad and won the best artistic achievement prize at the Venice Film Festival. Even some critics on the right in France could praise the rousing "Marseillaise" resistance scene and appreciate de Boeldieu's noble sacrifice as well as Maréchal and Rosenthal's resolve to return to battle. President Franklin Roosevelt famously screened it at the White House and touted its democratic message. However, during and immediately after World War II, Renoir's sympathetic portrayal of the Germans, from von Rauffenstein and Arthur the prison guard to the widow Elsa, became highly controversial, as did Maréchal's antisemitic outburst against Rosenthal. By the end of the 1940s, however, *Grand Illusion*'s artistic and humanistic legacy was assured by the ciné-club circuit and the renewed auteurist fervor practiced by Bazin and a new generation of cinephiles.

At the peak of his career, Renoir made three more features during the 1930s. Despite his triumphs, his dissatisfaction with the commercial system and mainstream politics alike continued. His next project offered a unique opportunity to challenge the status quo. He undertook a leftist interpretation of the French Revolution, *La Marseillaise* (1938), produced in partnership with the PCF and Ciné-Liberté. Advance subscriptions were sold to union members and others in exchange for eventual discounts or free admission. Ultimately, the budget was not adequate, and a more conventional production company had to be formed.

For their historical reconstruction, Renoir and his team worked to avoid nationalistic clichés and other conventions of fancy costume dramas. They minimized the roles of the usual major historical figures of the revolution. Instead, *La Marseillaise* concentrated on a cluster of people who band together, joining the revolutionary cause for justice as they organically spread the patriotic call to arms, "La Marseillaise," which had just played a key role in *Grand Illusion*: "*La Marseillaise* is an intervention in the long-running struggle to define the Revolution, the founding event of French political modernity, a struggle which established the principal faultlines that would dominate the country's politics well into the twentieth century" (O'Shaughnessy, *Jean Renoir* 133). *La Marseillaise* also pulled the national anthem back toward the side of the leftists and the people, reminding everyone on the right just where this powerful song originated.

A product of multiple political and aesthetic influences as well as detailed historical research, *La Marseillaise* reflected the Popular Front's ideology that workers could sweep aside a corrupt system through collective action. It also revealed Renoir's ongoing concern for women's social positions along with his trademark empathy toward most everyone, regardless of class. That King Louis XVI (Pierre Renoir) came off as a genial if awkward fellow and the aristocrats seemed genuinely frightened rather than cruel or villainous disappointed some on the left. The aristocrats fit in Renoir's sympathetic worldview as much as the pigeon-poaching peasant or patriotic fishwife. *La Marseillaise*, edited by Marguerite Renoir and Marthe Huguet, opened up the revolution's history into a series of self-conscious performances to be contemplated and debated by contemporary viewers. For Renoir, it was a marvelous, unorthodox experiment: "I breathed the exalted air of the Popular Front. For a short time the French really believed they could love one another. One felt oneself borne on a wave of warm-heartedness" (127). His version was hardly about re-creating the pitched battles of the revolution with impassioned public speeches and heads lopped off by the guillotine. For him, nation-building was a joyous, grassroots affair, but without compelling scenes of good versus evil, the narrative bogged down in its original length. *La*

Marseillaise was released in February 1938, as the Popular Front ideals were in decline, and it did not perform well in France, though it proved popular in a few international markets, especially the Soviet Union. The relative failure of *La Marseillaise* was quickly overlooked by many critics in part because *Grand Illusion* was just being released abroad to rave reviews. Thus, Renoir stood as one of France's most celebrated directors as he turned to adapting another novel, Émile Zola's *The Human Beast* (*La Bête humaine*, 1938), for Robert and Raymond Hakim's Paris Film Production company.

Gabin and the Hakims initially approached Renoir, asking him to adapt Zola's naturalist novel about betrayal and madness. Renoir quickly turned the highly detailed and descriptive novel into a taut screenplay. *La Bête humaine* proved to be one of Renoir's most striking cinematic works, much of it shot on location, on and around moving trains and in the Le Havre rail yard. Gabin even learned to operate the huge steam trains to play engineer Jacques Lantier, and Julien Carette mastered the fireman's job of stoking the engine for his role as Lantier's trusty partner, Pecqueux. The opening scene of their train trip from Paris to Le Havre unfurls like a poetic documentary with various

Gabin and Carette as engineers (*La Bête humaine*)

camera mounts providing spectacular mobile perspectives while demonstrating the labor of the actor-engineers. Lantier is a conflicted, doomed protagonist. A seemingly nice fellow, he has inherited violent tendencies, especially when he becomes emotionally aroused around women. His fear of hurting others has kept him single and isolated. Early on he nearly strangles Flore (Blanchette Brunoy), a young woman who has loved him since childhood. Luckily, he is roused from his murderous trance by a passing train, his other love. These bouts of madness allow Gabin to display crazed anger yet again.

Meanwhile, another troubled person is Séverine (Simone Simon), the flirtatious wife of Le Havre rail manager Roubaud (Fernand Ledoux). Since her teens, she has secretly been sleeping with her wealthy godfather, Grandmorin (Jacques Berlioz), as, apparently, had her mother before her. When her oblivious husband jokes that she may be the old guy's illegitimate daughter, the disgusted Séverine, apparently contemplating the possibility of incest for the first time, panics and confesses all. The outraged Roubaud hatches a plan to murder Grandmorin on the return train, which stops to pick up Lantier and his old friend, former convict Cabuche (Renoir). As the train races toward Le Havre, Roubaud and Séverine enter Grandmorin's compartment and pull the curtains; the camera remains in the corridor as the pair kill the old man. Lantier, the only witness to the couple on the train, keeps quiet when he gazes at Séverine's lovely face.

Throughout the second half of *La Bête humaine*, Séverine pursues Lantier to make sure he does not turn her in, exploiting his desire—"Don't look at me like that, you'll ruin your eyes"—and pretending to love him, claiming she had no part in the murder. Instead, the police wrongly arrest Cabuche, who had hated Grandmorin for seducing a girl he knew. Meanwhile, Lantier lets his guard down, falling for Séverine, although she warns him that she can never really love anyone, due to her past, in a scene that mirrors an earlier discussion Lantier had with Flore. Séverine paints Roubaud as an abusive lout and urges Lantier to kill him, but Lantier spares the pathetic husband. Séverine serves as a fascinating femme fatale. Half the time she is deceptive and manipulating, and the rest of the time she is quite honest, speaking from her damaged heart. In a fit of rage, Lantier finally kills Séverine in her apartment while everyone else is dancing nearby at the rail worker's ball to "Le Petit Coeur de Ninon," a song about a fickle woman (Conway, "Popular Songs" 213). Back in the apartment, the shot of Lantier glaring at himself in Séverine's mirror could be out of any of Gabin's tragic Poetic Realist roles. Back on the train to Paris, Lantier confesses his crime to Pecqueux. Following another stunning railroad montage to bracket the film, Lantier leaps from the speeding engine to his death, ending his crippling grief and guilt. Pecqueux stops the train and gently closes Lantier's eyes, much as von Rauffenstein had for de Boeldieu after his sacrifice in *Grand Illusion*.

La Bête humaine was another hit for Renoir and Gabin, and helped Simone Simon, who had been working in Hollywood for a few years, reconnect with her French audience. It was certainly Renoir's last big critical and box office success of the 1930s. While some critics and historians have complained that Renoir's politics were muddied and cynical here, others noted his ongoing sympathy for the plight of the working class and especially women. Georges Sadoul considers *La Bête humaine* Renoir's masterpiece and superior to *Grand Illusion* thanks to its editing, plot structure, acting, and representation of the workers' milieu (*Dictionary* 32). For locations and interior studio sets, the shadowing, depth, and use of passageways to evoke everyone's confinement all owe to Renoir's aesthetic choices and to a Poetic Realist context. Often the camera remains at a distance, peering around corners, observing characters

Simone Simon as the troubled Séverine (*La Bête humaine*)

cross a room or the rail yard before panning to follow them as if spontaneously trying to capture their movements.

Thus, while *La Bête humaine* is built on obvious thematic structures and
binary oppositions—Lantier has a loving stepmother, Séverine has an evil
godfather—the characters are embedded into a rich and realistic scenographic
space. Furthermore, the narration preserves ambiguity by providing just
enough background cues for the audience to become aligned with or at least
feel sympathy for every major figure. All the characters have their personal
demons and their reasons to act as they do. Unlike Zola's novel, Renoir's version remains relatively open-ended. It is unclear what became of Cabuche
and whether the pathetic Roubaud, last seen with Grandmorin's watch in his
hand near Séverine's body, will be caught for the old man's murder or even
hers. Lantier's rash suicide does not seem to help anyone else, unlike that
of de Boeldieu, or Lange's murder of Batala. Renoir's ending, which allows
Gabin to shift from calm resignation to suicidal mania, could be interpreted
as a symptom of the dire contexts of 1938 France and Europe. Renoir offered
a timely adaptation of a French classic as part of his ongoing brand of socially
responsible cinema.

Renoir's final movie of the 1930s, *The Rules of the Game* (*La Règle du jeu*, 1939),
is generally considered one of the greatest motion pictures of all time, though
it was hardly a triumph when it premiered on July 7, 1939. Initial reviews
included puzzled reactions to the uncomfortable mix of comedy, drama,
and satire. Even René Clair reportedly asked Renoir about his overall
point, though a few critics were immediate champions of the film, including
Georges Sadoul, who had visited the set and marveled at Renoir in a bear
suit directing actors. Maurice Bessy at *Cinémonde* declared it "100% Renoir,"
praising his perceptive auteurist vision (63). Yet *Rules of the Game* also benefited from Renoir's usual team, including Koch, Kosma, Marthe Huguet, and
Marguerite, as well as a cadre of recurring actors. Renoir and his crew drew
on personal anecdotes and pertinent theatrical influences: "From Marivaux,
Renoir drew an elegant cynicism and characters whose lives revolve around
love; from Musset, essential elements of his plot and an uneasy tragi-comic
tone; from Beaumarchais, the implicit critique of a smug ruling class on the
edge of a catastrophe and parallel love affairs between masters and servants"
(O'Shaugnessy, *Jean Renoir* 145). To ensure control over this production, Renoir
and his brother Claude, along with three friends and collaborators, formed
NEF (Nouvelle édition française), which they hoped to turn into a sort
of French United Artists, offering more opportunities for cooperatively

produced and distributed auteur films. They also secured a chateau in the Sologne region west of Paris, and set designer Eugene Lourie built interiors back in Joinville, including authentic wood doors and staircases to match the chateau. Lourie was apparently quite aware of Renoir's shooting style, requiring deep spaces and room for camera movement, so he created sets appropriate for these techniques (Thompson, *Breaking* 233). *Rules of the Game* was a prestige Renoir production, and thanks to the elaborate sets, Coco Chanel costumes, and unfortunate weather delays, it became the most expensive French film of the year.

Renoir's preferred mode of storytelling was to begin with personal observations, gradually grafting them organically onto a narrative structure. From the beginning, he described *Rules of the Game* as a tale built around women's limited options in society and their often untenable situation, being pursued by assorted men competing clumsily for their attention. He had recently met Nora Gregor, an Austrian in exile with her aristocratic husband, and selected her as the upper-class hinge pin of the drama, playing opposite her earthy maid, Lisette (Paulette Dubost). Gregor's life story as a reluctant immigrant influenced Renoir's ongoing development of her character. The ensemble cast included the naive aviator André Jurieux (Roland Toutain), who flew across the Atlantic to impress the married Christine (Gregor), and his old friend Octave (Renoir), who also has a crush on Christine. Her husband, the wealthy Robert de la Cheyniest (Marcel Dalio), becomes jealous enough over André to break off from his longtime mistress, Geneviève (Mila Parély). When they all leave Paris for a trip to Robert's country chateau of La Colinière, the servant class expands from the head of staff Corneille (Eddy Debray) and Lisette to include her brutish Alsacien groundskeeper husband, Schumacher (Gaston Modot), as well as the poacher Marceau (Julien Carette), now hired on as a footman. Marceau takes an immediate fancy to Lisette and Christine attracts additional suitors as well. At some point in the past, Christine's visiting niece Jackie (Anne Mayen) also fell in love with the clueless André. Frustrated desire is everywhere.

The idle upper-class rituals include a vast rabbit hunt and an elaborate costume party, which allow the interpersonal tensions and attempted seductions to surface, with parallel shenanigans erupting among the staff. Once Christine realizes that her husband has been betraying her with Geneviève, her three suitors each try to whisk her away in absurd romantic performances. Meanwhile, the jealous groundskeeper Schumacher chases Marceau through the party, firing his pistol, prompting Robert to ask Corneille to "stop this

Renoir plots out *Rules of the Game* (*Rules of the Game*)

comedy," to which Corneille replies, "Which one, sir?" André, who does not recognize the social rules, naively sets much of the chaos in motion. He is completely incapable of seeing the heroic role he is expected to play, just as Christine is tragically late in recognizing her part in her farce of a marriage. Even before the film was released, Renoir summarized Christine's character as mistaken, believing her romantic life is simple, when in fact desires are complicated. He also added, "In our era, only two options exist for women: Work for a job that absorbs her or clean up after the kids." He wanted Christine's life to be different (*Pour Vous*, January 25, 1939, 3). Dido Freire worked as script and continuity assistant.

Unfortunately for all, a case of mistaken identity over which wife is leaving with André soon motivates Schumacher to shoot the famous aviator, believing André is seducing Lisette. Christine, who had been on the verge of running off with André, or even Octave, limps back to Robert, who declares it all a terrible accident. Octave and Marceau, both crushed, head off in separate directions. Just as the worlds of the de Boeldieus and von Rauffensteins were falling apart in *Grand Illusion*, here the old social order is imploding, this time from within. Rather than offering a simple scathing attack, *Rules of the Game* provides an insightful lampooning and cynical contemplation of an unjust and confused social world. The upper crust may be idle snobs, but the narration appreciates them nonetheless, and the lower class can be just as foolish. Everyone struggles to find happiness, and characters' roles are determined by their cultural situation, personal motives, and illusory rules of conduct. Like it or not, as Octave explains to Robert, the awful thing about life on this Earth is that everyone has their reasons.

The soundtrack in *Rules of the Game* cleverly works to escape the theatrical limitations of a dialogue-heavy comedy of manners. Robert surrounds himself with a distracting array of noisy toys and music machines; gunshots punctuate the hunt and the party; Kosma's lyrical music underscores and

André arrives at the chateau (*Rules of the Game*)

comments on the class struggles and personal deceptions afoot. Yet *Rules of the Game*'s reputation rests chiefly on its array of visual strategies. Renoir has repeatedly claimed that as he learned his craft, he moved increasingly away from close-ups and shot/reverse shots, and *Rules of the Game* may best display this confidence in staging the action in complicated scenographic spaces. Cameras often dolly around corners and peek into doorways to uncover characters lurking about or already engaged in conversation. Martin O'Shaughnessy points out that in *Rules of the Game*, "depth staging and camera mobility repeatedly invite the spectator to see more than the characters, thus stressing the spatiotemporal limitations of their vision" ("Shooting" 21). Early on in Paris, when Octave visits Christine in her vast home, the camera takes off, independently tracking and panning to peer into her room from another doorway, like the point of view of an unseen witness. Similarly, when André arrives at La Colinière for an uncomfortable meeting in front of the guests, Renoir's camera arcs behind a pillar for a better view, and then Octave and Robert appear in the background plane of action reacting to André and Christine in the foreground as she awkwardly introduces him to the other guests.

Depth and longer takes for conversations and encounters between characters open up the space, placing great emphasis on the performers in their environment. For instance, when Schumacher discovers Marceau flirting with Lisette in the basement kitchen, Renoir stages him in depth, peering through a window toward the couple in the foreground. Later, when Marceau tries to sneak out of the kitchen undiscovered, Lisette distracts Schumacher while Marceau sneaks out in the background, until he stumbles, and the long comical pursuit begins that will disrupt the party upstairs. There, André and Robert carry a hysterical Geneviève up the staircase in a shot with multiple planes of action, including the gun-toting Schumacher in the middle ground searching for Marceau, who will be revealed hiding among the elegant guests. In every scene, the camerawork and blocking of actors exploit deep space and embedded frames, staging even highly farcical action in a naturalistic setting. Renoir's storytelling and stylistic arsenal of the late 1930s prompted Bazin to credit him with helping launch a revolution in cinematic style, as a director who placed his faith in reality, delighting the spectator with a dynamic field of vision that displays a refreshing spontaneity: "No one has grasped the true nature of the screen better than Renoir. . . . The suppleness, the mobility, the vital richness of form in his direction, result from the care and joy he takes in draping his films in the simple cloak of reality" (Bazin, *Jean Renoir* 87, 91).

Marceau and Lisette (*Rules of the Game*)

While Renoir liked to claim that during the premiere of *Rules of the Game* he saw someone in the audience trying to set the theater on fire, the film's reception was not all negative: "There were as many positive reviews as negative ones. . . . Among the favorable reviews, there were few without reservations (in particular about Nora Grégor and Jean Renoir's acting), whereas practically all the negative reviews were unqualified" (Gauteur 347). Among those celebrating the film was *Beaux Art*: "It is probably the most original, the most personal film that French sound cinema has yet produced" (Gauteur 350). Nino Frank admitted the movie was incredibly complex, warranting multiple viewings, and not for children, but he also claimed it was the best Renoir so far and would be discussed far in the future. Its story meanders and detours like a great river and follows a rhythm more associated with a great novel than a film, "revealing humanity in its pure state" (6). The rabbit hunt was cited as stunning and cinematically unprecedented (*L'Action Française*, July 7, 1939). However, many reviewers and audiences found it disappointing, ponderous, and ideologically confused, with a rare discord between the acting styles, which ranged from plausible to buffoonish. In addition to

Bessy's review, *L'Avant Scène Cinema* culled highlights from pertinent outlets. René Jeanne in *Le Petit Journal* suggested that Renoir should have teamed up with a veteran screenwriter such as Henri Jeanson and made the satire less violent (September 20, 1939), and *Le Petit Parisien* found almost nothing of interest in any of the characters (July 13, 1939). The narrative seemed splintered among multiple characters with obscure or contradictory motives. The opening setup in Paris was said to lack dramatic purpose and energy. Moreover, many critics over the years questioned the choice of Gregor for Christine, finding her performance stiff, hardly the stuff to inflame so many hearts. Meanwhile, Renoir has been both praised and criticized for his cartoonish Octave. Thus, its reception was uneven but allowed for a wide variety of engaged perspectives. Initially the print was 113 minutes long, then Marguerite tightened it to 100 minutes for the release, but immediately following the premiere, *Rules of the Game* was reduced to a 90-minute version and then another at 85 minutes. Gauteur suggests that the various truncations may partly account for some of the confusion over characterization and plot (347).

The distribution campaign for *Rules of the Game* was also poorly timed. NEF and Distribution Parisienne de Films decided to open at only two major cinemas during July, including one week with English subtitles, and then offer the wide release beyond Paris in November. *Rules of the Game* played for four weeks in Paris and in several hub cities, including Rennes, but France entered into war with Germany in early September 1939, closing most theaters. The strategy for a limited initial opening had proven a financial disaster, though *Rules of the Game* was released in a few outside markets, including North Africa. With the Occupation in 1940, hundreds of French films were officially banned, including those featuring prominent Jews, such as Marcel Dalio, which meant neither *Grand Illusion* nor *Rules of the Game* could be rereleased. In late 1940, Renoir and his companion, continuity person Dido Freire, managed to receive exit visas and left for New York. *Rules of the Game* had to wait until the postwar years for its series of revivals and rediscoveries.

French Cinema at the End of the 1930s

While *Rules of the Game* offered a cynical view of the state of the world, a few films provided more overt warnings about the rise of political uncertainty, fascism, and threats of war in Europe. One of the most politically engaged projects was André Malraux's *Days of Hope* (*Espoir*, 1940), based loosely on his book about the Spanish Civil War. Shot in Spain, including on war-torn locations, and completed in Paris, *Espoir* boasted real combatants as performers.

Given Malraux's dramatization of authentic events, *Espoir* anticipates the Italian Neorealist *Paisan* (Rossellini, 1946). Its premiere was set for September 1939. However, France's declaration of war led the government to ban *Espoir's* release, and it only appeared in June 1945, long after Franco had crushed the Republican cause in Spain.

The veteran Marcel L'Herbier had directed a string of star vehicles throughout the decade, including his own remake of *The Cheat* (*Forfaiture*, 1937) with Sessue Hayakawa and Ève Francis, and *Rasputin* (1938), featuring Harry Baur. But he ended the decade by launching the patriotic *Entente cordiale* (1939), a highly polished costume drama. *Entente cordiale* celebrates the daring 1904 alliance between France and England that was initiated by King Edward VII in the face of rising tensions with Germany and Russia. Once the two nations compromise over their colonial competition in Africa, with its "terrifying sun and unsettling atmosphere," they forge a union that will help them prove victorious in World War I. The movie boldly asserts that the French and British are strongest when they fight side by side, and it demonizes those who might consider any alliance with Germany. *Entente cordiale* was openly political, which undercut its chance to represent France at the 1939 Cannes Film Festival. Instead, features by Duvivier, Christian-Jaque, Feyder, and de Baroncelli were chosen for what proved to be an ill-fated festival.

In hindsight, 1939 can be seen as a devastating year for France and its cinema; war was declared in early September after prolonged threats. In the months leading up to war and the eventual Occupation, many in the film industry were buoyed by 1938's aesthetic and economic triumphs, which seemed to prove French cinema was healthy and resilient. During January, *Pour Vous* even proclaimed that "1939 will be a great year for French cinema." Although the entire nation faced a disastrous crisis by year's end, the initial confidence at *Pour Vous* was not entirely unjustified. France's decentralized studio system had reached a relatively mature stage, generating considerable international prestige along with economic stability. By the end of the 1930s, mainstream French cinema was built around a relatively small cadre of major stars, writing teams, and auteur directors and their recurring production crews. Producers had to compete for their participation, unlike the Hollywood studio system, where talent was under long-term contracts.

Auteur directors are always cited as the backbone of 1930s cinema, but the star system guaranteed reliable commercial genre films. During the period 1937–40, popular actors such as Raimu, Fernandel, Françoise Rosay, Arletty, and Marcel Dalio could appear in multiple feature films in a year. Jules Berry performed in eleven movies in 1938 alone, all with different production companies. France's fifty top actors starred in over a thousand films during the 1930s. For the historical drama *Chess Player* (*Le Joueur d'échecs*, Dréville, 1938), the salaries for Rosay and Conrad Veidt were said to account for more than half of the total budget. Talented screenwriters were also in high demand. Charles Spaak was hired by more than twenty productions during the late 1930s, working with a range of top directors and a variety of producers, from Germany's UFA to the one-film studio Gladiator. Rising costs for talent, studio space, and scripts increased the average budget for a French film, which doubled between 1935 and 1938. France's classical period was thriving with consistently high production values, an innovative range of stories and styles, and an array of exhibition circuits, which included 17.5mm for smaller towns and rural distribution. Many French producers and filmmakers were entering into new coproduction contracts with studios in Italy, Germany, England, and Monaco. The final years of the 1930s demonstrate just how well French cinema had adapted to the domestic and global marketplaces, where they were earning renewed international respect.

The French star system took advantage of the reputations of many famed performers moving from stage to screen throughout the decade. Louis Jouvet stands as a prime example of a major figure in French culture. He was regularly cited as helping bring high art aspirations and professionalism to popular cinema. After working with Feyder, Renoir, and L'Herbier, among others, Jouvet appeared as an acting teacher, Professor Lambertin, in Marc Allégret's *The Curtain Rises* (*Entrée des artistes*, 1938). The clever dialogue was written by Henri Jeanson. Allégret's movie foregrounds the labor of acting, where talent includes displaying perfect diction and a ready arsenal of literary quotations. Lambertin's dedication to the craft, stern advice, and paternalistic guidance for his conservatory students seemed to come from Jouvet himself, who often mentored and championed young talent in real life. *Entrée des artistes* also fit Allégret's oeuvre well. He had already directed a number of movies built around young adults and their hopes, fears, and struggles, and he was known for advancing the careers of new actors. For *Entrée des artistes*, Allégret and Jeanson acknowledge the competing contexts of theater and motion pictures. For instance, after students François (Claude Dauphin) and Isabelle (Janine Darcey) spend the night together, François jokes that if this were a movie it would reveal half-smoked cigarettes, an unmade bed, a pillow tossed on the floor, and her stockings dangling off a chair to signal a night of passionate lovemaking. Meanwhile, the camera scans the room to

Louis Jouvet as a demanding teacher (*Entrée des artistes*)

frame up each item he mentions. The film blurs the lines between play-acting and reality. In addition to self-conscious winks to the audience and frank references to sexual activity among the students, *Entrée des artistes* acknowledges risqué performances on other levels, with several young men moonlighting as male escorts.

While *Entrée des artistes* celebrates hard work and determination, it also reveals the inherent power structure and class divisions between the pretentious teachers and vulnerable students. The women students in particular are carefully examined for their appearance as much as their performance, with Lambertin inspecting them at close range with his opera glasses. Lambertin coaches the actors in life lessons and acting styles, erasing the differences between their roles and their selves, and the film includes dramatic high comedy and high tragedy, culminating with the substitution of real poison during a recital, which kills François's former girlfriend Coecelia (Odette Joyeux). Dalio, playing the police inspector, has to struggle to decipher clues from a host of suspects and witnesses comfortable with performing and deception before he can locate the real culprit. By the end, Lambertin uses

Coecelia's death on stage as just another learning experience about life, death, love, and acting, to bolster and challenge his students going forward. French critics praised the first-rate acting among the young performers, especially Dauphin and Darcey, though many regretted the overly melodramatic, "literary" ending with Coecelia's sudden revelations and suicide. Abroad, Jouvet's name commanded attention from reviewers. The *New York Times*, however, found Allégret's direction "routine," and while it praised the ending's realism, it lamented that Isabelle is not given a chance to prove herself after all her sacrifices, in the tradition of American drama films such as *Stage Door* (*La Cava*, 1937) (April 22, 1939, 15).

In addition to benefiting from a strong range of star performers, many classical French films of the late 1930s displayed a professional confidence in staging action in longer takes than American cinema. A number of films respected the context for the performance without relying exclusively on continuity editing and shot/reverse shots to deliver details. Even conventional genre films, whether based on original scripts or adaptations of stage plays or novels, incorporated creative solutions to avoiding the look of canned theater and formulaic continuity editing. The popular crime comedy *Fric-Frac* (Lehmann, 1939), based on an Édouard Bourdet play, typifies this strategy of using a mobile camera to open up the space, revealing characters in the off-screen space and reframing to follow their antics. It stars Arletty and Michel Simon as a pair of small-time crooks, Loulou and Jo. Their street slang and crude lifestyles intrigue a straightlaced jeweler, Marcel, played by Fernandel, who needs a distraction from the unwanted advances of his boss's daughter, Renée (Hélène Robert). This stylish comedy is aware of its status as entertainment and opens with the title sequence seemingly broadcast on a primitive television screen. The incompetent thief Jo even complains about unrealistic gangster movies that make robbery look too easy, and Marcel refers to a film he once saw as a guide for how Loulou can repent and change her ways. In broad caricatures, the three comic actors perform their parts with gusto. Marcel pursues Loulou while her abusive crook boyfriend sits in prison. But the persistent Renée wants Marcel to marry her and inherit the family business. When Loulou and Jo try to rob the jewelry store, Marcel gets stuck between the jewelers and his new friends, who convince him to stay in his world, marry Renée, and be the boss of his relationship and the store. Loulou claims that her boyfriend slaps her around and Marcel should do the same to retain Renée's respect. The women end up getting what they want in *Fric-Frac*, but only by allowing a strong man to take control of their lives.

A happy ending (*Fric-Frac*)

France's cinematic output for 1939 was on schedule to rival any other year of the decade. Projects were underway from veterans Gance, Diamant-Berger, L'Herbier, and de Baroncelli, among many others, as well as auteurs Feyder, Guitry, Duvivier, and Renoir, plus an array of younger directors in their thirties, such as Jean Boyer, Pierre Chenal, and Edmond T. Gréville. There were also many immigrant film professionals working in France, either as new permanent residents or temporary employees ready to flee Europe for England or North America if the situation changed. For instance, German director Robert Siodmak had become embedded in French production. In 1939, he directed *Personal Column* (*Pièges*), starring Maurice Chevalier, before leaving for Hollywood. Two other German émigrés, G. W. Pabst and Max Ophüls, were also among the more prestigious foreign directors working in France. In 1938, Pabst had directed Louis Jouvet in *The Shanghai Drama* (*Le Drame de Shanghai*), a tale about exile partly shot in Saigon as a stand-in for China. Next, his *Young Girls in Distress* (*Jeunes filles en détresse*, 1939) launched the teenaged Micheline Presle's career.

Ophüls, a new French citizen, adapted *The Novel of Werther* (*Le Roman de Werther*, 1938) from the Goethe stories, then *There's No Tomorrow* (*Sans lendemain*, 1939), starring Edwige Feuillère. He made the lavish costume drama *Sarajevo* (*De Mayerling à Sarajevo*, 1940), featuring elaborate studio sets and a cluster of Comédie Française actors. It follows the doomed Archduke Franz Ferdinand (John Lodge) and his wife, Sophie (Feuillère), as they practically sacrifice themselves for love and duty at Sarajevo, where their murder will ignite World War I. The production was interrupted by the contemporary crisis, however, and Ophüls entered the French army. He and his crew were allowed to return and finish the production, which premiered in May 1940, just a week before the German offensive. Ophüls, a Jew who broadcast "Goodnight to Hitler" anti-Nazi radio messages into Germany, fled to Switzerland before eventually settling in California.

In France, the government increased measures to regulate cinema more fully. During July 1939, the film industry, including its censorship, was placed under a new Information division along with propaganda services and newsreels. Cinema's political value and responsibilities were becoming increasingly clear nationally. In March, French troops were mobilized as Hitler invaded Czechoslovakia. By the end of March, Franco's forces had overtaken Madrid and Barcelona, ending the Spanish Civil War. Even though the threats of war remained high and Europe's situation increasingly dire, the summer 1939 box office broke records. By late August, the Soviets and Nazis signed a nonaggression pact. On September 1, 1939, Germany invaded Poland, triggering France and Great Britain to declare war on Germany two days later. The Cannes Film Festival shut down immediately. At least seventy feature films were in production at that point, but the government's censor office quickly put new conditions in place, including the prohibition of any demoralizing or pacifist films or any movies mocking the military. Positive stories were needed to bolster the domestic population and maintain a strong, proud image of French culture abroad. Initially, with so many actors and technicians being called up for service, some productions were forced to shut down temporarily or, as in the case of René Clair's new project, were canceled altogether. Writer-director Henri Decoin became a captain in the air force; Renoir, Jean Delannoy, and Chomette joined the military's film unit; and even Gabin was called to service. Strangely, even after war was declared, the government allowed films from UFA and other German studios to be distributed throughout France even as some French movies were banned.

As of February 1940, no new film projects had been approved, and only thirty of those seventy productions underway late in 1939 appeared during the first half of the year. Duvivier began filming the patriotic *Untel père et fils* (*Hearts of France*), a melodramatic saga about three generations of a French family forced repeatedly to fight German aggression over the years. However, Duvivier fled France, completing the project in the United States. Movie theaters had surprising new rules, including restrictions limiting audience sizes, exterior lighting, and night screenings. There was a fear of large loss of life in the event of a bombing raid. Attendance fell to six million entries during September, but gradually, as all-out war was delayed, some rules were relaxed, allowing attendance to climb to twenty-three million by November as the government recognized the value of entertainment and patriotic newsreels. From September 1939 until May 1940, France experienced what became known as the *Drôle de guerre*, or phony war. French and German soldiers were positioned on either side of the border, but no real conflict began. In May 1940, the Nazis invaded the Netherlands and Belgium, surprising the French military by circling up and around the famed Maginot Line of defense in the east. France was quickly overrun, with tragic results. Among the first cinema personnel to die was composer Maurice Jaubert, shot while helping blow up a bridge to stop the advancing Nazi army. In June 1940, the Germans were in Paris, and many in the film community were scattering to the south and abroad seeking refuge. What many called the golden age of French cinema had come to a very abrupt end.

CHAPTER 7

Occupation Cinema

A Fractured Nation and Film Community

Reorganizing the Industry: New Institutions and Collaboration

The impact of the German invasion and Occupation on French cinema was as complex as it was brutal. The Germans entered France in 1940 prepared for a quick transition, intent on securing the nation and forcing rapid political, economic, and social transformations for a stable, sustainable French state, dependent on the Third Reich. They realized in advance that they would need to work with as many local politicians and business interests as possible. Collaboration with French individuals and institutions was preferable to blunt dominance by force. German officials sought influential partners in government, industry, and education, many of whom saw few options other than to cooperate in the short term. The cinema was particularly vulnerable to such collusion. Throughout the 1930s, German French coproductions had forged many business alliances and working relations that the Nazis could now build on. The Germans also exploited Paris as a luxurious oasis for officers and soldiers taking refuge from their battles. Thus, entertainment was high on their agenda, including the exhibition of German-language movies and requisition of cinemas as *Soldatenkinos* for the military.

A Nazi-run film trade journal, *Le Film*, was launched in fall 1940 and quickly became a major voice for communicating the strict new policies aimed at reorganizing the industry. It was also preoccupied with convincing everyone that French cinema was rebounding rapidly after the Armistice. *Le Film* mapped the progress in bringing French film back to life, from Paris to Lyon to Nice, helping the Nazi propaganda machine and the collaborating French officials illustrate that local culture continued to thrive after the invasion. In reality, many theaters, studios, and distributors remained closed by the authorities or were slow to recover due to lack of materials, personnel, and utilities.

During June 1940, the aged World War I hero Marshal Philippe Pétain had formed a new French government, anchored in Vichy, which signed the Armistice allowing France to be divided into two zones. Germany retained direct control over the industrialized north and the strategic Atlantic coastline, while the Vichy government technically operated the remaining 40 percent of southeastern France, as well as the colonies, under what has been labeled a "pluralist dictatorship" of Pétain and his inner circle. Pétain claimed to be launching a national revolution and brought brutal crackdowns on "anti-French" elements, including Jews, communists, and Freemasons. Much of the film community joined the exodus from German-controlled Paris into Vichy's "unoccupied" southern zone as the lesser of two evils, with Nice and Marseille becoming hubs for film production. Over the next several years, *Le Film* went out of its way to publicize which cinemas were reopening and point out important productions getting underway. Its pages were full of gala premieres for new films. *Le Film* also heralded major French directors and stars who returned from the Vichy zone to work on projects in Paris: "Michel Simon is back in Paris to star in his next movie!" *Le Film* also featured photos of patrons waiting outside movie palaces as evidence that French cinema was almost back to normal. Movies were regularly said to be breaking post-Armistice box office records.

The Germans imposed immediate changes to nearly every aspect of the film industry, including placing cinema under their Propagand Abteilung division, responsible to Joseph Goebbels, Nazi minister of Propaganda. They also established a more localized Filmprufstelle (film control board) for France. Initially they refused to grant any permits for non-German productions. To regulate distribution, they prohibited the popular 17.5mm format, crippling thousands of small rural cinemas. Germany wanted to force their 16mm format onto France and thus better control the movies circulating in remote areas. The Germans also seized the holdings of all French distributors and banned all previous films from being screened until they had been approved. Before any exhibitor could reopen, they had to receive official permits from the head of the German military administration in France, with the forms filled out in triplicate in French and German. The paperwork included verification of the applicants' nationality, via their official identity card.

During the fall of 1940, censorship rules, including script approval, were put into place, as well as other strict procedures, including collecting license fees from distributors, actors, and technicians who had to apply and pay for the right to work. Even ticket prices were dictated by the committee. The German authorities wanted to get the film industry up and running as soon as possible, but not before guaranteeing fiscally responsible practices and purging Jews and other potential enemies from the entertainment business. In *Le Film*, for instance, one page could list which Jewish-owned enterprises were being seized, while the opposite page proudly announced that Tobis signed Fernandel to a new comedy or show Danielle Darrieux attending a lavish opening. *Le Film* also managed to publish in fancy colors, including gaudy advertisements and glamour photos, such as press releases of the blue-eyed Kristina Söderbaum, at a time when paper and ink were rationed and in short supply.

Initially, the only new movies available in occupied France for many months were German productions dubbed into French and newsreels. *Le Film* regularly inserted images proving that there were many French citizens lining up to see German-made films. For instance, *The Golden City* (*Die goldene Stadt*, *La Ville dorée*, Harlan, 1942), in Agfa color, was singled out repeatedly as it ran for thirty weeks in the Normandie cinema on the Champs-Élysées. *The Golden City* was one of the prestige pictures that Goebbels was counting on to win over French audiences. In the occupied zone, approved new French productions had to promise that several prints would be made available with German subtitles for the occupying forces. Any existing French film prints deemed unworthy or even dangerous were destroyed, typically recycled for the valuable materials, as were American and British prints pillaged from distributors. Henri Langlois, Georges Franju, and Marcel L'Herbier managed to save and hide innumerable prints, some in wine caves and cellars across France, while others were transferred to friendly archives abroad, including in Denmark and Italy. Many prints were secretly moved into underground vaults in the Palais de Chaillot, right across the river from the Eiffel Tower, thanks to a heroic German archivist, Frank Hensel. On more than one occasion, Germaine Dulac personally sought assurance from Hensel, who was also president of the International Federation of Film Archivist group, to protect prints that were at risk of being seized.

Throughout the Occupation, Langlois, Franju, Dulac, and others had to advocate for the Cinémathèque française and fight proposals to eradicate its collection or replace it with an alternate German-run film agency. Ironically, in some ways the Cinémathèque gradually became a more stable institution during the Occupation despite all the threats to its holdings, some of which were indeed seized by the Nazis, moved to Germany, or destroyed. But for the first time, regular government funding helped Langlois and his staff formalize and expand their mission as they also bought up and saved valuable collections, including a sizable cache of silent negatives and prints from Gaumont. The Cinémathèque was even allotted valuable film stock to transfer and preserve rare and vulnerable older reels.

But all around them, the industry was changing dramatically and dangerously. The Germans quickly launched a new vertically integrated studio, Continental Films, a subsidiary of UFA's parent company and allied with Tobis. The new studio fell under the control of Berlin's Max Winkler, head of Germany's film industry, who answered directly to Goebbels. Continental quickly boasted the largest, most profitable theater chain in France thanks to confiscated Jewish-owned cinemas and exhibition companies, including those of Jacques Haïk and León Siritsky. Tobis also commandeered and absorbed closed studio spaces and cinemas and then partnered with Pathé's circuit for increased first-run exhibitions. Continental, under the leadership of producer Alfred Greven, became the largest producer during the Occupation.

Moreover, the affiliated ACE (L'Alliance cinématographique européenne), which had formerly distributed all UFA films in France, now dominated French distribution, including forcing German newsreels onto all cinemas in both zones. From the start, the German-made newsreels met with jeers from audiences, leading officials in *Le Film* to warn that unless such public demonstrations were stopped, all cinemas in Paris would be closed. House lights were left on during newsreels to discourage people from protesting or mocking the content and to allow roving inspectors to arrest troublemakers. Fuel for the trucks needed to distribute film prints to theaters was carefully rationed, though ACE and Tobis received preferential allotments. These distributors also managed to purchase, at artificially low prices, formerly Jewish-owned laboratories for producing film stock and striking prints. As the Germans consolidated power in the industry, they also stripped some shuttered studios and labs of their equipment, shipping it to Germany to bolster their production at home.

Alfred Greven's goal at Continental was to ensure his studio's dominant position and help jump-start high-quality "French" film production by signing top talent and exploiting the best production facilities available. Greven regularly twisted arms and plotted to secure successful professionals and promising newcomers alike. He was well known for his manipulative tactics. For instance, André Cayatte, who had escaped a German prisoner of war camp, later explained that Greven was aware of his illegal status and insisted he work for Continental or he would be banned from all production. Cayatte delivered three successful genre films featuring stars like Danielle Darrieux and Michel Simon for Continental, including a lively adaptation and remake of Émile Zola's *Shop Girls of Paris* (*Au bonheur des dames*, 1943). Michel Simon stars as the proprietor of a small shop being displaced by a grand new department store, where his nemesis, played by Albert Préjean, hires his niece (Blanchette Brunoy) and connives with a wealthy woman (Suzy Prim) to destroy the competition. The settings are lavish, with spectacular costuming and a highly mobile camera, all evidence of Continental's vast resources.

In Greven's pursuit of revitalizing French film culture, he worried less about producing overt propaganda films and more about creating popular movies to replace the banned American releases. The result was a rather artificial situation with the illusion of creative freedom in a highly repressive context. As Evelyn Ehrlich notes, "Paradoxically, the greatest artistic liberty in occupied France was to be had under the aegis of the German production company" (46). Yet while Continental ended up producing some surprisingly inventive films with complex, even ambivalent ideological perspectives, it was ultimately a vital instrument of the Nazi regime intent on proving that German–French collaboration was good for France and its cultural vitality.

Already in the summer of 1940, German committees began assessing all French industries, including cinema and other forms of entertainment, for efficient ways to get the nation up and running while imposing strict new expectations and regulations. For filmmaking, practical concerns included how to allocate valuable electricity and film stock, quotas for how many titles could profitably be produced and distributed in a year, systems to guarantee that cinemas reported ticket sales accurately, and policies for who should be allowed to participate in the film industry. The Vichy government, eager to retain nominal control over France's cinema, met the challenge by installing Guy de Carmoy as director of their Service du Cinéma. De Carmoy had evaluated industrial and regulatory aspects of the French film industry during the mid-1930s, and even though he was opposed to collaboration, he agreed to direct Vichy's Film Office to keep the Germans from taking over all aspects of cinema (Ehrlich 14). The organization retained offices in Paris to allow close consultation between representatives of both regimes. Vichy's

goal was "to bring order to an industry notorious for turbulence and to promote filmmaking of distinction" (Nord 277). During his short and difficult
reign, de Carmoy negotiated regularly with Nazi officials, including during
their seizure and sale of Jewish-owned theaters and studios in France. When
the Germans agreed to allow the Vichy government to establish its committee to regulate French film production in 1940, de Carmoy's recommendation
for its director was Raoul Ploquin, who had worked with Greven previously
and participated in German French coproductions during the 1930s. Ploquin
took over the Comité d'Organisation des Industries Cinématographiques
(COIC) and helped introduce systemic changes in how movies were made,
distributed, and exhibited in France.

Greven and Ploquin were both opposed to dumping German films and
newsreels onto the captive French audience, and they wanted to revive
and guide French domestic output, within the limits imposed. They also
wanted to reopen repertory cinemas, but Vichy's Commission of Control
banned sixty-five classic French features as demoralizing or mocking the
military, including Renoir's *Tire au flanc* and *Lower Depths*, Carné's *Quai des
brumes* and *Le jour se lève*, plus the Gabin vehicles *Lady Killer* and *Pépé le Moko*.
Some of these banned titles could and did play in the Occupied zone. Nonetheless, while the German and Vichy governments wanted studios and cinemas to reopen and flourish, they agreed that consistently higher-quality new
French films could prove popular in France and compete successfully globally
in neutral markets against American and British product. A healthy French
industry would provide much-needed entertainment and cultural prestige while generating tax revenue. Gradually, under COIC supervision,
French production levels rebounded, and by 1942, France accounted for
80 percent of its own box office. The artificial elimination of competition
from Hollywood and beyond, plus the increasing war-time attendance,
created unique opportunities.

Another successful new program involved encouraging French-made animation, which was especially important due to the absence of American
cartoons. The COIC helped provide funding for animation and documentaries. French animation was particularly weak, so approved cartoons were
guaranteed national distribution, coupled with specific new feature titles. The
COIC's daunting mission was to stabilize an industry that was risky and
unpredictable even in normal times. The war, with its loss of markets, fleeing or imprisoned employees, bombardments, and acts of resistance and sabotage, forced the COIC to paint a positive picture as it constantly imposed

new regulations and clamped down on dissent, trying to manage a vast, unruly, and even volatile industry.

De Carmoy's initial leadership of the COIC allowed him to follow up on the motion picture management recommendations he had proposed in the 1930s. To guarantee a more sustainable and profitable number of productions, double bills were prohibited. A new precensorship policy was put in place, replacing the chaotic, localized practices of the past. Every script had to be submitted in advance for approval, and often censors cut scenes and prohibited specific dialogue and actions. Even location shooting had to be approved, and vast swaths of France, especially near the shorelines, were off limits, which affected what sorts of stories could be told and forced more productions to remain in the studios. COIC also required that key employees have a professional identity card, which had to be renewed annually. The approval process required evidence of adequate technical skills, but it also ensured that no Jews or other "enemies of the state" could work in the industry. COIC regulations tightened from year to year until everyone involved in production, including workers making titles as well as hairdressers and costume shop employees, needed a permit. The flexible employment model of the 1930s, when personnel, some from live theater, could pass in and out of cinema, was over.

To regulate finances, including tax collection, the COIC installed a new accounting system, ending the notoriously corrupt and unreliable self-reporting of box office sales during the 1930s. Now ticket prices were determined by the government, with physical tickets provided by COIC and the numbered stubs collected to prove sales. No cinema could open without adopting COIC's verifiable box office and reimbursement system, which helped the government-imposed distributors and made industry revenues more predictable. During 1942, a new 18 percent luxury tax on all movie tickets increased ticket prices further, artificially boosting the box office receipts. The cost of a ticket was closely governed by the COIC, with regular postings in Le Film, explaining which theaters could charge which amounts at which times. The increased production costs, steady stream of new taxes and ticket prices, plus the highest attendance levels of the war in 1942 increased box office revenue dramatically going into 1943, validating the COIC's policies to the Germans.

However, increasing problems with shortages of electricity and fuel for studios and theaters accumulated. Guidelines changed regularly under the COIC, which took many of its orders directly from both Vichy and the Nazi governments. For instance, cinemas in many towns had to reduce screenings down to once a day and close on Tuesdays. By spring 1943, the crises in utilities and other hardships cut into production and exhibition. New rules allowed studios to operate at night, when electricity needs were lowest, and special permit cards were issued to allow film employees to circulate during curfew. By April 1943, the film industry was ordered to decrease electricity use by 50 percent, across the board, from laboratories to studios to cinemas. COIC issued precise prescriptions right down to individual theaters. One half of Parisian cinemas had to close Tuesdays (the Pagode in Paris, for instance) while the other half closed on Fridays (the MacMahon). Some could only run three days a week, skipping every fourth Sunday (the Balzac and Normandie). Despite the electricity warnings, the COIC still required that theaters leave their house lights on low "to allow for safe evacuation" in an emergency, though the real reason was to spy on the audiences. *Le Film* even listed fines levied on specific cinemas that failed to project the required propaganda documentaries and newsreels, as well as other violations, such as who was behind in paying their taxes and other annual fees to the COIC.

With film stock, electricity, and other materials in short supply, the COIC increasingly restricted the number of production permits granted each year and limited feature films to ninety minutes in length, with a maximum run of thirty prints. The scarcity of silver oxide and other materials kept film stock supplies low and expenses high. In practice, German productions, especially those by Continental or Tobis, received more reliable shipments and better-quality film stock than French producers. The production rules, cumbersome script approval processes, and high costs necessitated ever more efficiency. Shooting scripts became strict outlines, with little stock for retakes. Directors relied more heavily on rehearsals, which some saw as providing increased professional rigor on set, while others regretted a marked loss of spontaneity.

Under the COIC, film projects were eligible for advance loans from the Crédit national bank. Up to 65 percent of a film's budget could be awarded, at a rate of 5 percent interest, which helped motivate a steady number of films in production and provided adequate funding to ensure acceptable technical quality. The approval committee considered the projects' budgets as well as their proposed personnel and especially their star power. Well-made and popular films yielded more predictable ticket sales and tax revenues. Beyond regulating film production, the COIC began supporting the Cinémathèque française with state funds, and it helped launch new film schools, first in Nice and then in Paris, founding IDHEC (Institut des Hautes Etudes Cinématographiques) in 1944. Marcel L'Herbier was appointed as the IDHEC school's first director. Further, the COIC offered two prizes a year for the best French movies exalting the family, with one prize for fiction and one for documentary. Thus, the COIC's reforms and interventions were vast and intended to address and satisfy as many institutional interests as possible.

While the years of the Occupation may be clearly delineated by the 1940 Nazi invasion and then the liberation of Paris in 1944 and the formal end of the war in 1945, the so-called Vichy cinema nonetheless remains a loose label. Some of the key films distributed during World War II were begun before the Occupation, and other films initiated during the war were not released until later. Moreover, with more than two hundred feature films, to say nothing of the hundreds of shorts produced under the COIC, it is always possible for critics to cherry-pick titles to demonstrate more thematic or stylistic coherence than the overall diversity of output warrants. Admittedly, there were scripts submitted that aimed to please censors with tales reinforcing family values and traditions, but one can also find themes and styles that could just as easily have appeared during the 1930s or later in the 1950s. As Pierre Billard points out, although one might argue that roughly 20 percent of Occupation films fit Vichy moral themes, most of these films touched on universal stories and probably would have been completed regardless. Not a single French feature film of the era had pro-German characters or themes; none demonized American or British society (*L'Age* 384).

Jacques Siclier also argues that there is no set core of Pétainist God, family, and tradition themes dominating Vichy-era commercial films, despite the repressive economic and censorship systems in both zones of French cinema. Further, he warns that film scholars rarely discuss the mainstream output of the period, further skewing their sample (23). For instance, the popular melodrama *The Blue Veil* (*Le Voile bleu*, Stelli, 1942) has been labeled a Vichy drama by some critics because Gaby Morlay's character sacrifices her own possible happiness to devote herself to caring for other people's children, helping instill religious and bourgeois values in their lives. However, she only becomes a nun-like nanny after her husband is killed fighting Germany in World War I and her baby dies soon after. Her life serving others is often harsh and thankless; most of the families she helps are flawed and unhappy. As she admits, "No child can ever replace my own." Even the supposedly reactionary *Blue Veil* is dominated by dysfunctional families and avoids simply reinforcing propaganda about the rewards of motherhood, though its ending does include Morlay's character finally recognized for her sacrifices, surrounded by the generations of children she has raised, an image that mirrors certain Vichy posters (Burch and Sellier 105).

One key trait of Occupation narrative cinema, in marked contrast to the wartime German or Italian output, is the surprising absence of overtly fascist themes of the sort being disseminated in French newspapers, newsreels, and state radio. Nova Films, which made the propaganda featurette *Forces occultes* (Mamy, 1943), attacking Freemasons, was a rare exception. Some in the Vichy regime even complained that their cinema was too independent and should be forced to present more virulent antisemitic and profascist propaganda (Bertin-Maghit 143). Similarly, while specific themes may have dominated Vichy and Nazi propaganda, including the central, patriotic role of motherhood for women (even arguing that to be truly healthy a woman should have at least four children), there are few plots of the era built around happy, large families. French narratives rarely engaged directly with Vichy ideology, although they regularly avoid problematic themes and plot points in favor of topics that could receive COIC approval and funding. Evelyn Ehrlich handily summarizes Vichy-era cinema as distinguished by material and cultural constraint and a resulting classicism with new attention to formal perfection in tales that avoid the realities of daily life: "It is as if the films of this period were played out under glass, the characters suffocating in an airless environment, observed from a detached, scientific distance" (97). The result may have been a *cinéma d'évasion*, dodging many real-world problems, but overt propaganda did not dominate French fiction of the Occupation.

There were rigid rules set in place by the Nazis and the COIC, but the Occupation involved an ongoing set of shifting, sometimes contradictory policies on both sides of the demarcation line, and the restrictions varied year to year. For instance, the German Occupation did not immediately lead to the expulsion or imprisonment of all Jews in France. Initially the COIC's task was to remove Jewish workers and financial interests from the industry itself. In 1940 and 1941, the Vichy government began arresting foreign Jewish refugees fleeing into the unoccupied zone and interning them temporarily in concentration camps on French soil. During 1942, French Jewish families were arrested and deported to death camps, with the Nazi and Vichy powers increasingly working in tandem. During the summer of 1942 alone, well over thirty thousand people were rounded up and sent to Auschwitz and other camps. Under the Vichy regime, Pathé's Bernard Natan, still in prison, was stripped of his citizenship and transferred to Auschwitz, where he was killed in 1943.

The roundups were vicious and ongoing, yet a few film personnel managed to hide and even contribute to some Occupation-era productions. Jean-Paul Le Chanois (real name Dreyfus), a major Resistance figure and founding member of the Committee for the Liberation of French Cinema (CLCF), found work as a scriptwriter for Continental thanks to evidence that his grandparents were Catholic, though his assumed Jewish heritage kept him from being awarded an assistant director work permit. Prominent Jews Joseph Kosma and Alexandre Trauner remained undercover throughout the war, secretly working on Marcel Carné's most prestigious productions. Jean Wiener wrote and sold film scores under an assumed name. Composers, designers, and writers had an easier time getting false identities and work permits than the more visible actors and directors. Henri Langlois even managed to hire Lotte Eisner under a fake name to help him catalog films hidden in a cache near Bordeaux.

As the war took a greater toll on Germany, the Nazis instigated various forced labor programs, requiring large numbers of skilled and unskilled laborers to be exported to German sites, and film workers were no different. Specific companies were required to deliver quotas for this *service du travail obligatoire* program, and there are estimates that in some German studios and labs as many as three-fourths of cinema technicians and employees were French by the end of the war. Thus, the lack of available film workers was due to several factors; many fled, others were banned or imprisoned, and some were sent as forced labor to Germany and Italy. For those willing and able to work in France under Occupation conditions, the absence of talent opened new doors. Some more opportunistic figures took full advantage of the antisemitic workplace rules. Director Claude Autant-Lara, for instance, later praised the new situation: "During the Occupation we got rid of a certain number of parasites and it was an era when the cinema could open up, creating a new sort of French school with directors who could finally work. The French worked for the French" (Bertin-Maghit 10). Not all collaborating directors were as blunt as Autant-Lara, who intertwined the 1930s-era nationalistic call for protecting the French industry with the antisemitic discourse of Vichy.

Many people working in the industry were Popular Front leftists quietly trying to preserve more than their own careers, subtly continuing French film practice under nearly impossible circumstances. Despite the multiple hurdles imposed by Nazi Occupation and Vichy collaboration, French cinema of World War II managed to survive with a startling variety of productions creating what Francis Courtade, Evelyn Ehrlich, and others label a "cinema of paradox," in which many complex and even masterful films were completed in this cruel, repressive atmosphere. In addition, some new institutions were formed that ultimately strengthened certain aspects of French cinema after the war. It is no wonder the Occupation and the assessment of French cinema "under the Nazi boot" continue to surprise, fascinate, and frustrate historians.

Transitional Occupation Cinema

One of the first cinematic triumphs of the Vichy system was Marcel Pagnol's *The Well-Digger's Daughter* (*Le Fille du puisatier*, Pagnol, 1940). Pagnol boldly situated his story in contemporary times, with the mobilization and fear of war as backdrop. Once France's armies collapsed, he had to adjust the screenplay. Set in Provence and shot at his southern studios, the tale involves Patricia (Josette Day), a dutiful daughter of the earnest well-digger Pascal (Raimu). His hapless employee Félipe (Fernandel) hopes to marry Patricia, but she has fallen for the wealthy local playboy and stunt pilot Jacques Mazel (Georges Grey). When war is declared, Jacques is off in the air force and Félipe is drafted as well. Just before Félipe leaves, he learns that Patricia is pregnant and frightened. He offers to marry her to solve the problem, much as Panisse had for Fanny in *Marius*, but she refuses. Next, her father finds out and confronts Jacques's parents, but the Mazels refuse to acknowledge the forthcoming child or inform their son. Jacques's mother, jaded by the demands of other young women seduced and abandoned by her son, destroys evidence of Jacques and Patricia's relationship. Disappointed, Pascal sends Patricia away to her aunt in another town to avoid scandal. Soon, Jacques is reported missing in action, shot down behind enemy lines. Meanwhile, Patricia has given birth to a son, naming him after both grandfathers. Ultimately, Pascal brings his "lost daughter" Patricia and her child home, and the mourning Mazels sheepishly meet their illegitimate grandson. After spirited discussions involving guilt and forgiveness, all the parties become reconciled. Then, the supposedly dead Jacques returns miraculously, uniting both families with the happy promise of two marriages, Patricia to Jacques and her sister Amanda to Félipe, in another folksy Pagnol tale about paternity, honor, and redemption.

The Well-Digger's Daughter premiered in December 1940 in Lyon and was a hit in the free southern zone before opening in Paris in spring. It was more closely anchored in social reality than any previous Pagnol film. It was even marketed as "a tale of our time!" The script had been completed during the winter of 1940 and filming began in May, just as the "phony war" turned real.

The original version, which played for months to huge crowds in Paris, even included Pétain's June 17, 1940, radio speech calling for the end of hostilities. That radio address comes near the end of the film as the two families are reconciled and makes it clear that the Armistice allows Jacques and Félipe to stay home permanently with their new wives, doubling the happy resolution. As a project begun under one government and completed under another, *The Well-Digger's Daughter* avoided some official restrictions, including its extended length. Pagnol and his film were praised for their authenticity, both for thematic points, including frustration and resignation over the war, and for the Provençal settings and accents (though much of the film was shot in his studio, built around extended conversations filmed in two- and three-shots). Pagnol embedded the anguish over the war into a family melodrama about reconciliation.

One of the major hits of the Occupation, as well as in foreign markets right after the war, *The Well-Digger's Daughter* continued Pagnol's brand of southern French *pagnolade*, with its erring daughters, comically crusty fathers with hearts of gold, and communities populated with colorful figures who must evolve, learning empathy from one another. Moreover, despite allowing sympathy for Patricia and Jacques's sexual indiscretions, Pagnol's film fit many traits of Vichy cinema. It emphasized a return to the land and the protective powers of faith and family, thanks to an enlightened patriarch and a young mother willing to sacrifice all for her child. Jacques's magical return seems to come about in part as a reward for his parents' new-found humility and their full recognition of and commitment to their grandchild. Alfred Greven repeatedly tried to sign Pagnol at Continental, but the fiercely independent Pagnol refused to collaborate. Instead, he waited for the liberation to release his next movie.

Jean Grémillon was another director with a project straddling the devastating mobilization and surrender. After completing *The Strange Monsieur Victor* (*L'étrange Monsieur Victor*, 1938), written with Spaak and starring Raimu and Viviane Romance, for UFA, Grémillon and Jacques Prévert began *Stormy Waters* (*Remorques*, Grémillon, 1941), based on a novel about a tugboat captain. As with *The Strange Monsieur Victor*, much of the action was to be shot on location. For Gabin to appear in *Remorques* as skipper André Laurent, he had to be decommissioned from his military service. The novel is largely set at sea, and Grémillon had hoped to include great deal of documentary-like footage. The declaration of war forced the production to shut down, then once Grémillon fled south with his footage, he was forced to wrap up with miniature boat scenes in the studio. The shores were off-limits. Nonetheless, the movie offers a rousing portrait of Laurent as a trusted and beloved leader of his crew and a fair competitor in the business of rescuing ships during storms. He is also a dutiful husband to Yvonne (Madeleine Renaud), who unbeknownst to him has a weak heart and fears dying alone while he is at sea. During one unfortunate sea rescue, he meets the crooked captain Marc (Jean Marchat). Marc's desperate wife, Catherine (Michèle Morgan), tries to escape her brutish husband, and in the process meets Laurent, who ferries her and other sailors back safely to shore. The couple find a new and powerful romance together, though fate will keep them apart.

Grémillon and Prévert efficiently reduce much of the drama to contrasting various married couples and their limited options. After a romantic interlude with Catherine, Laurent explains to his wife, who wants him to stop sailing and stay home with her, that he cannot quit his job yet because the ship, his crew, and the sea are too important to him. But when he tries to leave Yvonne for Catherine, during another storm, he learns his wife has collapsed from her illness. Laurent rushes to her deathbed, where Yvonne proudly reaffirms her faith in Laurent, while Catherine, realizing they have no future, leaves town. Destiny has ruined everyone's lives. With Yvonne's death comes another SOS, and the dejected Laurent leads the ship out onto the dark sea once more. Laurent's crushed but resigned final pose, pelted by rain at the helm, recalls Gabin's Poetic Realist performances, and this tale of an impossible romance reminded audiences of the doomed Morgan–Gabin pairing in *Quai des brumes*. Furthermore, Roland-Manuel's musical score adds an impressive liturgical dimension to this epic tale of destiny, love, and sacrifice. Ultimately, while men work, married to their ship and the sea, Grémillon's women have few options beyond waiting and suffering. As Catherine points out, "Women like me were made to disappear." Burch and Sellier celebrate *Remorques* as an ambiguous, psychological realist melodrama "about alienating masculinity and the social construction of gender roles, themes that were virtually unknown in the French cinema," beyond a few titles such as *Rules of the Game* (82).

When *Remorques* finally opened, Morgan and Gabin had both fled France for the United States. Soon, the COIC banned all Gabin movies because he helped the Resistance, though ironically the German Occupied zone did allow some of Gabin's "demoralizing" movies, including *Le Jour se lève* and *Quai des brumes*, to play in Paris during the war. Eventually *Le Film* announced that all Morgan films were banned to retaliate for her refusal to return to

Morgan and Gabin, reunited (*Remorques*)

occupied France. Ironically, Morgan was still featured on the cover of *Le Film* just months after her role in a Hollywood drama, *Joan of Paris* (Stevenson, 1942), in which she sacrifices herself to the Nazis after rescuing some British airmen in Occupied Paris. Morgan, Gabin, and other major figures, including Jean Renoir and René Clair, continued to haunt the public discourse about French cinema and its recent history even as the COIC and the Nazis struggled with how to erase them from the national memory.

Julien Duvivier also had a film in production during the 1939 season. His *Heart of a Nation* (*Untel père et fils*, 1943) was mostly shot in the Victorine studios in Nice and launched as a patriotic call to arms as it followed three generations of a French family and their hard-fought defense of their homeland over the decades. The French government's Ministry of Information initiated *Untel père et fils* deliberately to remind the resilient population of previous threats, battles, and sacrifices against Prussian and German invaders. The Froment family, based in Paris but with a rich uncle in Marseilles (Raimu), are meant to represent their nation. In 1871, the Prussians kill the father, which motivates the son Pierre (Louis Jouvet) and sister Marie (Michèle

Morgan) to remain devoted patriots over the years. Cold winters, hunger, and fear recur, as do references from the narrator to France's many cultural and political triumphs. One son's interest in early airplanes brings us to World War I, where he heroically volunteers to fly a mission for a decisive battle. He dies helping rout the Germans. Large titles announce the years as they roll past. The men fight and the women contribute as well, including Estelle Froment (Suzy Prim), who is given a medal for her selfless nursing of wounded soldiers. Meanwhile, Pierre drains swamps and builds bridges in the colonies. However, by 1939, just as a new generation is marrying and planning for the future, the Nazis threaten. At a wedding, the mayor encourages faith in the future, even though in his own lifetime France has been called to arms three times. The final image presents the grandparents, who have lost so much, kneeling in church praying that the righteous shall win and France may live again.

Duvivier completed most of the filming, but then fled to Hollywood, where he added some documentary footage for the American release as *Heart of a Nation* in 1943. Only after the war could *Untel père et fils* be shown in France, although by then its message was dated and its style was ridiculed as stagy and glacial rather than daring or inspiring. A much more successful project for Duvivier in Hollywood was *Lydia* (1941), his adaptation of "Un Carnet de Bal," filled with clever flashbacks to rework and update his previous script. Upon his return to France, Duvivier revived his reputation, working with Spaak to adapt a Georges Simenon novel into the stylish film noir *Panique* (1946), starring Viviane Romance and Michel Simon.

A similarly tortured production process occurred for Edmond Gréville's *Threats* (*Menaces*, 1940). Immediately after the 1938 Munich Agreement and Germany's annexation of the Sudetenland, Gréville launched a project about fleeing Europeans taking refuge at a hotel near the Pantheon in Paris. The caring Denise (Mireille Balin), a single woman working in fashion, helps everyone in the hotel feel like family and is especially concerned about Professor Hoffman (Erich von Stroheim), a former doctor now cut off from his family and homeland. Hoffman, wounded in World War I, wears a black mask to cover half of his face. As he explains, his nation no longer exists on any map, and his face signifies war and peace. Everyone in the building is tense, and the French police, highly suspicious of foreigners, keep watch over who comes and goes. *Menaces* is one of the only movies of the era to confront directly the ongoing political crisis and Gréville inserts discussions, newspapers, and radio reports assessing the Nazi aggression of the day.

Erich von Stroheim (*Menaces*)

Despite the welcoming atmosphere of the hotel, with its benevolent female owner, the mise-en-scène remains dark and claustrophobic, with heavy, attached shadows. Moreover, *Menaces* repeatedly demonstrates the high risks for independent women during this era of paranoia and desperation.

Gréville inserts occasional documentary footage of the chaotic Paris and advancing Nazi tanks. As catastrophe looms around them and though a temporary peace is brokered, Hoffman shoots himself in his room, leaving a note calling the supposed peace a "vain illusion." A mournful musical refrain reinforces this reference to *Grand Illusion*, and a voice-over announces that Hoffman was right. War is soon declared, and initially *Menaces* ended there, but the print was destroyed in a fire, so Gréville reshot much of the film and opened it briefly in 1940. However, *Menaces* was soon seized and destroyed. At the end of the war, Gréville, who remained in France and directed two more movies during the Occupation, compiled a new version from available prints and added an ending with liberation footage intercut with some of the actors looking overjoyed and returning to their beloved hotel. They also visit poor Hoffman's grave to be sure to remember what was lost.

Continental's Drive toward a New Studio System

As the German officials and the COIC had planned, Continental Films quickly became a major player at the center of French commercial filmmaking. One of the big film events of 1941 was the first Continental production, the first film completed entirely under the Occupation, Henri Decoin's *Her First Affair* (*Premier rendez-vous*), starring Danielle Darrieux. Decoin, who had enlisted to fight the Nazis, secretly cowrote the scenario with his Jewish colleague Max Kolpé. As the *Ciné-Mondial* magazine, which was funded by Germany, proclaimed after the lavish premiere at the Normandie cinema, Decoin's movie offered Parisians their own *premier rendez-vous*: this was the first French film released since the Armistice, and its huge crowds proved "not everyone has left town." The magazine's review credits *Her First Affair* with reawakening French cinema, providing appreciative audiences "a taste of French cinematic *terroir* that had almost been forgotten" (August 22, 1941, 5). Darrieux plays Micheline, an inquisitive young woman who sneaks out of her orphanage to pursue a mysterious man who has been corresponding with her. They exchange romantic letters, but it turns out that Nicolas (Fernand

Jourdan and Darrieux make music (*Her First Affair*)

Ledoux) is much older than he pretends and teaches boys her age. Eventually his farce falls apart when she meets his handsome young ward, Pierre (Louis Jourdan). By the end, the students in Nicolas's elite school bail Micheline out of her orphanage so she and her romantic ideal, the smitten Pierre, can run off on a train together.

The Catholic reviewers were upset that the young couple was leaving town with no mention of marriage. Nonetheless, Darrieux's feisty performance drew intense praise, and she sang the title song, "Premier Rendez-vous," which also became a hit. *Her First Affair* also lifted the dashing young Jourdan up to leading man status. Decoin's high-quality production deploys an impressive classical visual style, with many conversations handled in a single shot, plus fluid camera movements, convincing back projection, and even an Impressionistic insert or two. While the Parisian opening was heralded as a national triumph, Decoin, Darrieux, and a number of major French stars, including Viviane Romance, soon traveled to Berlin as part of a publicity tour for the film's German premiere, angering many fans back in France. Continental was proud to launch its slate of films with *Her First Affair*, the first of six films it released that fall, but it turned out to be the only French film released in Germany for the rest of the war.

Another popular release in fall 1941, Continental's *Who Killed Santa Claus?* (*L'Assassinat du Père Noël*, 1941), came from Christian-Jaque, who had directed a string of Fernandel vehicles in the 1930s. Christian-Jaque initially resisted Greven's pressure to work for Continental until he was assured that he could select his own scripts. In addition, he negotiated to alternate those productions with feature projects for French studios. Many top figures in the industry struggled to avoid being dependent on Continental, and some simply moved to Nice or Marseille, claiming they were under exclusive contract in the unoccupied zone. Christian-Jaque's contract was an unusual solution to the dilemma. Some of his colleagues and crew, including cinematographer Armand Thirard, resented working for Continental but found no other work in the industry since their demobilization. Thanks to the Poetic Realist touches, their somber *Who Killed Santa Claus?* offered an ominous tone worthy of the anxieties of the era.

Who Killed Santa Claus? was adapted by Charles Spaak and shot partly in Chamonix in the Alps. It opens with beautiful vistas and church bells and children excited about Christmas. Inhabitants of the snowy village include Léon (Robert Le Vigan) a free-thinking atheist schoolteacher; la mère Michel (Marie-Hélène Dasté), a confused woman, who wanders about searching for her lost cat; Gaspard Cornusse (Harry Baur), who sells hand-crafted globes, drinks a bit, and plays Santa every year; and his grown daughter, Catherine (Renée Faure), who lives in a childish fog awaiting her own Prince Charming. But this year the mysterious young playboy Baron Roland (Raymond Rouleau) returns to his chateau after a ten-year absence and, wanting to avoid their company, leads the locals to suspect he suffers from leprosy. Meanwhile, someone knocks out the priest and steals the priceless gem from atop the nativity scene, and Santa is found dead by two boys. It turns out the thief who stole the jewel had disguised himself in Gaspard's Santa suit but was then killed by his accomplice, the local druggist. By the end, the pure Catherine breaks free from her nearly comatose state, recognizing the baron as her Prince Charming; Gaspard, playing Santa again, motivates a crippled boy to stand; and the re-reinvigorated baron realizes it is best to remain at home helping take care of one's neighbors rather than looking for happiness elsewhere in the world.

Who Killed Santa Claus?, which is set in an isolated space, surrounded by snow, offered another Occupation-era allegory about patience, prayers, and faith in a reawakening. For the final scene, Christian-Jaque inserted a daring final plea by Baur's Santa that seemed to equate Sleeping Beauty waiting for Prince Charming with France awaiting Liberation. Christian-Jaque later argued he was referring to Charles de Gaulle, who, like the baron, would soon return, but he had to convince Continental that the scene was an innocent fairy-tale allusion. Greven, who wanted a lineup of films that built on successful genres, stars, and auteurs from France's prewar years, was willing to allow such creative freedom to ensure continued participation to top talent. With *Who Killed Santa Claus?*, Christian-Jaque managed to provide themes and locations dear to the audience's hearts in this popular, prestige picture, and supply Continental with another major hit.

Christian-Jaque's next film for Continental was a biopic of Hector Berlioz, *The Fantastic Symphony* (*La Symphonie fantastique*, 1942), starring Jean-Louis Barrault as the composer. This production famously caught the attention of Goebbels, who wrote in his diary that it was of "excellent quality and amounts to a first-class fanfare." Nonetheless, he opposed its release: "I am angry to think that our own offices in Paris are teaching the French how to represent nationalism in pictures. . . . I ordered Greven to come to Berlin from Paris to give him absolutely clear and unmistakable directives that . . . only light, frothy and, if possible, corny pictures are desired" (Ehrlich 141). *The Fantastic Symphony* was indeed released and played quite successfully in both French zones.

Santa cures the boy (*Who Killed Santa Claus?*)

Goebbels continued to caution Continental. He ordered that any French actors and technicians who could help build the quality of German cinema should be hired away to work in Germany. The war was taking a steep toll on all aspects of production back home. One actor to follow that course was the popular Harry Baur. He was sent to Berlin for a Tobis project, *Symphony of a Life* (*Symphonie eines lebens*, Bertram, 1943), triggering severe criticism from those in the Resistance. However, the Nazis were continually suspicious of Baur, convinced he had a Jewish background. Once Baur returned to Paris, he was arrested for "anti-German activities" and sent to prison, tortured, then freed. He died miserably in April 1943, partially paralyzed, distrusted by the Germans and free French alike. *Ciné Mondial* printed a tribute to Baur, based on the magazine's last interview in his apartment just days before his death. The story never mentioned his final film, which opened in Germany that month, or his arrest.

Among Continental's most controversial movies was *The Raven* (*Le Corbeau*, Clouzot, 1943), which is also one of six Occupation-era films celebrated by Pierre Billard as marking a new stage of creativity and high quality in French cinema. The others were *Douce* (Autant-Lara, 1943), *Angels of Sin* (*Les Anges du péché*, Bresson, 1943), *Love Eternal* (*L'éternel retour*, Delannoy, 1943), *The Sky Is Yours* (*Le Ciel est à vous*, Grémillon, 1944), and *Children of Paradise* (*Les Enfants du paradis*, Carné, 1945) (*L'Age* 385). Throughout the 1930s, Henri-Georges Clouzot had been a professional screenwriter, often adapting popular novels for such films as *I Will Be Alone after Midnight*, and he worked regularly in Germany, occasionally directing the French versions of his scripts. During the Occupation, he advanced from an important scriptwriter and adviser at Continental to a major director. Clouzot's *The Murderer Lives at Number 21* (*L'Assassin habite au 21*, 1942) fit the *policier* genre, but he also grafted comedy onto the mystery formula. Despite severe shortages of materials and film stock, Clouzot was furnished with all his costuming and decor requests, though he had to adhere to Continental's two-shot limit for retakes. He delivered his stylish first film quickly, to the delight of Greven. However, Greven still had to be convinced before approving *Le Corbeau*, a particularly dark crime drama.

Le Corbeau's plot revolves around a rural town that is gradually pulled apart by a series of poison-pen letters accusing a wide range of locals of immoral, illegal, or cowardly acts, all signed by the Raven. The Occupying forces encouraged and depended on such anonymous denunciations against Jews, black marketeers, and other enemies of the state, which sowed fear and anxiety among the population. This plot point made the entire project rather risky for everyone involved. Alan Williams sums up the widespread surprise that *Le Corbeau* could have been made at all: "How could they not reject a film in which the doctor-hero is an accused abortionist (he freely admits saving women's lives at the expense of their unborn children); his new lover is a promiscuous woman with a minor physical deformity (hence an offense both to Vichy moralism and to Nazi eugenics); and everyone else a fool, a knave, insane, or all three?" (*Republic* 260–61). Years later, François Truffaut recalled seeing *Le Corbeau* repeatedly: "The film seemed to me to be a fairly accurate picture of what I had seen around me during the war and the postwar period—collaboration, denunciation, the black market, hustling, cynicism" (3). Clearly, *Le Corbeau* was a timely, if unlikely, film, and it seems especially surprising that it should be produced by Continental. *Le Corbeau* became a lightning rod for criticism from all directions.

Originally written by Louis Chavance in the early 1930s, based on a real and vicious letter-writing spree, *Le Corbeau* offered a cynical picture of the French heartland and the nation as a whole. The movie opens with the grim but handsome Dr. Germain (Pierre Fresnay) having saved an expectant mother's life at the expense of her child. Not only does Germain coldly suggest that her husband can soon try to impregnate her again, but a neighbor lady whispers that another man had actually helped the woman get pregnant this time. Such references to abortion, adultery, and false paternity, all in the shadow of the village church, were what helped *Le Corbeau* earn condemnation from Catholic officials. Critics across the political spectrum remarked on the story's decadence, as it ridiculed most social institutions and perhaps French culture itself. Ultimately, hundreds of letters are distributed in *Le Corbeau*, infecting nearly everyone in the town, from the mayor to a young girl who tries to drown herself when she learns her father is not her real father. Throughout the film, everyone is a suspect, and everyone spies on one another as the tone of the letters becomes more severe and threatening.

Central to all the town's crazed suspicions is the cynical and aloof newcomer Dr. Germain, who seems to threaten the status quo, which is rotten to the core. He has become friendly with the attractive, seemingly sensitive Laura Vorzet (Micheline Francey), who is married to one of the leading figures in town, the elderly head of the hospital's psychiatric department, Dr. Vorzet (Pierre Larquey). Her jealous sister Marie (Héléna Manson), a cruel nurse, withholds and steals morphine from terminally ill patients to sell on the black market and give to Dr. Vorzet, an addict. Her schemes drive one patient to suicide. While everyone is guilty of something, the women are particularly active in the town's affairs, and male authority is systematically mocked. The slightly deformed, promiscuous Denise (Ginette Leclerc) lives above her one-armed brother's school and seduces Germain. Meanwhile, Laura continues to meet Germain behind her husband's back, and another woman tries to frame Germain as an abortionist. The exact relationship between the doctor and Laura is never clarified, but his secret medical motivation is revealed late. His wife died in labor, along with their child. Formerly a famous brain surgeon in Paris, he changed his name and became a country doctor, determined to save pregnant women at any cost. For most of the film, the sounds of children at play cause him pain.

By the end, Germain learns Denise is apparently pregnant with his child, and he discovers suspicious ink on Laura's hands. Germain is jolted back to life when Denise tries to end her own pregnancy by leaping down the stairs right when he realizes Laura may be the Raven. The treacherous Dr. Vorzet tricks Germain into helping send Laura to an asylum, but then Vorzet, the real Raven, is murdered by the vengeful mother of Marie's suicidal patient.

Dr. Germain treats Denise (*Le Corbeau*)

The mourning mother figured out the mystery before anyone else. *Le Corbeau* ends on a sudden, unsettling resolution that suggests Laura was both an initiator and a victim of the letter campaign. However, the twisted Vorzet's motives remain surprisingly unclear. Clouzot's ambiguous, bitter saga proved popular with wartime audiences fascinated by this unusually cruel contemporary film noir. With more theaters opening all the time, *Le Corbeau* set a new Occupation-era box office record during its first week in Paris.

The grim *Le Corbeau* impressed critics and viewers with its realistic performances and intense, poisonous atmosphere. Several reviewers took advantage of the storyline to rail against anonymous informants. Beyond the gripping storytelling, Clouzot and veteran cinematographer Nicolas Hayer's visual style inserted these morbid characters in a low-key film noir world of shadowy hallways and bleak exterior settings. Jean Cocteau, a friend of Clouzot's, praised the resulting film as remarkable: "Every shot is troubling, violent, and taken to the limit" (Billard, *L'Age* 406). Harsh lighting and extreme close-ups reinforce the claustrophobia. A single light bulb sways back and

Laura Vorzet and Germain (*Le Corbeau*)

forth when Vorzet confronts Germain about the absence of any clearly defined good or bad in the world. Even shots of Germain and Laura meeting secretly in the church look ominous. Many historians then and now consider *Le Corbeau* the masterpiece of the Occupation. Critic Audiberti wrote that it "proceeds with a skill that is nearly unbearable" (Mayne 72), and even those who found it demoralizing in the tradition of *Quai des brumes* praised its narrative power and naturalism. Unfortunately for Clouzot, Resistance reviewers attacked *Le Corbeau* in language that seemed to recall the right-wing assaults against Poetic Realism. They concentrated on the "degenerate" aspects of the story, arguing that Clouzot and Chavance were playing into the Nazis' hands. There is no pride, hope, or heroism here; all the French characters are shown to be weak or evil, including its "deceitful, perverted, and obscene girls" (Mayne 75). Ironically, Germany's censors rejected *Le Corbeau* on moral grounds. Even though Clouzot left Continental immediately following *Le Corbeau*, his unflattering depiction of small-town France and work as script supervisor there made him a target of the Resistance.

After the war, Clouzot's close association with Continental led to him
being punished as a collaborator by the liberation committee, along with a
number of other film professionals. It is still unclear how much Clouzot supported the Occupation, but his cinematographer, Hayer, secretly organized
a Resistance network among cinematographers even as he worked on *Le Corbeau*. After the war, the assessment of the themes, casts, crews, and styles
of all of Continental's movies, not just *Le Corbeau*, divided critics, historians,
and audiences for decades.

Continental Films remains at the center of all the controversies and historical reevaluation of wartime French cinema. With its thirty well-made features, including a mix of fantasies, comedies, mysteries, and crime dramas,
Continental, more than any other production company, shaped the era
on film. Greven had managed to establish a viable enterprise that rapidly
exploited its vast resources and notorious political power to provide the man-
dated evidence of a thriving French film scene. Moreover, Greven diligently
pursued projects right up to the spring of 1944. He even built a new studio
with an underground cellar for film negatives just west of Paris, hoping to
continue production if other studio spaces were bombed. However, soon
after the June 1944 Allied invasion, Greven moved Continental's official office
to Nancy before taking all its films and records to Germany later that summer when Paris was liberated. Continental's final film, *Majestic Hotel Cellars*
(*Les Caves du Majestic*, Pottier, 1945), opened in France more than a full year
later, in fall 1945, finally ending the German studio's unsettling legacy.

Adapting Georges Simenon

In addition to original screenplays for both realist dramas and escapist genre
movies, fully one-third of films made under the COIC were adaptations.
Clearly, producers believed that previously published novels and plays were
safer than contemporary material. Adaptations of cultural classics also
allowed the COIC to demonstrate that it was indeed bolstering French traditions. For instance, seven different Balzac stories were sources for movies
during the war, including playwright Jean Giraudoux's highly successful,
even feminist adaptation of *La Duchesse de Langeais* (De Baroncelli, 1942) and
Michel Simon's star performance in *Vautrin* (Billon, 1943). Balzac's tales may
have been tempting for many reasons, including his cynical critiques of society as a whole. Yet many of the plays and novels adapted during the Occupation came from mainstream commercial writers and turned into popular
genre films. The most frequently adapted French-language author was

Georges Simenon, with nine productions, five of which came from Continental: *Annette and the Blonde Woman* (*Annette et la dame blonde*, Dréville, 1942), *Strangers in the House* (*Les Inconnus dans la maison*, Decoin, 1942), *Picpus* (Pottier, 1943), *Cecile Is Dead* (*Cécile est morte*, Tourneur, 1944), and *Majestic Hotel Cellars*. Other notable versions included *The House with Seven Daughters* (*La Maison des sept jeunes filles*, Valentin, 1942), adapted by Charles Spaak; *Le Voyageur de la Toussaint* (Daquin, 1943); *Midnight in Paris* (*Monsieur La Souris*, Lacombe, 1942); and Decoin's gloomy *The Man from London* (*L'Homme de Londres*, 1943).

By the 1940s, the Belgian-born Georges Simenon had become France's (and some claim the world's) most prolific author, churning out hundreds of crime stories and gripping novels, often pounded out on his typewriter in just a few days. He became France's best-selling writer of the twentieth century. His direct style and vocabulary won him praise from critics and fellow writers, including Dashiell Hammett and André Gide. During the war, Simenon lived and wrote on the west coast of France. "The German occupation, in one of its many paradoxes, turned out to be a golden age for Simenon," who became Continental's star writer (Vincendeau, "Maigret" 168). That he repeatedly negotiated deals with Continental created great resentment among his critics, while his supporters argued that his very "French" tales entertained and reassured the populace during the dark days of the war. Nonetheless, charges of cultural insensitivity and even blatant antisemitism dogged Simenon for years.

Simenon's first sale to Continental was an uncharacteristically light-hearted story. Set in Cannes, *Annette and the Blonde* stars Louise Carletti as Annette, a lovesick young woman who wants to disrupt the romance between the wealthy American blonde Myriam (Mona Goya), just coming off her fourth divorce, and the suave attorney Maurice (Henri Garat). The adaptation comically caricatures the American and includes a parody of Hollywood gangster films, as it blatantly signals the superiority of French culture and romance. Yet the overall light farcical tone and plot points follow Hollywood romantic comedy conventions. Throughout the film, the scheming Annette weaves fanciful tales and causes repeated misunderstandings, even trying to get herself thrown into prison, until no one, including the handsome young visitor Bernard (Georges Rollin), believes anything she says. By the end, feigning despair, she leaps into the sea, forcing the elegant lawyer to rescue and propose to her, though she abandons him at the altar and leaves the church with the newcomer Bernard in a zany, comical twist.

Other than a brief, distorted dream sequence, Dréville's film unfolds in a
highly generic escapist formula built around familiar character types. *Annette
and the Blonde* was carefully packaged at Continental, with Decoin helping
adapt the Simenon novel and Greven personally insisting that Carletti play
the lead despite director Dréville's objections. *Annette and the Blonde* was a
hit and another film that concerned Goebbels due to its high quality: "It is of
the same levity and elegance as the Darrieux movie, *Caprices* [1942]. We shall
have to be careful about the French so that they won't build up a new moving-
picture art under our leadership" (Ehrlich 139). Goebbels feared the French
would surpass Germany's technical skills, though Greven's job was precisely
to build a successful new "German" studio in France and prove film culture
was thriving. *Annette and the Blonde* reveals many of the contradictions of
Occupation filmmaking, including its love/hate of prohibited Hollywood
genre films.

Decoin next adapted *Strangers in the House*, a more typical Simenon crime
drama. The adaptation, which included input from Clouzot, retains some of
Simenon's casual, even chaotic narrative structure; the novelist often claimed
he never began with any outline but made up the stories as he typed. Here,
Raimu plays a bitter drunk of an attorney, Hector Loursat, whose wife left
him long ago. Now he lives in a nearly empty old mansion with his independent daughter, Nicole (Juliette Faber), largely oblivious to her antics with a
gang of unruly petty criminal friends who come and go. When a dead body
is discovered in the house and Nicole's boyfriend is accused of the crime,
Loursat gradually regains his sense of decency and takes the case. During
the ensuing court case, he unearths the true villain, a "foreign" member of
the gang, played by Marcel Mouloudji. But the lawyer also launches into an
attack on bourgeois parents like himself who neglect their duties. Whose
fault is this lost generation? The French family itself. This call for responsible parenting and the film's representation of an amoral society, from its dis-
solute young people on up, outraged *L'Ecran* and other Resistance voices
who charged that *Strangers in the House* was blaming France as if it deserved
its current problems. It is worth noting that Decoin cast an Arab French actor
for the murderer, while in the book Simenon clearly labeled him Jewish.
As Pierre Billard notes, a number of Occupation movies, even some from
Continental, suppressed any Jewish references to avoid the issue altogether
(*L'Age* 384). Regardless, *Strangers in the House* was initially banned, alongside
Le Corbeau, after the war.

Another Continental director, Richard Pottier, had actually fled the Nazis and his home in Austria in the early 1930s. He changed his name from Deutsch, taking his French wife's last name instead. He fought and was wounded in the early days of the war, but once he was back in Paris, French producers were leery about hiring him. Ironically, it was ultimately COIC's Ploquin who got him a permit to direct, and Pottier soon ended up at Continental, where he directed two of their high-profile Simenon novels, *Picpus* and *The Majestic Hotel Cellars*. Both films featured Albert Préjean as Inspector Maigret, Simenon's most popular recurring character. For both movies, Pottier worked with two talented but risky writers, Jean-Paul Le Chanois and Charles Spaak. Le Chanois adapted *Picpus*, and Greven kept him employed at Continental even though he knew his real name was Dreyfus. Although Greven was aware Le Chanois was Jewish, he had no idea Le Chanois was a major figure in the French Communist Party (PCF), organizing cinema workers in the Resistance. The Continental censors did keep watch, even cutting the line he inserted into *Picpus* where a waiter serving a bottle of 1918 wine declares that it was a very good year (Leteux 35). Referring to the German loss was forbidden.

Le Chanois also wrote the screenplay for Maurice Tourneur's stylish *Carnival of Sinners* (*La Main du diable*, 1943) at Continental. It was another Occupation-era allegory about the Devil sowing chaos, this time told in a clever flashback structure. Finally, he adapted another Maigret detective tale for Tourner, *Cecile Is Dead*, before going into hiding. For the remainder of the war, Le Chanois continued to organize a vast network of film technicians. They stole film stock to make clandestine newsreels that were smuggled out to London for processing and distribution. He became a major figure in rebuilding the French industry after the liberation and he directed the documentary *In the Heart of the Thunderstorm* (*Au coeur de l'orage*, 1948), compiled mostly of their secret newsreels and German war and propaganda footage.

For *The Majestic Hotel Cellars*, Pottier worked with veteran writer Spaak. However, the Gestapo arrested Spaak, hoping he would lead them to his brother, Paul-Henri, former Belgian prime minister and a leader in the European Resistance movement. While Continental officials negotiated for Spaak's release, the Nazi guards allowed him to complete his screenplay from his prison cell. Both *Picpus* and *The Majestic Hotel Cellars* retain some of the loose aspects of Simenon's narratives in which suspects come and go as the complicated array of crimes are solved in a leisurely, even careless manner.

These adaptations benefit from André Gabriello's endearing performance as the detective's sidekick Lucas. Pottier even exploits a clever split screen in *Picpus* to help illustrate a dense crime plot summary by Lucas.

Perhaps the most adept of the Maigret films at Continental, however, was *Cecile Is Dead*. Maurice Tourneur's team methodically presents the tale of the paranoid Cécile (Santa Relli), who lives with her demanding wealthy aunt but fears something mysterious occurs during the nights there. She regularly pesters Maigret at his office with her vague complaints, until Cécile's decapitated cousin is discovered in a hotel, and her aunt is strangled. Next, poor Cécile is found murdered and stashed in a closet in the police station. It turns out the aunt owned a network of valuable brothels, and only Maigret can finally make sense of the killer's identity and motives. As with many Simenon stories, unexpected witnesses suddenly appear amid a string of surprising leads and confessions. Maigret's talent involves assessing the tales and coincidences as they accumulate before explaining all the convoluted facts quickly at the end. These Occupation-era Simenon films underscored the distinct pleasure of French pulp fiction and served as models for later European noir *policier* films.

Cécile at the police window (*Cecile Is Dead*)

The continued popularity of Simenon as a cultural figure during this period fueled the spate of adaptations, including several of his comic, romantic melodramas, including *The House with Seven Daughters*. Directed by Albert Valentin, this rather theatrical farce concerns a single father with seven marriageable daughters and a failing school for girls. Ultimately, after a series of jealous fits and misunderstandings involving verbal and physical humor, two daughters marry wealthy, rather ridiculous men, guaranteeing a solid financial future for the nice, ineffectual father, the remaining daughters, and the school. As with most Simenon tales, *The House with Seven Daughters* mocks social norms and conventions while finally reinforcing them. On the more somber end of the Simenon spectrum, Decoin's version of *The Man from London* features Jules Berry as a railway worker who witnesses a murder and retrieves a sack full of money. The discovery leads him into a paranoid, downward spiral, until he has lost everything, especially his family's respect. During the Occupation, the name Simenon was featured prominently in publicity as a sort of guarantee for an engaging narrative, whether for a light-hearted family drama or a gripping murder mystery. But none of Simenon's literary work of the period, much less the filmed adaptations, referred to any sort of real-world social issues. Simenon continued to write as if nothing had changed around him, a condition that made it quite safe for Continental and others to adapt his novels while profiting from his celebrity status.

Prestige Auteur Productions and Popular Occupation Cinema

Gradually, as some aspects of production rebounded in the early 1940s, the new realities of making movies in France under the COIC became clearer, and their systematic regulations managed to stabilize the shattered industry somewhat. Surprisingly to some, a recognizable resurgence in high-quality, popular French productions was indeed emerging. Some labeled it a new French school. The COIC's policies coupled with the realities of a wartime economy restricted the overall number of feature films to sixty, or roughly half the prewar output, concentrating scarce resources and helping ensure better financial returns for each title. These policies and restrictions on access to work permits dramatically reduced the number of jobs in the industry, further concentrating the labor among approved professionals. As the conditions of production slowly found a new equilibrium, many of the more significant projects during the Occupation were created by a cohort of veteran writers, cinematographers, and auteur directors from the 1930s. Nonetheless, there were opportunities for younger talent to take advantage of the political and industrial transformations, bolstering their careers with prestige, auteur projects as they filled in for others driven out or forced to flee.

Beyond the continuity in writers and directors, many top names from the late 1930s star system remained in place as well. The French industry continued to function as an array of small production companies. Despite the COIC's attempts to centralize the industry, most films were still made by small production houses. The seventy features produced in 1942 were made by forty-one different studios, and 1943's forty-nine films were created at thirty-four companies (Crisp, "Business" 124). All these producers were forced to compete for a relatively limited pool of successful writers, directors, and especially actors. Even Continental's success was largely dependent on acquiring established stars from pre-Occupation French cinema. Thus, despite the shrinking number of feature films being made, the opportunities for well-known popular entertainers could actually increase, in part by gaps left by fleeing Jewish actors. Marcel Dalio is exemplary. At what should have been the peak of his career, he ended up playing "Frenchy" roles in Hollywood, including running the roulette wheel in *Casablanca*, before returning after the war. By contrast, Jules Berry, one of the busiest actors prior to the war, starred in twenty-four features between 1940 and 1945 for twenty different production companies, from the tiny SPDF to André Paulvé and Eclair-Journal. Only one of his films was made by Continental, and several were Italian coproductions. The versatile Suzy Prim starred in eleven films during the same period. Albert Préjean was in ten, *Le Corbeau*'s Ginette Leclerc appeared in twelve movies, and Pierre Fresnay starred in eleven, four of which were at Continental, where Fernandel performed in three of his fourteen Occupation-era features. Michel Simon starred in nine films, one at Continental. Clearly, there was great stability in the French star system of the era, fueled in part by fan magazines such as *Ciné-Mondial* as well as actors' long-standing relations with successful producers and directors. Despite all the upheaval, French cinema settled into a new period of adjustment and persistence, adapting some practices from the past into the new realities of the Occupation.

After a busy decade in which he tried repeatedly to regain his footing in sound cinema, Abel Gance confronted the growing wartime anxieties with *Paradis perdu* (*Four Flights to Love*, 1940), a pacifist tear-jerker involving World War I made with high production values and a haunting song about impossible love. The protagonist, Pierrè (Fernand Gravey), must leave his pregnant young wife (Micheline Presle) when he is called to the front. She dies in childbirth. Years later, after devoting himself to their daughter, also played by Presle, Pierre sacrifices his own chance at a new romance, dying just as his daughter marries the love of her life. Next, after several failed plans to make nationalist and pacifist films in the face of the rising Nazi threats, Gance directed one of the first films shot in Nice after the French defeat, *Blind Venus* (*Vénus aveugle*, 1941), for J. J. Mecatti's studio, which inserted a Vichy-friendly "France nouvelle" logo at the front. Gance even began the movie with a handwritten dedication to Maréchal Pétain and the New France of tomorrow.

A Viviane Romance vehicle, *Blind Venus* includes many stereotypes of Vichy-era films that seem permeated with foreboding and stasis, as well as themes of self-sacrifice and redemption. Romance plays Clarisse, a beautiful cabaret singer and model stuck in a tough southern seaport. But she is losing her vision and does not want to become a burden on her true love, an adoring sailor, Madère (Georges Flamant), who lives with her in an abandoned cargo ship. Deciding to force him to abandon her and start a better life for himself, she lies, claiming to have another lover. A storm immediately explodes around them, and he beats her in a jealous rage, presented via a hectic montage. Neither of them knows that she is carrying Madère's child when he leaves her. Clarisse becomes another suffering single mother in French Occupation-era films, and Léonce-Henri Burel's flashy cinematography represents her deteriorating vision via Impressionistic devices. Gance's mise-en-scène also reveals debts to Poetic Realism, charting Clarisse's lonely journey through the seedy locales. She sinks into absolute despair with the death of her young daughter, whose funeral coincides with the christening of the newly married Madère's legitimate baby girl. Alone, Clarisse resorts to entertaining men with her erotic, sad realist songs. After completely losing her sight, Clarisse stands next to a crucifix, admitting that at least she will never again have to see the unpleasant life that surrounds her. Eventually, however, a regretful Madère returns in her life, along with his child, and wins her over in a fanciful series of events, including a pretend voyage on their old ship. By the end, Clarisse gets to live out her dream, reunited with Madère as his child replaces theirs.

Gance was an early fan of Pétain and saw *Blind Venus* as a populist work celebrating cooperation to overcome exceptional challenges: "Gance's New France . . . consists of an aesthetic renewal achieved collectively, guided by a powerful vision of the future" (N. King 174). But Gance's tale is also built around the spectacle of Clarisse's body, which is plastered all over town on posters and Venus cigarette packs: "*Blind Venus* describes the slow and painful

Viviane Romance as Clarisse (*Blind Venus*)

transformation of a pagan image . . . to a Christian icon (a blind woman sitting on a pedestal, around whom the whole community ends up rallying)"
(Burch and Sellier 106). Initially successful at the box office, *Blind Venus* has
been attacked by French historians and critics for its convoluted melodramatic
plot and its shameless attempts to please Vichy. Yet Romance's poor, suffering
Venus reverberated with audiences hungry for emotional and inspiring French
movies. Gance, never known for concise storytelling, had to cut *Blind Venus*
drastically to meet projection length restrictions in the Occupied zone.

    Claude Autant-Lara solidified his career during the Occupation by offer-
ing a trio of carefully crafted costume dramas with a recurring production
team, including writer Jean Aurenche, cinematographer Philippe Agostini
(of *Le Jour se lève* fame), and leading actress Odette Joyeux. Based on a popular
nineteenth-century novel, *The Marriage of Chiffon* (*Le Mariage de Chiffon*, 1942)
features Joyeux playing an ambitious and spunky teenager who repeatedly
defies conventions. Chiffon attracts the attention of an elegant colonel, who
soon proposes marriage, which greatly pleases her mother. However, Chiffon prefers her eccentric inventor "uncle," the brother of her stepfather, who

is nearly fifty years old and going bankrupt trying to create France's first airplane. By the end, he wins a big cash prize for his flying machine, which allows the old fellow to marry the adoring Chiffon.

This fast-paced comedy mocks upper-class pretensions with physical and verbal humor, in the style of Ernst Lubitsch. While each of Chiffon's romantic options has a long line of mistresses behind them, the men are nonetheless presented as true gentlemen, the products of a refined, traditional France. Chiffon accepts her situation eagerly in this patriarchal comedy. *The Marriage of Chiffon* was a beautiful (many said soothing) film at a time when French audiences were looking for escapist tales built on respect of France's past and a faith in its future. *Le Film* celebrated Autant-Lara's technical brilliance and picturesque version of turn-of-the-century France: "It is certainly one of the best French films since the Armistice" (November 20, 1943, 8). After liberation, it was included alongside *Douce* in Jean Painlevé's screening of the most innovative French movies of the Occupation.

Right after *The Marriage of Chiffon*, Autant-Lara and his team made *Love Letters* (*Lettres d'amour*, 1942), set in 1855 with Joyeux playing a pretty young widow who captivates Emperor Napoleon III, among others. She relishes her freedom as a widow rather than mourning her brief marriage. She agrees to receive secret love letters for her married best friend, though soon people suspect Joyeux's character is the one with loose morals. By the end, the independent young widow succumbs to a conventional resolution, declaring her love for one of her friend's past lovers. She dances off happily as part of a new, optimistic couple, reconciling their culture's moral divisions. In each script, the Joyeux character's goal is a stable relationship with a man who has not initially noticed or even desired her. She is the architect of their union, for better or worse.

For *Douce*, Joyeux played the title character, first seen in a confessional explaining that she is in love with a man who lives in her house and has a social stature far beneath hers, yet she plans to run away with him. The priest warns her that this relationship can only lead to tragedy, and we soon learn the man of her dreams is the family's steward, Fabien Marani (Roger Pigaut), a rather ghoulish and resentful fellow who seems to pay little attention to her. Douce's widowed father, a count (Jean Dubucourt), is a quiet, repressed man with an artificial leg who adores their governess, Irène (Madeleine Robinson), though for years she has been Marani's secret lover. The count's domineering mother rules the vast house and tries in vain to keep her son and granddaughter from their infatuations with the lower-class employees.

Mostly Douce is looking for a way to grow up and leave her sad family home. Finally, believing that Irène will marry the count, the jealous Marani whisks Douce away to a hotel room, where she recognizes they have no future together. Strangely, she naively decides that by sleeping with Marani and then abandoning him, she can take some revenge on him and his enduring love for Irène. However, before she returns home, they stop at a theater to watch a ballet, where a fire erupts, caused by a mysterious ogre of a nobleman who seems to be following her. Disoriented and lost amid the chaos, Douce, frozen with hysteria, is surrounded by flames. There is a suggestion that Marani may be able to save her, but the next scene shows him lumbering into the count's home to announce her death. The devastated count and his mother kick Irène and Marani out into the night, irrevocably united in guilt.

Unlike Autant-Lara's two light-hearted romantic comedies, *Douce* verges on the gothic, moving ineluctably from the priest's fateful warnings to tragic loss for every character connected with this family and their property. *Douce* benefits from evocative lighting and shadows, deep space, and lavishly detailed sets and costumes. As with many studio-bound dramas, the crew found creative ways to stage action, including placing the camera inside a fireplace or outside windows. *Douce* benefited from René Cloërec's romantic score as well. Reviews of the era noted its delicately handled melodrama and exceptional performances, with *Le Film* proclaiming it superior to Autant-Lara's previous two Joyeux films: "It is a true masterpiece" (20 November 1943, 7). Moreover, *Douce*'s nostalgic glimpse at fine foods, clothes, and even roaring fireplaces would surely have provoked awe and perhaps resentment during this era of shortages, unheated cinemas, and widespread hunger. On every level, *Douce*, one of only five features from Industrie Cinématographique, was a highly polished, prestige production. It had received advance funding from the COIC and won a cinéma d'art Grand Prix from Vichy's cinema committee (Montebello 37). It anchored Autant-Lara's reputation, although it was also the last movie he released during the war. As Noel Burch and Geneviève Sellier note, "In all three of Autant-Lara's films, Joyeux is a particularly striking emblem of female resistance and rebellion in a cinema that boasted many such figures, and *Douce* is her finest role" (198). Shifting studio contracts delayed Autant-Lara's fantasy romance *Sylvie and the Ghost* (*Sylvie et le fantôme*, 1946), another Joyeux vehicle, which was finally set to begin filming in August 1944 when the liberation of Paris postponed it anew. After the war, Autant-Lara was among the directors shunned by returning

Odette Joyeux shot from outside a window (*Douce*)

Jewish filmmakers and technicians for his antisemitic views, which persisted all his life.

Marcel Carné began the war in uniform, digging ditches and then sorting mail, until the Armistice arrived. He decided to remain in France rather than flee and was one of the highest-profile figures in the industry to continue working during the Occupation. After hastily entering a contract with Continental and then breaking it, Carné moved to the unoccupied south, funded by André Paulvé's independent production company. Greven and Continental resented Carné's maneuver. His personal life as a homosexual, along with his history of creative alliances with top Jewish talent and producers, made him a target of COIC threats. In Nice, Carné teamed up with Jacques Prévert to make a fairytale costume drama that would avoid any contemporary references, *The Devil's Envoys* (*Les Visiteurs du soir*, 1942). Many Occupation tales sought heritage stories and historical settings, in part to avoid censorship problems but also to emphasize the vitality and longevity of French traditions and culture.

The story by Prévert and Pierre Laroche is anchored around a medieval chateau. The castle set was built in southern France, where all the exteriors were shot. Most interiors were constructed and filmed in the Joinville studios near Paris. The production secretly employed Alexandre Trauner for set design and used Joseph Kosma's musical compositions. Both men were hiding in the southern zone. The extravagant settings, costumes, and props, including fine horses, proved especially challenging during an era of shortages and rationing. Once Arletty signed on as a lead actress, her fame and political connections helped secure material support and necessary permissions to complete the production. Veteran cinematographer Roger Hubert captured the fantasy and special effects, working closely with Carné to create a fairy tale from the Middle Ages. When it premiered in December 1942, *Les Visiteurs du soir* quickly garnered high praise from critics on the right and the left. Rave reviews highlighted Hubert's remarkable artistic compositions and debt to medieval illuminations. André Bazin cited it as the first Occupation drama to offer France "hope," exploding "like a revolutionary event," in sharp contrast to the other dreary films of that year (*French Cinema of the Occupation* 31, 44). Carné would always argue that he, his cast, and his crew were struggling to offer a source of pride for France under the Occupation, though others later charged that *Les Visiteurs du soir* fueled the German propaganda machine. Carné and his film continue to serve as flash points for historical summaries of the era.

Les Visiteurs opens with a manuscript page explaining that in 1485, the Devil sent two envoys disguised as minstrels, Dominique (Arletty) and Gilles (Alain Cuny), to Earth to seed despair. The pair, equipped with supernatural power, arrives at the castle of Baron Hugues (Fernand Ledoux) just in time to disrupt preparations for the marriage of Lady Anne (Marie Déa) and Count Renaud (Marcel Herrand). Anne, who is not really in love with her betrothed, is quickly struck by Gilles's voice and appearance, which helps his task of breaking up the wedding. The provocative Dominique sets about distracting and destroying Renaud as well as Anne's father. At one point, the troubled Renaud even tells Dominique that peace and happiness no longer matter to him. Throughout the spectacular film, a trained bear magically materializes, time slows and freezes, an ugly woman is transformed into a beauty, while the Devil (Jules Berry) appears and disappears before our eyes. It turns out Dominique and Gilles were ruthless seducers prior to death and are now exploited by the Devil to make other couples suffer. A trio of deformed little people, also in the Devil's service, cavort around them. Strangely, the baron

Alain Cuny and Arletty as the devil's envoys (*Les Visiteurs du soir*)

and several others initially believe Dominique, dressed in an androgynous outfit, to be male, which only increases her allure and troublesome effects among the inhabitants of the castle. Ultimately, the regretful Gilles falls for the innocent Anne and begs her to teach him how to live and love. Upset with this disruption of his plans, the Devil arrives to salvage their cruel mission, making sure that Gilles is discovered in the bedroom with Anne and that the baron kills Renaud in a duel over Dominique. For a time, Gilles is chained, and Anne, who repeatedly demonstrates her resistance and even rebellion against patriarchal expectations, voluntarily joins him in bondage. After Dominique entices the baron to give up his castle and follow her, Anne and the newly freed Gilles declare their eternal love, but the Devil quickly turns them into stone statues. He is then shocked to hear their hearts still beating within, overcoming his deadly powers. As with many Occupation dramas, the man who tries to dominate everyone is frustrated in the end, and more than a few viewers interpreted Berry's Devil as a reference to Hitler.

Les Visiteurs du soir became a huge hit in France with people lining up for hours during the bitter cold winter for a chance to witness this stylish fantasy. Historian Roger Régent, writing in the 1940s, recounts that from the day it opened, *Les Visiteurs du soir* became the event of the season, revered and debated in every bar, metro, and gathering: "It was the greatest artistic shock of the Occupation." Carné's story and style were so unexpected, "it was like a bomb had been thrown into our midst" (90–91). The COIC's *Le Film* helped with publicity, celebrating Carné's film for its exceptional poetic beauty, crowning it as "the most important and courageous French production since the Armistice," thanks to its technical polish, spectacular special effects, and dynamic performances (19 December 1942, 16). *Les Visiteurs du soir* also proved popular abroad after the liberation, where this luxurious prestige production surprised many who had last seen Carné and Prévert's names on dark and compelling Poetic Realist films, not high-budget fantasies. Hubert's camerawork, with its deep space compositions and striking mobility to capture dances, romantic trysts, and excursions through the rocky countryside, displayed a classical elegance far removed from Carné's 1930s films. Reportedly, Prévert was also a bit surprised, as he felt the treachery and violence of the characters had been masked by Carné's refined visuals and theatrical acting styles. For instance, when the Devil visits the chained Gilles and spouts his lines about how the executioner will torture him, Berry's jubilant performance undercuts the sadistic weight of his words. Carné's style revealed "a shift from the realist to the transcendent, from the intimate to the distant" (Driskell 63). *Les Visiteurs du soir* also helped open the door to other costume fantasies, including *L'éternel retour* (Dellanoy, 1943) and *Children of Paradise.*

Many subsequent accounts interpret *Les Visiteurs du soir* as an allegory and morality play about invasion and resistance, disguised as a historical costume drama. After all, late in the film, the Devil surveys the castle and decides this might be a nice place to remain for a while, or, as others saw it, a good place to occupy temporarily. It can also be seen as another Carné-Prévert movie critiquing a failed society "gone amuck" (see Turk 194–96, 205). Many mainstream critics, however, accepted the film as an apolitical, timeless treatment of tragic love, in the tradition of legends such as Tristan and Isolde. Clearly, as with most Occupation films, the audience would have seen the narrative from several pertinent perspectives at once. As Evelyn Ehrlich points out, even though the lovers must die in *Les Visiteurs du soir*, "love vanquished destiny . . . The message conveyed in this enormously popular film was not rebellion but reassurance—all is not lost; our destiny has not been determined" (103). While there were several negative French reviews at the time, including mention of incompatible acting styles and anachronistic dialogue, especially from Berry, they all showed great respect for Carné's mise-en-scène. With *Les Visiteurs du soir*, Carné consolidated his reputation as one of France's top auteur directors, which allowed him the opportunity to pursue his next extravagant production, *Children of Paradise*, at his leisure, as he tried to outlast the Nazi Occupation.

Jean Grémillon was another established auteur who managed to thrive during this era. Following *Remorques*, Grémillon directed two highly successful and respected films, *Lumière d'été* (*Summer Light*, 1943) and *Le Ciel est à vous*. These titles were included in Jean Painlevé's Grande Quinzaine, a two-week screening during December 1944 of the fourteen most artistically important French films of the Occupation. *Lumière d'été*, produced by Paulvé and written with Jacques Prévert, was filmed in Nice studios and on sun-drenched locations in the rugged mountain terrain nearby. Michèle (Madeleine Robinson) arrives at a remote hotel, near a dam construction site undergoing lots of dynamiting. The hotel is designed to resemble a fragile bird cage, bathed in the stunning Provençal light, but it is rattled by the ominous explosions. While Michèle awaits the arrival of her emotionally fragile artistic boyfriend, Roland (Pierre Brasseur), she attracts the attention of the wealthy cad Patrice (Paul Bernard), who is tiring of his lover Christiane, "Cricri" (Madeleine Renaud), the hotel's manager. (Renaud, who acted with the Comédie Française, only performed in films by Grémillon at this point in her career.) Another new resident, a handsome engineer for the dam project, Julien (Georges Marchal), also arrives and falls for Michèle. Once Roland appears, drunk, broke, and hostile, the romantic options multiply in Prévert's tale of shifting potential couples and opposing value systems. The earnest Julien rescues Michèle when she wanders despondently into a dynamite zone, Patrice fuels Roland's alcoholism to neutralize him as a rival, and Cricri struggles to hold on to Patrice and prevent him from seducing Michèle. It turns out that Patrice, a sharpshooter with an impressive chateau, shot his ex-wife and, with Cricri's help, made it look like a hunting accident. She knows not to trust him.

After Patrice throws a wild costume party (just one of the film's parallels with *Rules of the Game*), the central characters take a careening drunken car ride that ends in an accident near the construction site. Roland, dressed as Hamlet, dies from his wounds (recalling Renoir's André Jurieu), while the hard-working Julien undertakes a daring rescue of a dangling cable car. Patrice tries to shoot him, but the workers turn on Patrice, who tumbles to

his death over a cliff. Finally, Michèle walks off into the mountains with Julien
on her arm in a somber version of a happy ending. This is a woman-centered
story anchored around Michèle, who also has a career as a fashion illustrator waiting for her back in Paris. She shifts from passively awaiting one man
to leaving with a better man, motivating all aspects of the plot and every other
character's actions.

The movie's cynical representation of the murderous aristocrat Patrice,
along with its celebration of the working class who struggle day and night
while the rich throw extravagant parties, riled Vichy censor Paul Morand.
He initially withheld the film's release until the COIC forced him out of his
office. Grémillon's movie was released to strong reviews and box office, with
contemporary critics praising its technical polish, clever dialogue, and evocative use of locations, especially the mine scenes. Ultimately, *Remorques*,
Lumière d'été, and the subsequent *Le Ciel est à vous* assured Grémillon's status
as a major auteur, and his clever mix of sets with locations suggested he was
influenced by both *Toni* and *Rules of the Game*. He seemed to rise to the challenging restrictions and risks of the era, and he maintained a consistent team

Michèle and Julien take refuge at a work site (*Lumière d'été*)

of skilled professionals around him. He was also secretly active in the Resistance and soon became president of the Cinémathèque française.

Grémillon's *Le Ciel est à vous*, produced by Raoul Ploquin and written by Charles Spaak and Albert Valentin, was another movie set in contemporary times that nonetheless had to avoid the realities of the day. The story follows a middle-aged couple, Pierre and Thérèse Gauthier, played by Charles Vanel and Madeleine Renaud, who own a small automotive garage. The film's opening titles, added after the war, attest to the true nature of the story, based on a 1937 achievement by a woman pilot, but they also underscore the modest, hard-working nature of this heroic provincial family. The film opens with the Gauthiers forced to move into town to make way for a new airfield. The move starts poorly when their daughter's prized piano is smashed as the workers try to hoist it up to a window. This motif, the threat of things falling from the sky, reinforces the later theme of risky airplane maneuvers. Pierre is a talented mechanic, working alongside Thérèse, a strong, modern, yet devoted wife who drives her own car, keeps the family organized, and impresses everyone with her management skills. The pair make a rather unusual couple in French cinema of the era. They are a devoted, well-matched, romantic pair, with no tensions beyond earning a living, which comes fairly easily to them.

On the day the new airfield opens, Gauthier, who worked on airplanes in World War I, is called on to repair the engine for an attractive stunt pilot, Miss Ivry (Anne Vandène). Soon, however, Thérèse takes a job selling cars in Limoges, away from the family, while Pierre secretly begins flying dangerous air stunts, leading to the couple's first domestic strife. Thérèse sacrifices her job to return home to help care for the family and prevent Pierre from his risky flying. However, by the film's midpoint, Thérèse takes a plane ride and becomes hooked on the thrill as well, and her passion accelerates until the couple buys a small plane for her to enter flight competitions, including barrel rolls and time trials. The rest of the family takes a backseat as Therèse pursues her new dream as a pilot in women's air shows, aided by Pierre's mechanical abilities. However, many town officials discourage her, believing women should stay home. Clearly the film critiques these restrictive Vichy perspectives on women and family duties.

Undaunted, Pierre and Thérèse secretly sell their daughter's new piano to complete the plane's upgrades and prepare for her most dangerous flight: trying to beat the recent record for a woman flying from Marseille to Africa. After Thérèse takes off, however, time passes and there is no report of her

Vanel and Renaud as daring aviators (*Le Ciel est à vous*)

landing. She is assumed lost. Pierre has to return home defeated and inform the children that their mother is missing. The rest of the town turns on him, blaming him for putting his wife at risk, until news arrives that Thérèse is safe in Africa and has indeed broken the record. The final scene allows their unified, small French town to celebrate Thérèse's heroic triumph with an inspiring happy ending. Throughout *Le Ciel est à vous*, brave, ambitious women aviators are championed, with Thérèse continuing that proud history.

The theme of living dangerously to reach a personal, even obsessive goal was compelling to critics on the right and the left, who saw what they wanted in this skillfully made movie. *Le Ciel est à vous* garnered praise as an example of French realism and Occupation cinema at its finest, and as a rare, intelligent treatment of women in a modern French family: *"Le Ciel est à vous* comes out in favor of a 'new couple' based on equality and a job outside the home for both its members" but remains a relatively exceptional film for this era in revealing the contradictions faced by women who are both independent and married (Burch and Sellier 217). At the time, *L'Écran*'s underground review boasted that Grémillon's movie was saving the honor of French cinema with a courageous and authentic representation of French ideals and culture (March 10, 1943, 14). *Le Film* championed the "truth and emotions" of *Le Ciel est à vous*, declaring (as the publication often did) that this was the best and most artistic film since the Armistice. The journal also undercut the central feminist theme by assuring its readers that *Le Ciel est à vous* demonstrates that a woman's place is ultimately in the home and that her family is everything. The film's reception was indeed unusual, with a highly publicized special screening arranged for Pétain, proving this film's ideological usefulness for both the Resistance and Vichy (see Sellier 241).

With the liberation, Grémillon worked with a cooperative group creating newsreels and documentaries, culminating in his very personal and grim project, *The 6th of June at Dawn* (*Le 6 juin à l'aube*, 1946). Shot in his native Normandy after the invasion, it incorporated combat footage and postwar interviews with locals. Grémillon hoped a new, socially engaged cinema would rise from the devastation of the war, much like the Soviets after World War I, but he was disappointed. He never regained the auteur status and prominence he built up during the Occupation. However, he was one of the veteran professionals who had managed to make the transition successfully from decentralized, inventive, and often chaotic 1930s French cinema to flourish during the Occupation despite the restrictions and risks of filmmaking "under the Nazi boot" and the watchful eye of the COIC. He helped anchor what was seen as the new French style of the era. The Occupation also provided opportunities for a younger generation of ambitious writers and directors to compete alongside the established Préverts, Spaaks, Delannoys, Carnés, and Grémillons in France's continuing auteur and star-centered national cinema.

New Directors and Popular Occupation Cinema

Vichy cinema featured prestige and auteur productions, but escapist genre films were a large part of the production season. In competition with Continental, smaller producers fought for their share of the domestic market, which remained profitable, thanks in part to the COIC's policies and the lack of foreign competition. Many of these films displayed remarkably high production values, given the hardships, and also benefited from new faces or the rise of supporting actors from the 1930s into lead roles. One special case was the lively *Us Kids* (*Nous les gosses*, Daquin, 1941), which combined young stars Louise Carletti and Gilbert Gil with an array of talented character actors, including children playing the kids in a tough, poor neighborhood, just trying

Kids in a grown-up's world (*Nous les gosses*)

to get by. Roger Régent credited *Nous les gosses* with opening a completely new direction for French cinema of the era, providing a refreshing, purely cinematic energy (37). Its tale is centered around the need for unity of action in the community, including cooperation between rival gangs of children. It was written by a cluster of leftists from the October Group and Popular Front days, including Gaston Modot. Director Louis Daquin, still in his early thirties, was a communist and active in the Resistance. The romance and crime plot lines remain tangential to the real subject, which involves the kids trying to raise money and solve their own challenges in a gritty world where adults only seem to cause problems: "Daquin deliberately inserted several anti-authoritarian statements into *Nous le gosses*. . . . Much to his surprise, the film was passed without cuts" (Ehrlich 131). Despite being shot on Pathé's backlot, Daquin and his crew generated a naturalism built on traditions of 1930s French cinematic realism that looks quite rare during the Occupation. *Nous les gosses* became a surprise hit.

The most important new director to enter French production during 1943 may have been Robert Bresson with *Angels of Sin*. Although Bresson had directed a rather Surreal comic film, *Public Affairs* (*Les Affaires publiques*, 1934), *Angels of Sin*, a creative collaboration with Jean Giraudoux, cinematographer Agostini, and set designer René Renoux, began his auteur career. The purging of talent and dire need for new product motivated producer Roland Tual and his wife, editor and producer Denise Batcheff, to take on the project for their studio Synops, even though Bresson had no successful track record. Based in part on a story from a Dominican order, *Angels of Sin* begins with nuns staging an early morning rescue of Agnès (Silvia Monfort), a prostitute who is being released from prison. They want to get there ahead of the gang of pimps who want to enslave her anew. The quick mission is handled like a robbery, with shadowy images worthy of Agostini's best Poetic Realist compositions. Agnès is initiated into the order along with Anne-Marie (Renée Faure), a wealthy social reformer anxious to help women less fortunate than herself. One of Anne-Marie's assignments is to reform another difficult woman also recruited from prison, Thérèse (Jany Holt). Upon her release,

Jany Holt as the avenging angel Thérèse (*Angels of Sin*)

however, Thérèse murders the thief who had forced her to steal. She is given refuge in the convent before Anne-Marie or the others know of her crime. Meanwhile, the independent-minded Anne-Marie raises complaints and is dismissed from the convent, but instead of returning home, she hides out in the gardens until she is discovered, unconscious and very ill. As Anne-Marie dies, Thérèse helps her speak her vows, then descends the stairs to be arrested for murder in a scene that combines redemption, humility, and surrender.

For *Angels of Sin*, Bresson and his team manipulate the whites and blacks of convent life for striking graphic compositions featuring dynamic movements of contrasting habits positioned in the frame. The resulting intricate designs are reinforced with careful shadowing via, as Colin Burnett notes, elegant and minimal geometric patterns subtly reinforcing the symbolism of each space and action (157–58). Close-ups are reserved for special narrative moments, such as when Thérèse realizes Anne-Marie knows of her crime. Evelyn Ehrlich contends that *Angels of Sin* fits many visual traits of the era, with "glacial compositions," spare, poetic dialogue, and highly controlled, even cold performances, along with the themes of intense passion for characters shut away from the world: "This isolation, this remove from life, was a perfect metaphor of the *vase clos* that was the French cinema, and France itself" (119). *Angels of Sin* won the COIC prize for the best film of 1943; *Les Visiteurs du soir* had won for 1942.

Another important director to emerge during the war was Jacques Becker, who had worked as an assistant director for Jean Renoir. After returning from captivity in a prisoner of war camp, Becker was given an opportunity to direct a murder mystery titled *The Trump Card* (*Dernier atout*, 1942) by producer André Halley des Fontaines. This Mireille Balin vehicle was set in Latin America but shot in Nice and Paris, with sets by Max Douy. During the production, Becker began to forge connections in the Resistance, working with cinema contacts in both the northern and Vichy zones. His next film, *It Happened at the Inn* (*Goupi mains rouges*, 1943), fully established his reputation and proved his personal, naturalistic storytelling. Based on a novel by Pierre Véry, who helped with the adaptation, *Goupi mains rouges* chronicles the struggles in an extended family of peasants whose many faults may be partially due to inbreeding. Becker shot much of the film on location in the rugged hills of the western Charentes region, and Marguerite Renoir's editing preserved a sense of the naturalistic daily rhythms. Most of the costumes were purchased at flea markets or from local villagers to lend authenticity.

Goupi mains rouges presents a rustic, isolated world that is neither romanticized nor caricatured. The Goupi family all have nicknames, Goupi-
Moneybags, Goupi-Cancan, and so on. As the plot begins, one member of
the Goupis, the twenty-seven-year-old "Monsieur" Eugène (Georges Rollin),
is returning from Paris, where he was taken as a child by his runaway mother.
His uncle Leopold "Mains-Rouges" (Fernand Ledoux), whose hands really
are red, is suspicious of this gentleman, who turns out to be nothing more
than a salesclerk, to the disappointment of his miserly father. The Goupi
family inn is dark and smoky, but in the low-key lighting Becker manages to
compose painterly images with deep space staging. The gruff Leopold now
lives alone in the woods and resents his family for refusing years ago to allow
him to marry the love of his life, who then drowned herself in a well. Nonetheless, Leopold gradually proves to be the voice of reason and the guardian
of family values despite his reticence. *Goupi mains rouges* is filled with colorful characters and their lively storytelling and backgrounds, including the
unhinged Goupi-Tonkin (Robert Le Vigan), who is rattled from his military
service in the Indochina colonies.

The protection of the family's property and money is central to preserving the Goupis' patriarchal traditions and insulated way of life. Greed and
violence distinguish the dominant family members, while the meek relatives
are all kept in their place and mistreated. The feeble elder, Goupi-Emperor
(Maurice Schutz), is the only one who knows where the legendary secret
family fortune is hidden. Moreover, when the cruel, dominant woman in the
family is found murdered, the family nearly unravels, as most of the men rush
to find the treasure rather than the killer. Ultimately, Tonkin is revealed in a
short flashback to have struck Goupi-Tisane (Germaine Kerjean) violently for
beating a feeble family member. Pursued by the police, Tonkin climbs a tree
in a delirious panic and falls to his death. Meanwhile, Mains-Rouges has discovered the Emperor's secret fortune is in the old clock, but he leaves it
there, vowing it will only be revealed if the family ever needs to protect its
land. A tentative peace reigns at the end, including a surprising new romance
between Goupi–Lily of the Valley (Blanchette Brunoy) and her returning
cousin, Eugène. The family's secrets and inbreeding will continue.

André Bazin proclaimed *Goupi mains rouges* "a work of almost perfectly
uniform quality, of a firm and precise style in which the mastery of the director unhesitatingly asserts itself" (*French Cinema of the Occupation* 32). *Goupi
mains rouges* was deemed a great success in the popular press and generated

Tonkin and Mains-Rouges (*Goupi mains rouges*)

an impressive box office run, selling over 100,000 tickets at the Madeleine, which only had 660 seats. After the war, Becker's film's reputation continued and was included in Painlevé's Grande Quinzaine screening of films that had made France proud during the Occupation. Becker's movie was included in part because of "its critique of the Vichy regime's idealization of peasants" (Smoodin, *Paris* 129). Becker had been a member of the October Group of the 1930s and continued to be active in leftist politics. His final Occupation movie, *Paris Frills* (*Falbalas*, 1944), was a lavish costume drama, made when materials were scarce. Much of the studio work for *Falbalas*, a flashback drama starring Micheline Presle and Raymond Rouleau set in the world of fashion design during contemporary times, took place at night in the Pathé Studios, when electricity was more stable. Becker managed to use high-key lighting to glamorize the sets and clothes, but the film also foregrounds how the male designer's success depends on the women's creative labor and sexual exploitation. While this stylish study of gender and the fashion business was being shot, Becker and his colleagues were secretly distributing film stock and other supplies through the CLCF network for Resistance newsreels. *Falbalas*, another major accomplishment for Becker and his team, did not open until 1945, after the liberation.

In contrast to Bresson and Becker, veteran director Jean Delannoy had begun making accomplished genre films in the late 1930s before coming into his own during the Occupation. The much-respected *Pontcarral, colonel d'empire* (1942), built around a patriotic officer following the loss at Waterloo, who wants to regain his own and France's status in the early nineteenth century, pleased audiences with its tale of a defeated France rising anew. Delannoy's *The Eternal Return* became one of the celebrated productions of the watershed year 1943 and another triumph for producer André Paulvé. A sort of modern heritage film and costume drama, *The Eternal Return* was adapted and updated by Jean Cocteau from the popular medieval tale of the impossible love between Tristan and Isolde, which also served as an inspiration for *Les Visiteurs du soir*. The film's authorship is divided, opening with a hand-written note from Cocteau that helps assert his ownership of this adaptation. The striking visual compositions, including intricate camera movements, canted angles, and evocative lighting, were the product of cinematographer Roger Hubert, who returned to working with Carné for the prolonged shoot of *Children of Paradise*. The expressive music was composed by the prolific Georges Auric. *The Eternal Return* was devised as a high-quality, high-art production and marketed as one as well, and it established Delannoy's position as a major commercial director.

Cocteau's fanciful script for *The Eternal Return* inserts the medieval legend into a rather vague time and space where the occasional automobile or motorboat seems out of place in a world more fit for horses and sailboats. Jean Marais plays Patrice, a striking blond young man, living in a remote chateau with his ghoulish extended family, including a little person cousin, Achille (Piéral), who constantly pesters and betrays him. Patrice sets off in search of a young woman to marry his lonely uncle Marc (Jean Murat), returning with the statuesque blonde Nathalie (Madeleine Sologne) after being stabbed defending her honor in a rough bar. Nathalie is fated to marry Marc, though she and Patrice have fallen deeply in love, an attraction reinforced by a powerful potion. Chased from Marc's chateau, Patrice moves in with his friend Lionel (Roland Toutain) across the water and becomes engaged to Lionel's sister, a brunette also named Nathalie. The film, like the legend, is built around clear binary systems. When Patrice tries to visit blonde Nathalie one final time, Achille shoots at him. Wounded, Patrice is carried away by Lionel

Jean Marais and Madeleine Sologne as the forbidden couple (*The Eternal Return*)

back across the water. Nathalie arrives a moment too late and dies of grief, laid out next to his corpse in the garage as if they were two sarcophagi. Cocteau merged his own themes of death and beauty with the Tristan tale. Fans made sudden stars of Marais and Sologne, with young men seeking sweaters like his and young women copying her hairstyle. Despite its initial popularity, cinema history has not been as kind to *The Eternal Return*. The Aryan-looking lead couple and the evil dwarf fit too neatly into Nazi iconography.

The Occupation also saw a large number of popular genre films by reliable commercial directors who were finding new opportunities. *Mademoiselle Swing* (Pottier, 1942) is representative of productions trying to model themselves on the absent Hollywood genre films. Pottier managed to make *Mademoiselle Swing*, only the second movie by SUF studio, before working for Continental and directing six more features during the Occupation. The backstage musical *Mademoiselle Swing* features Raymond Legrand and his orchestra and stars the twenty-one-year-old Irène de Trebert as a bored, upper-class young woman in Angoulême who runs off with a swing band to pursue her career in Paris, writing songs, singing, and dancing. To avoid displeasing her family, Irène hides her identity behind a mask and stage name, Mlle. Swing, and becomes a major star. The narrative builds on generational conflicts and gender oppositions, proving that modern music and culture are empowering for women of the day, though the film's one apparently gay musician becomes the brunt of all the physical gags. The young woman's desires and talents completely drive the narrative, and her character even pushes off the looming heterosexual romance with entertainer Armand (Jean Murat) as a minor potential plot line. Her independent career comes first. Pottier exploits high-key lighting, polished sets, and Nicholas Hayer's trademark mobile camera, as well as back projection, split screens, and clever uses of offscreen sound to mimic Hollywood musical comedies. With an average shot length of nearly twenty seconds, *Mademoiselle Swing* mixes long takes and performance montages in a lively contemporary style and rhythm, offering a bold alternative to more traditional, staid music and movies. Initially, the German censors banned the film because of one song's lyrics, "One must defy destiny!" After a two-month delay, the ban was lifted (Burch and Sellier 144).

The Inevitable M. Dubois (*L'inévitable Monsieur Dubois*, Billon, 1943), like *Mademoiselle Swing*, was a fast-paced romantic comedy clearly intended to remind audiences of the Hollywood movies they were missing, while anchoring the tale in a very French context, including boulevard theater plot devices. The story starts off with a bang as a successful artist, Claude Orly (André Luguet), and his motorbike are run off a country road by the attractive and independent Hélène Mareuil (Annie Ducaux), the head of a prosperous perfume factory. Hiding behind the assumed name Dubois, Claude pretends to be just a bohemian Sunday painter. The hectic businesswoman wants to buy him off quickly to get back to her office, but he begs her to sit for a portrait then and there, to replace the painting ruined in the crash. Hélène abandons him, leaving a blank check, which fuels his frustrated desire and sets this screwball comedy rolling. Orly decides to insert himself into her life in Grasse, where everyone is aware that the respected factory director needs some romance in her life. After a rapid-fire series of back-and-forth skirmishes and misunderstandings, the couple ends up happy together, working side by side, though she is always one step ahead of him, in a comedy worthy of Irene Dunne and Cary Grant.

The Inevitable M. Dubois provides another tale of a proud, independent woman learning she needs a man, yet Hélène remains at least his equal throughout. Claude gradually gives up some of his independence, shifting

A screwball ending (*The Inevitable M. Dubois*)

from casual clothes to a suit and tie as he learns how challenging her business is and how accomplished she is as a manager. The witty banter and
playful sparring among mature adults eliminate any of the need for Vichy
themes of family or children. As with many American screwball romances,
the adults avoid turning into their stodgy elders. Even Hélène's beautiful
younger sister is more interested in horses, tennis, and parties than becoming a wife or mother. Based on a play by André-Paul Antoine, Pierre Billon
offered a smart and highly popular diversion in the form of a pastiche of Hollywood romantic comedies, including fancy convertibles, luxurious settings,
and lots of champagne. Even Orly's mustache is said to be "à l'américaine." As
with other contemporary tales, there is no reference to the war or any social
problems in this confident, reassuring, and very popular comedy.

It was thanks to films like *The Inevitable M. Dubois* and others curated by
Jean Painléve for his Quinzaine celebration of Occupation triumphs in storytelling, including *Nous les gosses*, alongside *Le Ciel est à vous*, *Goupi mains
rouges*, and L'Herbier's stylish *The Fantastic Night* (*La Nuit fantastique*, 1942),
that French cinema surprised foreign critics with its resilience and vitality.

As Pierre Billard points out, an American observer in 1946 noted that despite the horrors of World War II and the Occupation, "French cinema not only survived, it had reached a new level of perfection" (*L'Age* 386). French critics as opposed as the fascist Robert Brasillach and progressive André Bazin agreed that France's cinema defied all odds and thrived during the Occupation with its own isolated renaissance. Roger Régent went further, arguing that triumphant accomplishments such as *Nous les gosses*, *The Duchesse of Langeais*, *Angels of Sin*, and *Lumière d'été* proved that a true cinematic revolution was rattling the foundations of French film (109, 122).

Animation

While going to the movies became increasingly uncomfortable because of energy shortages and increasingly dangerous due to bombings and Nazi roundups, the publicity campaigns continued to tempt audiences with new spectacles. Thanks to the COIC's policies, animation was becoming an integral part of the evening program. The typical screening included a cartoon, in addition to required newsreels and propaganda shorts, before the feature. Animation in France had always been a frail venture, with most animators working independently for art films or on commercials and title sequences rather than ongoing cartoon series. Even with the COIC's aid and encouragement, Occupation-era animation remained quite uneven. Commercial artist André Rigal worked in comic strips before becoming an animator for newsreels and then creating several cartoons in a series, *Les Aventures de Cap'taine Sabord* (1943), about an inept sea captain's journeys. Rigal's animation owes much to the Fleischers' cartoon style, with rubber-hosed figures, cycled drawings, and a jazzy soundtrack. His sailor was seen as a response to Popeye. Rigal also regularly included racist, colonialist representations of exotic natives in foreign lands. COIC funds brought some consistency to his output and income. A *Cap'taine Sabord* cartoon was distributed nationally with *Goupi mains rouges*, along with a COIC-sponsored documentary on Rodin by the young René Lucot.

In the 1940s, Paul Grimault and André Sarrut continued their efforts from the 1930s to maintain a stable studio, finding funding from commercial sources, including Air France, as well as production loans and advances from the new COIC animation program. In November 1943, his *Passengers on the Big Bear* (*Les Passagers de la Grande Ourse*) premiered to kind reviews, with *Le Film* hailing it as an amusing fantasy and the first French animated film whose quality was comparable to the best foreign cartoons (November 6, 1943, 13).

In the same issue of *Le Film*, however, the COIC announced it was tightening participation in the industry further, now requiring all animators, even those working on title sequences, to get authorized work permit cards, verifying their identity and background. Germany also restricted the use of valuable Agfacolor in France, prompting Sarrut to travel to Berlin to plead for color negatives for their contracted cartoons (Roffat 159).

Animation was one of the areas the COIC pointed to with pride as it repeatedly sought to demonstrate its positive effects on the industry. It emphasized that Occupation-era animation belonged to a long cultural history. In December 1943, a gala event was organized to celebrate France's successful animation, including a retrospective screening in Paris of work by Émile Cohl and some shorts from the 1930s, such as *La Joie de vie*. Then nine films submitted for jury prizes were screened, among them Grimault's *The Scarecrow* (*L'épouvantail*, 1943), which won the Émile Reynaud award. This cartoon about a sensitive scarecrow who hides birds from an evil cat in a black suit who is hunting them down seems like clear condemnation of collaboration and naming names that the whole family could appreciate and understand. Nonetheless, *The Scarecrow* premiered in Berlin and was praised as a good example of the Ministry of Information and the COIC's influences on French animation. Once again it was clear that the same themes could be interpreted quite differently from competing ideological perspectives.

The Paris gala's jury prize went to a very refined yet static film, *Callisto, Diana's Little Nymph* (*Callisto, la petite nymphe de Diana*, 1943), by established illustrator André Édouard Marty. The beautiful Callisto, who has taken a vow of chastity to join Diana's commune, is seduced by the trickster Jupiter and becomes pregnant. Rejected by Diana, Callisto and her son are turned into bears and flung into the sky by the reluctant Jupiter, where they remain as Ursa Major and Minor. Despite *Callisto*'s prize, *Le Film* dismissed Marty's animation as dated and disappointing. The jury decided that none of these nine candidates were worthy of their planned first-ever Émile Cohl award (December 4, 1943, 5). By the next year, the COIC would be disbanded, so the prize was discontinued until it was resurrected in 1955.

Some of the COIC's financial support had lasting, positive effects on French animation going forward. This funding kept Grimault afloat and produced his bittersweet war-themed cartoon, *The Little Soldier* (*Le Petit soldat*, 1948), about a female toy harassed by a brute back on the home front in their toy store while her boyfriend has been drafted and taken away to fight. He returns wounded, and together they manage to defeat the evil figure. *Le Petit soldat* took several years to complete, in part because of problems finding color film stock, opening after the war and winning a prize at the Venice Film Festival. Another beneficiary of the programs was Jean Image, a recent immigrant. In 1941, Image joined the popular graphic artist Paul Colin, who was establishing a school for animators, vowing that the land of Cohl, great literature, and art would finally offer viable alternatives to American animation. Image was central to Colin's project, teaching animation to a new generation and pursuing small commercial projects on the side. Image's most significant short, *Rhapsodie de Saturne*, premiered after the war in 1946. It was the first French cartoon in Technicolor and had to be processed in London. Image was acutely aware of the Disney aura and was determined that French animation had to be brightly colored to appeal to children and shift away from high-art animation, such as Marty's *Callisto*. The cartoon emphasizes the vibrant range of Technicolor, especially via its abstract backgrounds. However, most characters remain black notes, resembling caricatures of minstrel-like black musicians. Visually, *Rhapsodie* is a very figurative cartoon, making little effort to develop character animation, and it includes many repetitive, cycled movements, avoiding Disney-style fluidity, much less depth, volume, or texture cues. *Rhapsodie de Saturne* won acclaim and was selected for inclusion in the Cannes Film Festival. Thanks to these new ventures, the CLCF proposed (unsuccessfully) that a special Center for Animation be established after the liberation to guarantee continued employment for that sector of film workers.

The March toward Liberation: *Children of Paradise*

In spring 1943, in a *Le Film* tribute to UFA and German cinema's long history, Joseph Goebbels declared cinema a key instrument of national education whose significance would continue to grow moving forward (March 20, 1943, 9). However, by summer of 1943 and into 1944, the COIC's official decrees in *Le Film* sounded increasingly grave with harsher penalties for anyone violating regulations. Projectionists (who needed work permits) were regularly reminded to clean their equipment and inspect and protect prints because fewer copies of each film were being struck and film stock was increasingly scarce and valuable. Vichy officials complained that there were too many destructive projection-room fires lately, some of which may have been sabotage. Collection of ticket sales, license fees, and taxes continued to preoccupy the regulators as well: "Fraud Is Public Enemy Number One" (*Le Film*, July 24, 6). On a positive side, the COIC initiated benefits and emergency funds to aid victims of bombings and shelling in the industry. Short announcements routinely acknowledged specific labs, studios, and cinemas that had been "pulverized" in the fighting.

Nonetheless, *Le Film* featured headlines boasting box office records for nearly every major release from Paris to Lyon to Nancy as well as images of stars at elegant premieres. For the 1943 holidays, it ran a series of photographs of packed houses full of laughing children attending Christmas specials. Even its already positive reviews seemed to get more glowing: "Très beau film . . . Ce grand film . . . Un film de qualité." The COIC's own declarations were quite contradictory, with positive assessments for the industry's health alternating with dire warnings about electricity shortages and stepped-up punishments for violating rules or being late with tax payments. Major cities were divided into strict zones to control where and when a movie could open, with a COIC official assigned to oversee their programming. Paris was cut down to ten zones, and no film was allowed to play at more than one cinema in each zone at the same time (instead of the previous five), without special permission. Fewer and fewer prints were available of popular new movies. *Le Film* acknowledged that the loss of external markets in North Africa and beyond were hurting the industry's income, without mentioning that Allied victories were the cause.

By winter 1944, the COIC announced that the führer had personally banned any construction or remodeling in French labs, cinemas, or studios without authorization. Everything was in short supply, so film studios had to stop taking vital materials away from war efforts. The skyrocketing cost of production was branded as unsustainable and unpatriotic. Given the lack of coal and electricity, the COIC granted special permission for cinemas to use portable space heaters, if available. As the Allied gains increased during 1944, the COIC began to emphasize its long line of positive contributions to the film industry, as if trying to defend itself to the French people, without acknowledging the end was near. It bragged in *Le Film* about arranging film shows for French prisoners in Germany (*Douce, Goupi mains rouges*), and it celebrated the first class of thirty students entering its new film school, selected by none other than Marcel L'Herbier, Charles Spaak, Roger Leenhardt, Jean Mitry, and a handful of other respected figures (February 5, 1944). Issues of *Le Film* got progressively thinner in 1944 as paper and ink became rare, but even after D-Day, with the war now on French soil, it argued that French cinema was more important than ever and must be protected. Finally, on July 1, 1944, *Le Film* listed all 220 films put into production under the COIC's watch. The next issue emphasized that eighty-two different directors, most very well known, had participated in French cinema and benefited under the COIC over the previous four years (July 22, 1943). *Le Film's* goal was to justify its own policies and existence, now couching the COIC as a sort of apolitical guardian of French cinema and culture, lending continuity and stability to the industry despite the disruption of the Armistice, Nazi Occupation, and imposition of Vichy.

Le Film was not alone. By the final double issue of *Ciné Mondial* at the close of July 1944, every article assessed the last four years, from miraculous triumphs in costuming and sets, despite the material shortages, to questioning why more movies did not acknowledge the ongoing war. It listed the top new stars, acknowledging that there were many more men than women at the top of the billings. Critic Pierre Leprohon even wrote a wrap-up titled "New Tendencies of French Cinema," arguing, as others also did, that the Occupation had ironically brought dramatic new developments in French film. He cites many of what became the canonical films of the war, including *Who Killed Santa Claus?*, *Angels of Sin*, *Goupi mains rouges*, *Le Ciel est à vous*, and

L'Herbier's high-quality Occupation-era style (*The Fantastic Night*)

L'Herbier's dazzling *Fantastic Night* as marking a new stage in French cinema's evolution. Leprohon contends that French films had become more expressive, realistic, and indeed poetic (3–4). Thus, even as the war was raging, the legacy of the COIC and French cinema's response to the crisis were being written. Roger Régent helped solidify many of these debates and observations in his influential 1948 history of the World War II years, *Cinéma de France*. His longest chapter, "Birth of a Style," details how the French industry rose to the challenges, especially in 1943, creating a surprising string of major artistic triumphs that forever changed France's cinematic storytelling. Many historians have followed suit, arguing that the Occupation forged a new school of French filmmaking that allowed both fantasy and realism in a high-quality, technically polished studio system.

As the tensions in France increased, producers still struggled to deliver well-made and engaging projects despite the hardships, many taking advantage of the remaining financial aid from the COIC. Few films had as tortured a production process or succeeded so well as Carné's *Children of Paradise*, which suffered a series of delays and challenges. It was mostly finished under the Occupation, but Carné purposely delayed its completion until after the liberation. *Children of Paradise* provides an important primer for French film practice of the era. It builds an isolated world unto itself, provides a tribute to nineteenth-century French culture and melodrama, and incorporates generic conventions from 1930s and 1940s French film. As with Carné, Prévert, and Trauner's rather eccentric *Les Visiteurs du soir*, *Children of Paradise* was conceived with production design at the center of the drama, although this time the setting and visual style were less static and more cinematic, despite much of the story being anchored on and around theatrical stages.

André Paulvé, still based in Nice, was willing to take on Carné's expensive and demanding new project because of the profits he had reaped from *Les Visiteurs du soir*, *L'Eternel retour*, and his other successful Occupation-era spectacles. *Children of Paradise* originated from several parallel ideas concerning French theater and early nineteenth-century Paris scandals. Carné became intrigued when actor Jean-Louis Barrault shared his interest in the famous nineteenth-century mime Jean-Gaspard Deburau, in part because Prévert was considering writing a script built around the dashing murderer Lacenaire from the same era. Carné traveled to Paris to undertake primary research and bring back illustrations and materials to provide inspiration. Trauner, hiding nearby under an assumed name, worked with Prévert and Carné as they blended these two projects into a single screenplay. Trauner designed the demanding settings as they went, though Léon Barsacq's name was listed as set designer with the COIC instead. As the stories became intertwined, with new composite fictional and real characters connecting the various plot lines, the script continually grew until they believed it might warrant two or even three movies. At a time of strict limits on film length, their improbable screenplay was more than three hours long. Ultimately, *Children of Paradise* premiered after the COIC's demise, with two parts and an intermission, plus a double admission price, thanks to a compromise with distributor Gaumont. It quickly became one of France's most celebrated movies. When it opened in the United States, *Children of Paradise* was marketed as France's response to *Gone with the Wind*.

Children of Paradise was a rare production on every level. From its very first announcement, it became a major topic in the press, which followed its progress every step of the way. Hundreds of performers and technicians participated in the production, the history of which is an epic in its own right. Faced with an unprecedented budget, including salaries of top stars Arletty, Barrault, and Pierre Brasseur, among others, and ever-increasing costs of production during the war, Paulvé found an Italian coproducer to share the risks. Arletty's continuing popularity with audiences and the COIC helped justify the budget. Filming began in August 1943. However, with the overthrow of Mussolini and the Allies landing in Sicily, the Italian coproducer withdrew and the Germans demanded that Carné's production move back to Paris, even before the mammoth Boulevard of Crime street set had been completed or used. Nazi sympathizer Robert Le Vigan, who was to perform the part of the rag dealer, fled to Germany and was replaced by Pierre Renoir. The Germans were suddenly suspicious of Paulvé and banned him from producing while they investigated his background. Pathé Consortium came on to guarantee that the high-profile project continued. Carné's reputation as well as that of his stars motivated robust publicity. Already in December 1943, the press revealed photos of the vast interior theater sets at Pathé's studios, which were built by skilled crews from live theater and could seat six hundred extras as spectators. After these scenes were completed, the company was finally allowed to return to Nice in February 1944, where the neglected exteriors needed extensive repair work. Once the Allies landed in June, Carné and his team continued to shoot, but at a measured pace, vowing to release their epic once France was completely liberated.

Children of Paradise opens with an appropriately grandiose title sequence and a curtain rising on section one, "The Boulevard of Crime," the nickname

Baptiste performs for pleasure (*Children of Paradise*)

for the bustling Boulevard du Temple in Paris, home to crowds seeking cheap diversions and entertainment at highly melodramatic theatrical shows. Arletty's Garance is introduced in a sleazy carnival setting, spinning naked in a tub of water for onlookers to peer in. She soon catches the attention of the ambitious actor Frédérick Lemaître (Brasseur) but is already entwined with the scoundrel Lacenaire (Marcel Herrand), "a thief by need, a murderer by calling." The mime Baptiste (Barrault) initially proves his skills by comically reenacting a theft involving Lacenaire and Garance, to the delight of the audience, as he demonstrates her innocence. He also falls under her spell, while the earnest actress Nathalie (Maria Casares) suffers from unrequited love for Baptiste. The chaotic Funambules theater ends up launching Baptiste's and Lemaitre's careers, as the pair pass the ultimate test, pleasing the popular audience, the "children of heaven," up in the cheap seats. The romantic Baptiste builds Garance into his show as his impossible object of desire. On stage and in real life, she chooses Lemaître as her lover, though she grows ever fonder of Baptiste. By the end of the first part, Lacenaire's antics have landed Garance in trouble, so she calls on a count (Louis Salou) to whisk her safely away, which opens the field for Nathalie to pursue Baptiste. Throughout, the screenplay relies heavily on clever, theatrical banter to develop characterization and weave in deceit, fate, and irony, while shifting our focus quickly from one character's plight to the trajectory of another. All the world is indeed a play here.

The second portion, "The Man in White," returns us to the Boulevard of Crime six years later, where Lemaître is now a major star, with women on each arm, but a pile of debts. Baptiste, now a successful mime, has begun a family with Nathalie. An older, humbled Garance has returned from her travels, harboring a hidden love for Baptiste as she watches his performances in secret. Lucenaire resurfaces, wanting money and help from his old acquaintances. When Baptiste learns that Garance is in town, he shuts down his show, depressed and lovesick. When they bump into each other at Lemaître's premiere of *Othello*, they slip out to spend the night together. In the morning, the jealous Lucenaire kills the count in the exotic setting of a Turkish bathhouse, triggering his own tragic end, even as the whole town dances in the streets to celebrate the carnival. Back in the apartment, Garance explains to Baptiste she must leave him to his family, as Nathalie walks in on them and learns that Baptiste has never stopped thinking of Garance. With that, Garance races out, disappearing into the crowd of revelers, and Baptiste charges past Nathalie and their son, becoming lost in the chaos as well. Confronted by the fatalistic, moralizing old rag man, he watches Garance's fancy carriage pull away. Neither Baptiste nor Garance know that her protective count is dead, but they recognize their own lives are ruined, as the children of paradise dance on, oblivious to their suffering.

Children of Paradise benefited greatly from Hubert's cinematography, panning, tracking, and dollying to open up the theatrical spaces. The lush musical score by Joseph Kosma heightens the melodrama throughout. Kosma had to work in secret, with Maurice Thiriet fronting for the compositions and directing the orchestra. A number of extras and other crew members worked under assumed names or with false permit cards, as the COIC's control began to slip, especially for monitoring such an extensive production shot in both zones. The story has been praised for its rich characterizations and savvy performances that synthesize theatrical and cinematic traditions. *Children of Paradise* also provides yet another example of an Occupation tale populated with weak male figures and suffering women. There is no strong patriarch or solid nuclear family to provide safety, happiness, or a conventional moral framework here. *Children of Paradise* was conceived and marketed as a bold

tribute to French culture and its resilience. As Jill Forbes points out, its premiere at the Palais de Chaillot was a major event: "It was a showcase, a tes-
timony to the French cinema's enduring qualities of imagination, and proof
that it could stand up to foreign competition" (9). The film ran for over a year
in Paris alone and was hailed as a high point in the careers of all the participants, even as Arletty's reputation was coming under fire for her very public
collaboration with German officials.

Liberation: From the COIC to the CLCF to the CNC

There were high hopes among members of the Committee for the Liberation of French Cinema (CLCF), including those writing in the pages of *L'Écran*,
that French cinema would be completely purged of collaborators and revitalized on liberation. The eventual recovery was quite complicated and varied from region to region, but a newly energized industry did slowly emerge
after filmmaking temporarily ground to a halt in 1944. From the June Normandy invasion on, nearly every facet of life became more dangerous as the
Occupation forces and collaborators grew more desperate and the Resistance
was emboldened. During June 1944, five hundred French cinemas closed.
Fighting, the loss of electricity, and accumulating troubles shipping prints
took a heavy toll on theaters, with most Paris screens going dark by August.
Paris was liberated at the end of the month, and the slow recovery began
from there.

The CLCF had been formed secretly in 1941, initially in Henri Langlois's
apartment, to monitor the industry and prepare eventually to replace the
COIC. Along with other Resistance and technician groups, they were anxious to take over the offices of the COIC, Continental, and the studio spaces,
starting with Buttes-Chaumont and Pathé, at the first opportunity. On
August 19, the CLCF began its offensive from its secret meeting site at La
Pagode cinema. Langlois sent his brother to guard the Cinémathèque's vault
in the Palais de Chaillot. Jacques Becker, Le Chanois, Pierre Bost, and others
had already organized clandestine filming of the battles and helped document
the final skirmishes in and around Paris. The resulting *Liberation of Paris* was
screened at the Normandie cinema within days. André Bazin's review cited
a cruel yet beautiful scene in which "a German soldier crawls along a deserted
street while all around him bullets spatter against the pavement like rain-
drops in a storm" (*French Cinema of the Occupation*, 101). Furthermore, when
the COIC offices on rue Messine were reclaimed, Langlois took over, calling
for executions in the name of the Cinémathèque.

The liberation and its immediate aftermath were an exhilarating and challenging time for the film community. For security reasons, many in one professional wing of the industry had no idea who else was in the Resistance. The electricians' cell may have been unaware of which editors, actors, or designers were active in their own disciplines. Moreover, the CLCF's hard-line leftists were suspicious of the more moderate Comité de résistance de l'industrie cinématographique (CRIC), which included people working at the COIC but secretly trying to protect French interests and prepare for a smooth transition when the Germans left. Even COIC director Louis-Emile Galey had begun harboring Resistance members in his office. The two major resistance groups and others had been quietly organizing film workers from the labs to the studios to government administrators. All wanted a lead role in jump-starting production. CRIC and Galey would argue that they had been crucial to propping up and supporting ongoing production and protecting Resistance members in the industry as best they could, while waiting and planning secretly for the liberation of French cinema. At the same time, the French Communist Party and its CGT unions held a strong hand immediately following the liberation of Paris and were establishing rules for who could and could not continue working in technical craft positions.

Charles de Gaulle and the Free French movement began compiling lists of enemies of France long before the Allies landed on French soil. Even as fighting raged in other parts of France, the provisional governments in Paris and liberated areas began the task of identifying, trying, and punishing collaborators as part of a fairly organized purification plan, meant to bring swift justice to those who betrayed France and profited from the Occupation. These liberating groups also hoped to reduce subjective retaliation and citizen-versus-citizen violence. Various civil and military courts were quickly formed to review charges against traitors and collaborators, and many regional and professional organizations including the CLCF had their own *commissions d'épuration*. Initially Pierre Renoir presided over the CLCF's sessions, and its committee helped funnel purification cases involving the film community into the larger regional or national systems where collaborators could be censured, fined, imprisoned, or even executed. For instance, the head of the Pathé studios at Billancourt was sentenced to five years in prison, was fined, and had his property confiscated. One common punishment for egregious collaboration was a charge of *l'indignité nationale*, for those found no longer worthy of full citizenship. Such a ruling of indignity could be leveled for serious offenses, such as making pro-Nazi documentaries, that did not necessarily involve specific criminal activities. Such a ruling could be combined with jail time or house arrest.

Military courts typically dealt with the most clear-cut cases of treason, while the Justice Department handled a vast array of offenses. One high-profile case involved the well-known film critic and writer Robert Brasillach, a dedicated Nazi sympathizer who had published names of Jews and Resistance fighters in hiding. Brasillach was also accused of pursuing homosexual relationships with German officers and officials. He was executed by firing squad. His colleague Maurice Bardèche was initially sentenced to death as well but was released from prison within a year. Other serious cinema-related trials included cases against those associated with *Forces occultes*. Director Jean Mamy was executed, and his screenwriter Jean Marquès-Rivière was sentenced to death in absentia. He was already hiding in a fascist Spanish enclave in Africa. Their producer at Nova was sentenced to three years in prison.

L'Écran, the CLCF's journal, had regularly pointed out its own targets for revenge and justice prior to the liberation, even printing warnings naming specific people and their offenses, including Clouzot for directing *Le Corbeau* at Continental. The committees for purification charged Clouzot with *indignité*, but he was never found guilty by the higher courts. Nonetheless, he was banned from working in the industry for several years, despite pleas from high-profile supporters, including Jean-Paul Sartre, that *Le Corbeau* was misunderstood and not anti-French or pro-Nazi at all. While still technically barred from the profession, Clouzot managed to direct *Quai des Orfèvres* (1947), a Louis Jouvet vehicle, and renew his career. Guilty sentences were in nearly constant review and were often weakened or overturned by subsequent hearings. Other *L'Écran* targets escaped serious consequences during the inquiries. Fernandel, who had made two Continental films and continued an active career singing and acting during the Occupation, underwent the embarrassment of an investigation but avoided any lasting sanctions. Similarly, the popular Danielle Darrieux had performed in three Continental films and traveled to Germany for a publicity tour, but she never faced any formal charges.

Arletty's fate in the *épuration* process was less clear-cut. She was arrested in September 1944. She had maintained a number of close professional and social relations with German officials and was tried and found guilty for a very public affair with a Nazi officer. Although Arletty never worked for Continental and claimed that she had never made any personal pro-German statements, unlike many others in the industry, she was initially sentenced to four months in prison, then eighteen months under house arrest. With the liberation, women denounced for "horizontal collaboration" in all walks of life were often publicly humiliated, often with their heads shaven, and made scapegoats for national guilt. Although many in the Resistance were openly suspicious and hostile toward women following the Occupation, one of de Gaulle's provisional government's earliest new decrees in spring 1944 granted women the right to vote, in part to acknowledge their heroic efforts in the Resistance. Women remained particularly vulnerable during the final days of the war and into the first months of liberation.

Beyond Arletty, a number of actresses were accused of "carnal collaboration" for their often highly visible relations with Nazi officials and soldiers. The COIC and Vichy public relations campaigns displaying gala premieres with actresses drinking champagne alongside German and Vichy representatives fueled resentment among the population, especially the Free French Resistance. Ginette Leclerc posed a special challenge. She and her husband, Lucien Gallas, ran a popular night club, patronized by German officers, plus her association with Le Corbeau and two other Continental films made her particularly open to attack. She was imprisoned for nine months, then was not allowed to act for three more months (Leteux 346). One of the most severe cases was Mireille Balin, who was arrested in September 1944 by Free French soldiers near Monaco as she tried to flee to Italy with her fiancé, a German soldier. He was apparently executed soon after. She was beaten, raped, and imprisoned under harsh conditions for several months. Her trial included censure for participating in a pro-Franco Italian-Spanish coproduction, The Siege of the Alcazar (Genina, 1940). Her director, Augusto Genina, who remained in Italy, was never punished. He later returned to make the Louis de Funès comedy Frou -Frou (1955).

Among male stars, Maurice Chevalier was arrested briefly for having sung in Germany to French prisoners of war, while Pierre Fresnay, star of Le Corbeau and president of the Vichy actors association, was imprisoned for six weeks, then placed under house arrest. Albert Préjean was jailed briefly and banned from working for one year. Suspects could be denounced by organized groups, including the CGT, or accusers could remain anonymous. Band leader Raymond Legrand was criticized for his radio shows and role in Mademoiselle Swing and received a six-month sanction. Among the more challenging cases was Sacha Guitry, still a major entertainer and personality across France. He was quickly arrested in August 1944 and sent to prison in Paris, but he was released after sixty days, and subsequent investigations failed to indict him formally. He defended himself by explaining he had turned down lucrative offers from Continental. Robert Le Vigan, who had fled with his friend Céline, was eventually arrested by French forces in Austria and found guilty of aiding in Nazi propaganda, including regular radio transmissions, and sentenced to ten years of hard labor. His sentence was suspended in 1948, and he eventually left Europe for asylum in Argentina.

In all, nearly two hundred cinema employees of the roughly one thousand investigated were purged and punished in some way (Bertin-Maghit 221). Most of the hearings required that suspects justify their behavior during the Occupation, including working at Continental. Michel Simon, Viviane Romance, Marcel Carné, and even Le Chanois appeared before various committees. Typically, sentences were rather light, and a number of accused, especially actors, tried to justify continuing to work and provide evidence that someone active in the Resistance could vouch for their character. The many exceptions created some resentment in the CLCF. André Sarrut, for instance, was the only animation producer called before the committees. He had to explain his close relations and contracts with COIC and Continental, and his travels to Germany. His coproducer Grimault, who had friends in the Communist party, was not questioned (Roffat 217–19). Ultimately, those in charge of the trials realized that their role was to balance retribution with bringing stability back to the industry. Motion pictures were the most popular form of entertainment, and they had helped provide a source of national escape and even pride during the war. Harshly punishing some of France's most popular figures, such as Guitry, Darrieux, or Fernandel, could be risky.

To revive the cinema as efficiently as possible, a number of Vichy and German institutions were retained, revised, or renamed. Pierre Blanchar presided over the CLCF and Jean Painlevé, a well-known scientific documentary filmmaker and leftist, became the director general of cinema, replacing Louis-Emile Galey. Painlevé and the CLCF quickly made plans for a smooth transition of the industry. They wanted a new, progressive committee to oversee film production, parallel to the renewal plans in other fields, but with a budget from the government. He and the CLCF had to work with de Gaulle's more conservative minister of Information, Pierre-Henri Teitgen, to adapt some of COIC's practical programs while safeguarding union control and ensuring creative freedom for above-the-line talent. As Alan Williams points out, "There was no question of returning to the chaotic, unbridled free market of the 1930s, for the recent reforms, however tainted their origins, had

been overwhelmingly beneficial to the industry" (*Republic* 276). In 1945, Teitgen replaced Painlevé with Michel Fourré-Cormeray, a functionary dedicated
to reorganizing the cinema sector more quickly. Fourré-Courmeray established the Office professionnel du cinéma (OPC) with a committee to revise
or replace most of the COIC's functions. However, the OPC was to be funded,
like the COIC, from mandatory membership dues from all participants, from
technicians to exhibitors to producers. These dues proved highly unpopular, as did other top-down decisions from Fourré-Cormeray, and the OPC lost
much support in the industry (Legrand 61).

The problems raised by OPC and ensuing wrangling between powerful
constituents in the industry threatened the cinema's recovery. During October 1946, the government launched a replacement, the new Centre National
de la Cinématographie (CNC), to take over centralized control of the industry, which it maintains to this day. The CNC was controversial from the
beginning, including for retaining Fourré-Cormeray as director, but it was
protected under the Ministry of Information. The CNC's charter granted its
director increased power for regulating and modernizing the industry, and
a budget for granting subventions to film production. One of the first changes
was to revise the ticket pricing and tax system, allowing aid and support for
movie theaters and producers, two groups who often disagreed about recent
financial policies (Legrand 64). The CNC board included members from
union and management.

Gradually, CNC funding for chosen quality projects allowed outright production subsidies, beyond the low-interest loans from the Crédit National.
Many saw this as a stabilizing improvement on the COIC's system. The CNC
oversaw permits and training for personnel and maintained the IDHEC film
school and the Cinémathèque française, including film preservation. France's
cinema was in many ways professionalized by the CNC, which disappointed
those (including some CLCF members) who preferred the looser opportunities of the 1930s. However, the CNC also helped promote French films on the
global market. The CNC is unusual in that government employees and industry professionals both participate, which has reinforced its flexibility and
authority over the years (Bertin-Maghit 278–79). No other single institution
has shaped French cinema more since World War II, and the CNC remains
a unique and inspiring model for other national cinemas today.

Despite new government supports, postwar French cinema still faced a
major threat. As movie theaters began slowly reopening in late 1944 into 1945,
it became clear that American and other foreign films, long absent, would

be dominating French screens for some time to come. As Eric Smoodin notes, initially only seven Paris movie theaters were open in fall 1944; the hit Deanna Durbin vehicle *It Started with Eve* (Koster, 1941) occupied two of them (*Paris* 126). Moreover, few new French movies were complete and ready to open after the devastation of 1944, further undercutting France's share of the box office. The government signed the Blum-Byrnes agreement in spring 1946, which only made matters worse for French filmmakers and technicians. This agreement, between the returning Léon Blum and US Commerce Secretary James Byrnes, was designed in part to help guarantee debt relief for France. The deal allowed free trade with no quotas on incoming American movies but required that cinemas reserve at least four weeks for French films out of each three months of screenings. Most everyone in French cinema complained, except theater owners, who wanted the flexibility to book the most popular movies, regardless of where they came from. Importantly, the French government had recently nationalized Continental and other German or collaborator-owned movie theaters into the Union Générale du Cinéma (UGC), which still exists, now as a private corporation. High ticket sales would thus help exhibitors and government coffers alike.

In response to France's weakened industry, a Committee for the Defense of French Cinema was launched, complaining that the Americans were invading French screens and dumping their movies at bargain prices, which was true. US studios had benefited from high domestic attendance during the war and now rereleased films that had already played well at home. French distributors and exhibitors were eager to profit from the pent-up demand for Hollywood movies. By summer 1946, movies as varied as *The Wizard of Oz* (Fleming, 1939), *Citizen Kane* (Welles, 1941), *The Maltese Falcon* (Huston, 1941), *Laura* (Preminger, 1944), and *Double Indemnity* (Wilder, 1944) all opened in Paris, among many others. The latter three helped motivate France's "discovery" of American film noir, thanks to the concentrated release of crime melodramas from the previous years. By contrast, the same market conditions were not benefiting France's backlog of wartime movies because the CNC could not be a strong advocate for distributing COIC-era films abroad.

While Hollywood's stockpile of live-action movies was most visible as an immediate threat to France's share of screen time, the Americans also inundated France with animation. During 1946 and 1947, Disney opened four features, *Pinocchio* (1940), *Fantasia* (1940), *Dumbo* (1941), and *Bambi* (1942), in under eighteen months. As the posters proclaimed each time: "Encore un chef d'oeuvre de Walt Disney." Thus, the Disney brand was at its peak in France immediately after World War II, while short cartoons from Warner Bros., MGM, and other studios were regularly part of the programs in theaters. The steady stream of competing movies led various unions for skilled and unskilled cinema workers to unite into a single powerful cinema syndicate, under leadership from the Communist Party's CGT. The PCF organized rallies and strikes against the Blum-Byrnes agreement, charging that Americans were forcing their culture onto Europe, crippling France's studios, and depriving French workers of a living. Big-name writers, directors, and stars, including Jean Grémillon and Louis Jouvet, complained as well, and talent as diverse as Gaston Modot, Françoise Rosay, Jacques Becker, and Claude Autant-Lara showed up at movie theaters to rally spectators behind their cause. In December 1947, a demonstration of ten thousand actors, directors, writers, and film technicians paraded across Paris (Courtade 248). France's feature film output had decreased from ninety-one films released in 1946 to just seventy-eight in 1947.

Finally, in 1948, the Blum-Byrnes agreement was renegotiated, placing a cap of 121 import visas on American movies, though 180 such visas had already been issued that year. It also required an additional four weeks of French films in theaters each year. But lasting damage had been done. Only 25 percent of the films shown in France in 1948 were French. Nonetheless, the industry was poised to develop new strategies for combining specifically French assets, including their ongoing star system, stable of respected auteurs, and supportive policies from the CNC, with the new realities of the post–World War II global marketplace. By 1949, CNC aid money began flowing to producers and reinforced the gradual increase in feature film production numbers into the 1950s. France still only created roughly 30 percent of the first-run movies shown, comparable to the 1930s, but those films often earned over half the box office. Moreover, European coproductions began to return, with producers like Paulvé reviving their French–Italian partnerships to secure higher budgets and international stars to counter British and American competition.

New market conditions and CNC regulations restrained the overall number of new French films that were released each year to an average of under 100 in the late 1940s, helping improve the odds of profitability over the 1930s business model even though most movies were still produced by small-scale production companies. A number of major stars and directors, including Michèle Morgan, Jean Gabin, Marcel Dalio, René Clair, and Julien Duvivier, returned, reinforcing the notion that French cinema was recovering and even thriving. Moreover, the CNC launched Unifrance in 1949 with a mission of actively promoting French films abroad. Thus, thanks to the CNC and France's specific cinematic environment, French cinema proved easier to rebuild after the Occupation than was the case for the industries of Italy or Germany. Despite renewed competition from Hollywood and beyond, French producers old and new reexamined their place in international cinema, audiences in France caught up on movies they had missed over the past few years, and French writers and directors assessed those global discoveries for new trends in storytelling. French cinema, as always, would synthesize influences from beyond its borders while striving to forge a vibrant and timely postwar film experience that was particular to France and its cultural contexts.

Epilogue

Toward a New Era in French Cinema

After World War II, French cinema stabilized rather rapidly, even as material shortages and rationing continued for several years after the liberation. Fortunately, its fifty-year history of institutional structures, flexible modes of production, and innovative aesthetic options provided firm foundations for French filmmaking's comeback in the postwar period. While the venerable Pathé and Gaumont, joined now with the government-owned newcomer UGC, dominated certain aspects of the industry (especially first-run exhibition), most films were still produced by small- and medium-sized companies. Despite the turmoil of the 1940s, France's industry continued to maintain and develop a strong array of star vehicles, genre films, and high-profile adaptations, which were revitalized by the postwar return of actors, writers, directors, and producers as well as an influx of new talent. French cinema supported alternative production models, including some daring individual auteur productions, thanks to favorable market conditions and a large, receptive audience looking for cinematic renewal after the war.

The number of ciné-clubs and *art et essai* cinemas exploded in the late 1940s and early 1950s. In 1946, Jean Painlevé helped establish the Féderation française des ciné-clubs to help advocate for and guide that expansion. This group soon began printing a newsletter for subscribers and art houses. In 1954, its more substantial journal *Cinéma* appeared, edited by critic and historian Pierre Billard, helping establish a critical environment modeled on and ultimately rivaling that of the 1920s. The fascination with French cinema's past was accelerated by retrospectives, including Henri Langlois's 1947 series "The Avant-Garde of Yesterday and Today" at the Cinémathèque, and the short-lived Objectif 48 and 49 ciné-club and its anti-Cannes Festival du film maudit, held in Biarritz, to present overlooked and avant-garde films (Burnett 70).

The Objectif group, which included Alexandre Astruc, André Bazin, Robert Bresson, and Jacques Doniol-Valcroze, among others, also attracted a lively young cohort of devoted followers, including François Truffaut, Jean-Luc Godard, Jacques Rivette, and Éric Rohmer. One of the key moments for this new generation of critics was an exemplary article, "The Birth of a New Avant-Garde: *La Caméra-Stylo*," published in *Écran* during 1948. In it, Astruc championed a cluster of films, including *Rules of the Game* and Bresson's *The Ladies of the Bois de Boulogne* (*Les Dames du bois de Boulogne*, 1945), for pointing out innovative directions for storytelling in which the camera would be the equivalent of a pen, forging a new cinematic language for what he predicted would be the age of the *caméra-stylo* (32). Astruc was still in his twenties. Along with the thirty-year-old Bazin, he helped jumpstart post–World War II aesthetic film criticism. Bazin, Doniol-Valcroze, and Joseph-Marie Lo Duca launched the powerfully influential *Cahiers du Cinéma* in 1951. Their rival, *Positif*, started publication in 1952, fueling the critical debates and excitement around contemporary cinema. Moreover, in 1948, the International Federation of Film Archives decided to maintain its headquarters at the Cinémathèque in Paris. Thanks to this cluster of activities, France was once again positioned at the nucleus of film culture globally.

As the critical landscape suggests, filmmaking of the late 1940s continued France's distinctive tradition of maintaining both a healthy mainstream cinema and a vibrant alternative auteur cinema. The CNC's policies, which were regularly updated and revised, had provided excellent support for technical upgrades in both studios and theaters. Many postwar films displayed highly polished, classical production values in a wide range of commercial and auteur projects, including studio-bound costume dramas. Moreover, much as during the 1930s, a recurring cadre of successful screenwriters, including Charles Spaak, Pierre Véry, and the team of Jean Aurenche and Pierre Bost, were much in demand. The resulting spate of prestige productions was soon labeled a "new" tradition of quality. Among the celebrated movies were Jean Delannoy's stylish adaptation of André Gide's *Pastoral Symphony* (*La Symphonie pastorale*, 1946), which won three prizes at the Cannes Film Festival that year, and Claude Autant-Lara's sentimental melodrama told in flashback, *Devil in the Flesh* (*Le Diable au corps*, 1947), which adapted a World War I–era story of forbidden love by Raymond Radiguet.

These titles represent a tendency toward high-profile versions of French literary tales. They feature doomed women who captivate the suffering male leads. The newly returned Michèle Morgan starred as the blind ward who

Morgan in *Pastoral Symphony*

fascinates a father and his son in *Pastoral Symphony*, disrupting her adoptive family. Micheline Presle played the adulterous woman of *Devil in the Flesh*, which also catapulted Gérard Philipe to stardom. *Pastoral Symphony* was produced by Russian immigrant Joseph Bertcholtz at Les Films Gibé, while *Devil in the Flesh* was produced by Paul Graetz, a German Jew who moved back to France after fleeing to the United States during the war. Graetz's Transcontinental Films joined other new ventures in seeking international and coproduction partnerships for bigger-budget projects.

While such mainstream classical tradition of quality films proved popular with audiences as well as the CNC and the commercial press, the shifting critical climate among passionate film fans and younger reviewers often celebrated the more adventurous alternative auteur productions. Leftist critics in particular became restless after the war, calling for more social realist films. The CLFC had in fact demanded a politically engaged production cooperative be formed as a response to the Occupation. However, the Occupation experience itself inspired few films, and France never created the equivalent of Italy's *Rome, Open City* (Rossellini, 1945) or ensuing neorealist

Gérard Philipe and Micheline Presle (*Devil in the Flesh*)

movement. Nonetheless, a few projects managed to address the Occupation-era and French resistance overtly. Among them was René Clément's *Battle of the Rails* (*La Bataille du rails*, 1946). Initially begun as a short documentary sponsored by the railroad union and former Free French resistance members, *Battle of the Rails* grew into a feature fiction film with real rail workers and nonactors performing alongside some professionals. Writer Colette Audry worked with Clément, helping compile railroad workers' tales about their exploits hiding Resistance members on trains, sabotaging operations, and disrupting Nazi supply lines. Given that the same railways had deported thousands of Jews and forced laborers to Germany during the war, the railway union was keen to highlight their Resistance efforts and counter the public charges of collaboration or complicity. As historian Sylvie Lindeperg reveals, from the beginning this production was shaped by competing agendas from the originating communist CLCF collective and the state-owned railroad company that wished to promote the myth of an idealized France without class or political divisions, united in its opposition to the Germans (142).

Battle of the Rails, filmed by Henri Alekan, includes compelling action scenes and dramatic montages of speeding and crashing trains as well as shots

Engineers on the job (*Battle of the Rails*)

of daring engineers. Many shots recall Jean Renoir's *La Bête humaine*. Bazin's review at the time applauded Clément's combination of rhythmic poetry and artistic honesty for a film that ultimately "makes us feel we know and love the auteur like a friend" (*French Cinema of the Occupation* 125). *Battle of the Rails* was the sort of cinema that many from the CLCF hoped would become a major component of French film practice, but it was a rare project. One of Clément's next films was the impressive *The Damned* (*Les Maudits*, 1947), starring Marcel Dalio and Henri Vidal, about a group of Nazis and sympathizers trying to flee Europe in a submarine destined for South America, only to be foiled by French heroism.

Another unusual post–World War II Occupation drama was Jean-Pierre Melville's *Silence of the Sea* (*Le Silence de la mer*, 1949), which was produced without CNC approval and adapted from a resistance book by Vercors, without the author's permission. Melville (a.k.a. Grumbach) was refused a professional director permit. Frustrated, he created his own production company, and, with some help from producer Pierre Braunberger, shot his film in 1947, defying union staffing rules. It was only after the author approved and the CNC relented that *Silence of the Sea* was shown commercially in 1949. The film involves a Nazi officer (Howard Vernon), billeted with a man (Jean-Marie Robain) and his niece (Nicole Stéphane) in a small French town. The uncle narrates the tale as a flashback. The pair "resists" by refusing to speak to or acknowledge the presence of the officer in their home. Unlike *Battle of the Rails*, *Silence of the Sea* acknowledges the role of women at the home front during the Occupation, here employing passive resistance. Melville's struggle to make and exhibit a film outside the CNC system demonstrated the limitations of experimentation and independent production that frustrated other filmmakers. Agnès Varda ran up against similar industrial hurdles with *La Pointe Courte* in 1954. Nonetheless, Melville's and Varda's creative production strategies inspired a new generation to find their own entry points into filmmaking when they started the French New Wave by the late 1950s.

Thus, French film conditions after the war allowed for a few surprising projects. One rather unique post-Occupation project was Georges Rouquier's naturalistic, semi-documentary *Farrebique* (1946), chronicling a year in the life of a proud peasant farm family and their immediate community in the Aveyron region. The film offers a heartfelt tribute to the bonds between the generations who have grown up and grown old there. Their connection to the land they cultivate and inhabit is nearly sacred. Photojournalistic shots of the family huddled around their table debating whether they can afford to repair their home and get electricity are alternated with deep space exterior scenes of the family working their land that recall Lumière. *Farrebique* includes striking time-lapse sequences and poetic seasonal montages, including extreme close-ups of buds and insects and even shots of sap flowing in the plants that recall the micro-cinematography of Étienne-Jules Marey and scientific documentaries by Jean Painlevé, who championed the project. Rouquier's film resembles Aleksandr Dovzhenko's *Earth* (1930) in places, but it is also firmly anchored in the history of French cultural heritage. *Farrebique* won the International Federation of Film Critics FIPRESCI prize at Cannes.

For the most part, postwar classical French cinema followed in the steps of the 1930s, allowing for a wide variety of commercial, auteur, and political niche productions. After the war, André Paulvé continued to produce a tradition of quality projects, such as Victor Hugo's *Ruy Blas* (Billon, 1948), starring Danièlle Darieux and Jean Marais, and Stendhal's *La Chartreuse de Parme* (Christian-Jaque, 1948), an Italian coproduction featuring Gérard Philipe. Paulvé also produced unique and personal auteur films, including Jean Cocteau's *Beauty and the Beast* (*La Belle et la bête*, 1946) and newcomer Jacques Tati's

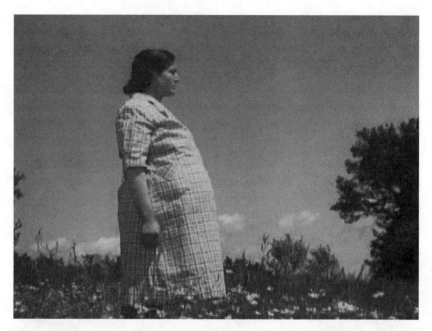

Graphic matches: pregnant woman (*Farrebique*)

Graphic matches: clothes on a line (*Farrebique*)

Jour de fête (1949). *Beauty and the Beast* continues Cocteau's penchant for creating distinct fantasy worlds set apart from normal experience. It benefited greatly from music by Georges Auric, lighting effects and cinematography by Henri Alekan, and Christian Bérard's magnificent sets. Josette Day and Jean Marais starred as the title characters. Much like *Children of Paradise*, *Beauty and the Beast* was quickly hailed as a masterpiece demonstrating the exceptional technical skill and the high quality of 1940s French cinema. It was very successful internationally, where it was praised as a rare poetic fantasy and a great cinematic accomplishment. Nonetheless, Noel Burch and Geneviève Sellier credit *Beauty and the Beast* with being more timely than its fairy-tale setting might suggest. It involves a weak father willing to sacrifice his daughter, something typical of Occupation dramas, and it features a young woman who must renounce her own freedom and desire to love a man who needs her: "It seems to be a luminous metaphor for the task assigned to women at the Liberation, which was to sacrifice themselves so that the male identity, twisted beyond recognition by the horrors of war, could reconstruct

Jean Marais and Josette Day in Cocteau's fanciful world (*Beauty and the Beast*)

itself" (266). Beyond Cocteau's personal input, *Beauty and the Beast* proves anew the creative power of producers in auteur cinema of the era. Within four years, André Paulvé had produced such high-profile films as *Les Visiteurs du soir*, *Lumière d'été*, *L'Eternel retour*, *Sylvie and the Phantom*, and now *Beauty and the Beast*. With the war over, he continued with big-budget costume dramas and took a chance on young talent such as Jacques Tati.

Jacques Tati links post–World War II French cinema back toward its silent comic roots, yet he also points toward the future of the 1950s and 1960s art cinema. A magician, actor, and comic, Tati won the Max Linder award for his short film *The School for Postmen* (*L'École des facteurs*, 1947), which was adapted and expanded into the feature film *Holiday* (*Jour de fête*, 1949) thanks to its producer, Fred Orain, and then Paulvé. Shot simultaneously in black and white and the additive color process Thomson Color, *Jour de fête* follows the antics of the rural mailman, played by Tati, who makes his rounds on a bicycle but tries to improve the local mail service by following a supposedly American model of efficiency. The slapstick performances and visuals are reinforced by the highly artificial soundtrack, which owes to Surrealism and

Tati's bicycle phone (*Jour de fête*)

René Clair. Sound levels and fidelity are constantly manipulated to amplify each carefully staged gag. Tati's storytelling involves a casual accumulation of motifs, gestures, and sounds. *Jour de fête* demonstrates the rich array of films possible in classical French cinema, and the significance that short films, encouraged by the CNC, played in encouraging new talent to enter the industry by the 1950s.

Film culture was indeed in a state of renewal following the liberation, with the return of ciné-clubs, the proliferation of new criticism, the wide range of movies suddenly available in France via retrospectives at art houses and the Cinémathèque, and new discoveries from around the world in commercial cinemas. French movie attendance hit a new high in 1947 and broke records with more than 420 million tickets sold, roughly 9 tickets per person, or nearly double the sales in the difficult 1944 (Crisp, *Classic* 68). Filmmakers, critics, and audiences alike participated in exploring and rejuvenating film practice. *Cinéphilia*, the passionate belief in the importance of films in French cultural formation, was ignited during the late 1940s. Building on critical traditions dating back to the 1920s, a new generation of critics and spectators placed cinema at the center of their cultural life. In 1946, Jean-Paul Sartre and André Bazin famously sparred over the merits of *Citizen Kane*, elevating film aesthetics to the level of philosophical debate and forcing audiences to rethink their own taste and even ethics.

As historian Antoine de Baecque points out, by 1948, French *cinéphilia* was firmly in place. Critics regularly appeared in person to introduce movies and lead discussions at commercial theaters and art houses. In Paris, spectators could spend Tuesday nights at the Studio Parnasse ciné-club and Thursdays at the Latin Quarter ciné-club, and even the sixteen-year-old François Truffaut began a "ciné-mania" club at the Cluny-Palace on Sunday mornings. There were the Objectif events and special screenings at *art et essai* houses such as the Pagode, Ursulines, or Reflet cinemas (de Baecque 36–37). French film criticism and *cinéphilia*, as much as French film production itself, placed Paris firmly at the center of film culture nationally and globally. France's cinematic reputation, including the significance of the Cannes Film Festival, continued to accelerate into the 1950s, culminating at the end of the decade with a cinematic rebirth: the French New Wave.

For readers of this book, it should come as no surprise that French cinema continued to thrive through and beyond World War II. The history of French film is an encouraging chronicle of how continual challenges were met with innovative economic, technical, and storytelling solutions. Since its beginnings, with the Lumières, Alice Guy, Georges Méliès, Charles Pathé, Léon Gaumont, and all the others, French film benefited from a unique array of institutions and aesthetic options, with the auteur-director at its core. Some of the later New Wave critic-directors liked to suggest that they knew film history and incorporated film references more than their predecessors, but such claims were certainly unfounded. France's writers, directors, producers, actors, and technicians were well aware of their historical context. Just as French animators today refer to the "two Émiles" (Reynaud and Cohl), live-action filmmakers understand their own modes of production continue and respond to the legacy of traditions before them, including commercial norms over the years and avant-garde's counterattacks. As we have seen, many films of the Occupation were influenced by and responding to Poetic Realism, which was influenced by and responding to Impressionism. Many of the various experimental tendencies of the 1920s were reacting against the dramatic conventions of the 1910s while incorporating some of the stylistic flourishes from that period's comedies. Global transmedia influences have proven significant for the development of moving pictures from the late nineteenth century on up through today. As this history of French film reveals, perhaps no other national cinema has more consistently and profoundly shaped film aesthetics and cinematic culture. Clearly French cinema by the end of World War II had proven cinema's importance and legacy and set the stage for what continued to be at the heart of cinematic storytelling, criticism, and theory as we know them.

Bibliography

Abel, Richard. *The Ciné Goes to Town: French Cinema, 1896–1914.* Berkeley: University of California Press, 1994.

———. *French Cinema: The First Wave, 1915–1929.* Princeton, NJ: Princeton University Press, 1984.

———. *French Film Theory and Criticism, 1907–1939.* 2 vols. Princeton, NJ: Princeton University Press, 1988.

———. *The Red Rooster Scare: Making Cinema American, 1900–1910.* Berkeley: University of California Press, 1999.

Andrew, Dudley. *Mists of Regret: Culture and Sensibility in Classic French Film.* Princeton, NJ: Princeton University Press, 1995.

———. "Praying Mantis: Enchantment and Violence in French Cinema of the Exotic." In *Visions of the East: Orientalism in Film*, edited by Matthew Bernstein and Gaylyn Studlar, 232–52. New Brunswick, NJ: Rutgers University Press, 1997.

———. *What Cinema Is!* Malden, MA: Wiley-Blackwell, 2010.

Andrew, Dudley, and Steven Ungar. *Popular Front Paris and the Poetics of Culture.* Cambridge, MA: Belknap Press of Harvard University Press, 2005.

Armes, Roy. "Cinema of Paradox: French Film-Making during the Occupation." In *Collaboration in France*, edited by Gerhard Hirschfeld and Patrick Marsh, 126–41. Oxford: Berg, 1989.

———. *French Cinema.* New York: Oxford University Press, 1985.

Astruc, Alexandre. "The Birth of a New Avant-Garde: *La Caméra-Stylo.*" In *The French New Wave: Critical Landmarks*, edited by Peter Graham and Ginette Vincendeau, 30–37. London: BFI Palgrave, 2009.

Aubert, Michelle, and Jean-Claude Seguin, eds. *La Production cinématographique des Frères Lumière.* Paris: Bibliothèque du Film, 1996.

Auzel, Dominique. *Emile Reynaud et l'image s'anima.* Paris: Dreamland, 1998.

Aumont, Jacques. *L'Oeil interminable: Cinéma et peinture.* Paris: Séghier, 1989.

Bakker, Gerben. "Selling French Films on Foreign Markets: The International Strategy of a Medium-Sized Film Company." *Enterprise and Society* 5 (2004): 45–76.

Banda, Daniel, and José Moure, eds. *Le Cinéma: Naissance d'un art, 1895–1920.* Paris: Flammarion, 2008.

Bardèche, Maurice, and Robert Brasillach. *Histoire du Cinéma*. Paris: Éditions Denoël, 1943.

Barrot, Olivier. *L'Ecran français 1943–1953: Histoire d'un journal et d'une époque*. Paris: Editeurs Français Réunis, 1979.

Bazin, André. *French Cinema from the Liberation to the New Wave, 1945–1958*. New Orleans: University of New Orleans Press, 2012.

———. *French Cinema of the Occupation and Resistance*. Translated by Stanley Hochman. New York: Frederick Ungar, 1981.

———. *Jean Renoir*. Translated by W. W. Halsey and William H. Simon. New York: Da Capo Press, 1992.

——— "Réalisme et genie de Renoir." *Avant-Scène Cinéma* 44 (1964): 44.

———. *What Is Cinema?* 2 vols. Translated by Hugh Gray. Berkeley: University of California Press, 1972.

———. *What Is Cinema?* Translated by Timothy Barnard. Montreal: Caboose, 2009.

Benghozi, Pierre-Jean, and Christian Delage. *Une histoire économique du cinéma français (1895–1995)*. Paris: L'Harmattan, 1997.

Benjamin, Walter. "Paris—Capital of the Nineteenth Century." *New Left Review* 48 (March/April 1968): 77–88.

Bertin, Célia. *Jean Renoir: A Life in Pictures*. Translated by Mireille Muellner and Leonard Muellner. Baltimore: Johns Hopkins University Press, 1986.

Bertin-Maghit, Jean-Pierre. *Le Cinéma sous l'occupation*. Paris: Olivier Orban, 1989.

Bessy, Maurice. "La Règle du jeu." *Avant-Scène* 52 (October 1965): 63.

Beylie, Claude. "Marcel L'Herbier ou l'intelligence du cinématographe." *Avant Scène du cinéma* 209 (1978): 27–42.

Bey-Rozet, Maxime. "From the Casbah to Père Jules's Cabin: Theorizing the Exotic-Abject in 1930s French Cinema." *French Screen Studies* 20, no. 2 (2020): 107–24.

———, ed. *Une histoire du cinéma français*. Paris: Larousse, 2005.

Billard, Pierre. *L'Age classique du cinéma français: Du cinéma parlant à la Nouvelle Vague*. Paris: Flammarion, 1995.

———. *Le Mystère René Clair*. Paris: Plon, 1998.

Bordwell, David. *Figures Traced in Light: On Cinematic Staging*. Berkeley: University of California Press, 2005.

———. *Filmguide to "La Passion de Jeanne d'Arc."* Bloomington: Indiana University Press, 1973.

———. *The Films of Carl-Theodore Dreyer*. Berkeley: University of California Press, 1981.

———. "French Impressionist Cinema: Film Culture, Film Theory, and Film Style." PhD diss., University of Iowa, 1974.

———. *On the History of Film Style*. Cambridge, MA: Harvard University Press, 1997.

Bordwell, David, Kristin Thompson, and Jeff Smith. *Film Art: An Introduction*. New York: McGraw Hill, 2017.

Bowles, Brett. *Marcel Pagnol*. Edinburgh: Edinburgh University Press, 2012.

———. "Renoir under the Popular Front." In *A Companion to Jean Renoir*, edited by Alastair Phillips and Ginette Vincendeau, 398–424. Malden, MA: Wiley-Blackwell, 2013.

Braun, Marta. *Picturing Time: The Work of Etienne-Jules Marey (1830–1904).* Chicago: University of Chicago Press, 1992.

Breton, André. *Manifestoes of Surrealism.* Translated by Richard Seaver and Helen R. Lane. Ann Arbor: University of Michigan Press, 1969.

Brownlow, Kevin. *The Parade's Gone By.* Berkeley: University of California Press, 1968.

Buache, Freddy. *Claude Autant-Lara.* Paris: Editions L'Age d'Homme, 1982.

Buchsbaum, Jonathan. *Cinema Engagé: Film in the Popular Front.* Urbana: University of Illinois Press, 1988.

Burch, Noel. *Marcel L'Herbier.* Paris: Seghers, 1973.

Burch, Noel, and Geneviève Sellier. *The Battle of the Sexes in French Cinema, 1930–1956.* Translated by Peter Graham. Durham, NC: Duke University Press, 2014.

Burnett, Colin. *The Invention of Robert Bresson.* Bloomington: Indiana University Press, 2017.

Bush, W. Stephen. "Germinal." *Moving Picture World,* January 24, 1914, 416.

Callahan, Vicki. "Representations 1890–1930: Mutability and Fixity in Early French Cinema." In *The French Cinema Book,* edited by Michael Temple and Michael Witt, 65–73. London: Bloomsbury, 2004.

———. *Zones of Anxiety: Movement, Musidora, and the Crime Serials of Louis Feuillade.* Detroit: Wayne State University Press, 2005.

Canudo, Ricciotto. "La Leçon du cinema." In *Le Cinéma naissance d'un art, 1895–1920,* edited by Danial Banda and José Moure, 491–95. Paris: Champs Flammarion, 2008.

Carné, Marcel. *Ma vie à belles dents.* Paris: L'Archipel, 1996.

Cayla, Véronique. *Du Praxinoscope au cellulo: un demi-siècle de cinéma d'animation en France (1892–1948).* Paris: Centre Nationale de la Cinématographie, 2007.

Chardère, Bernard. *Les Images des Lumière.* Paris: Gallimard, 1995.

Charensol, Georges, and Roger Régent. *50 ans de Cinéma avec René Clair.* Paris: La Table Ronde, 1978.

Chothia, Jean. *André Antoine.* Cambridge: Cambridge University Press, 1991.

Clair, René. *Cinema Yesterday and Today.* Translated by Stanley Appelbaum. New York: Dover, 1972.

Cohl, Emile. "Les Dessins animées et à trucs." *1895* 53 (December 2007): 301–5.

Conway, Kelley. *Chanteuse in the City: The Realist Singer in French Film.* Berkeley: University of California Press, 2004.

———. "Popular Songs in Renoir's Films of the 1930s." In *A Companion to Jean Renoir,* edited by Alistair Phillips and Ginette Vincendeau, 199–218. Malden, MA: Wiley-Blackwell, 2013.

Courtade, Francis. *Les Maledictions du cinéma français.* Paris: Alain Moreau, 1978.

Crisp, Colin. "Business: Anarchy and Order in the French Film Industry." In *The French Cinema Book,* edited by Michael Temple and Michael Witt, 73–80. London: Bloomsbury, 2004.

———. *The Classic French Cinema, 1930–1960.* Bloomington: Indiana University Press, 1993.

———. *Genre, Myth, and Convention in the French Cinema, 1929–1939.* Bloomington: Indiana University Press, 2002.

Cuff, Paul. *A Revolution for the Screen: Abel Gance's Napoléon.* Amsterdam: Amsterdam University Press, 2015.

Dagognet, François. *Etienne-Jules Marey: A Passion for the Trace.* Translated by Robert Galeta and Jeanine Herman. New York: Zone Books, 1992.

Daigle, Allain. "Lens Culture." *Les Cahiers d'histoire du cnam* 12 (2019): 17–44.

Daire, Joel. *Jean Epstein, une vie pour le cinéma.* Paris: La Tour Verte, 2014.

Dall'Asta, Monica. "Debates 1890–1930, Thinking about Cinema: First Waves." In *The French Cinema Book,* edited by Michael Temple and Michael Witt, 81–90. London: Bloomsbury, 2004.

Darmon, Pierre. *Le Monde du cinéma sous l'occupation.* Paris: Stock, 1997.

de Baecque, Antoine. *La Cinéphilie: Invention d'un regard, histoire d'une culture 1944–1968.* Paris: Fayard, 2003.

De Julio, Maryann. "Another Look at Germaine Dulac's *The Seashell and the Clergyman.*" *Senses of Cinema* 69 (December 2013).

Delluc, Gilles. *Louis Delluc, 1890–1924.* Périgueux: Pilote, 2002.

Deslandes, Jacques, and Jacques Richard. *Histoire comparée du cinéma II: du cinématographe au cinéma.* Brussels: Casterman, 1968.

Drazin, Charles. *French Cinema.* New York: Faber and Faber, 2011.

Driskell, Jonathan. *Marcel Carné.* Manchester: Manchester University Press, 2012.

Duckett, Victoria. "The Stars Might Be Smiling: A Feminist Forage into a Famous Film." In *Fantastic Voyages of the Cinematic Imagination: Georges Méliès's Trip to the Moon,* edited by Matthew Solomon, 161–81. Albany: State University Press of New York, 2011.

Dulac, Germaine. "The Aesthetics. The Obstacles. Integral Cinegraphe." Translated by Stuart Liebman. *Framework* 19 (1982): 6–9.

———. "Le Cinéma d'avant-garde." In *Le Cinéma des origins à nos jours,* edited by Henri Fescourt, 357–64. Paris: Éditions du Cygne, 1932.

Dulac, Nicolas, and André Gaudreault. "Circularity and Repetition at the Heart of the Attraction: Optical Toys and the Emergence of a New Cultural Series." In *The Cinema of Attractions Reloaded,* edited by Wanda Strauven, 227–44. Amsterdam: Amsterdam University Press, 2006.

Ehrlich, Evelyn. *Cinema of Paradox: French Filmmaking under the German Occupation.* New York: Columbia University Press, 1985.

Elsaesser, Thomas. *European Cinema: Face to Face with Hollywood.* Amsterdam: Amsterdam University Press, 2005.

Escoubé, Lucienne. "Sauvons les film de repertoire." *Pour Vous,* March 31, 1932, 3.

Ezra, Elizabeth. *Georges Méliès: The Birth of the Auteur.* Manchester: Manchester University Press, 2000.

Faucheux, Michel. *Auguste et Louis Lumière.* Paris: Gallimard, 2011.

Faulkner, Christopher. *The Social Cinema of Jean Renoir.* Princeton, NJ: Princeton University Press, 2014.

Fescourt, Henri, ed. *Le Cinéma des origines à nos jours.* Paris: Editions du Cygne, 1932.

Feyder, Jacques, and Françoise Rosay. *Le Cinéma notre métier.* Lausanne: Cailler, 1946.

Flinn, Margaret C. *The Social Architecture of French Cinema, 1929–1939.* Liverpool: Liverpool University Press, 2014.

Flitterman-Lewis, Sandy. *To Desire Differently: Feminism and the French Cinema.* Urbana: University of Illinois Press, 1990.

Forbes, Jill. *Les Enfants du paradis.* London: BFI, 1997.

Frank, Nino. "La Règle du jeu." *Pour Vous,* July 12, 1939, 6.

Frizot, Michel. *Avant le cinématographie: La Chronophotographie.* Beaune: Association des Amis de Marey, 1984.

Frodon, Jean-Michel. *La Projection nationale: Cinéma et nation.* Paris: Odile Jacob, 1998.

Garçon, François. *De Blum à Pétain.* Paris: Les Éditions du Cerf, 1984.

Gaudreault, André, ed. *Pathé 1900.* Sainte-Foy: Les Presses de l'Université de Laval, 1993.

———. "Theatricality, Narrativity, and Trickality: Reevaluating the Cinema of Georges Méliès." In *Fantastic Voyages of the Cinematic Imagination: Georges Méliès's Trip to the Moon,* edited by Matthew Solomon, 31–47. Albany: State University Press of New York, 2011.

Gaudreault, André, Catherine Russell, and Pierre Véronneau, eds. *The Cinema: A New Technology for the 20th Century.* Lausanne: Editions Payot, 2004.

Gauteur, Claude. "'Better than a Masterpiece': Revisiting the Reception of *La Règle du jeu.*" In *A Companion to Jean Renoir,* edited by Alistair Phillips and Ginette Vincendeau, 347–55. Malden, MA: Wiley-Blackwell, 2013.

Gauteur, Claude, and Ginette Vincendeau. *Jean Gabin: Anatomie d'un mythe.* Paris: Nouveau Monde, 2006.

Gautier, Anne, and Jean-Marc Lamotte. "L'Année 1895 et ses jalons." In *La Production cinématographique des Frères Lumière,* edited by Michelle Aubert and Jean-Claude Seguin, 15–21. Paris: Bibliothèque du Film, 1996.

Guido, Laurent. *L'Age du rythme: Cinéma, musicalité et culture du corps dans les théories françaises des années 1910–1930.* Lausanne: Payot-Lausanne, 2007.

Gunning, Tom. *D. W. Griffith and the Origins of American Narrative Film.* Urbana: University of Illinois Press, 1994.

———. "Phantasmagoria and the Manufacturing of Illusions and Wonder: Towards a Cultural Optics of the Cinematic Aparatus." In *The Cinema: A New Technology for the 20th Century,* edited by André Gaudreault, Catherine Russell, and Pierre Véronneau, 31–44. Lausanne: Editions Payot, 2004.

———. "Preface." In *Jean Epstein: Critical Essays and New Translations,* edited by Sarah Keller and Jason N. Paul, 13–22. Amsterdam: Amsterdam University Press, 2012.

Gustavson, Todd. *Camera: A History of Photography from the Daguerreotype to Digital.* New York: Sterling Innovation, 2009.

Hall, Mordaunt. "A French Musical Farce." *New York Times,* May 21, 1931, 37.

Harrison, Louis Reeves. "Weekly Comments on our Shows." *Moving Picture World,* February 20, 1909, 200.

Hayward, Susan. *French National Cinema.* London: Routledge, 1993.

Hayward, Susan, and Ginette Vincendeau, eds. *French Film: Texts and Contexts.* London: Routledge, 2000.

Hughes, Alex, and James S. Williams, eds. *Gender and French Cinema.* Oxford: Berg, 2001.

Jacobson, Brian R. *Studios before the System*. New York: Columbia University Press, 2015.

Jacquier, Philippe, and Marion Pranal. *Gabriel Veyre Opérateur Lumière*. Lyon: Institut Lumière, 1996.

Jeancolas, Jean-Pierre. "Beneath the Despair, The Show Goes On: Marcel Carné's *Les Enfants du paradis* (1943–5)." In *French Film: Texts and Contexts*, edited by Susan Hayward and Ginette Vincendeau, 78–88. New York: Routledge, 2000.

Jeanne, René. "L'Évolution artistique du cinématographe." In *Le Cinéma des origines à nos jours*, edited by Henri Fescourt, 169–248. Paris: Éditions du Cynge.

———. *Histoire du Cinéma français*. Paris: Nathan, 1995.

Kern, Anne M. "Renoir and the Ethics of Play." In *A Companion to Jean Renoir*, edited by Alastair Phillips and Ginette Vincendeau, 108–20. Malden, MA: Wiley-Blackwell, 2013.

King, Elliott. *Dali, Surrealism and Cinema*. London: Kamera Books, 2007.

King, Norman. *Abel Gance: A Politics of Spectacle*. London: BFI, 1984.

Koos, Cheryl A. "The Good, the Bad, and the Childless: The Politics of Female Identity in *Maternité* (1929) and *La Maternelle* (1933)." *Historical Reflections* 35, no. 2 (Summer 2009): 3–20.

Larson, Stephen. "Risen from the Ashes: The Complex Print History of Carl Dreyer's *The Passion of Joan of Arc* (1928)." *Moving Image* 17, no. 1 (Spring 2017): 52–84.

Lavédrine, Bertrand, and Jean-Paul Gandolfo. *The Lumière Autochrome: History, Technology, and Preservation*. Los Angeles: Getty, 2013.

Lécuyer, Raymond. *Histoire de la photographie*. Paris: Bachet et Cie, 1945.

Lefebvre, Thierry. "Internationalité, influences, réception: Le cas de la diffusion des films américains en France (1894–1916)." In *Théorème*, 55–66. Paris: Presses de la Sorbonne Nouvelle, 1996.

Leglise, Paul. *Histoire de la politique du cinéma français*. Paris: R. Pichon and R. Durand-Auzias, 1970.

Legrand, Pascal. "Le Centre national de la cinématographie des 'premiers temps' (1944–1954)." In *Le Cinéma: Une affaire d'État, 1945–1970*, edited by Demitri Vezyroglou, 59–69. Paris: Comité d'histoire du ministère de la Culture et de la Communication, 2014.

Leprohon, Pierre. "Les Nouvelles tendances du cinéma français." *Ciné Mondial* 149–50 (21 July 1944): 3–4.

Leteux, Christine. *Albert Capellani: Pioneer of the Silent Screen*. Lexington: University Press of Kentucky, 2015.

Leuba, Marion. *Marey: pionnier de la synthèse du mouvement*. Beaune: Musée Marey, 1995.

L'Herbier, Marcel. *La Tête qui tourne*. Paris: Pierre Belfond, 1979.

Lherminier, Pierre. *Louis Delluc et le cinéma français*. Paris: Ramsay, 2008.

Lindeperg, Sylvie. "Political and Narrative Ambiguities in *La Bataille du rail*." *Historical Reflections* 35, no. 2 (Summer 2009): 143–62.

Lonjon, Bernard. *Emile Reynaud: Le véritable inventeur du cinéma*. Polignac: Editions du Roure, 2007.

Lopez, Ana M. "Early Cinema and Modernity in Latin America." *Cinema Journal* 40, no. 1 (2000): 48–78.

Lumière, Auguste. *Mes travaux et mes jours.* Paris: La Colombe, 1953.

Mallet-Stevens, Robert. *Le Décor moderne du cinéma.* Paris: Massin, 1928.

Malthête, Jacques. *Méliès, Images et illusions.* Paris: Exporégie, 1996.

Malthête-Méliès, Madeleine. *Georges Méliès, L'Enchanteur.* Paris: La Tour verte, 2011.

Mannoni, Laurent. *The Great Art of Light and Shadow: Archaeology of the Cinema.* Translated by Richard Crangle. Exeter: University of Exeter Press, 2000.

———. *Histoire de la Cinémathèque française.* Paris: Gallimard, 2006.

Marie, Michel. "The Invention of French Talking Cinema: Language in Renoir's Early Sound Films." In *A Companion to Jean Renoir,* edited by Alistair Phillips and Ginette Vincendeau, 53–71. Malden, MA: Wiley-Blackwell, 2013.

Matz, Jesse. *Lasting Impressionism: The Legacies of Impressionism in Contemporary Culture.* New York: Columbia University Press, 2016.

Mayne, Judith. *Le Corbeau.* Urbana: University of Illinois Press, 2007.

McCann, Ben. *Julien Duvivier.* Manchester: Manchester University Press, 2017.

McCarron, Bernard. "*Brasier ardent* (1923): Ivan Mosjoukine's *Clin d'oeil* to German Expressionism." In *Expressionism in the Cinema,* edited by Olaf Brill and Gary D. Rhodes, 220–33. Edinburgh: Edinburgh University Press, 2018.

McMahan, Alison. *Alice Guy Blaché: Lost Visionary of the Cinema.* New York: Continuum, 2003.

———. "The Animation Paradigm." In *The Cinema: A New Technology for the 20th Century,* edited by André Gaudreault, Catherine Russell, and Pierre Véronneau, 373–80. Lausanne: Editions Payot, 2004.

Méliès, Georges. "Les Vues cinématographiques (1907)." In *Le Cinéma: Naissance d'un art, 1895–1920,* edited by Daniel Banda and José Moure, 95–107. Paris: Flammarion, 2008.

Mesguich, Felix. *Tours de Manivelle: Souvenirs d'un chasseur d'images.* Paris: Bernard Grasset, 1933.

Metz, Christian. *Le Signifiant imaginaire: Psychanalyse et cinéma.* Paris: Union Générale d'Éditions, 1977.

Meusy, Jean-Jacques. *Cinémas de France, 1894–1918.* Paris: Arcadia, 2009.

Mitry, Jean. *Histoire du Cinéma, I. 1895–1914.* Paris: Editions Universitaires, 1969.

———. *Histoire du Cinéma, III. 1923–1930.* Paris: Editions Universitaires, 1973.

———. *Histoire du Cinéma, IV. 1930–1940.* Paris: Jean-Pierre Delarge, 1980.

Montebello, Fabrice. *Le Cinéma en France, depuis les années 1930.* Paris: Armand Colin, 2005.

Moving Picture World. "Les Miserables." April 26, 1913, 362–63.

Murphy, Libby. *The Art of Survival: France and the Great War Picaresque.* New Haven, CT: Yale University Press, 2016.

Myrent, Glenn, and Georges P. Langlois. *Henri Langlois: First Citizen of Cinema.* Translated by Lisa Nesselson. New York: Twayne, 1995.

Nord, Philip. *France's New Deal: From the Thirties to the Postwar Era.* Princeton, NJ: Princeton University Press, 2010.

O'Brien, Charles. *Cinema's Conversion to Sound: Technology and Film Style in France and the U.S.* Bloomington: Indiana University Press, 2005.

———. "Relocating Renoir's Sound and Music." In *A Companion to Jean Renoir*, edited by Alastair Phillips and Ginette Vincendeau, 35–51. Malden, MA: Wiley-Blackwell, 2013.

———. "*Sous le toits de Paris* and Transnational Film Style: An Analysis of Film Editing Statistics." *Studies in French Cinema* 9, no. 2 (2009): 111–25.

O'Shaughnessy, Martin. *Jean Renoir.* Manchester: Manchester University Press, 2000.

———. *La Grande Illusion.* London: I. B. Tauris, 2009.

———. "Shooting in Deep Time: The *Mise en Scène* of History in Renoir's Films of the 1930s." In *A Companion to Jean Renoir*, edited by Alastair Phillips and Ginette Vincendeau, 16–34. Malden, MA: Wiley-Blackwell, 2013.

Phillips, Allistair. "People: Migration and Exile in the Classical Period." In *The French Cinema Book*, edited by Michael Temple and Michael Witt, 103–17. London: Bloomsbury, 2004.

Pinel, Vincent. "Chronologie commentée de l'invention du cinéma." *1895* (1992): 9–98.

Potonniée, G. *Les Origines du Cinématographe.* Paris: Paul Montel, 1928.

Powrie, Phil, and Eric Rebillard. *Pierre Batcheff and Stardom in 1920s French Cinema.* Edinburgh: Edinburgh University Press, 2005.

Puget, Clément. *Verdun, le cinéma, l'événement.* Paris: Nouveau Monde Éditions, 2016.

Ramond, Sylvie, ed. *Impressionisme et naissance du cinématographe.* Lyon: Fage, 2005.

Rasula, Jed. *Acrobatic Modernism: From the Avant-Garde to Prehistory.* New York: Oxford University Press, 2020.

———. *Destruction Is My Beatrice: Dada and the Unmaking of the Twentieth Century.* New York: Basic Books, 2015.

Régent, Roger. *Cinéma de France.* Paris: Éditions d'Aujourd'hui, 1948.

Renoir, Jean. *My Life and My Films.* Translated by Norman Denny. New York: Atheneum, 1974.

Rittaud-Hutinet, Jacques. *Letters: Auguste and Louis Lumière.* Translated by Pierre Hodgson. London: Faber and Faber, 1995.

Robinson, David. "Introduction." *Griffithiana* 43 (December 1991): 8–18.

Roffat, Sébastien. *Les Gémeaux: L'Histoire d'un studio d'animation mythique.* Paris: L'Harmattan, 2021.

Rony, Olivier. *Louis Jouvet.* Paris: Gallimard, 2021.

Roud, Richard. *A Passion for Films: Henri Langlois and the Cinémathèque Française.* New York: Viking Press, 1983.

Sadoul, Georges. *Le Cinéma français (1890–1962).* Paris: Flammarion, 1962.

———. *Dictionary of Films.* Translated by Peter Morris. Berkeley: University of California Press, 1972.

———. *Histoire du cinéma mondial des origines à nos jours.* Paris: Flammarion, 1949.

Salles Gomes, P. E. *Jean Vigo.* Berkeley: University of California Press, 1971.

Schrader, Paul. *Transcendental Style in Film: Ozu, Bresson, Dreyer.* New York: Da Capo Press, 1972.

Sellier, Geneviève. *Jean Grémillon: Le Cinéma est à vous.* Paris: Klincksieck, 2012.

Sesonske, Alexander. *Jean Renoir, the French Films, 1924–1939*. Cambridge, MA: Harvard University Press, 1980.

Siclier, Jacques. *La France de Pétain et son cinéma*. Paris: Henri Veyrier, 1981.

Sidhu, Maya. "Reconsidering Jean Renoir's *La Marseillaise* through Editor Marguerite Renoir." *French Screen Studies* 21, no. 1 (2021): 19–33.

Simon, Joan, ed. *Alice Guy Blaché*. New Haven, CT: Yale University Press, 2010.

Simsolo, Noel. *Sacha Guitry*. Paris: Cahiers du Cinéma, 1988.

Slavin, David Henry. *Colonial Cinema and Imperial France, 1919–1939*. Baltimore: Johns Hopkins University Press, 2001.

Smith, Susan, M. *The Cinema of Max Ophuls*. New York: Columbia University Press, 1995.

Smoodin, Eric. "Paris Cinema Project." *Paris Cinema Blog*, January 6, 2019. https://pariscinemablog.wordpress.com/2019/01/06/the-paris-cinema-project-44/.

———. *Paris in the Dark: Going to the Movies in the City of Light, 1930–1950*. Durham, NC: Duke University Press, 2020.

Solomon, Matthew, ed. *Fantastic Voyages of the Cinematic Imagination: Georges Méliès's Trip to the Moon*. Albany: State University of New York Press, 2011.

Spehr, Paul. *The Man Who Made Movies: W. K. L. Dickson*. New Barnet, UK: John Libbey, 2008.

Stam, Robert. *Film Theory: An Introduction*. Malden, MA: Blackwell, 2000.

Tariol, Marcel. *Louis Delluc*. Paris: Seghers, 1965.

Tavernier, Bertrand. "Commentary." In *The Lumière Brothers' First Films*, edited by Thierry Fremaux. New York: Kino Video and the Institute Lumière, 2003.

Tchernia, Pierre. "Préface." In Domique Auzel, *Emile Reynaud et l'image s'anima*, 5. Paris: Éditions du May, 1998.

Telotte, J. P. *Science Fiction Film*. New York: Cambridge University Press, 2001.

Temple, Michael. *Jean Vigo*. Manchester: Manchester University Press, 2005.

Temple, Michael, and Michael Witt, eds. *The French Cinema Book*. London: Bloomsbury, 2004.

Thompson, Kristin. *Breaking the Glass Armor: Neoformalist Film Analysis*. Princeton, NJ: Princeton University Press, 1988.

———. "Capellani trionfante." *David Bordwell's Website on Cinema*, July 14, 2011. http://www.davidbordwell.net/blog/2011/07/14/capellani-trionfante/.

———. "L'Inhumaine: Modern Art, Modern Cinema." *David Bordwell's Website on Cinema*, April 9, 2016. http://www.davidbordwell.net/blog/2016/04/09/linhumaine-modern-art-modern-cinema/.

———. "Ten Best Films of 1927." *David Bordwell's Website on Cinema*, December 27, 2017. http://www.davidbordwell.net/blog/2017/12/27/the-ten-best-films-of-1927/.

Thompson, Kristin, and David Bordwell. *Film History: An Introduction*. 2nd ed. New York: McGraw-Hill, 2010.

Truffaut, François. *The Films in My Life*. Translated by Leonard Mayhew. New York: Da Capo, 1994.

Turim, Maureen. "Poetic Realism as Psychoanalytical and Ideological Operation in Marcel Carné's *Le Jour se lève*." In *French Film: Texts and Contexts*, edited by Susan Hayward and Ginette Vincendeau, 63–77. London: Routledge, 2000.

Turk, Edward Baron. *Child of Paradise: Marcel Carné and the Golden Age of Cinema.* Cambridge, MA: Harvard University Press, 1989.

Usai, Paolo Cherchi. "A Trip to the Movies: Georges Méliès, Filmmaker and Magician (1861–1938)." In *Fantastic Voyages of the Cinematic Imagination: Georges Méliès's Trip to the Moon,* edited by Matthew Solomon, 25–30. Albany: State University Press of New York, 2011.

Véray, Laurent, "Pour une réflecture de l'histoire du cinéma français: L'exemple de la création de la section cinématographique de l'Armée en 1915." *Théorème* 4 (1996): 67–81.

Vincendeau, Ginette. "Forms: The Art of Spectacle: The Aesthetics of Classical French Cinema." In *The French Cinema Book,* edited by Michael Temple and Michael Witt, 101–11. London: Bloomsbury, 2004.

———. "Hollywood Babel: The Coming of Sound and the Multiple-Language Version." In *"Film Europe" and "Film America,"* edited by Andrew Higson and Richard Maltby, 207–24. Exeter: Exeter University Press, 1999.

———. "In the Name of the Father: Marcel Pagnol's Trilogy: *Marius* (1931), *Fanny* (1932), and *César* (1936)." In *French Film: Texts and Contexts,* edited by Susan Hayward and Ginette Vincendeau, 9–26. New York: Routledge, 2000.

———. "Maigret on Screen: Stardom and Literary Adaptation." In *French Literature on the Screen,* edited by Homer B. Pettey and R. Barton Palmer, 165–82. Manchester: Manchester University Press, 2019.

———. *Pépé le Moko.* London: BFI, 1998.

———. *Stars and Stardom in French Cinema.* London: Continuum, 2000.

Wall-Romana, Christophe. *Jean Epstein: Corporeal Cinema and Film Philosophy.* Manchester: Manchester University Press, 2013.

Wild, Jennifer. *The Parisian Avant-Garde in the Age of Cinema, 1900–1923.* Berkeley: University of California Press, 2015.

Williams, Alan, ed. *Film and Nationalism.* New Brunswick, NJ: Rutgers University Press, 2002.

———. *Republic of Images: A History of French Filmmaking.* Cambridge, MA: Harvard University Press, 1992.

Williams, Tami. *Germaine Dulac: A Cinema of Sensations.* Urbana: University of Illinois Press, 2014.

Yumibe, Joshua. *Moving Color: Early Film, Mass Culture, Modernism.* New Brunswick, NJ: Rutgers University Press, 2012.

Index

Belle Marinière, La (Lachman), 199
Belle Nivernaise, La (Epstein), 126
Benglia, Habib, 206
Benjamin, Walter, 5
Benoit, Pierre, 84
Benoît-Lévy, Jean, 205
Bérard, Christian, 342
Bergson, Henri, 127
Berlioz, Hector, 282
Berlioz, Jacques, 247
Bernard, Paul, 303
Bernard, Raymond, 79
Bernède, Arthur, 74
Bernhardt, Curtis, 162
Bernhardt, Sarah, 77
Berry, Jules, 117, 156–57, 219, 226, 234, 293–94, 300–303
Bertcholtz, Joseph, 337
Berthomieu, André, 215
Bessy, Maurice, 249, 254–55
Béte humaine, La (Renoir), 246–48
Between Calais and Dover (Méliès), 37
Beucler, André, 228
Big Five Agreement (1927), 161
Billancourt studio, 119, 182, 327
Billard, Pierre, 157, 178, 217, 271, 284, 286, 290, 317, 335
Billon, Pierre, 288, 315–16, 340
"Birth of a New Avant-Garde, The" (Astruc), 336
Birth, the Life and the Death of Christ, The (Guy), 52
Birth of a Nation (Griffith), 97
Bizarre, Bizarre (Carné), 230
Blaché, Herbert, 54
Black and White (Allégret and Florey), 193
blackface, 38–39, 196. See also minstrelsy
Blackton, J. Stuart, 55
Blanchar, Pierre, 330
Blavette, Charles, 188
Blind Venus (Gance), 295–96
Blood of a Poet (Cocteau), 167
Blue Beard (Painlevé), 169
Blue Veil, The (Stelli), 271

Blum, Léon, 218, 332
Blum-Byrnes agreement, 332
Boese, Carl, 171
Boireau series (Pathé), 55
Boitel, Jeanne, 207
Bonheur des dames, Au (Duvivier), 162
Bonjour Cinéma, 123
Borchard, Adolphe, 194
Bordwell, David, 70, 72, 75, 93, 99, 105, 134, 137, 151–52, 154, 164, 183, 233
Börlin, Jean, 109, 138–39
Bosetti, Romeo, 59–60
Bost, Pierre, 201–2, 326, 336
Boudu Saved from Drowning (Renoir), 186
Bourbon, Ernest, 60–61
Bourdet, Édouard, 259
Bourrache, Lucien, 229
Bowles, Brett, 239
Boyer, Charles, 106
Boyer, Jean, 260
Brabant, Andrée, 103
Brasier ardent, Le (Volkov and Mosjoukine), 112–14
Brasillach, Robert, 163, 317, 328
Brasseur, Pierre, 231, 303, 323–24
Braunberger, Pierre, 131–32, 163, 183, 235–38, 339
Braunberger-Richébé, 159, 162
Brechtian strategies, 179, 222
Breon, Edmund, 71
Bresson, Robert, 309–10, 313, 336
Breton, André, 135, 139, 145
British Urban Trading, 66
Broadway Melody, The (Beaumont), 158
Brooks, Louise, 159
Brunius, Jacques, 238
Brunoy, Blanchette, 247, 267, 311
Build a Fire (Autant-Lara), 164
Buñuel, Luis, 3, 128, 145–48, 165–66, 168
Burch, Noel, 342
Burel, Léonce-Henri, 86, 97–98, 295
Burnett, Colin, 310, 335
Byrnes, James, 332

WISCONSIN FILM STUDIES

The Film Music of John Williams:
Reviving Hollywood's Classical Style, second edition
EMILIO AUDISSINO

The Foreign Film Renaissance on American Screens, 1946–1973
TINO BALIO

Marked Women: Prostitutes and Prostitution in the Cinema
RUSSELL CAMPBELL

Depth of Field: Stanley Kubrick, Film, and the Uses of History
Edited by GEOFFREY COCKS, JAMES DIEDRICK,
and GLENN PERUSEK

Tough as Nails: The Life and Films of Richard Brooks
DOUGLASS K. DANIEL

Making Hollywood Happen: The Story of Film Finances
CHARLES DRAZIN

Dark Laughter: Spanish Film, Comedy, and the Nation
JUAN F. EGEA

Glenn Ford: A Life
PETER FORD

Luis Buñuel: The Red Years, 1929–1939
ROMÁN GUBERN AND PAUL HAMMOND

Screen Nazis: Cinema, History, and Democracy
SABINE HAKE